# CARELESS PEOPLE

MURDER, MAYHEM AND THE INVENTION
OF THE GREAT GATSBY

SARAH CHURCHWELL

virago

VIRAGO

First published in Great Britain in 2013 by Virago Press
This paperback edition published in 2014 by Virago Press
Reprinted 2014

A CIP catalogue record for this book
is available from the British Library.

ISBN 978-1-84408-768-6

Typeset in Goudy by M Rules
Printed and bound in Great Britain by
Clays Ltd, St Ives plc

Papers used by Virago are from well-managed forests
and other responsible sources.

MIX
Paper from
responsible sources
FSC® C104740

Virago Press
An imprint of
Little, Brown Book Group
100 Victoria Embankment
London EC4Y 0DY

An Hachette UK Company
www.hachette.co.uk

www.virago.co.uk

S... standing of the Humanities at the University of East Anglia. She is the author of *The Many Lives of Marilyn Monroe* (Granta, 2004), co-editor of *Must Read: Rediscovering the Bestseller* (Continuum, 2012), and author of various scholarly articles, chapters and introductions. Her journalism appears regularly in the *Guardian* and the *New Statesman*, among others, and she frequently appears on television and radio, discussing arts, culture and all things American. Raised in Chicago, she now lives in London with her English husband.

'Churchwell brings ... a lively curiosity, a gift for making connections, and an infectious passion for Fitzgerald and his greatest novel ... A suggestive, almost musical evocation of the spirit of the time'

Thomas Powers, *London Review of Books*

'The wonder of *Careless People* ... is that it rewinds the years and allows the reader to appreciate again just how well Fitzgerald reflected his times'

Nicholas Blincoe, *Sunday Telegraph*

'An excellent book ... [that] even manages to find fresh facts that escaped previous scholars ... She's earned the right to play on [Fitzgerald's] court. Prodigious research and fierce affection illumine every remarkable page'

*Kirkus*

'A treasury of new material. Churchwell adds considerably to our understanding of the early 1920s, and how life for Fitzgerald played into the development of his art ... Engaging deeply with the facts on the ground, the richly chaotic matrix that was Fitzgerald's life, Sarah Churchwell's *Careless People* takes us back there'

Jay Parini, *Literary Review*

'Churchwell ... holds in counterpoint the sprawling stuff of Fitzgerald's daily life and the gleamingly taut prose poem that emerged from it ... Fitzgerald offered the year 1922 as the chief exhibit when he tried to explain the meaning ... worth looking at very carefully. C... and panache'

*New Statesman*

'[Churchwell] evokes the jazz age in all its splendid glamour and reckless-ness ... She excels at providing rich period details ... the book highlights how accurately Fitzgerald intuited what was to come'

*Publishers Weekly*

'Part memoir, part painstaking historical research, part personal journey, *Careless People* brings to vivid life prohibition era New York and will make you rethink almost everything you thought you knew about F. Scott Fitzgerald and his most famous work'

*Harper's Bazaar*

'... an extremely complex re-rendering of the world according to Fitzgerald, but with delicious analysis all Churchwell's own'

Catherine Clinton, *Times Higher Education Supplement*

'Churchwell is especially successful in showing how Fitzgerald confidently produced a masterpiece (though it was not recognized as such when it was published) despite the excesses of his glamorous life ... This well-written and entertaining study is highly recommended for anyone who wants to know how a great work of art evolved out of disparate materials, as well as those who are interested in the history of the United States in the 1920s'

*Library Journal*

To WJA

'You've got [the] gift of going after the beauty that's concealed under the facts; and goddammit, that's all there is to art.'

Deems Taylor to F. Scott Fitzgerald, 1925

'The fancy cannot cheat so well
As she is fam'd to do ...'

John Keats, 'Ode to a Nightingale'

# CONTENTS

# PREFACE

On Thursday 14 September 1922, in St Paul, Minnesota, a popular young writer named F. Scott Fitzgerald and his glamorous wife Zelda were finishing their preparations to move to New York. Fitzgerald had wired his agent the day before, promising that a short story he was finishing called 'Winter Dreams', which he would later describe as a 'sort of 1st draft of the Gatsby idea', would reach the agency's Manhattan office by Monday. A few months earlier, he had told his editor of his dreams for his next novel: 'I want to write something *new* – something extraordinary and beautiful and simple and intricately patterned.' For the last two years, Fitzgerald's writing had been popular, highly paid, and celebrated. But now he wanted to do something different, more ambitious: 'the very best I am capable of ... or even as I feel sometimes, something better than I am capable of'. It would take him another two years to finish the book he would eventually call *The Great Gatsby*.

The same Thursday, a thousand miles to the east, a pretty young woman sat in a hot, cramped upstairs apartment in New Brunswick, New Jersey, reading a novel. At thirty-four she didn't look old enough to have teenaged children, or to have been married for seventeen years. She was wearing her favourite dress, dark blue with cheerful red polka-dots, and was avoiding the housework, as usual, to finish the book. She always lost herself in romances, but this one was special: it had been given to her by the married man with whom, for three years now, she had been having an increasingly passionate affair. They shared what they read with each other, talked about running away and poured their feelings into letters that they exchanged when they met. That night, she would wait for her lover at their usual rendezvous near an abandoned farmhouse on the outskirts of town, carrying letters filled with the dreams that had been inspired by the novels she loved.

That moonless night Eleanor Mills and her lover would both be shot through the head; their bodies were discovered together two days later under a crab-apple tree, their love letters scattered around the corpses. Eleanor Mills would never read the novel F. Scott Fitzgerald was beginning to plan, but as he made his way across America Fitzgerald would read about her.

This book is about the world that prompted F. Scott Fitzgerald to write *The Great Gatsby*, tracing the relationship between that world and the novel that it inspired, including the largely forgotten story of the brutal slaying of an adulterous couple, a murder mystery that held all of America spellbound at the end of 1922.

Fitzgerald began drafting *The Great Gatsby* during the summer of 1923, while he and Zelda were living in Great Neck, Long Island. He was also revising a play and writing magazine fiction, and he and Zelda were enthusiastically partying, all of which made work on his third novel sporadic. In the spring of 1924 the Fitzgeralds sailed for France, where he began writing in earnest his novel about modern America. He published *The Great Gatsby* a year later, in April 1925. After some hesitation about dates, he had eventually decided to set his story across the summer and into the autumn of 1922.

I started with a simple question: why 1922? A conventional answer has been that Fitzgerald wanted to signal his allegiance to the *annus mirabilis* of literary modernism, the year that began with the publication of James Joyce's *Ulysses* and ended with the publication of T. S. Eliot's *The Waste Land*. But while that may be part of the answer, the meanings of 1922 in relation to *The Great Gatsby* are far more expansive than that. It was a remarkable year, both in artistic and historical terms; an astonishing number of landmark events occurred, some (but by no means all) of which this book retraces. In his 1931 essay 'Echoes of the Jazz Age', Fitzgerald would 'offer in exhibit the year 1922!' for anyone hoping to understand the roaring twenties: 'it was an age of miracles, it was an age of art, it was an age of excess, and it was an age of satire'.

As *Gatsby* was inspired by the Fitzgeralds' eighteen months in Great Neck, beginning in late 1922, I tried to find the exact date of their return to New York that autumn, but no biographer or scholar had fixed it. Some said it was mid- or late September, most that it was October. On 22 September 1922 their friend Edmund Wilson wrote a letter saying he'd seen Scott and Zelda the previous night at the Plaza, and they'd been in town for 'several days', but that still left us approximating. Eventually I found a telegram from Fitzgerald in the Princeton archives, dated Monday 18 September 1922, informing his editor, Max Perkins, that they would arrive in New York two days later.

This date might seem insignificant, but it was the day after the story broke of the murders of Eleanor Mills and Edward Hall, as papers across America detailed the lurid events in New Brunswick, a town just up the road from Fitzgerald's alma mater, Princeton University. As the weeks passed, the story grew ever bigger; it would dominate the nation's headlines for the rest of the year.

One of the first histories of the 1920s, written in 1931, declared that the killing of Eleanor Mills and Edward Hall had been 'the murder of the decade': 'The Hall–Mills case had all the elements needed to satisfy an exacting public taste for the sensational ... It was grisly, it was dramatic (the bodies being laid side by side as if to emphasize an unhallowed union), it involved wealth and respectability, it had just the right amount of sex interest – and in addition it took place close to the great metropolitan nerve-center of the American press.' The author concluded with a description of the case's eccentric details: 'It was an illiterate American who did not shortly become acquainted with De

Russey's Lane, the crab-apple tree, the pig woman and her mule, the precise mental condition of Willie Stevens, and the gossip of the choir members.'

The Hall–Mills case has, until now, been considered in relation to *The Great Gatsby* only by a handful of scholars in brief articles, and in a few footnotes, but it is my contention that this remarkable story amplifies and enriches the story of *Gatsby* in many more ways than have yet been appreciated. Everyone knows that *The Great Gatsby* offers a connoisseur's guide to the glamour and glitter of the jazz age, but the world that furnished *Gatsby* is far darker – and stranger – than perhaps we recognize.

When *Gatsby* was published most of its initial reviewers dismissed it as mere melodrama, the type of story found in the movies or in the papers every day; here was a novel that surely would not stand the test of time, they sniffed. As far as its first readers were concerned, *The Great Gatsby* was covered in newsprint – and for many, this made it disposable and ephemeral, a mere tabloid tale. Even positive reviews returned repeatedly to the sense that it was a story ripped from the newspapers: 'You pick up your morning paper and see a headline,' wrote one typical assessment: 'NEW EVIDENCE IN SMART SET'S MURDER. "The Great Gatsby" is a perfect picture of the life that produces those headlines. It is the story that the morning paper never gives you.' The reviewer imagined that Fitzgerald had said to himself as he started *Gatsby*, 'The newspaper tells [the reader] what happened, but it never makes it clear enough. The reader wants to know *why* it happened. He wants to know how in thunder such a thing *could* happen. I'll show him how!'

In a sense, this book reverses that imaginary process, trying to suggest how, and why, *The Great Gatsby* could have happened. *Careless People* began as a species of biography – the biography of a book – seeking the origins of *Gatsby*, especially in relation to 1922 and to the role these notorious murders may have played in its inception. But along the way it became about something more: it also reconstructs a remarkable moment in America's history, at the dizzying centre of which stood Scott and Zelda Fitzgerald, trying to navigate their unsteady way through it.

Using newspaper reports, biography, correspondence, the Fitzgeralds' scrapbooks and other archival material, I piece together a collage of the Fitzgeralds' world, to tell not only their story but also that of the other remarkable people and noteworthy events swirling around them. This factual account is threaded through with Fitzgerald's fictional account in *The Great Gatsby*. The two mirror, reflect and amplify each other, a kind of two-part invention in which fact and fiction are in contrapuntal relation.

Although this book brings to bear original research into the news stories of 1922, as well as previously unused and newly discovered archival material about the Fitzgeralds and *The Great Gatsby*, it is by no means the case, of course, that all of the sources I use in this book are new. I have depended greatly on the work of other scholars, and in addition to the notes and bibliography, a word on sources at the end will explain in a bit more detail my debts to and departures from these sources. Many of these sources are known only to scholars, however, and even readers familiar with them will find here, I believe, new facts, new documents and new connections. Newspapers obviously became central to my story, as I traced not only that autumn's events, but more specifically some of the daily journalism that Fitzgerald himself was reading at the time.

Scott and Zelda kept careful scrapbooks, preserving every mention of his books and career – and of their well-publicized escapades – that they could find, but they almost never dated those clippings and only infrequently jotted down the papers from which they came. Working through the New York papers from the autumn of 1922, I was able to identify the sources and dates of many of Fitzgerald's anonymous clippings. It seems reasonable to assume that he at least glanced at the newspaper from which they came – like most writers then, Fitzgerald subscribed to a clipping service for national and international papers, but he also read the New York papers regularly. Radio would explode into American homes at the end of 1922, but it would not broadcast news for several more years; Americans depended almost entirely upon print journalism for information. Everyone read the papers, often more than one a day, and for a writer like Fitzgerald they were a vital source of news and gossip. Throughout the book I have used headlines from the New York papers – all taken from the jazz age, between 1920 and 1929 – to help suggest the ways in which Fitzgerald was often reflecting and reworking the myriad stories around him, and to help the reader navigate the various streams of the story.

Although 1922 is the crux of the tale, it will sometimes shift and jump in time, just as discussions of the novel will not be fixed by the progression of Fitzgerald's plot. *The Great Gatsby* is a hymn to language, a book about its possibilities, and so this book is also sometimes about language. Some of my allusions to Fitzgerald's language are less signposted than others: scattered throughout the book I've used some of Fitzgerald's phrases in other contexts, to suggest other ideas, for one of the themes of this book is the importance of context to determine meaning. (I have silently corrected his notoriously bad spelling, except in the case of the fictional gangster Meyer Wolfshiem, as the convention is to spell his name as it was first printed. Readers who are interested can find Fitzgerald's original spellings reproduced verbatim in biographies and published collections of his letters.)

Filaments of fact and fiction shed different lights on each other, and also throw shadows back on us. One of *The Great Gatsby*'s greatest pleasures is its suggestiveness: even if one could pin all its meanings down, such an effort would flout the entire spirit of the novel. Instead of trying to be definitive, what follows mixes explication with intimation, trying to suggest how inspiration might have worked. It would be foolhardy for anyone to promise to tell the whole story about Fitzgerald's masterpiece, but it does seem possible to tell *a* whole, true story about its creation, and about the chaotic, fugitive world from which it sprang. 'I *insist* on reading meanings into things,' Fitzgerald told Max Perkins near the end of his life, an idea which this book takes as an article of faith.

Most of my story occurs over the last four months of 1922, a period that reveals an amazing amount about Fitzgerald's novel. Although some of his sources and inspirations date from 1923 and 1924 it is also the case that nearly all of the significant sources connect back in one way or another to that year, a year that proves to have been a turning point.

In fact, the story of that autumn in 1922 is so remarkable that it would deserve retelling in its own right, even if Scott Fitzgerald had not arrived there first. But Fitzgerald usually arrived first. In addition to his sheer talent for writing, a gift that made other writers admire and envy him in equal measure, Fitzgerald often had an uncanny ability to guess right, an intuition that could be staggeringly prescient.

In 1920, when Fitzgerald was only twenty-three years old, a friend noted in his diary: 'Fitz argued about various things. Mind absolutely undisciplined but guesses right, – intuition marvelous ... Senses the exact mood & drift of a situation so surely & quickly – much better at this than any of rest of us.' Eventually, Fitzgerald came to understand this about himself as well, later telling Zelda: 'for all your superior observation and your harder intelligence I have a faculty of guessing right, without evidence even with a certain wonder as to why and whence that mental short cut came'. The Great Gatsby is a marvel of intuition, of this faculty for guessing right; it reveals Fitzgerald's instinctive grasp of the meanings of the era he has come to epitomize – and it is also a prophetic glimpse into the world to come.

The problem with guessing ahead of everyone else is that events have yet to prove you right, and this is the wall of incomprehension into which Fitzgerald would run headlong when The Great Gatsby was published. Review after review called the book 'superficial'. Blinded by the novel's resemblance to their moment, its first readers remained lost on the surface of Fitzgerald's tale, unable to fathom how deeply he had seen into the heart of his nation. Fitzgerald could sense that America was poised on the edge of a vast transformation, and wrote a novel bridging his moment and ours. The Great Gatsby made manifest precisely what Fitzgerald's contemporaries couldn't bear to see, and thus it is not only the jazz-age novel par excellence, but also the harbinger of its decline and fall. The exuberant year of 1922, for all its fun and frolic, was in an important way the beginning of the end – almost before the jazz age got going in earnest. It was a season of changes, a time of turmoil and reinvention for all the participants. Their story would prove that if you make yourself up, you can be undone, as well: being self-made risks unravelling. '*Evenements* accumulated,' Zelda wrote later, looking back on their Great Neck days. 'It might have been Nemesis incubating.'

The Fitzgeralds liked to be at the centre of things, but when the centre cannot hold, as Yeats observed in 1921, things fall apart. At the end of 1923 the play upon which Fitzgerald had been pinning his financial hopes flopped disastrously at its Atlantic City tryout; surveying the professional detritus of the previous twelve months, Fitzgerald realized 'with a shock' how little he'd achieved amid all the fun. Just before they sailed for France, he wrote to Perkins confessing 'how much I've – well, almost *deteriorated* in the three years since I finished *The Beautiful and Damned*'. Over the course of 1922 and 1923, he lamented, 'I produced exactly *one* play, *half a dozen* short stories and three or four articles – an average of about *one hundred* words a day. If I'd spent this time reading or travelling or doing anything – even staying healthy – it'd be different but I spent it uselessly, neither in study nor in contemplation but only in drinking and raising hell generally.' Looking back on his twenty-sixth year, the year this book documents, Fitzgerald summarized their time on Long Island as 'a comfortable but dangerous and deteriorating year at Great Neck. No ground under our feet'.

Going abroad was intended to ground them: Fitzgerald was bent on serious work at last, so they went to France to get away from the circus that their lives had become in New York, 'because there were always too many people in the house', as Zelda recalled. But while Fitzgerald was hard at work on the novel that meant so much to him, Zelda drifted toward someone else. Feeling neglected and bored, she became deeply attracted to a handsome French aviator named Edouard Jozan.

What Fitzgerald would call a 'big crisis' in their marriage arrived in the midst of his work on the novel, a crisis that almost certainly found a way into its pages. *The Great Gatsby* began as a story of illusions and ended as a novel about disillusionment. 'The novel finished,' Fitzgerald wrote in his ledger for September 1924. 'Trouble passing away.' That may have been wishful thinking, however, for many years later he would write, 'That September 1924, I knew something had happened that could never be repaired.' But it was also the month Fitzgerald finished the novel in which he believed passionately, a book he called 'a wonder'. Critics have long discussed the role that Zelda's rumoured adultery may have played in the novel's genesis, but that story, too, acquires new inflections when considered within the context of the various stories about faith, fidelity and cheating that were everywhere around, and especially against the murders of the adulterous Hall and Mills.

*Careless People* is an *histoire trouvé* about what was in the air as Fitzgerald wrote *The Great Gatsby*, including the unfolding of a remarkable tale of murder, adultery, class resentment, mistaken identity, and the invention of romantic pasts. In telling the story of the autumn of 1922, *Careless People* also tells the story of an extended party, what Fitzgerald called their 'Bacchic diversions, mild or fantastic'. In June 1922, a *New York Times* article condemned a worrying new phenomenon known as the cocktail party, at which 'inebriate' persons of both sexes gathered; soon 'animosities develop, quarrels arise, and not infrequently the end of the "party" is some sorry form of the tragical. Somebody gets shot or stabbed, or private disgraces become public because of a death over which the Coroner's jury ponder long in an effort to determine whether it was "natural" or a murder.' Jazz-age parties reached their literary apotheosis with the publication of *The Great Gatsby*, which predicted the party would come crashing to an end.

But despite the fact that the party inevitably ends with violence, private disgrace, or even murder, *Gatsby* made us all desperate to be invited. And so this book becomes a detective story, too, looking for what's been left behind, the evidence of history. We are searching for the clues dropped by careless people.

One crucial clue that Fitzgerald left to *The Great Gatsby* was an outline list he scribbled in the back of a 1938 book by André Malraux called *Man's Hope*. It is an old list now, barely legible, but we can still read the grey names, lightly scrawled in hard pencil. Spelled with Fitzgerald's usual approximation, it says:

    I. Glamor of Rumsies + Hitchcoks
   II. Ash Heaps. Memory of 125th. Gt Neck
  III. Goddards. Dwanns Swopes
  IV. A. Vegetable days in N.Y.
      B. Memory of Ginevras Wedding
   V. The meeting all an invention. Mary
  VI. Bob Kerr's story. The 2nd Party.
 VII. The Day in New York
VIII. The Murder (inv.)
  IX. Funeral an invention

The outline at the back of *Man's Hope* recollects a few key sources for each of *Gatsby*'s nine chapters, and has been known to Fitzgerald scholars for decades, but it is never more than a footnote to discussions about the documentary sources for *Gatsby*, offering a catalogue of people and places that Fitzgerald knew.

In order to piece together the chaotic and inchoate world behind *Gatsby*, I have taken the *Man's Hope* outline as my starting point, a springboard from which to dive into history. Each of my nine chapters begins with Fitzgerald's corresponding note as its title; while explaining the meanings of the listed references, each of my chapters also draws on the chronological events of the Fitzgeralds' lives beginning on 18 September 1922, and is in conversation with its parallel chapter in *The Great Gatsby*. Over the years after *Gatsby*'s publication, Fitzgerald cheerfully admitted many of his historical sources for the novel, including the real people upon whom he'd modelled Gatsby's gangster boss Meyer Wolfshiem, Daisy's golfing friend Jordan Baker, and Jay Gatsby himself, who borrowed some of the mannerisms and histories of actual people, including at least one bootlegger, whom Fitzgerald knew. None of these are included in the *Man's Hope* outline, but they needed to make their way into my story; and it will become clear as my story progresses that, important as it is, the *Man's Hope* outline is also enigmatic and incomplete.

Nor did Fitzgerald ever suggest, in any documentary source, that the murders of Hall and Mills had anything to do with *The Great Gatsby*, and in the *Man's Hope* outline he might even seem to deny it. This is doubtless why the few scholars who noticed some compelling parallels between *The Great Gatsby* and the Hall–Mills case didn't pursue those correspondences very far. The *Man's Hope* outline declares that the murder in *Gatsby*'s eighth chapter was '(inv.)': invented. The meanings of 'invention', and its relationship to discovery, will be considered more closely throughout, especially in my eighth chapter. For now, suffice to say that a notorious double murder might well have worked its way into Fitzgerald's mind, its details and themes resonating with his novel, without his even being aware of it. Nor did Fitzgerald necessarily believe that an artist ever fully apprehended his own material: 'What one expresses in a work of art is the dark tragic destiny of being an instrument of something uncomprehended, incomprehensible, unknown,' he wrote later.

The problem with trying to think intelligently about the relationship between life and art is that it is so easy to think unintelligently about it, to make literal-minded, simplistic equations between fiction and reality. Such literalism is reductive and unimaginative, can be deeply tiresome, and often misses the point of fiction entirely. But nor can we simply eliminate life and history from the tale, as if they have nothing to do with the genesis of fiction. If at its best fiction can transform reality, that doesn't mean that its history has nothing left to teach us. Art does not shrink when it comes into contact with reality: it expands.

And most readers also remain stubbornly as interested in the facts about great authors as in their great books. The eminent critic H. L. Mencken would call *The Great Gatsby* 'a glorified anecdote', but it was Dr Johnson who famously said, 'Sir, the biographical part of literature is what I love most. Give us as many anecdotes as you can.'

When *The Great Gatsby* was published, Fitzgerald's friend Deems Taylor, the composer and journalist, wrote a letter at four o'clock in the morning saying he'd just finished *Gatsby* and was 'dazzled' by it: 'You've got [the] gift of going after the beauty that's concealed under the facts; and goddammit, that's all there is to art.' Fitzgerald's art was so successful that its beauty has increasingly concealed the facts behind it. Some of them are lost to the passage of time, but there is another story to be told, about careless people in the autumn of 1922.

# GUEST LIST

## THE GREAT GATSBY

Nick Carraway, narrator, the only honest man he knows
Jay Gatsby, bootlegger and idolater, who springs from a Platonic
    conception of himself
Daisy Buchanan, the woman he loves, with a voice full of money
Tom Buchanan, millionaire playboy, Daisy's malicious husband
Myrtle Wilson, social climber, a woman of tremendous vitality
    and Tom Buchanan's mistress
George Wilson, her husband, mechanic, a spiritless, anaemic man
Jordan Baker, cheating golfer, Daisy's friend and Nick's sometime
    girlfriend
Meyer Wolfshiem, gangster, Jay Gatsby's partner

## NEW YORK

F. Scott Fitzgerald, writer
Zelda Sayre Fitzgerald, his wife
Edmund Wilson, Jr, writer and critic
Burton Rascoe, literary editor, *New York Tribune*
John Dos Passos, writer

Ring Lardner, writer
Carl Van Vechten, writer and photographer
Ernest Boyd, Irish writer and critic
Herbert Bayard Swope, editor, New York *World*
Deems Taylor, music critic, New York *World*
Dorothy Parker, writer
Gene Buck, Broadway producer and songwriter
Helen Buck, his wife
Edward E. (Ted) Paramore, playboy

## NEW BRUNSWICK

Eleanor Reinhardt Mills, wife, mother, choir singer, murder victim
James Mills, janitor and church sexton, her husband
Charlotte Mills, their daughter
Edward Wheeler Hall, husband, rector of church of St John,
    murder victim
Frances Stevens Hall, his wife
Willie Stevens, her brother
Henry H. Stevens, her other brother
Mrs Jane Gibson, the Pig Woman
Jenny, her mule
Raymond Schneider, roustabout
Pearl Bahmer, his girlfriend
Nicholas Bahmer, her father, bootlegger
Inspectors Beekman and Mott, prosecutors

And assorted gate-crashers, including Joseph Conrad, Fyodor
Dostoevsky, Albert Einstein, Friedrich Nietzsche, Tallulah Bankhead,
Ernest Hemingway, Benito Mussolini, Adolf Hitler, the Ku Klux Klan
and a host of bootleggers . . .

# 1924

At 10 a.m. on 3 May 1924, armed with seventeen pieces of luggage and a full set of *Encyclopedia Britannica*, F. Scott Fitzgerald, his wife Zelda and their two-year-old daughter Scottie departed from Pier 58 on the North River in New York for Cherbourg, France, on board the SS *Minnewaska*. The ship's brochure promised 'richly decorated public rooms and staterooms' and a full orchestra; some cabins came with private sitting room and bath. There was no steerage; the *Minnewaska* was entirely first-class, which is how the Fitzgeralds preferred things. After four years, off and on, in New York, Scott and Zelda had tired of dissipating across the islands of Manhattan and Long Island Sound. They would leave that side of paradise for France, where Americans were rumoured to live well on the strength of the postwar dollar.

When they boarded the *Minnewaska*, Fitzgerald had with him a few draft chapters of his third novel. In the summer of 1922 he had written to his editor, Max Perkins, his initial ideas about his next book: 'Its locale will be the middle west and New York of 1885 I think. It will concern less superlative beauties than I run to usually & will be centered on a smaller period of time. It will have a catholic element.' But he was also working on a play and the high-paying magazine stories that (almost) supported his family in their luxurious lifestyle. And then there were the parties: an art deco world of kaleidoscopic cocktails in basement dives, rooftop nightclubs and estates in the forested hills of Long Island.

In April 1924 Fitzgerald told Perkins: 'much of what I wrote last summer was good but it was so interrupted that it was ragged & in approaching it from a new angle I've had to discard a lot of it'. The new angle most likely involved abandoning 1885 and the 'catholic element', and shifting to a modern setting. It was time to put the devil and temptation behind him, and get back to work. He'd spent four months writing enough magazine stories to save seven thousand dollars, and he and Zelda were sailing for Europe, where he was going to write his new novel; it would be 'purely creative work – not trashy imaginings as in my stories but the sustained imagination of a sincere yet radiant world', 'a consciously artistic achievement'. Leaving for Europe meant they'd 'escaped from extravagance and clamor and from all the wild extremes among which we had dwelt for five hectic years', he said later that year. 'We were going to the Old World to find a new rhythm for our lives, with a true conviction that we had left our old selves behind forever.' Their old selves still seemed in fine fettle on board the *Minnewaska*, however: they drank champagne cocktails and had to apologize to an old lady they kept awake.

When they landed, they made their way south to the Riviera, ending up at St Raphaël, which Scott described as 'a red little town built close to the sea, with gay red-roofed houses and an air of repressed carnival about it; carnival that would venture forth into the streets before night'. They bought a car that they were assured was six horsepower – although 'the age of the horses was not stated' – and in nearby Valescure found Villa Marie, clean and cool, on a hill overlooking the town. 'It was what we had been looking for all along. There was a summerhouse and a sand pile and two bathrooms and roses for breakfast and a gardener,' who called Fitzgerald 'milord'.

His existence having acquired this gratifyingly seigneurial tone for the bargain price of about eighty dollars a month, Fitzgerald settled down to serious work on his novel. With his neat stack of loose white paper in front of him on the table, a pile of freshly sharpened pencils ready, he began to remember the familiar 'Long Island atmosphere' of two years before and to 'materialize it beneath unfamiliar skies'.

At the Villa Marie, the breeze floated up from the blue-drenched sea, while her husband's artistic sensibilities 'rose in wild stimulation on the barbaric juxtapositions of the Mediterranean morning', Zelda wrote later. Serrated terracotta cliffs stretched down to the water; twisted silver trees made pointed gestures among the dusty roses. A winding gravel drive extended back out into the world, and a terrace of blue-and-white Moroccan tiles overlooked the sea. Lemon, olive and pine trees mingled with the scent of roses in the air. They drank Graves Kressmann at lunch, and got into political arguments with the English nurse.

While he composed, Fitzgerald tended to pace around the room, trying words and phrases aloud, impelled by the urgency of putting language into motion, as if the ideal words lurked in the corners, awaiting discovery. Most of the novel's earliest drafts have been lost, and Fitzgerald didn't date the subsequent ones, but the novel appears to have been composed roughly in sequence. As Fitzgerald imagined its opening scenes, he would not have found it difficult to summon the swampy heat of a New York summer two years earlier, while staring out over the baked-clay cliff-tops of Southern France.

Fitzgerald had always been a fast, extravagant writer, propelled by humour and his zest for words into shooting off in all directions. Now he was writing more carefully than ever before, sculpting prose out of a past so recent it was hardly past at all. 'My novel grows more and more extraordinary,' Scott wrote to a friend. 'I feel absolutely self-sufficient & I have a perfect hollow craving for loneliness, that has increased for three years in some arithmetical progression & I'm going to satisfy it at last.' His fierce appetite for the gorgeous was being nourished by his romantic surroundings; white palaces glittered over the water and glass doors opened over terraces to which they were loosely bound by a breeze blowing through, as he evoked the mansions of Long Island. Blue after blue stretched into the sea of the happy future. He would call his novel, he thought, 'Among the Ash Heaps and Millionaires'.

# SEPTEMBER 1922

If you read the papers, you know there was a big sensation.

# I. GLAMOUR OF RUMSEYS
## AND HITCHCOCKS

In my younger and more vulnerable years my father gave me some advice that I've been turning over in my mind ever since.

'Whenever you feel like criticizing any one,' he told me, 'just remember that all the people in this world haven't had the advantages that you've had.' He didn't say any more but we've always been unusually communicative in a reserved way, and I understood that he meant a great deal more than that. In consequence I'm inclined to reserve all judgments . . .

When I came back from the East last autumn I felt that I wanted the world to be in uniform and at a sort of moral attention forever; I wanted no more riotous excursions with privileged glimpses into the human heart. Only Gatsby, the man who gives his name to this book, was exempt from my reaction . . .

*The Great Gatsby*, Chapter 1

## FACT AND FICTION.

This is a book about possibility.

In the spring of 1922, Nick Carraway moved from the Middle West to Manhattan, having consulted with his family, who deliberated the decision as if they were choosing his prep school. At last they agreed, and he moved east to work for a brokerage firm with a name that might not worry the naive: Probity Trust. Nick found a cottage fifteen miles from New York City, amid the mushrooming mansions built by new-found wealth, surrounding himself for about eighty dollars a month with the consoling proximity of millionaires. He would study finance, learning the secrets of Midas and Morgan and Maecenas. In an era of booming stock market fortunes everyone was making money: why shouldn't he? America was embarking on a spree; the world was rich with promise and there was always more money to be made: 'Bonds were the thing now. Young men sold them who had nothing else to go into.' Nick was ready for a fresh start, enjoying 'that familiar convic-tion that life was beginning over again with the summer'. He didn't yet know that fresh starts can become false starts: it all depends on the ending.

In the autumn of 1922 another young man moved from the Middle West to Manhattan, arriving four days before his twenty-sixth birthday. Unlike Nick Carraway, F. Scott Fitzgerald was not his own fictional cre-ation – at least, nowhere near to the same degree – and he really did move to New York City, in late September 1922. He was not in finance; indeed, he was usually in financial difficulties. He, too, was young, optimistic, fairly pleased with himself; but his own artistic aspi-rations far exceeded his character's modest admission that he was 'rather literary in college'. Unlike the alter ego he created to tell the story of his novel about greatness, Scott Fitzgerald wanted to be one of the greatest writers who ever lived. His ambitions, he wrote later, 'once so nearly achieved', were to be 'a part of English literature', a part of our inheritance.

Although later readers would persistently confuse them, the simi-larities between Scott Fitzgerald and Nick Carraway are mostly superficial. Both came from middle-class Midwestern families and acquired Ivy League educations – although Fitzgerald sent Nick to Yale, a university for which, as a loyal Princeton man, he had some com-petitive contempt. Both Fitzgerald and Carraway tended toward judgementalism, but also, correlatively, toward idolatry. Both were susceptible to glamour, and both were anxious about its capacity to corrupt. Both enjoyed material luxury but were also moralists who worried about its spiritual poverty.

And both moved to Long Island in 1922, where they would live through an extraordinary sequence of events. They were not exactly the same events, not identical, but their symmetry tilts toward the feeling of a design. For those who could sense the design as well as Fitzgerald, symmetry begins to shade toward prophecy. Art cannot, perhaps, impose order on life – but it teaches us to admire even the unruliest of revelations.

---

# PARTIES BEGIN.

Scott Fitzgerald wired Max Perkins on Monday 18 September that he and Zelda were coming to Manhattan after a year's sojourn in the bored, sprawling Middle West. They were keeping their return a secret: 'Arrive Wednesday tell no one.' He also requested that Perkins wire a thousand dollars to his account, to pay for their trip and for establishing themselves in New York. The next day Scott and Zelda left Scottie with her nanny in St Paul and boarded the train for the two-day journey to New York.

The bard of the jazz age, Fitzgerald heralded its arrival two years earlier with the publication of his first novel, *This Side of Paradise*, and his marriage to Zelda Sayre exactly a week later. The jazz age 'bore him up, flattered him and gave him more money than he had dreamed of, simply for telling people that he felt as they did, that something had to be done with all the nervous energy stored up and unexpended in the War', he wrote later. 'A whole race going hedonistic, deciding on pleasure', it was all part 'of the general decision to be amused that began with the cocktail parties of 1921'. In early 1922 he had published his second novel, *The Beautiful and Damned*, and they had spent an uproarious summer at the Minnesota resort of White Bear Lake, before they were asked to leave and take their uproar with them. Wearied of such provincialism, they decided to head back to the white chasms of Manhattan, taking a suite at the Plaza Hotel while they searched for a house near the city. On the train going back to New York they had a 'violent quarrel', Zelda remembered later, although by then she had forgotten why.

On the first night of a long train journey, Zelda said, 'there is a feeling of accomplishment that you are installed in your apple-green compartment, moving in a phosphorescent line' through the flickering night. 'The dining car glistens with bright new food; the train is still a part of its advertising pamphlets and has not yet settled down to its own dynamic ends. You can still smoke without tasting brass cartridges in the back of your mouth ... We were both fascinated by the limitations of life on a train.' In the morning, in preparation for arrival, a porter was available to steam and press travelling suits, and the *Twentieth Century* employed a professional barber, who could give a man a close shave with a straight razor while hurtling along at seventy miles an hour.

About to turn twenty-six, Francis Scott Fitzgerald was a slender young man, with dark golden hair and glittering 'hard and emerald eyes'. With his 'sophomore face and troubadour heart', he was 'such a sunny man', friends remembered; another recalled, 'Fitzgerald was pert and fresh and blond, and looked, as someone said, like a jonquil'. Pencil sketches and medallion-sized cameo photographs of his classic profile were regularly printed in the new gossip magazines and Sunday supplements. Just the week before, on 10 September, the New York *World* ran a large feature naming Fitzgerald one of America's Dozen Handsomest Male Authors.

Fitzgerald was so tall and straight and attractive, remembered H. L. Mencken, 'that he might even have been called beautiful'. At five feet eight inches (his passport added another half-inch), Scott Fitzgerald was not tall, but he was dapper, and exuberant with early success. 'Fitzgerald is romantic,' his friend Edmund Wilson had written earlier that year, 'but also cynical about romance; he is bitter as well as ecstatic; astringent as well as lyrical. He casts himself in the role of

F. Scott Fitzgerald, 1921

playboy, yet at the playboy he incessantly mocks. He is vain, a little malicious, of quick intelligence and wit, and has an Irish gift for turning language into something iridescent and surprising.'

His good looks and charm had helped propel Fitzgerald to instant fame when *This Side of Paradise* sold out its first printing in twenty-four hours: the novel 'haunted [their] generation like a song, popular but perfect'. It was so popular that a newspaper reported the story of a schoolboy who was asked to name the author of *Paradise Lost* and replied unhesitatingly, 'F. Scott Fitzgerald'. Fitzgerald clipped the item and pasted it in his scrapbook.

His wife, chic, provocative Zelda, was considered a great beauty, a woman of 'astonishing prettiness', although it is agreed that photographs never did her justice, failing to convey 'any real sense of what she looked like ... A camera recorded the imperfections of her face, missing the coloring and vitality that transcended them so absolutely.' Zelda's honey-gold hair seemed to give her a burnished glow and her éclat was soon legendary.

Her greatest art may have been her carefully cultivated air of artlessness; Zelda understood the aesthetics of self-invention, describing

Zelda Fitzgerald, 1922

the flapper as 'an artist in her particular field, the art of being – being young, being lovely, being an object'. Her behaviour was calculated to shock. Meeting Zelda for the first time nine days after her marriage to Scott, his friend Alec McKaig wrote in his diary, 'Called on Scott Fitz and his bride. Latter temperamental small town, Southern Belle. Chews gum – shows knees. I do not think marriage can succeed. Both drinking heavily. Think they will be divorced in 3 years. Scott write something big – then die in a garret at 32.'

Zelda's intelligence was unquestionably acute and she had a singular way with words, a gift for inventive and surprising turns of phrase, said Edmund Wilson. 'She talked with so spontaneous a color and wit – almost exactly in the way she wrote – that I very soon ceased to be troubled by the fact that the conversation was in the nature of free association of ideas and one could never follow up anything. I have rarely known a woman who expressed herself so delightfully and so freshly; she had no ready-made phrases on the one hand and made no straining for effect on the other.' Her conversation was 'full of felicitous phrases and unexpected fancies, especially if you yourself had absorbed a few Fitzgerald highballs'.

On the cloudy, cool morning of Wednesday 20 September 1922, as

their train pulled from the grey-turning light into the cavernous gloom
of Grand Central terminal, disembarking passengers were greeted
by the sensations of the nation's busiest train station: motor-driven
baggage-trucks, glaring arc-lights, red-capped porters, steam whistles,
shouting conductors, hurrying passengers, and the high-pitched cries
of the 'newsies'. Every front page in New York that morning was
still headlining the lurid murder mystery that had broken three days
earlier.

# HALL MURDER CLUE
# SOUGHT IN OLD HOUSE

Across the Hudson River in New Jersey, a double murder had stunned
the small town of New Brunswick. If the headline weren't enough to
catch the Fitzgeralds' attention that morning, the location of the crime
scene would have: New Brunswick was only a few miles up the recently
completed Lincoln Highway from Princeton, which the Fitzgeralds still
visited regularly to attend football games and cocktail parties.

The initial details were gruesome, and the press was doing everything it could to sensationalize them. Within four years America
learned to call this process 'hype', but in 1922 they called it 'ballyhoo',
or 'jazz journalism'.

Edward W. Hall, the well-to-do Episcopal minister of St John the
Evangelist church in New Brunswick, had been found dead in a field
outside of town on Saturday 16 September. Beside him was the body
of Eleanor Reinhardt Mills, a woman who sang in the choir in the
rector's church. Both victims were married to other people, but they
'had long been friendly', the *New York Times* insinuatingly reported,
and both had disappeared from their homes on the previous Thursday
evening. There were two wounds in the back of the rector's head, said
the *Times*, and one in Eleanor Mills's forehead; the rector's watch and
wallet had been stolen.

The dead bodies were found in an artful tableau: his arm was cradling her head; her hand rested intimately on his thigh. 'Their clothing was arranged as if for burial,' said the *Times*: his panama hat was over his face and a brown silk scarf covered hers. The bodies were found beneath a crab-apple tree near the abandoned Phillips Farm in De Russey's Lane, popular with locals for lovers' rendezvous. Love letters were scattered around their bodies, and the killer had added the piquant, theatrical touch of propping the rector's own calling card on his shoe.

The scandalous murders of Hall and Mills were impossible to miss. They would be front-page news across the country for the rest of 1922 and become one of the most famous murder mysteries of a murderous decade.

---

# New York Vistas

From Grand Central Terminal, the Fitzgeralds took a taxi that Wednesday morning up Fifth Avenue to the elegant alabaster Plaza, their favourite hotel in New York: 'an etched hotel, dainty and subdued', Zelda called it, which means it was the wrong place for the Fitzgeralds. Their cab might have been yellow, but probably wasn't. The Yellow Taxi Company had just been incorporated at the beginning of 1922, and would not achieve a monopoly of New York cabs for decades. In the 1920s, New York taxis came in harlequin colours: moonlight-blue taxicabs, 'discreetly hooded', appealed to those seeking 'a degree of privacy in pairs'; there were grey cabs, and green ones, and black-and-white ones; Fitzgerald put a lavender taxi into *The Great Gatsby*. Elegant open roadsters in varying styles and colours were marketed at chic women like Zelda, who were encouraged to think of them as accessories: a car in 'Sultan red' was promised to suit 'the florid color of the Latin type of woman', while various shades of blue and grey were recommended for blondes.

In 1922, Fifth Avenue, like all of New York City, was far less

2            THE NEW YORK TIMES BOOK REVIEW AND MAGAZINE. SEPTEMBER 24, 1922

## The Iliad of a Taxi Driver

thickly forested with buildings than it would become; the old island of Manhattan that had once welcomed Dutch sailors was not hard to imagine. The new beaux-arts buildings were creamy and unblemished, the city's wide avenues offering 'all the iridescence of the beginning of the world', Scott recalled. New York City then was still crisp and white, as if freshly laundered. The city air was salted by the ocean; rivers flowed fast on either side. 'New York was more full of reflections than of itself,' wrote Zelda a decade later in her autobiographical novel, *Save Me the Waltz*. 'New York is a good place to be on the upgrade.' The Fitzgeralds, glowing and celebrated, were riding the prow of America like the spirit of ecstasy on the hood of a red Rolls-Royce. 'America was going on the greatest, gaudiest spree in history,' Fitzgerald wrote: a spree that peaked, he said, in 1922.

The old world was deliquescing; the new world was delirious. Pleasure had become a principle and a promise – Dr Freud, whom everyone was quoting, said so. Four years after the end of the Great War, two years into prohibition, America was learning to party.

The old patrician rules still bonded high society together, but social barriers were proving soluble in alcohol. The Volstead Act, prohibiting the production, sale and transport of 'intoxicating liquors', became law on 17 January 1920. Prohibition didn't prohibit much, and incited a great deal. By September 1922 it was already obvious that prohibition (usually spelled with a small 'p' in the 1920s), known with varying degrees of irony as The Great Experiment, was experimenting mostly with the laws of unintended consequences. Its greatest success was in loosening the nation's inhibitions with bathtub gin – what they called 'synthetic' liquor.

Bootlegging was rapidly becoming a national joke, if a disreputable one. A popular wisecrack said that the safest way to get three sheets to the wind was to go to sea, because in the early days of prohibition you could drink in international waters. The day after Eleanor Mills and Edward Hall disappeared, the *Tribune* printed a comical piece about an 'Old Soak' lamenting how much more he drinks during prohibition, and requesting the repeal of the 18th Amendment so that he can return to his more temperate ways. The punchline is that although the Old Soak drinks far too much now, at least he doesn't drink as much as one of Scott Fitzgerald's heroines. By 1922 a flotilla of boats, known as 'Rum Row', was anchored three miles off Long Island Sound, safely in international waters, with holds full of liquor brought up from the West Indies. Under cover of night, bootleggers would chug out in motor-boats and make their purchases from what was effectively a floating liquor store. Some men wait for their ships to come in, it was said – and others meet them beyond the three-mile limit.

Looking back from deep within the Depression, Fitzgerald remembered 'a gala in the air'. Life was a 'gay parade', a carnival of bright colours, lavish and exuberant. Around the same time, he jotted a recollection in his notebooks: 'Laughed with a sudden memory of Hopkins where going to a party he had once tried taking gin by rectum, and the great success it had been until the agony of passing great masses of burned intestine.'

On this side of paradise, sins needed to feel original. That autumn a girl attracted crowds in Manhattan by strolling along Fifth Avenue in transparent pajamas, walking four cats on leads. The cats were also wearing pajamas. A crowd gathered; the police were called. Eventually an observant policeman worked out that the girl was enacting a current bit of slang, putting on a show of 'the cat's pajamas'. The police dismissed it as an example of that unsettling new phenomenon, a 'publicity scheme', and made the girl go home.

There was no sign of someone trying to be 'the cat's meow' or 'the bee's knees', other popular superlatives of the decade. In early February, Fitzgerald noted the 'adjectives of the year – "hectic," "marvelous" and "slick"'. Zelda remembered her own list of 'current adjectives, "hectic and delirious and killing"'. 'And how!' exclaimed the young men, as they announced they were becoming slaves to highballs; young women advised each other of 'the new and really swagger things' to do in the city. 'It was slick to have seen you,' Fitzgerald told Max Perkins that autumn, while Zelda wrote to a magazine editor, 'Thank you again for the slick party,' apologizing for her behaviour at it: 'But you know how it is to be a drinking woman!'

In 1921 H. L. Mencken published a revised version of his ground-breaking *American Language*, with a whole section devoted to slang and a separate chapter for war slang, including words like 'slacker', which originally meant draft-dodger. In 1925 Virginia Woolf would remark in her essay 'American Fiction': 'The Americans are doing what the Elizabethans did – they are coining new words. They are instinctively making the language adapt itself to their needs ... Nor does it need much foresight to predict that when words are being made, a literature will be made out of them.'

A list of the words first recorded in English between 1918 and 1923 reads like a jazz-age divination of the century to come, a catalogue of the origins of our life:

cool (1918)

motherfucker (1918)

teenage (1921)

wimp (1920)

debunk (1923)

encode (1919)

hypermodern (1923)

multi-purpose (1920)

power play (1921)

existentialism (1919)

columnist (1920)

cartwheel (1920)

extrovert (1918)

fantasist (1923)

Fascist (1921)

publicized (1920)

mass media (1923)

feedback (1920)

slenderize (1923)

slinky (1921)

sadomasochistic (1921)

homosexually (1921)

post-feminist (1919)

biracial (1921)

racialized (1921)

race-baiter (1921)

to ace (1923)

French kiss (1923)

fucked-off (1923)

psyching (1920)

tear-jerker (1921)

fundamentalism (1923)

bagel (1919)

ad lib (1919)

mock-up (1920)

prefabricated (1921)

atom bomb (1921)

supersonic (1919)

ultrasonic (1923)

hitch-hike (1923)

comfort zone (1923)

junkie (1923)

market research (1920)

off-the-rack (1920)

food chain (1920)

nutritionist (1921)

check-up (1921)

comparison-shopping (1923)

devalue (1918)

white-collar (1919)

posh (1919)

upgrade (1920)

ritzy (1920)

swankiness (1920)

nouveau poor (1921)

sophisticate (1923)

cross-selling (1919)

inflationary (1920)

deflationary (1920)

merchant bank (1921)

arbitrage (1923)

subprime (1920)

The year 1922 alone added brand-name, Hollywood, moviegoing, rough cut, performative, robot, sparkly, schlep, dimwit, no-brow, oops, multilayered, rebrand, mass market, broadcasting and broadcaster, finalize, lamé, sexiness, transvestite, gigolo, to proposition, libidinal, post-Freudian, cold turkey, quantum mechanics, polyester, vacuum, notepad, duplex, Rolex, entrepreneurial and party-crashing to English. In December 1922, E. E. Cummings would give us the first use of 'partied' as a verb, in a letter describing a night spent with the New York literary crowd. And in *This Side of Paradise* Scott Fitzgerald was the first to record the words T-shirt, Daiquiri, hipped ('I'm hipped on Freud and all that') and the use of 'wicked' as a term of approval. Amory Blaine, the novel's protagonist, is advised to collect the new, and told: 'remember, do the next thing!'

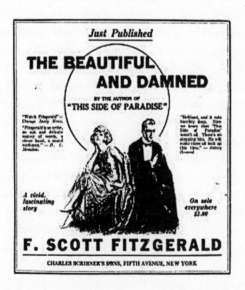

The Fitzgeralds always remembered to do the next thing. An article in March that year, responding to *The Beautiful and Damned*, remarked that Scott Fitzgerald's 'up-to-dateness is one of his chief assets. He believes in the vivid present, the immediate moment'. The Fitz, as they were sometimes known in the early years, danced on tables and rode on the top of taxicabs; both later noted, ruefully, that it costs a good deal more to ride outside cabs than in them. In the early hours of the morning Fitzgerald jumped, fully clothed, into the fountain in front of the Plaza, which was appropriately named 'Abundance'. He insisted he wasn't boiled: the stunt was inspired by sheer exuberance. Never to be outdone, Zelda danced in the fountain at Union Square. They knew that 'a chorus of pleasant envy followed in the wake of their effortless glamour', Scott wrote. 'They thought of themselves as a team, and it was often remarked how well mated they were.'

Zelda boiled the jewellery of partygoers in tomato soup; she rode out of hotel rooms in laundry wagons and was seen involved in 'goings-on' at parties with men who weren't her husband because, she announced, she admired their haircut or was charmed by their nose. Wilson recorded in his diaries that at one party Zelda so inflamed a mutual friend that he likened himself to a satyr, claiming, 'I can feel my ears growing pointed!' 'He became so aroused,' Wilson noted glee-fully, 'that he was obliged to withdraw to the bathroom. He was found in a state of collapse and murmured: "She made provoking gestures to me!"' Wilson also noted Zelda's propensity for kissing Scott's friends after they were married: 'When Zelda first began kissing John [Bishop] and Townsend [Martin], Fitz tried to carry it off by saying: "Oh, yes, they really have kisses coming to them, because they weren't at the wedding, and everybody at a wedding always gets a kiss." But when Zelda rushed into John's room just as he was going to bed and insisted that she was going to spend the night there, and when she cornered Townsend in the bathroom and demanded that he should give her a bath, [Fitz] began to become a little worried and even huffy.'

If there was no other way to add a bit of fun to the proceedings, Zelda was reportedly quite willing to take off her clothes. During their honeymoon, Zelda and Scott went to the *Follies* and the *Scandals*, and, moved perhaps by a spirit of homage to such titles, insisted on laughing loudly at the wrong parts and once began undressing in their seats. The writer Carl Van Vechten, whom they met that autumn, became very fond of both Fitzgeralds, but he felt a special affection for Zelda: 'She was an original. Scott was not a wisecracker like Zelda. Why, she tore up the pavements with sly remarks.' Scott 'was nasty when he was drunk, but sober he was a charming man, very good looking, you know, beautiful almost. But they both drank a lot – we all did, but they were excessive.' Fitzgerald was also known for his truculence when drunk. Of the Playboy Ball in April 1923 Wilson remarked: 'Fitz blew up drunk, as usual, early in the evening and knocked Pat Kearny unconscious in the lavatory.' As H. L. Mencken observed: 'Unfortunately, liquor sets him wild and he is apt, when drunk, to knock over a dinner table, or run his automobile into a bank building.'

At the beginning of the Fitzgeralds' marriage Alec McKaig recorded in his diaries their reaction to some well-meant advice: 'Suggested to Scott and Zelda they save – they laughed at me. Scott said – to go through the terrible toil of writing man must have belief his writings will be eagerly bought forever. Terrific party with two Fitz . . . ' A month later McKaig tried again to urge caution: 'Evening at Fitz. Fitz and I argued with Zelda about notoriety they are getting through being so publicly and spectacularly drunk. Zelda wants to live life of an "extravagant."' After a year of marriage, Zelda became pregnant and they moved back to St Paul to avoid bringing a baby 'into all that glamour and loneliness' in Manhattan. By January 1922 Fitz was writing to Edmund Wilson that he was 'bored as hell' in the Midwest; nine months later, they were returning to New York.

Fitzgerald was writing a play that he was sure would make their fortune, a satire of America's accelerating faith in success stories; it made sense to be near Broadway producers to try to get it staged. Scott and Zelda told each other that they were ready to settle down and be responsible. Their assurance of this intention was that they would stop going out with members of the opposite sex to make each other jealous. With this praiseworthy plan for married life, Scott was confident he could do some serious work at last. His latest collection of short stories, *Tales of the Jazz Age*, would be published by Scribner's in a few days, on Friday 22 September. And meanwhile Fitzgerald thought he might also get to work on the new, extraordinary, beautiful, simple, intricately patterned novel he had promised Perkins to write.

---

# RECTOR AND SINGER CLAWED BY WOMAN BEFORE THE MURDER

Throughout the week following the discovery of their bodies, details emerged daily about the murder of Edward Hall and Eleanor Mills. Hall had married a wealthy woman from South Carolina whom the *Times* said had inherited a fortune of a million dollars from her mother. Frances Stevens Hall had two brothers, one of whom, Willie Stevens, lived with her and the rector, and was locally known to be 'eccentric'. Eleanor Mills, 'a slight and pretty woman', was ten years younger than Edward Hall. Their bodies had been discovered early Saturday morning by a couple the *Times* reported as 'two children'. On the night of the murder, a woman in a light-grey polo coat had been seen entering the Hall mansion in the small hours, a detail made much of in the press. Soon Mrs Hall admitted that she had been out looking for her husband the night he disappeared, and had been wearing just such a coat: 'MRS HALL, THE "WOMAN IN A POLO COAT," SAYS SHE VISITED CHURCH', shouted the headlines.

One of the jazziest of the jazz-age newspapers, the New York *World* said that Eleanor Mills had been known locally for her vigorous personality, to the point of being pushy: 'Mrs Mills, twenty-eight and the mother of two children, was a woman of artistic tendencies, who had by sheer personality come to be a member of the best circles.' The

*Tribune* wasted no time in characterizing the principals in the story in their front-page coverage: the rector had a 'rich wife' at home, while James Mills was 'a pale, nervous little man', who worked as a janitor and sexton at Reverend Hall's church, and 'never did understand' his forceful, ambitious wife. On the night of the murder Eleanor Mills had left her house around 7.30 p.m.; when her meek husband asked her where she was going, she taunted him, 'Why don't you follow me and find out?' She had then rushed out of the house and never returned.

The *New York Times* reported that, in addition to being shot, both Hall and Mills appeared to have been 'clawed' by 'deep finger-nail scratches', which indicated, it was felt, that a woman must have attacked the couple first, before they were 'killed by a companion, probably a man'. But then the papers admitted that the bodies had so deteriorated from exposure that the wounds might have been made with a weapon, or even acid, instead of fingernails. 'The marks on the clergyman's hands and arms, being similar to the supposed scratches on Mrs Mills's face, indicated that he threw himself between the two women and was clawed by the other woman in her tigress fury. It was this moment, it is believed, that the other man drew his pistol. Now was heard a woman's scream ... this is taken to mean that the second woman was surprised at the sight of the pistol and attempted to prevent the murder.'

The report is circumstantial, eager and untrue, almost pure speculation. In fact, there was no evidence at all to suggest the sex, or number, of killers. But once the rumour had started the story was off and running, and the idea of the guilty woman would never leave it again.

Papers also eagerly reported on Mrs Hall's brother. Willie Stevens spent most of his time lurking around the local fire station, where he was tolerated as a harmless near-simpleton. On Friday 15 September, the day after Hall and Mills disappeared but before their bodies had been discovered, Willie had rushed into the fire station, blurting out: 'Something terrible is going to happen,' but refusing to say anything further, 'because I am tied by my sister's honor and that of my family'. Witnesses reported having heard screaming out beyond Buccleuch Park on the night of the murders.

When Nick Carraway introduces himself as *The Great Gatsby* opens, he explains that his family has 'a tradition that we're descended from the Dukes of Buccleuch, but the actual founder of my line was my grandfather's brother', a merchant who came west in 1851, 'sent a substitute to the Civil War and started the wholesale hardware business that my father carries on today'. As it happens, Nick is greatly concerned with honour too, although this may be a coincidence. But fraudulent family origins will return the story to the vicinity of Buccleuch Park before long.

---

## THE AGE OF JAZZ.

Strolling along wide New York avenues, young men with pompadours or hair parted in the middle and slicked straight back under jaunty white straw hats wore the standard three-piece suit with stiff collar and tie. Women flicked past in vivid colours and low heels; they, too, wore hats. The women were using talcum powder to keep themselves 'hygienic'; Listerine had recently invented something called halitosis and told women to avoid it by using their mouthwash. Zelda later imagistically described a yellow chiffon dress, a dress as 'green as fresh wet paint', a white satin dress and a 'theatrical silver dress' from those days in New York. That Sunday, below a headline breaking the story of the Hall–Mills murder, the *New York Tribune* had advertised 'Draped Frocks of Classic Lines', explaining that the new mode was returning to silhouettes of the past, while the *New York Times* showed 'Fall Frocks for Women':

Dresses in 1922 were not as short as received knowledge holds: in fact, that year hemlines lengthened considerably, to much comment. That Sunday, the *New York Times* ran a feature called 'The Long and

WE WILL HOLD MONDAY AN EXTRAORDINARY

*Sale of Fall Frocks for Women*

—of Poiret Twill, Crepe de Chine, Satin and Canton Crepe—

for which the August imports have served as inspiration, so
that one is assured that the models are the very, very newest.

17 September 1922

Short of New York', remarking on the surprising fact that skirts had
lengthened so much, and virtually overnight.

Working away at *Gatsby* across the summer and through the autumn
of 1924, Fitzgerald looked out at a world in which fashion had only
briefly flirted with hemlines as high as most people today picture them;
in the bold days of early 1920 and 1921, hemlines had suddenly flown
up to the knees, in what Fitzgerald later called 'the first abortive shortening of the skirts' – but not beyond, for any but the most daring. And
then skirts dropped again. In 1922, they were nearly down to the
ankles.

And that summer, dresses were white. On 11 June 1922 the *New
York Times* reported that white was 'the smartest summer color': 'the
vogue for [white] this year is much more than a natural [summer] tendency. It is a passion. It is a fad. It is a necessity ... This Summer the
evening dresses are white, the afternoon dresses are white, the morning dresses are white, the suits are white, the coats are white, the capes
are white.'

As *Gatsby* opens, Nick Carraway tells us that his story begins one
evening in June 1922, when he visited his cousin Daisy Buchanan and
her husband Tom at their stately home on Long Island, ten days before

11 June 1922

the longest day of the year. Nick finds Daisy and her friend Jordan Baker both dressed all in white, with their skirts fluttering around them in the breeze. It is one of the most evocative passages in American fiction, a setpiece that flirts with the surreal, a lingering picture of a claret-coloured room and the two women floating on a sofa in the centre of it.

Jordan is a golf champion, we soon learn, but Nick can't place her, and finds it surprising to discover that she's 'in training', which means she is not wearing a *sportif* little golfing number. What one wore mattered in a world that still judged character by conduct and appearance. In 'Echoes of the Jazz Age', Fitzgerald remarked that 'gentlemen's clothes' were a 'symbol of "the power that man must hold that passes from race to race"'. Clothes may make the man, but he has to know which clothes to buy; the mark of aristocracy is the assurance of knowing the rules. For the less certain, there were manuals like Mrs Post's bestselling *Etiquette*, first published that July, offering instructions for arrivistes trying desperately to arrive, including the useful suggestion that gentlemen keep an old tuxedo suit for informal dining at home. *Etiquette* is a shopping catalogue of silverware, napkins, wine glasses and stationery, talismans of the good life. Fitzgerald once 'looked into Emily Post and [was] inspired with the idea of a play in which all of the motivations should consist of trying to do the right thing' – and failing.

Not knowing the rules is a dead giveaway. Tom Buchanan will recognize Jay Gatsby as an impostor because of the gauche way he dresses: 'An Oxford man! ... Like hell he is! He wears a pink suit.' When Gatsby comes to woo Daisy, he wears a silver shirt and a gold tie: his clothes are as gaudy as his dreams.

---

## 'The Passing Show of 1922'

In September 1922 *American* magazine had just published Fitzgerald's facetious 'autobiographical' essay, 'What I Think and Feel at 25', in which he said that, placing 'one hand on the Eighteenth Amendment and one hand on the serious part of the Constitution', he would offer his own articles of faith. They included such essentials as whether to have your front teeth filled with gold (no), and an injunction to 'dislike old people' because 'most of them go on making the same mistakes at fifty and believing in the same white list of approved twenty-carat lies they did at seventeen'. What he feared most in life, Fitzgerald said, was 'conventionality, dullness, sameness, predictability'. The most important lesson he'd learned was to have faith that he knew more about his own work than anyone else.

Over the summer, Scott had been mulling over an offer to star, with Zelda, in a film adaptation of *This Side of Paradise* – the first, and perhaps last, time in history a celebrity author was asked to star as a fictionalized version of himself in the film adaptation of his own autobiographical novel. The new 'mass media' meant that clippings provided an easy way to calibrate a person's significance. Scott and

Zelda carefully collected every magazine and newspaper account about them in what Zelda described as 'four bulging scrapbooks full of all the things people envied them for'. Gatsby also keeps clippings about Daisy and shows them to her as a tribute to his faithfulness when they reunite at last. If you are 'Mr Nobody from Nowhere', as Tom dismissively calls Gatsby, then you must compensate for your exclusion from the old order: being original might substitute for a lack of origins.

Gatsby later fears that people will think he is just some 'cheap sharper', but in fact Gatsby also resembles a stalker, an idea that would have been available to the novel's characters, although Fitzgerald never uses it: a 1923 *Harper's* magazine article referred to a young woman who enjoyed rubbing shoulders with the rich and famous as a 'celebrity stalker'. Similarly, Gatsby cannot extricate his relentless desire for Daisy from her glamour and her wealth. Her voice was 'full of money', he tells Nick. 'That was it,' Nick agrees. 'I'd never understood before. It was full of money – that was the inexhaustible charm that rose and fell in it, the jingle of it, the cymbals' song of it . . . High in a white palace the king's daughter, the golden girl . . . '

In her scrapbook Zelda kept a clipping noting the novelty of rumours about the Fitzgeralds: 'We are accustomed enough to this kind of rumor in regard to stage stars, but it is fairly new in relation to authors. The great drinking bouts, the petting may be what the public expects of Fitzgerald whose books told so much of this kind of life.' From the beginning, Fitzgerald's books were inspiring public interest in his life, an interest that could be traded upon.

Gossip was beginning to acquire a life of its own. When Nick comes to dinner at the Buchanans' that night in mid-June, Daisy asks him about rumours of his engagement back home, insisting, 'We heard it three times, so it must be true.' Nick protests that he had 'no intention of being rumored into marriage'. Rumours aren't just active and abroad: they're coercive, prophets of self-fulfilment, and any phantom suspicion can be rumoured into fact. Gatsby himself consists only of a patchwork of rumours and myths for much of the novel. Rumour is an act of interpretation, however incomplete or inaccurate: gossip is careless fiction for careless people, and it fuelled the celebrity culture driving through America.

In 1922 Zelda began writing for the first time, publishing a few magazine pieces that traded on her celebrity name, including a tongue-in-cheek review of *The Beautiful and Damned*, and an article in June called 'Eulogy on the Flapper', in which she defended the right of a woman 'to experiment with herself as a transient, poignant figure who will be dead tomorrow'. 'Flapperdom,' she declared, 'is making them intelligent and teaching them to capitalize their natural resources and get their money's worth. They are merely applying business methods to being young.'

Zelda understood early that fame was something that could be sold. In *Save Me the Waltz*, when the heroine Alabama learns from the newspapers that she and her husband are famous, she spends the morning 'dancing happily about . . . feeling very graceful and thinking of ways to spend money'. In fact, Zelda was breathtakingly extravagant, 'as proudly careless about money as an eighteenth-century nobleman's heir', and her reckless improvidence worried all of Scott's friends. Women tended to be held accountable for such things: in fact Scott was spendthrift too. Their heedless profligacy was their trademark and their bond: as Edmund Wilson remarked, 'If ever there was a pair whose fantasies matched it was Zelda Sayre and Scott Fitzgerald.' A note Fitzgerald once made about drinks could serve as a sketch of the shape of things to come: 'You can order it in four sizes; demi (half a litre), distingué (one litre), formidable (three litres), and catastrophe (five litres).' From distingué to catastrophe was only a matter of measurements.

Earlier in the year, the New York *World* had run a film-strip montage of photos to headline an interview with Scott Fitzgerald, in a regular feature they called 'Evening World Ten-Second News Movies'. Beneath each picture were memorable quotations extracted from the piece: the sound bite had arrived.

'New York is crazy!' the interview began. Drinking had become a

status symbol, Fitzgerald observed, while young people no longer 'believe in the old standards and authorities, and they're not intelligent enough, many of them, to put a code of morals and conduct in place of the sanctions that have been destroyed for them'. After he read the piece, Fitzgerald politely wrote to the reporter, Marguerite Mooers Marshall: 'I liked your interview immensely. Thank you for the publicity which it gave to me.'

For almost two years, the papers had been declaring Fitzgerald 'the recognized spokesman of the younger generation – the dancing, flirting, frivoling, lightly philosophizing young America', who would soon be dubbed 'Flaming Youth' after Warner Fabian's 1923 bestseller. One clipping that Fitzgerald kept asked: 'Does the "younger generation" mean, perhaps, F Scott Fitzgerald alone, with his attendant flappers, male and female?' On the same scrapbook page a review of *The Beautiful and Damned* observed: 'for a man of imagination young Fitzgerald is strangely lacking in ideas outside his own as yet rather uneventful life. Every scene he writes seems to be personal experience; and one who knows him recognizes in certain minor characters acquaintances of his that he has dared to transfer to the printed page just as they are ... He invents little.' The New York *World* agreed: 'Yes, *The Beautiful and Damned* is true ... Some day, when he has outgrown the temptation to be flippant, Mr Fitzgerald will sit up and write a book that will give us a long breath of wonder.'

It was clear to everyone that Fitzgerald invented little, according to their definitions of invention, although being original is not simply a matter of making people up. They were continually recording their impressions of Fitzgerald's sources; one of the most frequently invoked models was Zelda, consistently identified as her husband's muse and inspiration, the model for all of his women. In 1923 a Louisville paper interviewed Zelda, and asked her to name her favourite of her husband's characters. "I like the ones that are like me!' she responded. 'That's why I love Rosalind in *This Side of Paradise* . . . I like girls like that . . . I like their courage, their recklessness and spendthriftness. Rosalind was the original American flapper.' 'Is She His Model?' asked the article breathlessly. 'Is Zelda Sayre Fitzgerald, wife of Scott Fitzgerald, author of flapper fiction stories, the heroine of her husband's books? . . . If so, is she the living prototype of that species of femininity known as the American flapper? If so, what is a flapper like in real life?' Soon Zelda would help inspire another of her husband's heroines, Daisy Fay Buchanan, who hails from Louisville.

They were 'plagiarising their existence', one critic said. In search of originals and prototypes, readers were finding their models in fiction and writers were finding their models in life. Jay Gatsby sprang from his Platonic conception of himself, says Nick: people reinventing themselves need a prototype, an ideal towards which they aspire.

As the days passed, the murder of Edward Hall and Eleanor Mills continued to dominate the nation's headlines, but the investigation was making no headway at all. Reporters were scouring the crime scene, as were the curious, all of whom were wandering around at will. Sightseers arrived by the carload. On the day the bodies were discovered, the authorities had made no effort to cordon off the scene or protect it from reporters and gawkers, who picked up the rector's calling card and dropped it again, and read the letters before scattering them on the ground; it was impossible to know whether any letters had been taken or lost. The forensic validity of the relatively new technique of fingerprinting was still disputed. Whether because of uncertainty or carelessness, no effort was made to preserve fingerprints, nor were any photographs or notes taken. The funeral of the rector had been held two days after the bodies were found; the Mills family held a service for Eleanor the next day in an undertaker's shop.

The prosecutor's office announced that police were searching for a light green car in connection with the murder. 'This case is a cinch,' a detective said breezily, 'but we have not enough evidence on which to act.' Meanwhile the county coroner's physician firmly refuted a growing rumour about how many bullets had been found in the bodies: 'Mrs Mills was slain by a bullet which entered her head above the right eye and not by four bullets, as has been reported by a physician in New Brunswick,' he told the *New York Times*.

At the end of *The Great Gatsby*, the police will also be told to look for a light green car in connection with a homicide. A tiny detail, too small to qualify as circumstantial evidence, it is probably just another coincidence, but coincidence has its own beauties. Even such small historical symmetries can suggest there are patterns all around us, reminders of how expansive the possibilities truly are.

## FLAMING YOUTH.

The night after they returned to New York, Edmund Wilson visited the Fitzgeralds at their suite at the Plaza Hotel. Universally known by his childhood nickname of Bunny, Wilson had been working at *Vanity Fair* and the *New Republic*, and was rapidly becoming one of America's most influential critics. He was also enjoying the hectic gaiety of the age of jazz as much as anyone. Recovering from a painful affair with Edna St Vincent Millay, Wilson was now seeing the actress Mary Blair and writing in his notebooks analytic descriptions of his many sexual encounters with other women. Not yet inclined to corpulence, and still a handsome

young man with red hair and large, intent eyes, Wilson had his own ideas about his success with women: he said he talked them into bed.

He was learning a great deal about the art of persuasion from the handsome, rakish Ted Paramore, with whom he shared an apartment. Paramore spent most of his time drinking and 'wenching' and regaled Wilson with the raunchy stories he gleefully recorded in his diaries, such as a room littered with partygoers who were out cold: there were so many people passed out on the floor that the place 'looked like Flanders Field'. The Yale Club was constantly trying to throw Paramore out, Wilson said: 'the room was always swimming in gin and garlanded with condoms'. When a previous roommate asked Wilson to send on a few things he had left behind, as a joke Wilson included an old box of condoms and the friend quipped, 'I wonder you can spare them.' Another friend received a package of condoms for his birthday: 'he was tickled to death,' said Wilson, 'and went around showing them to everybody at the Harvard Club' by blowing them up. Of one man he particularly admired that year, Paramore reported, 'You couldn't have him in the room with a girl fifteen minutes but you'd find a condom behind the clock.' They were all getting wise, as they said: modern young women wore 'wishbone' diaphragms, which were no more reliable than their name suggests. That winter, the scandal sheet *Town Topics* ran a story featuring an ultra-modern young flapper who pertly informs her mother, 'I suppose I'd be a nicer girl if I thought that birth control had something to do with the Pullman Company.'

Paramore's own favourite stratagem for seduction was to deploy the new fad for sex manuals, which were promoting what sociologists in 1924 termed 'companionate marriage', a new vision of marriage as a partnership based on egalitarian ideals including mutual pleasure and the novel possibility of a female orgasm. During the Great War, the US government had launched a national sex-education campaign to combat the spread of venereal disease, which, combined with modern theories about marriage and the increasing popularity of Freud's ideas, meant that anyone who wanted to be cool was talking about sex. 'One of Ted's principal pastimes,' Wilson wrote, 'was seducing his more inexperienced girlfriends.

His principal instrument for this was a pioneer guidebook to sex ... by a certain Dr Robey, which aimed to remove inhibitions by giving you permission to do anything you liked. He would put "old Dr Robey" into the hands of the girls and count upon their yielding reactions.'

The first time Edmund Wilson had met Zelda had been just after she married Scott; they drank orange blossoms and he found her 'very pretty and languid'. She told Wilson that hotel rooms excited her 'erotically'. Although he was deeply unimpressed by this Freudian pose and was at first inclined to view Zelda with suspicion – he wrote to John Bishop saying he hoped she'd run off with a bellhop – Wilson soon appreciated her vivacious charm and sharp wit, not to mention her beauty.

On Thursday 21 September the three friends sat high in their white tower as the early evening clouds bloomed red above New York, with what Wilson called 'the rumorous hum of summer' coming up through the windows, and talked about their plans for the future. 'Fitz goes about soberly transacting his business and in the evenings writes at his room in the hotel,' Wilson wrote to John Bishop the next day, with some astonishment. 'I had a long conversation with him last night and found him full of serious ideas about regulating his life.' The Fitzgeralds had even stopped drinking, a temporary state of grace that Wilson predicted would prove a 'brief interregnum' in their quest to make life an eternal party. You could only tell the story of the Fitzgeralds, Wilson wrote later, if you somehow did justice to the exhilaration of those days.

---

## SAYS NEWSPAPERS AID FICTION WRITING

The next day the Fitzgeralds prepared to celebrate the publication of Scott's fourth book and second collection of short stories. *Tales of the Jazz Age* collected the magazine fiction that was enabling the Fitzgeralds to pursue life as extravagants, and it was obvious to its first readers that here was a chronicle of their era. One far-sighted reviewer predicted that if 'any scholar of the future shall seek to learn the habits and conditions of this age and its people in something of the way that a scholar of to-day might study the stone age, let this advice be recorded for him now: in F. Scott Fitzgerald's "Tales of the Jazz Age" he will find an invaluable source for his researches'. Another clipping said that Fitzgerald's 'fiction will be the treasure trove of the antiquarian of the future, when the flapper, like les precieuses, is imbedded in the amber of time, so graphically does it reproduce the eccentricities of a perverse, hysterical, pleasure-crazed age'.

In June Fitzgerald had sent Perkins a few suggested blurbs (themselves a new advertising concept, not yet ten years old) to market *Tales of the Jazz Age*: 'In this book Mr F has developed his gifts as a satiric humorist to a point rivaled by few if any living American writers. The lazy meanderings of a brilliant and powerful imagination.' If that didn't suit, how about: 'Satyre upon a Saxophone by the most brilliant of the younger novelists'? Fitzgerald concluded: 'That's probably pretty much bunk but I'm all for advertising it as a cheerful book.' It was only six years since Henry Ford had declared in the *New York Times* that history was bunk, so why shouldn't a young man of ambition write himself into it? The reason for the great popularity of Fitzgerald's work, said another clipping he kept, was its portrait of 'a certain phase of life that had not been portrayed before. In other words, what we are looking for is news. We want to know, as accurately as possible, what is going on.'

Fitzgerald was always excited by a new publication, which is presumably why they arrived in New York in time to celebrate *Tales of the Jazz Age*. Wilson had been taken aback when Fitzgerald ingenuously announced during their undergraduate days: 'I want to be one of the greatest writers who have ever lived, don't you?' John Peale Bishop was also amused by Fitzgerald's ambition: 'even then he was determined to be a genius, and since one of the most obvious characteristics of genius was precocity, he must produce from an early age. He did, but wanted through vanity to make it even earlier.' Fitzgerald may have been prone to posing, but his aspirations were also serious, and none of his friends yet fully appreciated that those ambitions were as artistic as they were commercial. It was during this time that Wilson jotted in his notebooks something that Fitzgerald had told him:

When I'm with John [Bishop], I say: 'Well, John, you and I are the only real artists,' and when I'm with Alec [McKaig], I say: 'You and I are the only ones who understand the common man' and when I'm with Townsend [Martin], I say: 'Well, Townsend, you and I are the only ones who are really interested in ourselves,' but when I'm alone, I say: 'Well, Fitz, you're the only one!'

From the Plaza it was a stroll of just ten blocks down Fifth Avenue to the Scribner's building at the corner of West 48th Street, with the offices of the publishing house on the top floors and a bookshop on the ground floor. It is hard to imagine that Scott, who admitted to lingering in Fifth Avenue bookstores in hopes of hearing someone mention his books, neglected the opportunity to mark the occasion – especially as it was just two days before his twenty-sixth birthday. His career was still beginning: he must have felt that it was about to flame into life. Scribner's doubtless featured in its shop window the new book by one of its most famous writers, with its eye-catching, modern dust jacket, courtesy of illustrator John Held, Jr, of bobbed-haired, smoking flappers and young philosophers dancing while jazz musicians play in the background.

The word jazz, as Fitzgerald explains in 'Echoes of the Jazz Age', first meant sex: out of discretion or ignorance he neglects to mention that the word probably derives from 'jism'. Jazz was as disreputable as the term that spawned it: 'the flapper springs full-grown, like Minerva,' wrote Zelda in 1925, 'from the head of her once-déclassé father, Jazz, upon whom she lavishes affection and reverence, and deepest filial regard'. In 1922 Fitzgerald's association with déclassé jazz still damned him in the eyes of many readers: 'The unholy finger of jazz holds nothing sacred – leaves nothing untouched ... What Irving Berlin has done to music, F. Scott Fitzgerald and his like are doing to literature ... Fitzgerald is master of his school. He is the acme of all that is jazz. He is attune [sic] with jazz. His foundations are jazz. He can never rise to the things that are bigger; because his rhythm is jazz.' In fact, Fitzgerald was writing a jazz history of America, but the nature of his composition eluded most of his audience.

---

# CHARLES C. RUMSEY DIES IN AUTO CRASH ON JERICHO TURNPIKE

As the Fitzgeralds awoke at the Plaza on the morning of Friday 22 September, preparing to welcome the publication of *Tales of the Jazz Age*, headlines announced that a car crash had occurred the previous evening, while they were enjoying their surprisingly sober chat with Bunny Wilson. At a train station about twenty miles east of Manhattan the famous sculptor and polo player Charles Cary Rumsey had climbed into the back of an open roadster with some friends he'd invited to dinner. His wealthy wife, Mary Harriman Rumsey, was at a wedding at the estate of Clarence H. Mackay nearby. Rattling along the old Jericho turnpike a few miles south of the village of Great Neck, their car approached a bridge under the Long Island Rail Road. Pulling up to pass another car – the driver later insisted he'd been driving at moderate speed – their car clipped the other vehicle. Rumsey's roadster spun around and he was thrown out of it, hitting his head. He died at the scene, about ten minutes later.

Pad Rumsey, as he was known, was a hard-drinking playboy sculptor and polo player who had married the daughter of the Gilded Age robber baron E. H. Harriman. When Harriman died in 1909, he controlled the Union Pacific and the Southern Pacific railroads, which together were worth $1.5 billion, and employed more men than the standing army of the United States. Harriman was one of the richest men in America, and nationally famous for his cut-throat feud with the St Paul tycoon James J. Hill.

22 September 1922

Rumsey was frequently commissioned by the polo and hunting set to model their horses in bronze; one of his better-known sculptures was for his friend and teammate, Thomas Hitchcock, Jr, a war hero who had been awarded the Croix de Guerre and the most famous polo player in America. In September 1922 Hitchcock was preparing to move back to Manhattan: he had returned to America that summer after a year studying at Oxford on a scholarship offered to officers after the Armistice. Regularly likened to Babe Ruth and other sports heroes, Hitchcock was the first American player to popularize polo. When Scott Fitzgerald mused over the origins of *The Great Gatsby* twenty years later, beginning his outline in *Man's Hope* with the 'Glamour of Rumseys and Hitchcocks', these were the people he was remembering.

That autumn, Tommy Hitchcock moved into a townhouse on East 52nd Street with George Gordon Moore, a businessman alleged to be mixed up in various shady deals. Before long, rumours began to circulate that Moore was using Tommy Hitchcock as a front man for his disreputable ventures. Speakeasies had false fronts, barrels had false bottoms, drunk drivers gave false names to the police and upstarts depended on making false impressions. When Tom Buchanan first brings Nick Carraway to George Wilson's wretched garage, Nick thinks that the 'shadow of a garage must be a blind and that sumptuous and romantic apartments were concealed overhead'. Everyone was putting on airs; anything could be purchased, even the past – or, at least, the illusion of the past.

This was as true on the Gold Coast as anywhere else. During the late nineteenth century, the tycoons of Manhattan – the Astors, Vanderbilts, Fricks, Guggenheims, Harrimans, Morgans – had built vast estates along the North Shore of Long Island where they could indulge their imperial fantasies, recreating factual imitations of Old World aristocracy, complete with fox hunting and exact replicas of castles from Ireland or chateaux from Normandy. New York's rich and powerful moved out to Long Island to acquire the space to enjoy – and flaunt – their fortunes by building extravagant mansions with manicured, tumbling lawns, sundials and brick walls and sunken Italian gardens, topiary mazes, and ha-has, swimming pools, beaches, tennis courts and golf courses. Long Island was a moneyed idyll, rapidly become a familiar national symbol of aspirational wealth, an object lesson in mendacious traditions.

A 1926 *New Yorker* profile registered Scott Fitzgerald's critical interest in America's new aristocracy. The reporter explained that Fitzgerald's 'research is in the chronicles of the big business juntos of the last fifty years; and the drama of high finance, with the personalities of the major actors, [E. H.] Harriman, [J. P.] Morgan, [James J.] Hill, is his serious study. He saw how the money was being spent; he has made it his business to ferret out how it was being cornered.' And Fitzgerald predicted, all too accurately, what would happen to an America that accepted the creed of unbridled capitalism, an ignorant, credulous faith espoused by the negligible Henry C. Gatz, Gatsby's father, who continues to believe in his son's potential for greatness, even after the sordid fact of his murder: 'If he'd of lived, he'd of been a great man. A man like James J. Hill. He'd of helped build up the country.' Nick 'uncomfortably' admits that Gatz is right, for he feels that this is nothing to brag about. Hill, 'the empire builder', is also admired by the equally ineffectual father in Fitzgerald's 1924 story 'Absolution', originally composed as part of the first draft of *Gatsby*.

Fitzgerald saw clearly the damage being done to American society by making money the measure of all its values. This is the mistake made by Jay Gatsby – whose name suggests not James J. Hill, but Jay Gould, one of nineteenth-century America's most corrupt financiers and robber barons. When Jay Gould died in 1892, Mark Twain declared: 'The gospel left behind by Jay Gould is doing giant work in our days. Its message is "Get money. Get it quickly. Get it in abundance. Get it in prodigious abundance. Get it dishonestly if you can, honestly if you must."' Fitzgerald knew his Twain, and has Jay Gatsby believe in the same gospel of wealth as he goes about His Father's business, the service of a vast, vulgar and meretricious beauty.

Fitzgerald recognized the Gilded Age tycoons and financiers for the glorified crooks they were. Many years later, he remarked in his notebooks, 'Rockefeller Center: that it all came out of the chicaneries of a dead racketeer', and warned his daughter to beware of a certain type of 'Park Avenue girl': 'Park Avenue girls are hard, aren't they? My own taste ran to kinder people, but they are usually the daughters of "up-and-coming" men and, in a way, the inevitable offspring of that type. It is the Yankee push to its last degree, a sublimation of the sort of Jay Gould who began by peddling buttons to a county and ended with the same system of peddler's morals by peddling railroads to a nation.' Fitzgerald later claimed that he 'would always cherish an abiding distrust, an animosity, toward the leisure class – not the conviction of a revolutionist but the smouldering hatred of a peasant . . . I have never been able to stop wondering where my friends' money came from.'

Knowing where their money comes from tells a great deal more about their character than knowing where their families come from. The American east-coast aristocracy saw itself as fitting into the mould of European aristocracy. But what it took the Europeans centuries to accrue, families like the Morgans and the Harrimans did in a generation, sufficient time in America's rapidly cycling class system. The difference between old and new money is, after all, purely relative: it just depends on when you start counting.

After Pad Rumsey's death Mary Harriman bought an estate on Sands Point, at the tip of Manhasset, Long Island, and spent several years building a replica of a Norman castle. In April 1923 Scott and Zelda would attend lavish parties at Mrs Rumsey's estate, where they also met Tommy Hitchcock. When he was transposed into fiction Hitchcock would retain his first name and his skill at polo but not his honour, becoming a frequently acknowledged model for the dishonourable and malicious Tom Buchanan. 'The Rumseys and Hitchcocks' are a frequent footnote to the genesis of *The Great Gatsby* (although many erroneously say that the Fitzgeralds knew Charles Rumsey, when they only knew his widow) but merely explaining who these people were overlooks a gleam in history: that two days after his return to New York, on the very day *Tales of the Jazz Age* was published, Fitzgerald was reading of Charles Rumsey's death in one of the car crashes that were becoming all too common on Long Island in 1922.

---

# A FRESH START.

Sunday 24 September was a sudden bright, hot, humid day in the midst of two weeks of mild weather. Cecil B. DeMille released a film called *Manslaughter*, about a reckless society woman who runs over a man with her car, which would become one of the biggest cinematic hits of 1922. That Sunday was also Scott Fitzgerald's twenty-sixth birthday, and although the Fitzgeralds left no clues as to their activities on this day, a friend of theirs did.

Burton Rascoe was the literary editor of the *New York Tribune*, one of the two newspapers that Fitzgerald names in *The Great Gatsby*. (The *Tribune* was founded by Horace Greeley, remembered in American history for four famous words, 'Go west, young man,' a catchphrase that symbolizes much of Jay Gatsby's life.) Rascoe was one of the Fitzgeralds' most enthusiastic supporters, writing that *This Side of Paradise* 'bears the impress, it seems to me, of genius', and hiring Zelda to add some 'sparkle' to his pages by reviewing *The Beautiful and Damned*. Rascoe also wrote a weekly Sunday column called 'A Bookman's Day Book', in which he listed notable literary happenings of the previous week: mostly they involved the authors with whom he had partied. Just four years older than Fitzgerald, Rascoe had a fine critical intelligence, and an inclination towards name-dropping. In fact, Burton Rascoe was an inveterate gossip.

Rascoe's column that Sunday opened, as current literary conversations often did, with a reflection on the state of American letters in 1922: 'Aspiration and discontent are the parents – if not of paradise, then – of change ... No serious book is written in America nowadays which does not carry its implied or direct criticism of our ideals, our scheme of life, our cultural attainments.' That night, Rascoe reported in his next column, he went over to the house of Thomas R. Smith, editor-in-chief at Boni & Liveright and a friend of Scott Fitzgerald's. Finding other literary friends there, he had a fine evening, but Smith soon 'proved too generous a host', and Rascoe's wife Hazel had to help get him home. He was in bed by 9 p.m.; then, 'at 12:30 [a.m.] F. Scott Fitzgerald called up. He and Zelda, Mary Blair, and Edmund Wilson Jr. wanted to come out, or have us join them, I forget which, but I was too sleepy either to encourage the one or consent to the other.'

Fitzgerald cut out Rascoe's mention of their merrymaking that night, and saved it in his scrapbook. Undated and unattributed, the tiny piece of paper offers no hint that it was a birthday present from burgeoning celebrity culture – or that it might be a gift to the future, an inkling of how Scott Fitzgerald celebrated his twenty-sixth birthday.

---

## Sacred Objects

As the first chapter ends, Nick returns home after dinner at the Buchanans' and in the distance sees his neighbour for the first time, 'Mr Gatsby himself, come out to determine what share was his of our local heavens.' But just as Nick thinks he will call out and introduce himself he hesitates, watching Gatsby, 'trembling', stretch out his arms toward the dark water of Long Island Sound. Looking to see what he is reaching toward, Nick can distinguish 'nothing except a single green light, minute and far away, that might have been the end of a dock'. The green light has become one of the most famous symbols in literature, as readers debate its various meanings: green for envy, for hope, for spring, for the colour of money? Did green mean 'go' in 1922?

Having reached out to the green light that he couldn't grasp, Gatsby vanishes, leaving Nick alone 'in the unquiet darkness' as the tender night begins to fall.

## II. ASH HEAPS. MEMORY OF 125TH. GT NECK

About half way between West Egg and New York the motor-road hastily joins the railroad and runs beside it for a quarter of a mile, so as to shrink away from a certain desolate area of land. This is a valley of ashes – a fantastic farm where ashes grow like wheat into ridges and hills and grotesque gardens where ashes take the forms of houses and chimneys and rising smoke and finally, with a transcendent effort, of men who move dimly and already crumbling through the powdery air. Occasionally a line of grey cars crawls along an invisible track, gives out a ghastly creak and comes to rest, and immediately the ash-grey men swarm up with leaden spades and stir up an impenetrable cloud which screens their obscure operations from your sight.

*The Great Gatsby*, Chapter 2

## YOUNG WRITERS, OLD CRITICS.

Accidents will prove decisive, and there is much about which we can't be certain. But it's also true that certainty isn't all it's cracked up to be. 'It was a matter of chance', Nick Carraway tells us, 'that I should have rented a house in one of the strangest communities in

North America'. But it was not a matter of chance that the Fitzgeralds went there. It was time to find somewhere to live and a coherent mode for living, and where else should the golden boy and his golden girl live but as near to the Gold Coast as they could get? They would mingle with the millionaires on Long Island's North Shore, the better to calibrate their success. But first, maybe throw a party.

A few days after Scott's birthday, he and Zelda invited two writers he admired, John Dos Passos and Sherwood Anderson, to lunch in their suite at the Plaza. With a certain lack of foresight, the Fitzgeralds also booked an appointment to go hunting for a house in Great Neck, about fifteen miles outside Manhattan and just west of the Gold Coast, later the same day. There may have seemed little reason to worry about sobriety when looking at a house, given that they wouldn't often be sober when they were living in it. The brief interregnum was over, and cocktails were once again reigning supreme: the Fitzgeralds ordered champagne and the popular Bronx cocktails (equal parts gin, vermouth and orange juice, said to be named for the zoo) from a good bootlegger, to be served by one of the Plaza's discreet waiters. They added the hotel's trademark lobster croquettes to a sumptuous table set by the windows overlooking Central Park and awaited their guests.

It was a crisp day, showing the signs of early autumn: a high friendly sky, brightened by the fresh air, hung over hungover New York, as John Dos Passos walked up Fifth Avenue to meet the nation's literary good-luck charms. Writing about his memory of the day forty years later, Dos, as he was known, thought the encounter must have occurred in October, because of the chilly air with a scent of the fall to come. Fitzgerald's ledger, a kind of capsule autobiography that he first began keeping as a running account in 1922, put the lunch in September. However, Fitz frequently mixed up the months in his ledger, which he often recorded retrospectively.

Dos Passos's often-quoted versions of this encounter (he told it twice in the 1960s, slightly differently) attribute to his younger self all the foresight made possible by almost half a century of hindsight. Born earlier in the same year as Fitzgerald, Dos Passos served in the ambulance corps during the First World War with his friend Edward Cummings (who would soon begin signing some poems 'e e cummings'). In 1920, Dos Passos had published *Three Soldiers* to much acclaim; Fitzgerald admired the novel, although he was concerned to make clear that his own fine story 'May Day', also about demobbed soldiers, had been written before Dos Passos's novel. Still, in 1922 Dos Passos was a promising talent and Fitzgerald was, until the end of his life, notably interested in supporting young writers and celebrating those he admired.

Arriving at the Fitzgeralds' suite, Dos suspected they had hired it for the day to impress their visitors. (They had not: he overestimated their cynicism and underestimated their extravagance.) Sherwood Anderson, author of the much admired *Winesburg, Ohio*, was there in a 'gaudy Liberty silk necktie'; Dos thought he had a 'selfindulgent [*sic*] mouth' (he sounds like Hemingway 'worrying' about Fitzgerald's 'delicate long-lipped Irish mouth' in *A Moveable Feast*; watching each other's mouths seems to have been something of a preoccupation). Dos objected to the lobster croquettes – 'Scott always had the worst ideas about food' – and disapproved of what seemed to him the Fitzgeralds' fame-chasing: they were 'celebrities in the Sunday supplement sense of the word. They were celebrities, and they loved it.'

The Fitzgeralds commenced playing one of their favourite games, amusing themselves by asking their guests discomfiting personal questions. Scott, in particular, had a reputation for awkward prying. Some put these interrogations down to drunkenness, others to gaucherie, still others to a clumsy attempt at research: he would demand whether a man still had sex with his wife, or whether a woman was a virgin when she was married, or what method of birth control a couple preferred. Edmund Wilson noted in his diaries Dos's suggestion that 'Scott was by no means always so drunk as he pretended to be, but merely put on disorderly drunken acts, which gave him an excuse for clowning and outrageous behavior'. Wilson thought Dos was probably right, although he acknowledged that Fitz 'also had an act as Prince Charming, and I have been assured by a lady who had met him only once that in this role he was quite irresistible'. Too often, however, 'the sloppy boor took over', a role with which many of Fitz's acquaintances were all too familiar. Zelda did it too: she would tell a dancing partner that he danced badly, or mock a writer for using a joke she declared outmoded.

Dos Passos disapproved: 'Their gambit was to put you in the wrong. You were backward in your ideas. You were inhibited about sex. These things might perfectly well have been true but my attitude was that they were nobody's goddamned business.' The Fitz probably thought it was all very funny, a variation on their sporadic efforts to *épater les bourgeois* – when they weren't trying to emulate them. Fortunately, the freely flowing champagne that afternoon was making it easier for Dos to feel friendly toward the pair, even if they were trying to wrong-foot him: 'I couldn't get mad at him and particularly not at Zelda: there was a golden innocence about them and they were both so hopelessly goodlooking.' This is the leitmotif of the writing about the Fitzgeralds in the early years. Dorothy Parker said they always looked as if they had just stepped in out of the sun.

Although Sherwood Anderson was generally quite willing to enjoy good cocktails, he said he had another engagement that afternoon, and excused himself after lunch. Scott and Zelda told Dos of their plans to go house-hunting in Long Island and, determined to have his company, pressed him to join them. The accommodating Plaza supplied a chauffeur-driven, bright-red touring car to ferry them out to the forested haunts of the leisure classes, and Scott provided for the party by stashing a bottle of whisky under his seat. Having tanked up a good deal at luncheon, and with the Queensboro Bridge and the white spires of the city rising up behind them, the trio bounced off in search of a house to serve as a background for his ambitions and her efforts to stay amused.

# MRS. MILLS KILLED BY JEALOUS WOMAN, HER DAUGHTER SAYS

### Slayer of Rector and Choir Singer Wanted Revenge, Charlotte Declares.

Across the Hudson in New Brunswick, the murder investigation was making little progress. But the newspapers were not about to let that stop them. The story could easily be fed: if facts were in short supply, fiction would fill the gap, and speculation was in the air.

The papers began characterizing the people in the case, searching for culprits. Within a few days of the discovery of the bodies, the *World* told its readers that the one to watch was the widow's brother, Willie Stevens. 'BROTHER HINTED AT TRAGEDY NEXT DAY,' declared its headline as the story broke: '"Something Terrible is Going to Happen," He Said Hours After Killing.' Initial press accounts strongly implied that James Mills was too apathetic to have committed such brutal murders. He was described as 'a humble man of an unusually credulous type of mind' convinced that 'no sin could have been committed by his wife and the clergyman'. He was a colourless man, grey and dispirited; 'before his wife's death', explained the *Times*, Mills had been 'dominated' by his wife, who ruled over their household. On the night of Eleanor's death, Mills discovered a page missing from his edition of the *Evening World*. When his wife failed to come home that night he went to Reverend Hall's church, where she helped with office work, to see if she were there. On the rector's desk he found the missing page of his *World*, an article discussing a prominent bishop's views on divorce.

The Millses' daughter, sixteen-year-old Charlotte, seemed to have inherited some of her mother's force of character and was happy to share her theories. The woman who had killed her mother, Charlotte was certain, must have had 'queer, terrifying eyes', an idea the *Times* liked enough to feature in a headline. This frightening and quite imaginary woman, Charlotte felt, must have had 'many masculine traits', including 'the strength of a man and with a mind like a man's'. By no coincidence, Mrs Frances Stevens Hall, the rector's widow and Charlotte's former Sunday school teacher, might be said to match this unflattering description, at least physically: pictures show a woman with thick, dark eyebrows and steel-grey hair pulled back in a bun. Charlotte also made no bones about the animosity she felt toward Mrs Hall: 'Mrs Hall does not like flappers,' she explained, 'and I'm a flapper.' She added that wealthy Mrs Hall was 'snobbish' in relation to the 'humble' Mills family.

Eleanor Mills's sister, Elsie Barnhardt, maintained that her sister's letters to the rector were just romantic nonsense. In fact she went further, and tried to persuade reporters that they hadn't even been addressed to the rector. The letters were just fiction; Eleanor was 'highly imaginative', 'fond of reading, and of expressing thoughts and ideas derived from her reading by writing imaginary letters to imaginary characters'. The letters found at the scene were written to 'nobody', certainly not to a man who wasn't her husband. Her insistence that her sister had done nothing wrong was somewhat at odds, however, with the memories of other people in New Brunswick who knew Eleanor Mills. The church choir had long been 'a hotbed of trouble': 'Mrs Mills was the cause of it all. She had pushed herself forward, it was said.'

Meanwhile crowds were pouring from the tram stop at Buccleuch Park and over to the abandoned Phillips Farm on De Russey's Lane, peering into every nook and cranny, offering the police much needed advice and trampling over everything. Since the day the bodies were found, bystanders had been stripping bark from the crab-apple tree to take away and sell as souvenirs. There were still no police posted at the crime scene.

## Traffic Signals.

After the car carrying the Fitzgeralds and Dos Passos to Great Neck crossed out of Manhattan, the speed limit was 30 mph. In an open roadster with no seat belts, rattling along partially paved roads without lane markings or traffic signals, it was hardly a sober pace. The only rule at intersections was to remember to look out for other cars, and often drivers forgot. But speed, like wealth, is relative. In a 1923 story, Fitzgerald describes the noise made by the cars of the wealthy, the 'triumphant put-put of their cut-outs cutting the warm September air'.

Instead of traffic signs, most intersections had a speed limit for turning corners, which New York City had raised that April to 8 mph. Many roads outside the city were still unpaved and the city had only introduced signals for major thoroughfares over the last year: throughout 1922, 23-foot-high ornamental bronze signal towers were being built on Fifth Avenue, and would be unveiled in December. Open at the granite base to allow a clear view of traffic, each tower had a small room at the top in which a policeman sat, using a lever to open and close glass windows on all sides, displaying different coloured signals.

The signals, however, were confusing. In the autumn of 1922 a letter was sent to the *New York Times* complaining that the railroads had long used signal colours consistently, and everyone knew the code: red for stop, yellow for caution, and green for proceed. So why, then, was it the case that on the new Fifth Avenue signal towers, the green light indicated 'a cross movement or a side-shoot of some kind', whereas yellow seemed to mean proceed? They all knew that green should mean go: but when they got to New York, the meaning of the green light seemed mysteriously to change.

By 1924, New Yorkers were demanding that the city adopt 'traffic signal uniformity': 'At Broadway there was a green light on the tower, and for once I remembered that green in this city when displayed on a tower means stop, so I stopped, only to find that when green is displayed to the east and west it means "go."' Another letter-writer interpreted the signals differently: 'our signal system provides an orange light for go, a green signal really for stop ... and a red signal which may mean stop, but is actually taken as a "getaway" signal'. No wonder they kept having accidents.

Fitzgerald very possibly saw these letters from the autumn of 1924. Although he and Zelda had been on the Riviera since May, they received the *New York Times* from Paris and read it religiously. In September 1924 Fitzgerald published a facetious article explaining expatriate American life in France: 'as he struck a Swedish match and lit an American cigarette, he remarked sonorously that the trouble with most Americans in France is that they won't lead a real French life. They hang around the big hotels and exchange opinions fresh from the States. "I know," his wife agreed. "That's exactly what it said in the *New York Times* this morning."'

While New Yorkers were writing letters complaining that the meaning of green lights was eluding everyone, Fitzgerald was finishing a novel that is driven by Gatsby's faith in the green light and the promise of progress it seems to make: 'He believed in the green light, in the orgastic future that year by year recedes before us. It eluded us then, but that's no matter – tomorrow we will run faster, stretch out our arms farther ...' Jay Gatsby, the young man who misreads the green light when he moves to New York, is confused by it into thinking he has permission to proceed from west to east, when in reality it's telling him to stop. A collision becomes inevitable: if only America's signals were less mixed, their meanings more consistent.

New York City passed a law ensuring that green would forever mean go on 27 April 1925 – two weeks after *The Great Gatsby* was published.

By 1929, the traffic towers had been dug up by the roots out of Fifth Avenue and disappeared without a trace. 'Life is slipping away, crumbling all around us,' wrote the *New Yorker*, reporting on the towers' demolition. 'There's no telling what could be removed from New York and not be missed.'

---

# THE JUST, UNSEEING EYE.

In 1922 Long Island remained a series of small villages deep in farmland, connected by country roads along which horse-drawn carriages clopped, slowing down the shiny new roadsters. The Long Island Expressway would not be constructed for decades: the red touring car took the Fitzgeralds and Dos Passos along Jackson Avenue, Route 25A, now Northern Boulevard. Past cobbled slums presided over by the dark saloons of the previous century, they drove through rolling hills. The population of Queens gradually thinned as the land extended east, from the small working-class neighbourhoods edging New York City just across the bridge, through large swathes of land unburdened by buildings. Jackson Avenue carried them into Flushing, one of the first of the Dutch settlements on Long Island, after driving through Astoria, where Nick and Gatsby would scatter light with fenders spread like wings.

About halfway between New York and Great Neck, just beneath Flushing Bay, stood the towering Corona Dumps, vast mountains of fuel ash that New York had been heaping on swampland beyond the city limits since 1895, in a landfill created by the construction of the Long Island Rail Road. By the time the ash dumps were levelled in the late 1930s (and eventually recycled to form the Long Island Expressway), the mounds of ash were nearly a hundred feet tall in places; the highest peak was locally given the ironic name Mount Corona. Created to protect the city's inhabitants from the constant grime of coal ash on the streets, the Corona Dumps were soon piled high with all manner of refuse including manure, and surrounded by stagnant water. By 1922 desolate, towering mountains of ashes and dust stretched four miles long and over a mile across, alongside the road that linked the glamour of Manhattan to the Gold Coast. In the distance could be seen the steel frames of new apartment buildings braced against the sky to the west. Refuse stretched in all directions, with goats wandering through and old women searching among the litter for some redeemable object.

Past the ash heaps, looming like a corner of the Inferno beside the Long Island Rail Road, emerging from the clinging grime, through the dry, fallow fields dotted with occasional white-frame Victorian farmhouses, past the outpost of an isolated garage planted along the side of the two-lane road, a red gas-pump sprouting in front of it, they drove four miles north of where Charles Cary Rumsey had been killed in a car crash just a few days earlier.

They would also have driven past that new industrial object, the billboard. It was the age of advertising, but Americans were already

beginning to resist the defacement of their countryside by these eye-
sores, reported the *New York Times* that autumn. 'With the general
trend of opposition to billboards developing over the country ... it can
be but a question of time until the American public will take things
into its own hands and find some means for the abatement of this nuisance.' Fitzgerald's guess was better: he put a billboard at the centre of
*Gatsby*'s network of symbols, rightly predicting that the billboards
would mushroom as fast as Americans' faith in what they sold. Zelda
wrote in *Save Me the Waltz*: 'We grew up founding our dreams on the
infinite promise of American advertising. I still believe that one can
learn to play the piano by mail and that mud will give you a perfect
complexion.'

And so Fitzgerald plants a billboard among his ash heaps, painting
the giant eyes of Dr T. J. Eckleburg dominating the grey land and its
spasms of dust. Eckleburg's blue eyes look out of a pair of enormous
yellow spectacles created by an oculist in Queens, who was trying to
improve his business before he abandoned his sign to the ashes. By the
end of the novel these colossal, bespectacled eyes will be mistaken for
God: the false god of advertising, worshipped by sad, ghostly men like

Queen's Boulevard, Flushing, March 1922

Myrtle Wilson's husband George, who runs an unlovely garage under those sightless eyes.

Zelda later observed, 'almost all the superfluous wealth of America goes into display. If this is decadence, make the most of it – but I should think the sign of decadence would be surfeit, and not a lust for more and more' in 'this busy, careless land, whose every acre is littered with the waste of the day before yesterday'. *The Great Gatsby* emerges from a world strewn with wreckage and that debris is the novel's material – sullied, but with the hope of something redeemable glinting among the ash heaps.

---

# JAIL GIRL WITNESS WHO FOUND BODIES OF HALL AND SINGER

A week after the bodies of Hall and Mills had been discovered the breezes of rumour surrounding the murders of Hall and Mills abruptly shifted direction toward the couple that had done the discovering. 'Because of the carelessness with which the authorities handled the bodies,' reported the *World*, 'they were forced to-day to begin their investigation all over' and the couple was brought 'to the courthouse for exhaustive examination'.

First described as 'children' who were mushroom-picking, the couple was revealed to be a teenaged girl and a young married man. Twenty-three-year-old Raymond Schneider was reportedly not living with his wife; his companion in the early hours of a Saturday morning, near a notorious lovers' lane, was fifteen-year-old Pearl Bahmer, who was arrested on charges of 'incorrigibility' preferred by her father, Nicholas Bahmer, who was listed in the phone book as a confectioner, but whose shop was a blind for a saloon. Bahmer was, in fact, a well-known local bootlegger.

Schneider and Pearl Bahmer had not only been at the crime

scene on the morning of Saturday 16
September; they had also been seen
near there two nights earlier, when the
murders were committed. In addition,
Schneider lived two doors down from
Buccleuch Park.

The authorities remained 'convinced that jealousy was the motive and
that a jealous woman played a leading
rôle in the tragedy'. The *World* finally
explained why the authorities were so
certain that a woman must have been
involved, despite the complete lack of
evidence: 'The precise manner in which
the bodies were laid out in the field of goldenrod has convinced all
investigators that a woman must have been one of the accomplices.' Of
this much, at least, they were sure: a man would have been careless
about the bodies. Only a woman, however homicidal, would be careful
to ensure that her corpses were neatly laid out in a field of flowers. That
the killer might have intended some meaning to be read into the scene,
rather than simply composing an attractive tableau, seems not to have
occurred to anyone.

*Saloon of Nick Behmer, until the mur-
der a considerable factor in New
Brunswick town politics*

Bahmer's Saloon

Gossip continued to be revealed about 'dissension' in the New
Brunswick community because of Mrs Mills's reputation for 'officious'
behaviour. The papers reported on 26 September that James Mills
had asked Mrs Hall the morning after the rector and his wife disappeared whether she thought the couple had eloped. Rumours began
to circulate that they were planning a trip to the Orient. It was a year
for such dreams: Rudolph Valentino's performance as *The Sheik* was
still thrilling audiences across the country and in November Howard
Carter and Lord Carnarvon were about to discover the tomb of a
young pharaoh named Tutankhamun and start a craze for all things
Egyptian.

Although police had not yet bothered to interview Mrs Hall's other brother, Henry H. Stevens, reporters had. He spoke freely, saying he had nothing to hide. On the night of the murder he'd been at his summer home on the Jersey coast having dinner with friends with whom he'd been fishing all day, some fifty miles from New Brunswick. When he was informed on Saturday 16 September that his brother-in-law had been found dead, no mention was made of the manner of death; Stevens later said he'd assumed the rector had been killed in an automobile accident. He caught a train to his sister's house the next day, and only learned about the murder by reading the newspapers en route.

Jay Gatsby's father will learn of his son's murder in the same way. 'I saw it in the Chicago newspaper,' Henry C. Gatz tells Nick Carraway. 'It was all in the Chicago newspaper.'

## LONG ISLAND TOURING

At the foot of a forked peninsula that stretches up into Long Island Sound, the touring car carrying the Fitzgeralds and Dos Passos turned north at Lake Success (the name itself an intimation, as well as a touching relic of the original settlers' shamanistic literalism) toward Great Neck, a former fishing village that in the early 1920s found its proximity to New York was tempting those flushed with new success into building their own ancestral estates.

By 1922 the next generation of the newer rich was beginning to migrate east out of the city, encroaching upon Long Island's Gold Coast to the west, the barbarians knocking at the tycoons' gates. They settled across the bay, especially in Great Neck, a small fishing village across the narrow inlet from Sands Point and home of some of the most opulent mansions of them all. Great Neck had suddenly become host to that new category of the rich and famous: celebrities. So many Broadway producers, vaudeville actors and movie stars, directors and songwriters, magazine illustrators and successful writers thronged there that *Town Topics* had reported in August (using a new phrase, 'the show business'): 'Great Neck is becoming known as "the Hollywood of the East", because of the number of men and women in "the show business" who pass their summers there.'

This is the 'slender riotous island' where Nick Carraway settles, in a village Fitzgerald renames West Egg to reinforce both America's symbolic geography of east and west and the importance of origins to the story of *Gatsby*. (The name also reflects the currency of 'egg' as slang in the early 1920s, a term of which Fitzgerald was very fond. His stories have many 'good eggs' and 'bad eggs', and a 1924 story was titled 'The Unspeakable Egg'.) Fitzgerald later told his daughter that the term 'egg' 'implies that you belong to a very rudimentary state of life'.

West Egg sits across the bay from East Egg, Fitzgerald's reinvented Manhasset and Sands Point, as western new money begins outfacing eastern old money. Nick Carraway's 'eyesore' of a cottage has been overlooked by the parvenus nearby: 'I lived at West Egg, the – well, the less fashionable of the two, though this is a most superficial tag to express the bizarre and not a little sinister contrast between them. My house was at the very tip of the egg, only fifty yards from the

Sound, and squeezed between two huge places that rented for twelve or fifteen thousand a season.'

In 1922 Great Neck was a boisterous town with a population of about twelve hundred mingling in its heady atmosphere of ambition, talent and partying. Manhattan's skyscrapers, where any enterprising young man could hope to make a fortune on Wall Street, were still visible fifteen miles to the west, a mirage floating on the far horizon. In an early draft of *Gatsby* 'the tall incandescent city on the water' could be seen at night from Jay Gatsby's house.

When they arrived in Great Neck that brisk autumn afternoon, the Fitzgeralds and Dos Passos collected a real estate agent, who took them along to view 'several ritzy mansions'. Scott and Zelda began mocking the salesman's pretension, mimicking 'his way of saying "gentleman's estate" until I was thoroughly disgusted with them', Dos Passos wrote. Deciding that 'nothing pleased them' – or more likely, that they saw nothing they could remotely afford – 'they wearied of tantalizing the real estate man' and decided to pay a call on Ring Lardner, whose writing they had been discussing all the way across Long Island: 'Scott and I had been agreeing that no one handled the American lingo better.' In her scrapbook Zelda kept a card from Frank Crowninshield, the editor of *Vanity Fair*, on which he had scrawled, 'Introducing Scott Fitzgerald to Ellis and Ring Lardner'.

One of the most famous writers of the day, Lardner earned a reputed hundred thousand dollars a year, allowing him to live in an elegant colonial house overlooking the narrow bay on the east edge of Great Neck. The Lardners had only finished building their house, which Ring called 'The Mange', the previous year, and Fitzgerald was a great admirer of Lardner's writing – as were most writers and readers. H. L. Mencken praised Lardner's 'authentic American' voice, and in 1925 Virginia Woolf singled him out as offering 'the best prose that has come our way' from America, in a list that included Sherwood Anderson, Sinclair Lewis, Willa Cather and even Edna Ferber – but not F. Scott Fitzgerald, whom she did not mention.

The Lardners' house – which Dos likened to the houses they had been viewing – stood on a rise on East Shore Road, overlooking Manhasset Bay. Just beyond it, behind a new apartment complex, one can still see right across the narrow courtesy bay to the docks that continue to jut out into the great wet barnyard of Long Island Sound (although they have no green lights on the end of them).

Ring was a famously hard drinker even in the thirsty days of prohibition, and when the Fitzgeralds and Dos Passos arrived at Lardner's house in the early evening, Ring was already so 'helplessly drunk', Dos said, he could barely talk; 'when his wife tried to get him to speak, he stared at us without seeing us. He was literally out on his feet.' After an abortive attempt at conversation, and drinking some of Ring's whisky, they all piled back into the touring car and Scott, clearly very drunk himself by this point, began repeating that 'Ring was his private drunkard; everybody had to have his private drunkard.' Perhaps that seemed a mark of distinction in an age of increasingly public drunkards.

As they were chauffeured back into Manhattan, the trio passed a carnival with 'whirling lights, a calliope playing'. Radiant jewel colours dotted the grounds; the Ferris wheel, a bracelet of yellow lights, rolled slowly against the deepening gas-blue sky. Zelda and Dos 'clamored to be allowed to take some rides'. Scott sulked in the car, taking belts from the whisky bottle he'd stashed under the seat and moodily watching his drunk, flirtatious wife and the attractive dark-haired young writer as they revolved lazily on the Ferris wheel.

According to Dos Passos, writing almost half a century later, Zelda said something during that ride that made him think that she was 'mad', although he couldn't later remember what she'd said that was so insane. But he'd suddenly realized, Dos claimed, that there was a 'basic fissure in her mental processes': 'though she was so very lovely I had come upon something that frightened and repelled me, even physically'. Still, despite her erratic behaviour, 'she was never a girl you could take lightly'. As for Scott, his bad taste generally, Dos felt, was compensated for by his brilliance on the subject of literature: 'When he talked about writing his mind, which seemed to me full of preposterous notions about most things, became clear and hard as a diamond ... He had no taste for food or wine or painting, little ear for music except for the most rudimentary popular songs, but about writing he was a born professional. Everything he said was worth listening to.'

A few days after their meeting Dos Passos was bemused to see himself depicted as part of a new literary scene on an overture curtain for the 1922 Greenwich Village Follies. Fitzgerald, Edmund Wilson, John Peale Bishop, Gilbert Seldes and Dos Passos were all in a truck racing toward Washington Square, where Zelda, at the centre of the curtain in a white bathing suit, stood poised, forever young, forever ready to dive into the fountain. In June, Burton

*Les Enfants Terribles—By Gene Markey*

(John Dos Passos and F. Scott Fitzgerald)

Rascoe's *Tribune* book section had published a cartoon naming the two writers *les enfants terribles*: Fitzgerald clipped it and saved it in his scrapbook.

---

## New Witness On Grill in Hall Murder

Ten days after the bodies of Hall and Mills were discovered and a week after they were buried, the New Brunswick authorities began seriously discussing the possibility of exhuming their corpses. The bodies had been found on the county line between Somerset and Middlesex counties, and disputes about jurisdiction (and therefore which county should bear the costs of investigation and trial) would complicate the case for months. And in an especially awkward development, the county physicians had grown increasingly 'at variance' over the number of times Eleanor Mills had been shot: 'While Dr Cronk says she was shot three times, Dr Long said she was shot only once.'

By Friday 29 September the New Brunswick authorities could no longer pretend that they had the investigation into the murders of Hall and Mills under control. They 'admitted yesterday that their investigation had failed to consider the importance of a careful autopsy on the bodies'. In fact, Dr Long, the Somerset county physician, was forced to concede, reluctantly, that he had not performed an autopsy on the rector at all. Pressed to explain the reason for such negligence, he said, 'It was self-evident that Hall had been murdered, and that was all there was to it.'

In the early 1920s, most US states did not have medical examiners; nor did they license coroners, who were often drunk and so notoriously corrupt that for a nominal bribe many would write 'heart attack' on the death certificate of a corpse with a bullet hole in its forehead. The city of New York had only appointed its first chief medical examiner four years earlier, in 1918, and the Mayor's office still objected to paying his salary. In 1922 New Jersey didn't have a medical examiner at all; it fell upon the county physician to examine the bodies, and from Dr Long's short perspective there was nothing in doubt medically. He had two corpses with bullets in their heads. What did it matter how many bullets? They had been shot in the head and they were both dead.

Under intense pressure from the press and public, the authorities decided to exhume Mrs Mills's body and perform a new autopsy to 'remove all doubt as to the manner in which the woman was slain'. After exactly two weeks of fruitless investigation, the body of Eleanor Mills was exhumed. The results were startling, to say the least.

> ## SECOND AUTOPSY SHOWS ATTEMPT TO BEHEAD MRS. MILLS
>
> Report Also Discloses That Woman Slain With Pastor Was Shot Three Times.
>
> ### HER THROAT WAS CUT.
>
> Believed Couple Were Standing in Close Embrace When Shots Were Fired.

Not only had Dr Long missed two of the three bullet holes in the victim's head, he had also failed to notice that her throat had been slashed from ear to ear, so deeply that it exposed her vertebrae. Eleanor Mills had been shot above one eye, again in her right cheek and the third time in her right temple. The bullet holes Dr Long missed weren't even in the back of her head; all three were full in her face. 'Following this discovery,' the *Times* reported, Dr Long, 'who had announced that Mrs Mills had been shot only once and had said nothing about her throat being cut, admitted that he had never performed a regular autopsy, but had merely made a superficial examination.' That was putting it mildly: to miss one bullet wound might be regarded as a misfortune, but to miss two, and a throat slashed from ear to ear so deeply that it nearly severed the victim's head from her body, looks like carelessness.

In fact, Dr Long hadn't performed autopsies on the bodies at all, explaining that the county prosecutor had not requested them; the prosecutor, in turn, said he simply assumed Dr Long had performed autopsies. Now that the bodies had finally been examined, the pathologists reported that 'the position of the bullet holes in the woman's head did away with the possibility of murder and suicide or a suicide agreement'. Some had argued that a murder and suicide might explain the deaths, despite the fact that no gun was found at the scene.

Gossip began to murmur that Frances Stevens Hall was being treated with kid gloves by the authorities. The rector's widow had been reported from the outset as the wealthy heir to a fortune from Johnson & Johnson, the pharmaceutical company headquartered in New Brunswick. Mrs Hall was a respected member of a prestigious family and rumours were increasing that she was using her vast wealth to quash the investigation.

---

# A BELATED DISCOVERY.

Burton Rascoe reported in 'A Bookman's Day Book' that on Saturday 30 September he and a friend called upon John Dos Passos in Manhattan.

'Finding him out, we climbed into his studio through a window and left him a note.' A little later that night, Rascoe visited the actress Mary Blair, who would marry Edmund Wilson in less than six months; they went together to the apartment of Seward Collins, who would later have a serious affair with Dorothy Parker, 'where we found Zelda and Scott Fitzgerald and Dos Passos. They had all been house-hunting for the Fitzgeralds and had rented one in Great Neck. Dos was dancing about in gay abandon with a piano lamp on his head and Zelda was imitating Gilda Gray. Scott was apathetic, observing once that I danced as badly as George Jean Nathan and bestirring himself later to inquire whether I was "going to pieces."'

That Saturday was a bright, fresh day, in the cool sixties for the most part, although it reached 80°F at its hottest. Was it the last day in September that Dos remembered and Fitz documented, or had they gone back to Great Neck again for another look? In Dos Passos's account, there is no mention of actually renting a house, while he strongly implies that they found nothing suitable; and although Zelda later said they were tight when they signed the lease on Gateway Drive that hardly narrows down the timing. Nor did Dos say anything in his censorious memoir about cavorting around later that night with a piano lamp on his head.

It seems somehow to have slipped his mind, while Rascoe's column slipped into the cracks of history. Scott may have missed this one: it's not in his scrapbook.

---

## PROGRAMS OF ASPIRATION.

One night in late September 1922 a Scottish writer named James Drawbell, who had recently come to New York, was in an expensive speakeasy in Manhattan. An aspiring journalist, he had just acquired the most desirable of all reporting jobs: he was writing for the New York *World*.

That night he was, as usual, warily watching his American friends, 'true children of Prohibition', simply knock back their drinks – 'home-made, questionable, loaded with poison'. The tables were jammed together so tightly that the drinkers were practically in each other's laps as the speakeasy tried to capitalize on every inch of space. After a while, Drawbell realized a complete stranger was watching him, who suddenly demanded, 'You Scotty, too?' Someone explained to the stranger that it was just a nickname, because Drawbell was a Scot. The man laughed, and introduced himself as Scott Fitzgerald.

At first no one believed that they were sitting next to anyone so famous, said Drawbell; someone retorted derisively, 'And I'm Babe Ruth!' But on a closer look, 'there was no mistaking the green-blue eyes and the yellow hair of the handsome young half-tipsy god who had joined up with us. He was indeed Scott Fitzgerald, the already leg-endary author', whose escapades and practical jokes, 'riotous drinking' and 'reckless dissipation of himself and his money and his talents' had already made him 'the American *enfant terrible* of the early twenties. He himself had named it the Jazz Age. It was right and proper', Drawbell decided in his memoir decades later, 'that I should meet him in a speakeasy.'

They began talking, Drawbell wrote, 'in the luxurious stews of that expensive speakeasy', amid the racket and the smoke and the heat. 'Isn't this the hell of a way of living?' Fitzgerald asked, and Drawbell laughingly replied, 'This side of paradise.' Fitzgerald laughed too: 'Touché,' he said, adding, 'My world, you mean?' After a bit more chat, Fitzgerald said, 'Let's get the hell out of here!' and stood up, 'not doubting in his attractive arrogance that I would follow him'. They moved to the locked and guarded door of the speakeasy, with Fitzgerald strewing dollar bills on their way out 'to every minion who crossed his path'.

As they left, Fitzgerald told Drawbell: 'Parties are a form of suicide. I love them but the old Catholic in me secretly disapproves. I was going on to the world's lushest party tonight', but instead they ended up at Drawbell's apartment, where they talked about writing and drank boot-leg Scotch. 'He was a wild one,' Drawbell thought. 'You could tell by the eyes, and the high-strung nervous tension about him that made him seem to be acting a part, and the drinking.'

Fitzgerald spoke about his social anxieties, Drawbell said, confessing that 'he was always trying to live up to the men who had all the money and social advantages . . . "I was always trying to be one of them! That's worse than being nothing at all!"' Drawbell concluded, 'Fitzgerald had a greater need to conform than I had. I only wanted to belong in the social order. His need was to be it.' This is only one side of the story, however, in addition to the forty years of hindsight that might have been shaping Drawbell's recollection. To paraphrase what T. S. Eliot once said of another poet, Fitzgerald was also an instinctive critic of a society in which he was the most perfect conformist. Fitzgerald said that it was 'nice to get away from the gang and meet another bewildered and despairing human soul'. When Drawbell demurred ('Bewildered, yes . . . '), Fitzgerald said: 'The rest will come. Wait till you're successful.'

Drawbell was embarrassed about his shabby boarding-house room, but Fitzgerald told him: 'Don't be stuffy. You're not the only one. I put up at a dreadful hole once.' This 'hole' was a grim room in a boarding house on Claremont Avenue, near 125th Street in Morningside Heights, where Fitzgerald had lived for four dreary months in 1919 while he worked in advertising and tried, with assurances of future literary glory, to convince a sceptical Zelda to marry him. He had hoped to write for a metropolitan newspaper, to 'trail murderers by day and write short stories by night', but no one had given him a chance to trail murderers and so, to pay the bills, he had been forced to write bad advertising slogans, like the one he produced for a laundry in Muscatine, Iowa: 'We keep you clean in Muscatine.' That immortal verse earned him a raise. He later said, 'advertising is a racket, like the movies and the brokerage business. You cannot be honest without admitting that its constructive contribution to humanity is exactly minus zero.'

The 'drab room in the Bronx' where Fitzgerald lived during these months made a profound impression on him. In his admittedly autobiographical 1924 story 'The Sensible Thing', Fitzgerald described it as 'one room in a high, horrible apartment-house in the middle of nowhere'. The city had not yet expanded that far north; a few isolated apartment houses stood alone, surrounded by empty stretches of road. Fitzgerald always remembered that room in the Bronx as a recurring threat of what life could be if all were lost, so much so that a dingy apartment on Claremont Avenue is precisely the location to which he condemns Anthony Patch in *The Beautiful and Damned*, when he loses everything through dissipation. When Amory Blaine contemplates poverty in *This Side of Paradise*, he has a similar image: 'He pictured the rooms where these people lived – where the patterns of the blistered wall-papers were heavy reiterated sunflowers on green and yellow backgrounds, where there were tin bathtubs and gloomy hallways and verdureless, unnamable spaces in back of the buildings; where even love dressed as seduction – a sordid murder around the corner, illicit motherhood in the flat above.' As far as young Scott Fitzgerald was concerned, Claremont Avenue and 125th Street was where the damned ended up.

Fitzgerald's outline in *Man's Hope* makes it clear that he was thinking of this same 'hole' when he endowed Myrtle Wilson with a 'love nest' in Washington Heights paid for by Tom Buchanan for their trysts, a hole that for Fitzgerald always recalled his feelings of social exclusion, his fear of failure. Poor Myrtle Wilson, consigned to the same neighbourhood, is also assigned the same anxieties, but without Fitzgerald's education, charm, or intelligence, let alone his genius.

Myrtle, Tom and Nick have driven up to her apartment in a lavender-coloured taxi with grey upholstery after she lets several less impressive vehicles pass them by. The lavender taxi helps signal Myrtle's pretension, as does the magazine she is clutching, *Town Tattle*, a burlesque of *Town Topics*, which called itself a 'Journal of Society'. Fitzgerald had been likened to the magazine earlier that year, derided as 'a male gossip, an artistic edition of *Town Topics*'. Gossip is in the air as they all head to Myrtle's 'love nest' for the first, and seamiest, of *The Great Gatsby*'s three great party scenes.

*Town Topics* had been writing snidely about the Fitzgeralds for two years. That summer they had printed some unflattering gossip from St Paul, and it wasn't the magazine's first (or last) uncomplimentary word on the couple. Scott kept grudges – years later he recorded a 'snub list' – and he and Zelda also kept clippings of *Town Topics*' reports on their exploits. Neither Scott nor Zelda, said the magazine, had made 'much of a hit' in Minnesota:

> The women are jealous of Zelda's looks and of her soft voice ... and both men and women fear lest Francis should lampoon them in some *a clef* novel. The elder men especially dislike Francis's outspoken socialism ... The Fitzgeralds have not been at White Bear Yacht Club long nor do I think theirs will be a long stay there ... Francis behaves in a patronizing way to people who have known him all his young life, and that does not add to his social popularity. To justify his airs his literary baggage should be far less frothy than it is.

If Fitzgerald was known for using life in his art, sometimes barely disguising his models, his books weren't really *romans-à-clef*: many forms can be made out of originals. His characters were frequently inspired by real people, but the story was always Fitzgerald's. Whether in revenge for its continued critical remarks about him, or out of distaste for its social pretensions, Fitzgerald put an *à-clef* version of *Town Topics* into vulgar Myrtle's hand for the taxi ride up to her apartment, where will be found more copies of the affected magazine whose hauteur she tries to adopt.

Myrtle's raucous gathering grounds the later glamour and magic of Gatsby's festivities. Fitzgerald had been told that the destruction of his wealthy protagonists at the end of *The Beautiful and Damned* had not seemed authentically tragic: many readers thought the novel's ending was ironic, a flippant commentary from a writer known in 1922 as a satirist. To intensify the tragedy at the end of *Gatsby*, Fitzgerald brought another America into the story: the tawdry dreams of Myrtle Wilson as a counterpoint to the grandeur of Jay Gatsby's visions.

Myrtle's guests are pathetic facsimiles of the unrefined people who will frequent Gatsby's parties: Myrtle's sister Catherine, strident and ersatz, with a sticky bob of dyed red hair; Mrs McKee, 'shrill, languid, handsome, and horrible'; Mr McKee, a photographer, who says he is in 'the artistic game', a phrase that Fitzgerald viewed as a category error (art is neither a game, nor a racket). Myrtle spends the party putting on airs, becoming 'more violently affected moment by moment' as she minces, flounces and raises her eyebrows at the shiftlessness of the lower orders. It is telling that Catherine was recently at West Egg attending the party of a man named Gatsby: anyone can get into his parties, even the taste-less Catherine.

It was much remarked at the time that prohibition parties were breaking down old barriers: men and women were suddenly getting drunk together, with predictable results. Different social classes were also mingling, but what Myrtle Wilson's sordid little evening shows is that this was hardly the same thing as social equality. The fraternizing of rich and poor may, after all, simply serve to highlight economic dis-parity, underscoring the power of the wealthy. Dissatisfaction was the result; Myrtle is dissembling, but she isn't fooled. She wants what Daisy has. Myrtle is the mirror image of Gatsby, who wants what Tom has. They are both upstarts, trying to foist themselves upon high society, poseurs who lead double lives. But Myrtle, according to the code of the novel, lacks Gatsby's greatness, while her party, although cheaper than Gatsby's, shares (and foreshadows) the crassness and violence that will come at the end of his.

It is at this typical prohibition party that Nick offers his famous image of being a vicarious participant, both within and without the gathering simultaneously, enjoying the party but listening to the secret priest within who disapproves: 'Yet high over the city our line of yellow windows must have contributed their share of human secrecy to the casual watcher in the darkening streets, and I was him too, looking up and wondering. I was within and without, simulta-neously enchanted and repelled by the inexhaustible variety of life.' Before long, Tom has broken Myrtle's nose with the flat of his hand for saying Daisy's name; they stanch the blood with copies of *Town Tattle* to keep it from ruining the pretentious toile de jouy of her upholstery.

Myrtle informs Nick that when she first began her affair with Tom all that ran through her head was a modernist *carpe diem*: 'You can't live forever … you can't live forever.' When she makes a list at the party of all the things she's got to get, they end with ashes and death, 'one of those cute little ashtrays where you touch a spring, and a wreath with a black silk bow for Mother's grave'. Ashes open the chapter and they close it too: ashes mingling with dust.

Parties were a form of suicide and yet, after talking for a few hours with James Drawbell that late September night in 1922, and getting drunker, Fitzgerald 'looked round mockingly. The party was over. His path lay elsewhere. He was off to the bright lights, purged. The lushest party in the world would still see him. A little late, perhaps, but that was his usual way of arriving. He would soon catch up.'

# OCTOBER 1922

Suddenly one of these gypsies in trembling opal, seizes a cocktail out of the air, dumps it down for courage and moving her hands like Frisco dances out alone on the canvas platform. A momentary hush; the orchestra leader varies his rhythm obligingly for her and there is a burst of chatter as the erroneous news goes around that she is Gilda Gray's understudy from the 'Follies.' The party has begun.

# III. GODDARDS, DWANS, SWOPES

There was music from my neighbor's house through the summer nights. In his blue gardens men and girls came and went like moths among the whisperings and the champagne and the stars. At high tide in the afternoon I watched his guests diving from the tower of his raft or taking the sun on the hot sand of his beach while his two motor-boats slit the waters of the Sound, drawing aquaplanes over cataracts of foam. On week-ends his Rolls-Royce became an omnibus, bearing parties to and from the city, between nine in the morning and long past midnight, while his station wagon scampered like a brisk yellow bug to meet all trains. And on Mondays eight servants including an extra gardener toiled all day with mops and scrubbing-brushes and hammers and garden-shears, repairing the ravages of the night before ...

*The Great Gatsby*, Chapter 3

## THE REAL PROHIBITION PARTY.

How do you tell the story of a party? A guest list is one way to start. But as Americans invented 'partying', they found that the uninvited kept turning up. A new phrase was needed: crashing the gate, first recorded in 1922. If your party's gate is crashed, the guest list is retrospective, recording those who came rather than those who were expected. History resembles a guest list, in that sense, of the invited and the gate-crashers, the people for whom we have been waiting, and those whose presence takes us unawares. Sometimes the gatecrashers prove to be the life of the party.

In the case of the parties that inspired *The Great Gatsby*, the revel-ries Fitzgerald exalted in fiction but recorded at the back of *Man's Hope* as 'Goddards. Dwanns Swopes', the guests have grown fugitive with time and we're still awaiting an introduction to some of our hosts. Goddard, for example, may have been Great Neck resident and play-wright Charles W. Goddard, or perhaps it was Charles H. Goddard, a real-estate broker – we can't be sure. History is prone to mistakes in identity, and facts are not always solid things. The Goddards must be dispensed with, but they served their purpose.

The servants have been at work, and Fitzgerald has reminded us to mark their labour in repairing the ravages of the previous night's fes-tivities. But his notice of workers as he begins to describe Gatsby's parties does not mean Fitzgerald was more compassionate or egalitar-ian than his contemporaries. He might only have been thinking of how expensive servants were: they just couldn't get good help, he and Zelda kept finding, although being hopeless with money and drunk all the time might have had something to do with the problem.

Meanwhile, the bootleggers, having delivered their crates of smug-gled champagne, vanished into the whispering trees, hotfooting it away from the authoritative record.

If history starts as a guest list, it has a tendency to end like the memory of a drunken party: misheard, blurred, fragmentary. We're not always sure what happened, or who was there. We have some dropped hints and our own tacit – often mistaken – assumptions. Sometimes history appears to have been so inebriated that it blacked out com-pletely and we have no idea what a mysterious trace means at all.

But the vicarious pleasure of Fitzgerald's words and images remain: the ornate rooms, glowing to receive a thousand guests; the nightingale singing in the garden above the floating rounds of cocktails, which must have come over from Europe on the Cunard or the White Star Line because America doesn't have nightingales. (Unless it flew in from Keats's tender night, or Milton's paradise.) The silver jazz trumpets play a song that sounds plaintive now: 'In the morning, in the evening, ain't we got fun?' If they sing it often enough, perhaps they can convince themselves.

Gatsby delights so many readers in part because it is a book of symbolic senses, carefully designed to make the pleasure we imagine palpable. Food is drenched in music, lights burn in deep jewel colours, people drink mint juleps or luminescent champagne. Enchanted objects defy the laws of physics: houses and women alike tend to float, while cocktails glide, disembodied, through gardens. When Daisy arrives at Nick's house in the rain her hair is like a smear of blue paint across her face, and when Gatsby sits with her in Louisville he kisses her 'dark hair', but Fitzgerald also implies that Daisy is blonde, for she says her daughter inherited her 'yellow' hair. Scholars have debated the meanings of this discrepancy, but whether deliberate or not, the inconsistency adds to the mystical quality of the novel. Daisy's hair is both colours, for she is a figment of universal beauty, living in a world of spectroscopic gaiety, in which colours refract and shift. Fitzgerald merges different sensory experiences to create prose that is rich with synaesthesia. Voices in this novel don't speak, they are 'glowing' with sound. Colours nearly always suggest scents or tastes as well: Gatsby's house is decorated in rose and lavender silk; his tear-jerking shirts are in coral and apple-green and lavender and faint orange. Music has a tendency to liquefy: silver scales float over a body of water called the Sound while banjoes 'drip' their tinny tunes.

There's just enough reality in Gatsby's parties to keep them from being entirely surreal, but they are phantasmagoric, a night scene from El Greco, who imperiously decreed that only the masters should be permitted to use colour. Gatsby is washed in colour: leaves are blue, shirts are silver, cocktail music is yellow. Prodigal laughter fills the gardens; champagne glasses are as big as finger bowls; women wear trembling opal. Even turkeys are bewitched to a dark gold. Changing the world's colour alters its potential, as colour makes Gatsby's romance with possibility perceptible to the reader: anything can happen now.

Nick says the story of Gatsby begins the night he first went to the Buchanans', but for many readers it begins the night he dresses up in white flannels and strolls across to his neighbour's crowded lawns, complacent in the knowledge that he's one of the few guests who was actually invited to the party. When Nick is finally introduced to Gatsby three chapters in to the novel that bears his name, he tells us that Gatsby is not what he expected. Mistakes about identity continue to be made: Nick thought 'Mr Gatsby would be a florid and corpulent person in his middle years'; instead he's an attractive man of Nick's age, with a sudden, magical smile. But he is also obviously a tough attempting to appear cultivated, who could have sprung from the slums of New York's Lower East Side, or from the backwaters of Louisiana. 'I was looking', Nick says, 'at an elegant young rough-neck, a year or two over thirty, whose elaborate formality of speech just missed being absurd. Some time before he introduced himself I'd got a strong impression that he was picking his words with care.' Carefulness is a suspect trait among careless people; it means you're trying too hard.

Nick expects Gatsby to be a pompously successful tycoon. We expect someone great, because we know the book's title. Fitzgerald toys with great expectations, leaving the reader like Owl-Eyes, the stout man in glasses Nick and Jordan encounter in the library later that evening who has been drunk for a week, and thought it might sober him up to sit in a library. Owl-Eyes is marvelling over the realism of Gatsby's books: 'as a matter of fact you needn't bother to ascertain. I ascertained. They're real,' he announces. 'It's a bona fide piece of printed matter. It fooled me. This fella's a regular Belasco. It's a triumph.' Even Owl-Eyes can see through Gatsby's flimsy charade: they all know he's a fake. 'What thoroughness! What realism! Knew when to stop too – didn't cut the pages. But what do you want? What do you expect?'

What we expect helps shape what we will find; through fictions of self we create fact. 'If personality is an unbroken series of successful gestures,' Nick says of Gatsby, 'then there was something gorgeous about him.' Mark the doubt of that 'if', however: Gatsby lives in the conditional mood, as aspirants must. The plot may hinge on bad faith, but the book is bona fide: that much has been ascertained.

---

# A Century Before
# Scott FitzGerald

According to Burton Rascoe, on the night of Saturday 30 September the Fitzgeralds were partying at Sew Collins's apartment with Bunny Wilson, Mary Blair and John Dos Passos and his piano lamp, after signing a lease in Great Neck. The next day the *New York Times* ran a book review about modern college life with the large, misspelled headline: 'A Century Before Scott FitzGerald'. Alec Woollcott, an Algonquin regular (who looked, Max Perkins once remarked, 'like a petulant owl'), took the time to mock the possibility that the 'well-advertised gin-swigging finale-hopping' college boys of 1922 'could be sent to any American college as it was a century before the Scott FitzGerald age', for it was obvious to anyone that these modern young men 'could not possibly pass the entrance examinations' of a century earlier.

Scott may have been 'apathetic' and 'going to pieces' in the small hours of the previous night, but as he and Zelda read the *New York*  *Times* the next morning, perhaps he was enlivened to discover that he had made literary headlines again. If it was irritating to be held to symbolize the flippancy and igno- rance of the younger generation, it was also bewildering, he later said. Fitzgerald clipped the headline 'A Century Before Scott FitzGerald' and put it in his scrapbook – twice. He must have discovered himself in syndication.

Eight days later, the Fitzgeralds moved into a cottage at 6 Gateway Drive, in Great Neck, where they would live, tumultuously, until they set sail for Cherbourg in May 1924. The house they settled into was a recently built suburban cottage, part of a new development just outside Great Neck village. It has since been expanded; when the Fitzgeralds lived there it was a modest bungalow and, they and their friends agreed, amusingly bourgeois. They paid $300 a month rent, bought a second-hand Rolls-Royce, and hired servants: a live-in couple at $160 a month, a nurse for Scottie at $90 a month, and a part-time laundress for $36 a month. All this, and the consoling proximity of millionaires.

Zelda called the Gateway Drive house their 'nifty little Babbitt-home at Great Neck', a nod to Sinclair Lewis's bestselling new novel, published on 14 September, the day that Edward Hall and Eleanor Mills were murdered. Zelda wrote a letter urging the Kalmans, good friends in St Paul, to come for an autumn visit: 'Think of the ride through the dusty blue twilight to New York and the chrysanthemums and the sort of burnt smell in the air – and the liquor.' Soon Bunny Wilson was writing to John Bishop: 'Fitz and Zelda have struck their perfect milieu in the jazz society of Great Neck, where they inhabit a brand-new suburban house. Zelda plays golf, and Fitz is already acquiring pompous overtones of the successful American householder.' This impression of suburban conventionality was largely tongue-in-cheek, and Wilson added, 'They are still one of the most refreshing elements at large, however, and it would take me pages to do justice to their pranks.'

Zelda took a train back to St Paul to collect their daughter, in time for her first birthday. 'I brought Scottie to New York. She was round and funny in a pink coat and bonnet and you met us at the station,' she wrote to Scott years later, reminiscing. Zelda fired the nurse Scott had hired, 'and since then I have had the Baby myself. Now I have another one (nurse, not baby),' she told the Kalmans. With the rigours of several days of full-time parenting out of the way they could resume their fun.

The family settled in – but they did not settle down. Keeping house was neither Zelda's forte nor her aspiration, and Scott loudly objected to her failure to keep his shirts clean. Asked in 1925 to contribute to a collection of 'Favorite Recipes of Famous Women', Zelda explained how to make breakfast: 'See if there is any bacon, and if there is, ask the cook which pan to fry it in. Then ask if there are any eggs, and if so try and persuade the cook to poach two of them. It is better not to attempt toast, as it burns very easily.'

Zelda had no intention of being a self-sacrificing helpmeet and she was already contributing to Scott's art more than she may have liked: a few celebrated passages in both *This Side of Paradise* and *The Beautiful and Damned* were lifted almost straight from her letters and diaries, and Scott often put many of Zelda's wittier or more memorable lines in the mouths of his female characters. A practice he would continue through *Tender is the Night*, it would eventually lead to great acrimony. For now, Zelda's response was flippant. In her review of *The Beautiful and Damned* for Burton Rascoe earlier that year, she had facetiously observed, 'Mr Fitzgerald – I believe that is how he spells his name – seems to believe that plagiarism begins at home.'

Soon after the Fitzgeralds' marriage, Alec McKaig noted in his diary: 'Went to Fitzgeralds. Usual problem there. What shall Zelda do? I think she might do a little housework – apartment looks like a pigsty. If she's there Fitz can't work – she bothers him – if she's not there he can't work – worried what she might do ... Zelda increasingly restless – says frankly she simply wants to be amused and is only good for useless, pleasure-giving pursuits; great problem – what is she to do?' Zelda was only twenty when he wrote this; perhaps she had no more idea what she wanted to do than many twenty-year-olds. In *Save Me the Waltz*, Alabama is left alone on the Riviera, drifting with ennui, while her husband pursues artistic greatness. 'What'll we *do*, David,' she asks, 'with ourselves?' He never answers the question. Fitzgerald had given the same question to Daisy Buchanan ten years earlier: '"What'll we do with ourselves this afternoon," cried Daisy, "and the day after that, and the next thirty years?"'

Does the artist have to invent, or is discovering a fugitive theme original enough? Such invidious questions were for the future. For now, it was hard to take anything very seriously. Scott would say later that in those years he thought life was something you dominated if you were any good. Zelda thought life was simply to be enjoyed. She couldn't understand why Scott wasn't satisfied writing high-paying stories for the *Saturday Evening Post*. 'I always felt a story in the Post was tops; a goal worth seeking. It really meant something, you know – they only took stories of real craftsmanship. But Scott couldn't stand to write them.' When they'd visited New York earlier that year for the publication of *The Beautiful and Damned*, Mencken had written to a friend: 'Fitzgerald blew into New York last week. He has written a play, and [George Jean] Nathan says that it has very good chances. But it seems to me that his wife talks too much about money. His danger lies in trying to get it too rapidly. A very amiable pair, innocent and charming.'

Success in 1922 was beginning to be measured in what advertisers would later teach us to call 'lifestyle'. It was also measured in time, defining the leisure class; if you couldn't make time, you just borrowed it. Edmund Wilson lamented how few of his compatriots believed they 'had something left to live for beside a high standard of living'. Teaching its citizens to fashion themselves through emulation, and passing it off as a theory of moral sentiment, America was settling down to the serious business of selling pleasure.

Scott now placed the Fitzgeralds squarely and ironically among the 'newly rich': 'That is to say, five years ago we had no money at all, and what we now do away with would have seemed like inestimable riches to us then. I have at times suspected that we are the only newly rich people in America, that in fact we are the very couple at whom all the articles about the newly rich were aimed.' Their money may have been new, but there wasn't, in truth, enough to warrant it being termed riches, as Fitzgerald admitted in 1923: 'Thirty-six-thousand [a year] is not very wealthy – not yacht-and-Palm-Beach wealthy – but it sounds to me as though it should buy a roomy house full of furniture, a trip to Europe once a year, and a bond or two besides. But our $36,000 ... bought nothing at all.' No matter: money seemed to blow in on the trade winds off Long Island Sound. 'Even when you were broke, you didn't worry about money,' he said later, 'because it was in such profusion around you.' They paid for fun with a promissory note, 'checks written in disappearing ink', confident that the world would never collect on the debt.

---

# THE BELATED AUTOPSIES.

On Sunday 1 October, as Scott Fitzgerald read about himself in the *New York Times*, headlines announced 'STAR TROOPERS AID IN HUNT FOR SLAYER OF HALL AND WOMAN: STATE'S CRIME EXPERTS PUT TO WORK ON MYSTERY'. The New Jersey State Constabulary sent a trio of policemen with Dickensian names – Sergeant Lamb, Corporal Spearman and Trooper Dickman – to New Brunswick to take over the investigation. Not only had local authorities missed a few bullet holes and a near-decapitation; they had also failed to interview anyone in the vicinity of the crime scene. More than two weeks after the bodies were found, police finally began canvassing the area of Buccleuch Park and the Phillips Farm, searching for the weapons used to kill the minister and his lover. They were energetically assisted by the ever-growing crowds of thrill-seekers, who 'tore down the front porch of the old house, while others ripped apart the platform at the rear'. Someone else 'tore out a windowpane, entered, and opened the front door. Hundreds of persons went through the rooms, all furnished, and in the search for souvenirs, destroyed a quantity of furnishings.' Quite possibly they destroyed a quantity of evidence as well.

Questions continued to be asked about the bungled investigation. Defending his failure to demand an autopsy, Prosecutor Beekman explained: 'Dr Long notified me on Monday 18 September that he had examined Eleanor Mills's body and had found a single bullet had gone completely through the head. He declared also that he had cut open the abdomen, and I naturally assumed that he had made a full autopsy.' This small detail went unremarked: although Dr Long had not performed a full autopsy, and had missed two bullets in the face and a slit throat, he had not neglected to ascertain whether the female victim was pregnant. She wasn't.

Charlotte Mills and Florence North, 11 October 1922

Disgusted with the inept investigation, Charlotte Mills wrote to the governor demanding his help and retained 'a woman lawyer', Florence North, who understood publicity – before she became an attorney, Miss North had been a boxing promoter. Charlotte and her 'good looking young, smartly dressed' lawyer sold the love letters her mother had kept from the rector for a rumoured five hundred dollars to William Randolph Hearst's *American* magazine, rather than turning them over to the state as evidence.

The case was becoming scandalous enough to interest *Town Topics*, who declared that New Brunswick's 'authorities have shown themselves guilty of the most amazing neglect, their conduct being such as to create a widespread impression that they have been endeavoring to shield the perpetrators of this particularly brutal and unsavory double murder'. It seemed as if 'the Hall–Mills double murder were destined to [a] process of hushing up'.

The following weekend, the front pages headlined a potentially salacious new angle to the story: 'RECTOR HALL SENT SINGER "SPICY" BOOKS'. Eleanor Mills's letters to the rector revealed that 'he had been in the habit of purchasing sensational books for her'; in one she had written, 'I am sorry you bought me that spicy book. It fired my soul and wafted me into the spiritual world – Oh, goodness!' If you are having an illicit affair with a rector, it may be convenient to confuse the erotic and spiritual, and Eleanor Mills was clearly susceptible to vicarious pleasures.

---

# 'SATYRICON' AGAIN UP FOR PROSECUTION

On the mild evening of Friday 6 October, as clouds gathered over the New York night sky, Scott Fitzgerald attended a literary dinner party at the publisher Horace Liveright in Manhattan; wives were not invited. His friends the critics Ernest Boyd and George Jean Nathan were present, as was Carl Van Vechten, who would be remembered as the most prominent white patron of the Harlem Renaissance and whom Fitzgerald met for the first time that night. Van Vechten noted in his diary that the party included this memorable introduction, adding that during it Liveright 'pushes me off a piano stool, & breaks my arm'. It doesn't seem to have broken up the party.

Also on the job was Burton Rascoe, who described the dinner in his Day Book column, not neglecting the party's nonchalant violence: 'There were many mock speeches of the hands-across-the-sea variety ... Liveright pushed Van Vechten off a chair and broke his collar-bone; Evans played the "Oh, My Gawd" prelude by Rachmaninoff, to which I gave a terpsichorean interpretation, and Evans, Brackett and I bundled into a taxicab, declaring one another to be "the life of the party," and singing "God Save the King," and "Columbia, the Gem of the Ocean" ... It was a great day for literature.' Fitzgerald saved Rascoe's notice in his scrapbook.

Rascoe's facetiousness aside, it was a great day for modern literature, although he had no way of knowing it. Across the ocean in Sussex, Virginia Woolf had begun thinking about a novel that would use a magnificent summer party as a symbol of modern life. On 6 October 1922 she jotted down 'Thoughts upon beginning a book to be called, perhaps, At Home: or the Party'; it would consist of 'six or seven chapters, each complete separately ... And all must converge upon the party at the end.' From November, Woolf kept a notebook for the novel, which began: 'Suppose the idea of the book is the contrast between life and death. All must bear finally upon the party at the end; which expresses life, in every variety and full of conviction.' Woolf would publish Mrs Dalloway in May 1925, exactly a month after Scott Fitzgerald published his own novel about parties that symbolize modern life and death. A simple chime, Mrs Dalloway reflects at one point in her story, can remind us of the beauty in ordinary things. Beauty is everywhere, even in the small chimes of history.

Fitzgerald's friend Tom Smith, Liveright's editor-in-chief, was also at the party. He had just commissioned a new translation of Petronius's

*Satyricon* and John Sumner, secretary for New York's Society for the Suppression of Vice, had been trying to have the book banned for obscenity, with the result that the papers debated the literary value of the *Satyricon* throughout the autumn. (Sumner was not necessarily paranoid in seeing the seductive potential of books: men like Ted Paramore were deliberately using them to provide a respectable pretext for unrespectable conversations.) That year a number of 'spicy' books faced obscenity charges, including James Joyce's *Ulysses*, published on 2 February, which also alluded to the *Satyricon*. Throughout 1922 *Ulysses* circulated in underground copies across literary America; Edmund Wilson told Fitzgerald where to buy one and in June Fitzgerald received his copy from the Brick Row Bookshop, which had branches in Princeton and in New York. He wished, Fitzgerald told Wilson as he read it, that *Ulysses* had been set in America: 'Half of my ancestors came from just such an Irish strata or perhaps a lower one. The book makes me feel appallingly naked.'

In late September, a magistrate dismissed the case against the *Satyricon*, observing that if it was obscene, so was the Bible: 'The *Satyricon* is a keen satire on the vulgarity of mere wealth, its vanity and its grossness.' Undeterred, on 15 October Sumner presented the book to the New York attorney-general in yet another (futile) effort to have it proscribed. Later that month Tom Smith shared with Rascoe 'a prize remark' made by the prosecuting attorney in the censorship case, who had been told that the *Satyricon* had long been prized by scholars and historians as 'a literary and documentary classic'. The lawyer responded, 'Well, just because it was a classic two thousand years ago doesn't make it a classic now.'

At Liveright's literary dinner amid these court cases (Liveright also sued Sumner for libel), it seems hard to imagine that they would have failed to discuss this controversy. Most conversations were focusing on one of the fragmentary *Satyricon*'s most intact episodes: the opulent banquets of the former slave Trimalchio, a parvenu who amassed a fortune that he flaunts with eager vulgarity. Lavishly entertaining sybaritic friends and neighbours, he enjoys being the subject of their gossip. Comparisons between ancient decadence and jazz-age America were already ubiquitous: New York was called the 'Modern Babylon';

Zelda would soon be writing that they partied like 'ancient Rome *and* Nineveh'. Wilson likened one 'regular orgy' he heard about to 'a Roman banquet or something', while *Manslaughter*, DeMille's film about a society woman who runs over someone with her car, similarly underscored the debauchery of modern parties by cross-cutting them with Roman orgies.

More than one letter to the papers that October commented on the *Satyricon's* currency: 'Trimalchio's famous dinner party and the characters introduced by the author will interest the cultured reader ... particularly by the resemblance with those well known types of our ripe civilization, the nouveau riche and the profiteer.' Fitzgerald had spent 1922 writing stories about the nouveau riche and the profiteer, including his great satire of monopoly capitalism, 'The Diamond as Big as the Ritz'. Two years later, when Fitzgerald sent his novel about nouveaux riches and profiteers to Max Perkins, he was oscillating among several titles for it, including 'Trimalchio at West Egg'. He was eventually persuaded to choose an alternate, *The Great Gatsby*, instead, but Trimalchio gave Fitzgerald an image for his heroic parvenu that survived in the final draft, although only as a signal that the party is over: 'It was when curiosity about Gatsby was at its highest that the lights in his house failed to go on one Saturday night – and, as obscurely as it had begun, his career as Trimalchio was over.'

Trying to reinvent himself, Trimalchio is given to false claims. He tells boastful, self-aggrandizing tales of his life among the rich and powerful, and, in an ancient instance of name-dropping, claims to have spoken with the Cumaean Sibyl, mythical prophetess of the ancients. His banquets are adorned by tales of burnished gems and unfaithful women, roasted birds in gold plumage, a wife wearing a magnificent strand of pearls who 'lifts adulterous legs', insatiable luxury, a cauldron of gluttony, a chest of rubies glowing with their crimson-lighted depths. Reflecting on the meaning of literature, Trimalchio quotes a favourite passage: 'The emerald green, the glass bauble, what mean they to thee? Or the fire of the ruby?' They are beautiful but insubstantial; Trimalchio repeats a refrain about infidelity and the meaninglessness of wealth. Reluctantly agreeing to call his novel *The Great Gatsby*, Fitzgerald wrote to Perkins: 'It's O.K. but my heart tells me I should have named it *Trimalchio*.'

Fitzgerald was an indifferent classics scholar at best, flunking Latin three times at Princeton. His personal library contained a 1913 translation of the *Satyricon*, but Fitzgerald didn't need to read Latin to recognize the currency of Trimalchio in 1922: he only needed to read the *New York Times*.

In a few weeks T. S. Eliot would publish 'The Waste Land', which opens with an epigraph from the *Satyricon*. Drunkenly boasting at a party, competing with his guests amid grandstanding tales, Trimalchio claims: 'And then there's the Sibyl: with my own eyes I saw her, at Cumae, hanging up in a jar; and whenever the boys would say to her "Sibyl, Sibyl, what would you?" she would answer, "I would die."'

Art, Eliot wrote, is a guide to perception. It shows us how to look – or where to look – and then leaves us, as Virgil left Dante, to go beyond where the guide can take us.

---

On Monday 9 October the New Brunswick prosecutor's office triumphantly announced an arrest in the Hall–Mills case: a young man named Clifford Hayes had been taken into custody. The authorities remained certain that jealousy was central to the plot, but now they said the killer had shot Edward Hall and Eleanor Mills in a case of mistaken identity.

It made for a great day of selling newspapers, but no one outside the New Brunswick police department believed in Hayes's guilt for a minute – and it seems unlikely that many within the department believed it either. Raymond Schneider, the young man who had been with Pearl Bahmer when they discovered the bodies of Hall and Mills, had been grilled for twenty-four hours over the weekend, at which point he accused his friend Clifford Hayes of the killings.

The story was this: Schneider had been loitering with Hayes and another friend on the night of the murders, when they saw Pearl Bahmer walking with a drunken man. Jealous of Pearl, Schneider convinced his friends to follow the couple to Buccleuch Park, only to discover that the drunk man was Pearl's bootlegger father. Schneider's friends concurred with his story up to this point, but then said they'd parted company. Under police pressure Schneider changed his account, claiming they'd all remained near the park, later coming across a couple near the Phillips farmhouse, whom they again took to be Pearl and her father. At this point, Schneider said, Clifford Hayes fired four shots at the pair, only to discover that it was the wrong couple and that he had murdered two strangers – who turned out to be Edward Hall and Eleanor Mills. The tale was preposterous, but the police had a culprit at last.

The press immediately pointed out the gaping holes in this new 'official theory'. It failed to explain why or when Eleanor Mills's throat was cut, why the bodies were staged together so carefully, why the rector's watch and wallet had been stolen, why their love letters were found scattered around the bodies, why Raymond Schneider would have returned to the dead bodies with Pearl Bahmer two days later and reported their murder to the police, or why Hayes would have murdered two people for his friend's sake. They were all good questions. Hayes indignantly protested his innocence, insisting that he wasn't stupid enough to have killed the wrong people and then hung around, awaiting arrest.

When Nick Carraway asks if George Wilson objects to his wife's frequent disappearances, Tom answers dismissively, 'He thinks she goes to see her sister in New York. He's so dumb he doesn't know he's alive.' Tom is no genius himself, but he finds it a simple matter to manipulate Wilson into killing the wrong man. From Raymond Schneider's swapping of one man for another, to the Carraway patriarch who sent a substitute to the Civil War to die for him, to George Wilson's killing

Gatsby instead of Tom Buchanan, impersonations had a tendency to end in violence.

---

# A New Party.

As they settled into Great Neck, Fitzgerald noted in his ledger the high points of October 1922: 'Met Lardners, Bucks, Swopes.' Their new cottage in Great Neck was not far from Ring Lardner's gracious white house overlooking the narrow inlet in the bay and before long the two writers had become close friends and drinking companions. Lardner would inspire a character in *Tender is the Night*, 'the entirely liquid' Abe North. Lardner was older, more cynical and experienced than the frolicking young Fitzgerald, but they shared an acidic sense of humour, critical intelligence and a serious commitment to the craft of writing, although Lardner always deprecated his efforts and Fitzgerald tended in the early years to boast. They also shared an undercurrent of satirical disapproval of the absurd place in which they found themselves; Lardner derisively called Great Neck 'Wonder City'.

The false dawn of the Fitzgeralds' experiment with sobriety had made way for a roaring noon, and they were remaining well and truly lit. 'We seem to have achieved a state of comparative organization at last, and, having bought loads of very interesting flour sieves and cocktail-shakers, are in a position to make a bid for your patronage,' Zelda wrote to the Kalmans. 'We have had the most terrible time – very alcoholic and chaotic. We behaved so long that eventually we looked up Engalichoff which, needless to say, started us on a week's festivity.' These were the revels she declared to have been 'equaled only by ancient Rome *and* Nineveh!'

Behaving too long could only lead to revolution, this time with Prince Vladimir Engalitcheff, the son of a Russian prince who had escaped the Bolsheviks and married a Chicago heiress. Engalitcheff, known as Val, had become friendly with the Fitzgeralds the previous year on a voyage to Europe. Engalitcheff would die less than six months later. Newspaper obituaries in March said the twenty-one-year-old's cause of death in his Fifth Avenue mansion was heart disease, but in his ledger for January 1923 Fitzgerald noted: 'Val Engalitcheff kills himself'. Biographers have accepted this assertion, but Fitzgerald must have written it retrospectively, for his account places the death two months early, and he gives no reason for his belief that Engalitcheff committed suicide. Engalitcheff's death certificate, dated 6 March 1923, names heart and kidney failure. Whatever Engalitcheff's illnesses may have been, the doomed young prince does not appear to have exercised a sobering influence, but he would inspire 'Love in the Night', the first story that Fitzgerald wrote after completing *Gatsby*. In the midst of their autumnal bacchanal, the Fitzgeralds moved into the house at Great Neck.

Instead of sharing their new address, Fitzgerald jotted a thank-you note offering only their new phone number: G.N. 740. Telephones were still new enough to warrant comment, and to require only a location and three digits. 'Everybody said to everybody else,' Zelda later wrote, '"We're having some people ... and we want you to join us. We'll telephone." All over New York people telephoned. They telephoned from one hotel to another to people on parties that they couldn't get there – that they were engaged.'

They went 'on' parties, not to them: going on a party was like going on a voyage, an indefinite trip in search of eternal pleasure that tended to end on the rocks. That August, the *New York Times* reported that a woman who had married under the influence was able to have her marriage annulled: 'They went out on a party before the marriage and drank all night and next day and didn't sleep any. The cocktails, highballs and other mixtures, she said, deprived her of her mentality and she didn't know she was getting married.' The annulment was granted not on the grounds of intoxication, however, but of 'fraud and misrepresentation' as her new husband had claimed he didn't drink. Earlier in the year, a woman from Great Neck also tried to divorce her husband for misrepresentation: he'd told her he was a writer, but he just drank all day long and was never published. On Scott Fitzgerald's birthday, the *New York Times* had reported that another woman divorced her husband for 'excessive drunkenness' – although no one had established how much drunkenness was reasonable in a husband.

That summer the *Times* published an editorial deploring the new, debauched meaning that 'party' had acquired that year: it now denoted a gathering of 'inebriate' persons who could enjoy themselves only with the aid of illicit 'strong waters'. The day before, a man had taken a taxi home from a party at dawn, fallen down his front steps, rolled down a terrace and drowned in 'an all too convenient river'. Or what of another party, in which 'a mysterious revolver was brought into play', and a wounded man wandered off, without any of the other guests giving him another thought until they had to rush him to the hospital and embark upon embarrassing explanations? 'Perhaps the most light on "parties,"' the article concluded disapprovingly, 'is cast by F. Scott Fitzgerald's *The Beautiful and Damned*, that remarkable book being largely devoted to what manifestly are accurate descriptions of them, of the sort of people who give and attend them, and of the usual consequences.' Fitzgerald saved the notice; another review suggested the novel should have been called '"The Boozeful and Damned," by F. Scotch Fitzgerald'.

Although he wasn't the first to use 'party' as a verb, Fitzgerald does appear to have been the first to conjugate 'cocktail' as one, in a 1926 letter declining an invitation to a cocktail party: 'As "cocktail", so I gather, has become a verb, it ought to be conjugated at least once, so here goes:

| | | |
|---|---|---|
| **Present** | I cocktail | We cocktail |
| | Thou cocktail | You cocktail |
| | It cocktails | They cocktail |
| **Imperfect** | I was cocktailing | |
| **Perfect** | I cocktailed (past definite) | |
| **Past perfect** | I have cocktailed | |
| **Conditional** | I might have cocktailed | |

| Pluperfect | I had cocktailed |
|---|---|
| Subjunctive | I would have cocktailed |
| Voluntary Sub. | I should have cocktailed |
| Preterite | I did cocktail |
| Imperative | Cocktail! |
| Interrogative | Cocktailest thou? (Dos't Cocktail?) (or Wilt Cocktail?) |
| Subjunctive Conditional | I would have had to have cocktailed |
| Conditional Subjunctive | I might have had to have cocktailed |
| Participle | Cocktailing |

'I find this getting dull,' he concludes, 'and would much rather talk to you, about turbans.'

Two years before Fitzgerald conjugated cocktails, a contest was held to see who could invent the best word to describe the 'lawless drinker of illegally made or illegally obtained liquor'. The winner was the neologism 'scofflaw'; less than two weeks later the *Chicago Tribune* reported that Harry's Bar in Paris had invented the Scofflaw cocktail (a mix of rye, vermouth, lemon juice and grenadine), and it was already 'exceedingly popular among American prohibition dodgers'. The same day the Scofflaw cocktail found its way into the papers, Ring Lardner offered his own thoughts on prohibition: 'the night before it went into effect everybody had a big party on acct. of it being the last chance to get boiled. As these wds. is written the party is just beginning to get good.'

In his immensely popular magazine fiction, the rather liquid Mr Lardner addressed themes of great currency in jazz-age America: not only drinking and scofflaws, but also social climbing, fraud, self-deception, profligacy, self-aggrandizement and snobbery. Lardner had

started out as a sports journalist, and was famously one of the first reporters to suspect that the 1919 World Series had been fixed, in the Black Sox scandal. He was tall, dangling and stooped, characteristically deadpan with large dark eyes that stared owlishly out of a face that seemed a permanent parody of solemnity.

The resemblance was so marked that the Chicago White Sox started calling Lardner 'Old Owl-Eyes'. The name stuck: supposedly when Lardner first realized that the White Sox seemed to be throwing the World Series, he told his companion, 'I don't like what these old owl eyes are seeing'; the account circulated widely in the papers. In early October 1922 Burton Rascoe recorded an encounter with Lardner in his column, observing, 'Month by month Ring is getting more owl-eyed in every way.'

Some scholars have decreed that the character called Owl-Eyes whom Nick and Jordan encounter in Gatsby's library can have nothing to do with Lardner, because Lardner was thin and Owl-Eyes is stout. Others have maintained that Owl-Eyes is chronically drunk because Lardner was chronically drunk. But Owl-Eyes doesn't have to 'be' Lardner, or even a misrepresentation of him, to have been endowed with his memorable nickname, or to be drunk, or to have a wide-eyed expression that continually suggests astonishment and wonder. Owl-Eyes is a satirical chorus, a drunken wise fool whose vinous pronouncements let Fitzgerald offer some of his novel's verities, including the importance of distinguishing the real thing amid a host of fakes.

# Lost Causes.

Next door to Lardner in Great Neck, in a large brown Victorian farm-house that later burned down, lived Herbert Bayard Swope, the famous editor of the New York *World*, 'the Parnassian daily' paper of the 1920s. When Fitzgerald recalled the Goddards, the Dwans and the Swopes as the sources of *Gatsby*'s third chapter in his *Man's Hope* outline, it was Herbert Bayard Swope of whom he was thinking. Swope's lot joined Lardner's across a small, unbounded field; it wasn't obvious where Swope's land ended and Lardner's began. From Swope's lawn on East Shore Road one could also look out toward Sands Point, across the bay dividing the hopes of new money from the carelessness of old. Bon vivant, raconteur, man about town, Swope was renting the large house, which Lardner said looked as if it had been built by a man with a scroll saw and too much time on his hands, adding for good measure that living there made it impossible to work and even more difficult to sleep: 'Mr Swope of the *World* lives across the way, and he conducts an almost continuous house party.' Swope's parties soon became legendary: 'Herbert Bayard Swope operated a continual talk-fest at his keep on Long Island,' remembered the veteran reporter Ben Hecht. A cynical man who found little to rhap-sodize about in this world, Hecht waxed effusive about Swope. 'There was a name in the twenties and thirties! And a newspaperman worthy of the Chicago tradition. Swope had, moreover, a nose for literature as well as murder, and a passion for culture as deep as for scoops.'

Tall, red-haired, garrulous and booming, Swope was forty years old in 1922, already one of the most famous and successful newspapermen of his day. Burton Rascoe wrote that the mere name Swope 'seems inadequate, ineffectual, limp, somehow. It ought to be SWOPE, like an explosion; he's that dynamic or kinetic.'

Born in St Louis to German-Jewish immigrants who changed the family name from Schwab, Swope shed the trappings of his Jewish background in an anti-Semitic age, but he also commissioned a ground-breaking exposé of the Ku Klux Klan and hired the first black columnist to write for a mainstream white paper.

Six years later, in 1928, Swope moved across the bay to the old-moneyed eastern peninsula, near Mary Harriman Rumsey. When Swope's Sands Point mansion (renamed Land's End after he left it) was demolished in 2011 the erroneous news circulated that it was Fitzgerald's model for Gatsby's house. But Fitzgerald's description of Gatsby's house bears no similarity to either of Swope's Long Island residences, first a brown Victorian farmhouse on the western peninsula and then the massive white colonial on the eastern point. Neither resembles Gatsby's faux Norman chateau – and in any event, Swope didn't move to Sands Point until three years after *Gatsby* was published.

For Gatsby's opulent house in West Egg, Fitzgerald presumably had something in mind more like Falaise, Harry Guggenheim's 216-acre estate, which was finished in 1923. The mansion is now part of the Sands Point Preserve, which describes the house as 'French eclectic'. Based on a thirteenth-century Norman manor house, Falaise is a pastiche of Gothic revivalism, boasting an enclosed cobblestone courtyard, mortared brick walls, a round tower, arches, thick wood beams, textured walls and carved stone mantels. There is no specific evidence that Fitzgerald went to Falaise, but it's clearly the sort of thing he had in mind when Nick describes his neighbour's house, 'a colossal affair by any standard – it was a factual imitation of some Hôtel de Ville in Normandy, with a tower on one side, spanking new under a thin beard of raw ivy, and a marble swimming pool and more than forty acres of lawn and garden. It was Gatsby's mansion.'

But obviously Gatsby's mansion isn't really Falaise either, given that Gatsby didn't really exist. In an age of proliferating copies like ours, originals become intensely valuable, while materialism can tempt people into seeking the 'real thing', certain that everything of value must be tangible, locatable. This impulse – which echoes Gatsby's tragic error – relates to literalism, but it is also a way of realizing vicarious pleasures, so we can believe in our splendid fictions.

---

## Lost and Found

Swope helped inspire not Gatsby's house, but his parties. Everyone who was celebrated or witty was invited to the Swopes' renowned gatherings. The Fitzgeralds were great favourites for a time until, rumour has it, at one party Zelda took off her clothes and chased Mrs Swope's shy, sixteen-year-old brother up the stairs. He locked himself in the bedroom and for the rest of his life would be teased for the opportunity he passed up. Mrs Swope, it is said, banned the Fitzgeralds from returning to her house.

But all that was yet to come – if it is true. In the first heady months of their festivities among the Swopes and their guests the Fitzgeralds, thronged by a crowd of admirers, would stroll out to the gardens, where they would settle down with a few bottles of Swope's first-rate bootleg whisky: he claimed never to serve alcohol that hadn't first been tested by chemists. People would picnic out on the grounds or stroll across the quiet road down to the beach. In the late afternoon sun they would stretch out on the porch or in the garden and go to sleep. When they woke, the band would have arrived; they'd change into evening clothes and the next stage of the festivities would commence. Songwriter

Howard Dietz said the Swopes' parties were so dependable that if you were in Great Neck and 'happened to be hungry at four in the morning, you could get a steak. Everybody drifted Swopeward.'

In addition to cascades of gin rickeys and mint juleps, Swope's parties were renowned for his games, as Swope was also a compulsive, high-stakes gambler. He was especially fond of cut-throat croquet tournaments; when it got dark the guests turned their cars toward the lawn and switched on the headlamps. They played charades and twenty questions, and set up treasure hunts with sapphire cufflinks and gold-lined dressing boxes as party favours, sending urban sophisticates crashing through shrubbery to find them. Gatsby's parties are similarly punctuated by games – 'wild routs that resolve themselves into "hide-and-go-seek" or "sardines-in-the-box" with all the house thrown open to the game' – although the guests at Gatsby's parties don't play two of the Swopes' favourites, 'Who Am I?' and 'Murder'. But then in *The Great Gatsby* mistakes in identity and murder are serious business.

The Swopes had spent the summer of 1922 in Paris, where Alec Woollcott visited them at the Ritz; he and Margaret Swope shot craps to amuse themselves. Woollcott sent Edna Ferber, the popular novelist, an account of the afternoon at the Swopes's suite, enclosing a letter from Deems Taylor, a friend of Swope's and the music critic for the *World*, in which he described the high life as 'living like Swopes'. Soon after the Swopes returned to Great Neck, the Fitzgeralds moved in and began visiting Lardner. Before long they had drifted Swopeward.

---

As the Fitzgeralds began enthusiastically living like Swopes, the *World* and the other New York papers were reporting mounting anger in

New Jersey. Indignant citizens protested against the 'framing' of Clifford Hayes, a new enough term that the *New York Times* framed it in quotation marks; a hostile crowd chased a deputy policeman down a New Brunswick street, hurling stones and other missiles at him. When a reporter asked Prosecutor Beekman if he believed the truth of Schneider's confession, Beekman snapped, 'Truth? We are not trying to determine the truth of his statement. I don't have to do that. All I have to do is to look for a reasonable basis for prosecution.' The magnificently literal Beekman would stand defiant in his resistance to interpretation: the prosecution doesn't judge, it prosecutes – anyone it can find. As moral philosophies go, this is fairly limited.

Meanwhile the papers focused their scepticism on the character of Raymond Schneider, 'shiftless at twenty-three', said the *World*, and 'mentally deficient'. They were equally dubious about Pearl Bahmer, a girl who, noted the *Times*, 'has exhibited a willingness to tell almost anything to almost anybody'. One of the things Pearl told the police resulted in her father's immediate arrest. The accusation was evidently not 'fit to print' in the *New York Times*, which said first that Pearl accused her father of an 'abuse' that had recently led her to attempt suicide and then became more specific, quoting Pearl saying that a judge had told her father 'to stop bothering me': 'Father never wanted me to go out with a single fellow. I never knew a girl who had to go out with her own father.'

The *World* was clearer, although it too stopped short of the word 'incest'. Fifteen-year-old Pearl, reported the *World*, 'admitted to the judge that she had been intimate with Schneider for a year and also with her father'. Arrested on a charge the *Tribune* called 'the most despicable that can be lodged against a father', Bahmer 'flung up his arms and cried that Pearl was his own flesh and blood, that her charges were untrue'. He admitted to carrying a .45 revolver on the night of the murder, but Hall and Mills were both shot with a .32. He had been drinking heavily for several days; pressed by reporters, Bahmer drunkenly admitted, 'I was gunning for Schneider.' He also insisted that he could 'prove' that his daughter's charges were untrue: 'he would bring to bear competent testimony to show that he could not have been guilty'. No one speculated in print as to what such proof might be, but the papers suggested the law's attention might be swinging toward the bootlegger.

---

## DISAPPOINTED HOPES.

Parties were a matter of infinite hope; one came to them ready to perform. The guests did stunts, tricks, songs, variety acts, dances, recitations of poems or disaster, tricks, cartwheels and cabarets: show business people called it 'doing your stuff'. Fitzgerald, too, did his stuff. He liked to sing a mock-tragic song called 'Dog, Dog, Dog', that he'd composed:

> Dog, dog – I like a good dog –
> Towser or Bowser or Star –
> Clean sort of pleasure –
> A four-footed treasure –
> And faithful as few humans are!

Before long, Fitzgerald's song made Rascoe's Day Book column. 'Fitzgerald, Wilson said, composed these idiotic songs all day long and sings them to himself – one of them going, as he ran up the stairs to shave in the morning: "The Great Fitzgerald goes up stairs; the Great Fitzgerald goes up stairs. Oh, the Great Fitzgerald!" Ring Lardner, who is Fitzgerald's neighbor, is also addicted to this pastime, and the two of them compose the lyrics to impromptu songs.' Fitzgerald saved Rascoe's account in his scrapbook.

Instantly recycling the story, the popular columnist O. O. McIntyre embroidered the myth, adding that Lardner answered Fitzgerald's songs with his own: 'Soon across the space booms the voice of Lardner: "The mighty Lardner prepareth to shave. Soapsuds and lather! Oh, the beautiful, sylphlike Lardner." Neighbors have been trying to mitigate the annoyance, but to no avail, for Fitzgerald and Lardner continue their rhyming fooleries at intervals all during the day.' They must have had loud voices: the Fitzgeralds and Lardners lived almost exactly two miles apart. Fitzgerald saved this notice too.

That reality tends not to live up to our myths, or our memories, is the truth that destroys Jay Gatsby. There is a photograph of the Fitzgeralds and their friends at a party during their Great Neck days, which Zelda preserved in her scrapbook, writing in the names of most of the guests. It was taken in the Fitzgeralds' modest living room. The men are mostly, but not all, in dinner suits; Zelda, in profile on the far left at the back, wears a bracelet on her upper arm, the most iconically jazz-age accessory in the picture; her face is obscured by her bobbed hair falling forward. Fitzgerald lounges on the floor, third from left on the bottom, looking louche.

In *The Great Gatsby* Fitzgerald invented the perfect mythical party, which is why this photo comes as something of a disappointment. Where is the insatiable luxury, the Babylonian decadence, the glam-

our, the glitter? Where are the saturnalian revelries? The sequined dresses, feathered headbands, sumptuous grounds, cigarette holders, jazz orchestras and finger bowls of champagne? The flowers, the lights, the colour, the people twinkling like diamonds? Where is the magic?

Pinning our hopes on the idea that the real glamour was found at the phantom Goddards', at the Rumseys' and Hitchcocks', or among the Swopes' treasure hunts would leave us as lost in nostalgic fantasy as Gatsby. Alternatively, we could cultivate the Hall–Mills prosecutor's cavalier disregard for higher truth, but that would mean being trapped in his literalism, content with the merely plausible.

If reality disappoints, art seems all the more necessary. In his lovely, neglected 1929 story 'The Swimmers' ('the hardest story I ever wrote', he told his agent, 'too big for its space'), Fitzgerald wrote 'There was even a recurrent idea in America about an education that would leave out history and the past, that should be a sort of equipment for aerial adventure, weighed down by none of the stowaways of inheritance or tradition.' He realized how foolhardy this idea was: if America forgot its past, there would be no meaning in its future. History might be a stowaway, but we need the ballast it provides.

Friday 13 October 1922 was an auspicious day. As New York honoured Columbus by arguing over whether he had been Italian, Spanish or even Jewish, construction began on a 'vehicular tunnel' running under the Hudson River to Jersey City, which would become the Holland Tunnel. It was also reported that America would spend an estimated three hundred billion dollars over the next six years on the 'electrification' of the nation: in 1922 even

New York City was not fully electrified, and neon lights would not be introduced until the end of the decade. They thought their city was blindingly bright, and toweringly high, but to us it would seem shrouded in darkness, with scattered, enormous signs blinking their electric bulbs over abbreviated buildings.

And in New Brunswick the news went round that Clifford Hayes had been cleared of all charges as Raymond Schneider retracted his accusation that Hayes had killed Hall and Mills, saying he realized 'what a skunk I was in framing him up like that'. Stumbling on the bodies of the murdered lovers had proven disastrous for the hapless Schneider and his girlfriend. A local judge issued two warrants for Schneider's arrest, for perjury against Hayes and for the statutory rape of Pearl Bahmer, who would also be arraigned for 'incorrigibility', while her father would be arraigned on Pearl's accusation of incest. Amid this imbroglio of charges and counter-charges, the delightfully nicknamed 'Happy' Bahmer, Pearl's brother, was to be brought in for questioning. Happy had been arrested eight times that year on minor charges; a few years earlier, the

papers added for good measure, 'a negro roustabout was acquitted of a murder charge' after 'disemboweling "Happy's" uncle'. The jury decided the homicide was justifiable; no one explained what Happy's uncle had done that a jury of his peers thought warranted his disembowelment.

The *Times* reported that Schneider's story was 'considered the height of absurdity', as well it should have been. Unfortunately, their reasons for disbelieving Schneider were almost as weak as his story. The tale was considered ridiculous 'by those who had believed ever since the bodies were found that the circumstances pointed to jealousy as the motive and a woman as one of the participants in the crime'.

Pearl Bahmer in jail　　There was still no evidence that a woman was one of the criminals, but the story had made up what little mind it had left.

Ten days later, Pearl Bahmer was committed to a girls' home, having recanted the accusation against her father, which she said she had made for fear of being 'committed to a correctional facility because of her relations with Raymond Schneider'. The case would continue to backfire against many of its principals, but Nicholas Bahmer walked 'jauntily out of the courthouse' and within ten minutes was 'back behind the bar of his George Street tavern'.

---

# BROADCASTING AND FORE-CASTING.

The first known instance in English of the phrase 'mass market' was recorded two days later, on 15 October 1922. Signs of the mass market are littered throughout *Gatsby*: magazines, newspapers, reporters, photographers, movie stars, directors and especially advertisements abound. Consumption in *Gatsby* is very conspicuous indeed, a catalogue of possessions from Gatsby's spectacular Rolls-Royce to Daisy's $350,000 rope of pearls, to the gas-blue gown with lavender beads Gatsby sent a girl who tore her dress at his last gathering. We never learn her name, but we know the dress cost $265 because Fitzgerald attaches a price tag. They called such items 'goods' for a reason: purchasing was acquiring a moral valence.

The phrase 'mass media' soon followed 'mass market', in the 1923 business manual *Advertising and Selling*, and the biggest news in mass media across 1922 and 1923 was radio. Until 1922 radio was strictly a military device, used primarily by the world's navies, but by the end of that year an estimated 1.5 million radio sets were in American homes alone, and spreading rapidly abroad. The papers reported a plethora of inventions inspired by radio, many of which uncannily predicted today's devices: engineers foresaw wireless movies on trains; a French inventor created a mobile radio device to fit in parasols so that women out promenading could phone home while listening to music; another inventor patented a 'reading machine' designed to 'enable anybody to carry with him many copies of books without even bulging out his pockets'. Broadcasting would acquire great significance for political candidates, the *Times* said prophetically on 15 October 1922, because 'a cartoon carries its story more quickly than an argument'; three days later Great Britain established the BBC. In 1926 the *New York Times* reported that radio had added more than three thousand words to the English language.

Fitzgerald does not mention radio in the final version of *Gatsby*, but on the first page of the earliest surviving manuscript draft, radio suddenly appears as a metaphor: 'the intimate revelations of young men or at any rate the terms in which they express them vary no more than the heavenly messages ~~from Paradise~~ which reach us over the psychic radio'. When he revised his manuscript, Fitzgerald wisely changed young men from psychic heavenly radio operators to plagiarists ('the intimate revelations of young men or at least the terms in which they express them are usually plagiaristic and marred by obvious suppressions,' Nick complains). But the ghost of radio lingers in a book that guessed very early the ways in which mass media and mass markets would alter America.

The earliest use of the term 'brand name' also occurs in 1922. That summer, the *New York Times* wrote about the sudden explosion of branded goods, including 'Madame Bovary Lipstick', 'El Cid gloves' and 'Beau Nash shaving cream'. Even bootleggers, the article joked, were getting in on the act: 'Suicide Club and Borgia Brew are among their best sellers.' Marketing departments cheerfully used celebrity names to endorse their products, usually without bothering to get permission, so that 'the author of the latest bestseller may read without warning an advertisement which features him as a new kind of summer underwear for men'. Although Fitzgerald might have been amused to find himself fronting underwear, he was also fastidious enough to have objected. Soon after *Gatsby* was completed he asked

Max Perkins to remove a proposed blurb from *All the Sad Young Men*: please 'delete the man who says I "deserve the huzza's of those who want to further a worthy American Literature,"' he wrote. 'Perhaps I deserve their huzzas but I'd rather they'd express their appreciation in some less boisterous way.'

Stars were soon fighting back against the practice of taking their name, or selling power, for free. According to *Town Topics*, in late September Gilda Gray was trying to stop other stars from dancing the shimmy, which had made her famous and was now sweeping America: 'Gilda Gray, Ziegfeld Follies beauty, is out with double-barrelled charges. She accuses Bee Palmer of stealing the "shimmy" from her, and her husband, a Milwaukee bartender, of being untrue to her.'

Gatsby's first party begins with the rumour that the girl dancing out onto the canvas platform is Gilda Gray's understudy from the 1922 Ziegfeld Follies. Dancing 'individualistically' and 'moving her hands like Frisco', a popular vaudevillian with a stylized dance routine, the girl is not doing the Charleston, a dance that Fitzgerald never mentions in *Gatsby*. He was quite specific about when the Charleston first appeared. In the only murder mystery he wrote, a 1926 story called 'The Dance', Fitzgerald's narrator happens to see someone dance the Charleston in 1921: 'I had never seen anything like it before, and until five years later I wasn't to see it again. It was the Charleston – it must have been the Charleston. I remember the double drum-beat like a shouted "Hey! Hey!" and the unfamiliar swing of the arms and the odd knock-kneed effect. She had picked it up, heaven knows where.' When he finished *Gatsby* at the beginning of 1925, Fitzgerald had not mentioned the Charleston because mainstream America was not yet dancing it, and he probably hadn't heard of it. At the end of August, the *New York Times* would note that the Charleston had spent the summer 'prancing into favor', four months after *Gatsby* was published, and three years after its story is set.

The Charleston has nonetheless jazzed its way into countless images of *The Great Gatsby*, although the girl on Gatsby's dance floor is more likely doing the shimmy. Perhaps she didn't imitate Gilda Gray as well as Zelda had while Dos Passos danced with a piano lamp on his head.

---

## Using Assumed Names

As Broadway producers, stars and actors drifted into Great Neck, so did movie stars and film directors, thanks to the film studios that would remain around New York for several more years before the film industry moved decisively to the west coast. One of the film directors who moved to Great Neck in the early 1920s was a Canadian named Allan Dwan, and in 1923 Gloria Swanson, one of the biggest movie stars in the world, descended from the stratosphere to Long Island to work with Dwan at the Astoria studios. Zelda saved an invitation from Gloria Swanson for dinner and dancing on Thursday 27 March 1923, at ten o'clock at the Ritz Carlton. A few months later, in July 1923, Fitzgerald's ledger reads: 'Parties at Allen Dwans. Gloria Swanson and the movie crowd.'

Fitzgerald gave Great Neck the name West Egg in part to suggest that it was the home of west coast dissipation on the shores of Long Island. By 1922 the film industry had become so notorious for its depraved parties, routinely likened to orgies, that it had just received its own censor, Will Hays, who rode in on a wave of moral outrage. At the end of 1921 Roscoe 'Fatty' Arbuckle became embroiled in the scandal that would destroy his career, when he was accused of the rape and manslaughter of the starlet Virginia Rappe. On 2 February 1922, the same day that James Joyce published *Ulysses*, the director William Desmond Taylor was found dead in Hollywood, shot in the back. As the mystery unfolded, it was discovered that Taylor had reinvented himself, ruthlessly abandoning his former identity. Born William Deane-Tanner, he had abruptly deserted his family in 1912, changing his name to the more aristocratic-sounding William Desmond Taylor as he moved to Hollywood and began his social ascent. The biggest murder story of 1922 until it was supplanted by the Hall–Mills case, Taylor's homicide was never solved.

America was invented out of a desire for rebirth, for fresh starts. It was the place where a man could be the author of himself, reinventing himself as an aristocrat, but somehow these stories of renaissance kept ending in murder.

***

## CARELESS DRIVERS WARNED.

Gatsby's first party disintegrates into accident and mayhem. Women quarrel with men said to be their husbands; jealous wives appear like angry diamonds and hiss 'You promised' at husbands flirting with chorus girls. A drunk woman sings a song she finds so sad that her mascara runs in inky rivulets down her face; young men engage in 'obstetrical conversations' with the dancers they are trying to talk into bed. Women are carried bodily, kicking in protest, out of Gatsby's house. Owl-Eyes is driven off in a car that ends in a ditch; attempting drunkenly to explain that he wasn't the driver, he tells the gathering crowd that he wasn't even trying. Such recklessness astonishes the onlookers: 'a bad driver and not even *trying!*'

After Gatsby's party ends, Nick tells us that Daisy's friend Jordan Baker is also a 'rotten driver', who 'ought to be more careful'. Jordan lightly explains that she depends upon the carefulness of strangers, in another exchange that is said to have originated with Zelda:

'They'll keep out of my way,' she insisted. 'It takes two to make an accident.'

'Suppose you met somebody just as careless as yourself.'

'I hope I never will,' she answered. 'I hate careless people. That's why I like you.'

Not only is Jordan a careless driver, she is incurably dishonest, Nick adds, remembering a rumour that she had cheated in a golf tournament. The gossip nearly reached the newspapers, and approached the proportions of a scandal, before it died away. Fortunately, cheating doesn't matter much to him: 'dishonesty in a woman is a thing you never blame deeply', Nick declares, before telling us he's the only honest person he knows. We may feel at liberty to disagree.

Zelda was something of a reckless driver herself, as (by no coincidence) is Gloria in *The Beautiful and Damned*, whom Fitzgerald describes as 'a driver of many eccentricities and of infinite carelessness'. Remembering their sojourn in Westchester the first year they were married, Zelda wrote: 'There were people all along the Boston Post Road thinking everything was going to be all right while they got drunk and ran into fireplugs and trucks and old stone walls. Policemen were too busy thinking everything was going to be all right to arrest them.' Despite their unconcern, Zelda still somehow managed to get arrested once as 'the Bob-haired Bandit' while crossing the Queensboro Bridge, said Fitzgerald. Before long he was driving Max Perkins into a pond on Long Island, a story that lost nothing in the telling.

Jordan was also the name of a popular model of cars in America in the early 1920s. On 15 October 1922 Sherwood Automobiles took out a large advertisement in the *New York Times*, selling 'The Blue Boy in Blue Devil Blue'. A young man races along in a Jordan, 'like some wonderful somebody who has an account with Abercrombie and Fitch'. Shop at the right stores, drive the right car and you might be transformed into some wonderful somebody. That casual indifference to specifics admits infinite possibilities. Advertising was selling the hope of becoming a wonderful anybody.

As fate – or as it's also known, history – would have it, New York City declared the week of 8–15 October 1922 its first ever Safety Week, sponsored by the newly formed and optimistically named Society for the Prevention of Accidents. Posters and badges had been

N YORK TIMES, SUNDAY, OCTOBER 15, 1922.          xx      9

**The Blue Boy in Blue Devil Blue**

It is dressed like some
wonderful somebody
who has an account
with Abercrombie
and Fitch.

Sherwood Automobile Corporation,
1702 Broadway, New York City

# JORDAN

organized with slogans including, 'How many of the people killed by
automobiles last year were pedestrians?' and 'How many motorists
have been convicted of manslaughter?' That week the papers
reported that out of over four hundred deaths in New York caused by
reckless driving over the previous year not a single one of the culprits
had been jailed and few licences had been revoked. Automobile
dealer associations were teaming up with the *New York Times* to
demand an investigation into 'the carelessness and negligence' of so
many drivers.

Meanwhile, on that same unlucky Friday, a motorist in New
Jersey was killed, smashing his car into a telegraph pole an hour after
he'd been pulled over and fined for reckless driving. The papers
reported that he had won the Croix de Guerre and the Distinguished
Service Medal during the war. We shouldn't be surprised if we begin
to see the ghost of some wonderful somebody hovering in the margins of the newspaper reports, for Jay Gatsby, Daisy tells us, 'resembles
the advertisement of the man ... You know the advertisement of
the man.'

That day the *Times* announced the arrival of a new play by Luigi Pirandello called *Six Characters in Search of an Author*, about reality and illusion, incest and murder. By the end of the month one of Pirandello's characters had told American audiences for the first time, 'Life is full of infinite absurdities, which, strangely enough, do not even need to appear plausible, since they are true.'

# IV. A. VEGETABLE DAYS IN N.Y.
# B. MEMORY OF GINEVRA'S WEDDING

On Sunday morning while church bells rang in the villages along shore the world and its mistress returned to Gatsby's house and twinkled hilariously on his lawn. 'He's a bootlegger,' said the young ladies, moving somewhere between his cocktails and his flowers. 'One time he killed a man who had found out that he was nephew to von Hindenburg and second cousin to the devil. Reach me a rose, honey, and pour me a last drop into that there crystal glass.' Once I wrote down on the empty spaces of a time-table the names of those who came to Gatsby's house that summer. It is an old time-table now, disintegrating at its folds and headed 'This schedule in effect July 5th, 1922.' But I can still read the grey names and they will give you a better impression than my generalities of those who accepted Gatsby's hospitality and paid him the subtle tribute of knowing nothing whatever about him.

*The Great Gatsby*, Chapter 4

# THE STREETS OF NEW YORK.

Edmund Wilson jotted a fragment in his notebooks: a skeleton in a taxicab rides through the streets of New York, from Rutgers Place to Riverside Drive. Wilson did not identify his destination, but the skeleton might have enjoyed the Furnace Room ('the hottest place in town'), or – if he had a dinner jacket – perhaps he startled the other patrons of the Paradise Roof on Eighth Avenue at 58th Street. But presumably the skeleton would have been most at home in the city morgue, communing with some corpses.

Although the skeleton in the taxi was Wilson's idea, spending a night at the morgue was Scott Fitzgerald's. One night of partying with Scott and Zelda is said to have begun at a Broadway nightclub and progressed to a Washington Square speakeasy, before ending uptown at a Harlem cabaret. At five in the morning, their hilarious party arrived back at Fifth Avenue and 57th Street, two blocks from the Plaza, where they breakfasted at Child's, one of America's first chain restaurants. As dawn broke Fitzgerald led his party back out into another taxicab, and drove off to Bellevue, where they ended the festivities at the morgue, convincing the sleepy clerk to let them look at cadavers.

Sightseeing was on the rise in the 1920s and Fitzgerald was always exemplary: he was hardly the only one to indulge in a bit of necrotourism. Motorists were coming in from all over the country to gawk at the crab-apple tree where the bodies of Hall and Mills had been found. Topping off one's evening in a morgue, however, was probably less common – or at least less voluntary.

---

# Revising Our Beliefs.

When he was thirty, Fitzgerald gave an interview claiming that Nietzsche's *The Genealogy of Morals* had been 'the greatest influence on my mind' at the age of twenty-four; at twenty-six, his first year in Great Neck, it was Dostoevsky's *The Brothers Karamazov*. (His favourite teacher at Princeton would say that Scott Fitzgerald reminded him of all the brothers Karamazov at once.) Art, said Nietzsche, is a question of necessary lies and voluntary lies, while Dostoevsky urged, 'believe to the end, even if all men went astray and you were left the only one faithful'. Perhaps it is no coincidence that Fitzgerald came to believe that the test of a first-rate intelligence is the ability to hold two opposed ideas in the mind at the same time and still be able to function.

When Jay Gatsby collects Nick to drive him into New York for lunch, Gatsby tells Nick a series of absurd lies about his background: that he is an Oxford-educated aristocrat from the 'Middle West' of San Francisco; that he lived like a young rajah in the capitals of Europe collecting jewels – 'chiefly rubies' – and hunting big game, trying to forget an unspecified tragedy. Nick restrains incredulous laughter with difficulty and wonders whether Gatsby is pulling his leg: listening to these fictions 'was like skimming hastily through a dozen magazines'. But Gatsby is not joking (he has many virtues, but it must be admitted that a sense of humour is not prominent among them).

Then Gatsby shows Nick a picture of himself at Oxford, as well as some authentic medals from the war, and Nick suddenly believes it is all true. 'I saw the skins of tigers flaming in his palace on the Grand Canal; I saw him opening a chest of rubies to ease, with their crimson-lighted depths, the gnawings of his broken heart.' Nick continually loses faith in Gatsby only to regain it: 'I had one of those renewals of complete faith in him that I'd experienced before.' But Gatsby's faith is a constant: he believes to the end although everyone else goes astray.

As they drive toward the white glacier of Manhattan, Nick thinks that in New York anything could happen, anything at all. 'Even Gatsby could happen, without any particular wonder.'

---

# THE MAKING OF LISTS.

In the autumn of 1922, Fitzgerald wrote his cousin Cecilia a name-dropping letter, listing all the celebrities he and Zelda knew in Great Neck:

> We are established in the above town very comfortably and having a winter of hard work. I'm writing a play which I hope will go on about the 1st of Jan. I wish you could arrange to come up for the opening. Great Neck is a great place for celebrities – it being the habitat of Mae Murray, Frank Craven, Herbert Swope, Arthur Hopkins, Jane Cowl, Joseph Santley, Samuel Goldwyn, Ring Lardner, Fontaine Fox, 'Tad', Gene Buck, Donald Bryan, Tom Wise, Jack Hazard, General Pershing. It is most amusing after the dull healthy Middle West. For instance at a party last night where we went were John McCormick, Hugh Walpole, F.P.A., Neysa McMein, Arthur William Brown, Rudolf Friml & Deems Taylor. They have no mock-modesty & all perform their various stunts upon the faintest request so it's like a sustained concert.

Fitzgerald's list reads like a feuilleton; gossip magazines and newspapers often shared similar roll calls of people attending parties or events. The first half of every issue of *Town Topics* was a catalogue of prominent names, and Myrtle Wilson, the avid reader of *Town Tattle*, also keeps lists. Not lists of people she's met, as she still only aspires to enter society, but rather of the things she's 'got to get', which are the same as the things she's got to do. For people on the make, like Myrtle, getting was becoming the only thing worth doing.

Bunny Wilson was also a careful maker of lists. In February 1922, he solemnly recorded a list of current slang: ratty, crocko, squiffy, boiled to the ears. Dumbbell, upstage, lousy, high-hat, rat-fuck. What's the dirt? Spill the dirt? 'He's always doin' his stuff.' Razz: the Royal Spanish raspberry. Bozo. Cuckoo. Flop. Everyone was always doing their stuff, upstaging each other, spilling the dirt – not to mention getting crocko, squiffy and boiled to the ears.

A few years later, Wilson compiled 'A Lexicon of Prohibition', contemporary terms for drunkenness in order of 'degrees of intensity' and 'beginning with the mildest stages', including:

| | | |
|---|---|---|
| lit | tanked | paralyzed |
| squiffy | stinko | ossified |
| oiled | blind | embalmed |
| lubricated | stiff | buried |
| owled | tight | blotto |
| edged | pickled | lit up like the sky |
| jingled | spifflicated | lit up like a church |
| piffed | primed | fried to the hat |
| half-screwed | organized | slopped to the ears |
| half-shot | featured | stewed to the gills |
| half-crocked | pie-eyed | boiled as an owl |
| fried | cock-eyed | to have a slant on |
| stewed | wall-eyed | to have a skate on |
| boiled | over the Bay | to have a snootful |
| zozzled | four sheets in the | to have a skinful |
| sprung | wind | to pull a Daniel |
| scrooched | crocked | Boone |
| jazzed | loaded | to have the heeby- |
| jagged | leaping | jeebies |
| canned | lathered | to have the |
| corked | plastered | screaming-meemies |
| corned | soused | to have the whoops |
| potted | bloated | and jingles |
| hooted | polluted | to burn with a low |
| slopped | saturated | blue flame |

*The Great Gatsby* offers its own famous catalogue: on a timetable dated 5 July 1922, a day suggesting that dreams of America's future are in its past, Nick Carraway writes down a list of all the people who came to Gatsby's house that summer despite knowing nothing about him. They are politicians and movie stars, racketeers and tycoons, chorus girls and plutocrats, and none of them comes to any good.

Gatsby's guests have burlesque names, suggesting tastelessness, violence, bathos. There is the unctuous Doctor Civet, and fishy people including the Leeches, Hammerheads, Fishguards, and Beluga, the tobacco importer. There are the more aristocratic-sounding Willie Voltaires, Smirkes, and a snobbish clan Fitzgerald calls 'Blackbuck' in a bit of passing racism that seems aimed to cut the elitists down to size. There are men whose homosexuality is hinted at by their floral names, such as Ernest Lilly and Newton Orchid, the film producer. Many of the guests meet violent ends: one man's brother 'afterward strangled his wife'; another killed himself by jumping in front of a subway train; Doc Civet will drown. Bootleggers, recognizable by their nicknames (James B. 'Rot-Gut' Ferret), are mingling with the guests, and a woman comes with a man 'reputed to be her chauffeur', as well as 'a prince of something whom we called Duke'. This is café society, the promiscuous mingling of old and new money, aristocracy and industry, debauchery and criminality, comedy and death.

After *Gatsby* was published, Ring Lardner sent the Fitzgeralds a letter about a Great Neck celebrity party they'd missed: 'On the Fourth of July, Ed Wynn gave a fireworks party at his new estate … After the children had been sent home, everybody got pie-eyed and I never enjoyed a night so much. All the Great Neck professionals did their stuff, the former chorus girls danced … the imitations were all the same, consisting of an aesthetic dance which ended with an unaesthetic fall onto the tennis court.' Fitzgerald had already invented his own Fourth of July party in West Egg by the time he received this letter, but it was clear that imitations were becoming a way of life.

## Slain Rector and Choir Singer Found Illicit Love Prototypes In Novel "Simon Called Peter"

Four weeks after the murders of Hall and Mills, the *World* condemned the 'Tragedy of LIES' in 'this grim New Brunswick drama of passion, jealousy, hatred, envy, murder'. All of New Brunswick 'seems to have been lying about the Hall–Mills murder since it was first discovered ... It is a whole town of Babbitts.'

The papers had begun to reveal the contents of the love letters exchanged by Edward Hall and Eleanor Mills. On the last day of her life Eleanor had written to the rector about two bestselling novels he'd given her, *Simon Called Peter* and *The Mother of All Living*, both by Robert Keable, also an Episcopalian minister. *Simon Called Peter*, one of the most sensational books of the year, tells of an upright British minister, engaged to a proper young woman, who encounters an experienced 'woman of the world' in France during the First World War. They fall desperately in love and embark upon an illicit affair that makes him question both his engagement and his spiritual calling.

An enormous bestseller in 1922, *Simon Called Peter* is the book that Nick Carraway reads in Myrtle Wilson's flat while she sneaks off for some quick sex with Tom Buchanan. Nick is unimpressed: 'Either it was terrible stuff or the whiskey distorted things, because it didn't make any sense to me,' he complains. *Simon Called Peter* does seem terrible stuff now, nearly unreadable. Fitzgerald loathed it (in 1923 he called it a 'really immoral book'), but maybe Myrtle Wilson isn't entirely to blame for her bad taste. As Nick caustically notes of Tom Buchanan, 'the fact that he "had some woman in New York" was really less surprising than that he had been depressed by a book'. Perhaps Tom found books less depressing when they were titillating – as evidently did the not-very Reverend Hall.

On the day of Eleanor Mills's murder she finished reading Keable's latest, *The Mother of All Living*. Another story of adulterous love, it tells of an unhappily married woman and her passionate affair with a better-educated, sophisticated man who reveals to her life's romantic possibilities. After she finished it, Eleanor wrote to her lover about searching for a more romantic mode of life. Like Edward, she said, Keable was a man of the cloth who understood that true spiritual connections must be physically expressed. Their affair was no sordid liaison, she implied; it was a pure expression of God's love. 'I don't want to read such books again ever,' she ended. 'They make me dream. Yearning for what perhaps I miss in this life … I hate to come back to realities – as I always have to. Reading books (oh, I love them) makes me yearn.' The press ridiculed these letters 'from a woman in humble life who looks up to the man above her', mocking Eleanor's handwriting, her stationery and her heartfelt response to the novels she loved, jeering that she was trying to become a literary critic.

'SLAIN RECTOR AND CHOIR SINGER FOUND ILLICIT LOVE PROTOTYPES IN NOVEL "SIMON CALLED PETER"' declared the *World*, headlining an article by Marguerite Mooers Marshall, who had interviewed Fitzgerald earlier that year. The similarities between the affair of Hall and Mills and the fictional one in *Simon Called Peter* were striking. The novel offered a clear 'parallel to the passion which finally led to a double crime in New Brunswick'. The rectors' churches even had the same name in fact and fiction: both were called St John's.

Marshall wrote several articles detailing the symmetries between Keable's novels and the Hall–Mills affair. In *The Mother of All Living*, the heroine is persuaded into adultery by a man who insists that her marriage is 'a mocking sham'. Marshall demanded: 'Was this the logic which the Rev. Edward Hall of New Brunswick, NJ, used?' The heroine's lover continually demands that she admit to never having loved her husband: 'You don't love Hugh at all, you know you don't … You're mine, not his … It only remains for us to take our destiny in both hands and step out upon it.' Jay Gatsby is also a reader of sentimental novels, and makes a remarkably similar casuistical argument about his love for Daisy. 'Of course she might have loved him, just for a minute, when they were first married – and loved me more even then, do you see?' he says, before adding that in any case, 'it was just personal'. 'I don't think she ever loved him,' Gatsby insists, after trying unsuccessfully to get Daisy to repudiate her husband. 'He wanted nothing less of Daisy,' Nick realizes, 'than that she should go to Tom and say: "I never loved you."'

The connection of *Simon Called Peter* to the Hall–Mills case made headlines throughout the autumn, as John Sumner decided the novel should be proscribed:

## SUMNER DENOUNCES BOOK IN HALL CASE

Says "Simon Called Peter," Given to Mrs. Mills, Looked Innocent, but Was Insidious.

### NASTY, SAYS MAGISTRATE

Best Homes Invaded by Such Books Under Sanctimonious Titles, Says Sumner.

*Simon Called Peter* 'is the kind of book that certain men present with a smug expression in the hope that it will open up a field of conversation which is ordinarily forbidden', Sumner charged. Such books were 'aids to seduction'; their dangers were amplified by the apparent role *Simon Called Peter* had played in inspiring, or justifying, the affair that had provoked a double homicide. Sumner warned that the novel's link to the Hall–Mills murders 'may lead to a further effort to prosecute the book'. If the book had led to murder then it, too, should be prosecuted – an accessory after the fact.

After he submitted his manuscript of *Gatsby*, Fitzgerald asked Max Perkins, 'In Chap II of my book when Tom & Myrtle go into the bedroom while Carraway reads Simon Called Peter – is that raw? Let me know. I think it's pretty necessary.' He had good reason to fear that censors might consider this scene too coarse, not least because the allusions to *Simon Called Peter* would remove any doubts about the activities of Tom and Myrtle in the bedroom. For men like John Sumner, merely reading *Simon Called Peter* was to be caught *in flagrante delicto*.

## Winning Success in Modern Life

" The question was, ' How can I make a million dollars?' "

Throughout 1922, while he contemplated his third novel and wrote short stories to support his family, Scott Fitzgerald had also been writing a play, which he was confident would be such a hit that it could easily subsidize his serious novels. At Princeton, Fitzgerald's work on the annual Triangle show contributed greatly to the university's polite suggestion that he withdraw before he flunked out, but he had not given up on the idea of theatre. One of the first stories in *Tales of the Jazz Age*, 'Porcelain and Pink', is written in play form and was staged in New York in April 1923, while both *This Side of Paradise* and *The Beautiful and Damned* incorporate long sections written as plays (Joyce would later use the same technique in *Ulysses*).

Having first titled his play *Gabriel's Trombone*, Fitzgerald decided to name it *The Vegetable* – an inauspicious choice. He attributed the title to a quotation from an unnamed 'current magazine': 'Any man who doesn't want to get on in the world, to make a million dollars, and maybe even park his toothbrush in the White House hasn't got as much to him as a good dog has – he's nothing more or less than a vegetable.' It appears to have been a half-remembered quotation from a 1922 Mencken essay called 'On Being an American': 'Here is a country in which it is an axiom that a businessman shall be a member of the Chamber of Commerce, an admirer of Charles M. Schwab, a reader of the *Saturday Evening Post*, a golfer – in brief, a vegetable.' Moving to Great Neck was meant to help Fitzgerald meet Broadway producers so that he could stage the satire he was certain would make his fortune.

These were the 'Vegetable Days in New York' that Fitzgerald remembered in his outline in *Man's Hope*, a year of meeting producers and actors, lunches in speakeasies and dinners on rooftop cafés, of keeping a sharp eye out for the satirical potential and ironies of the world around him. An irony that Fitzgerald seems to have been less alert to – or less willing to admit – was that the play he was writing to mock America's faith in ambition also constituted his own get-rich-quick scheme, a dream that was just as doomed as that of any of his characters.

*The Vegetable* is a political satire centring on Jerry Frost, a railway clerk who dreams of being a postman but is nagged by a dissatisfied wife to aspire to greater things. After an encounter with a bootlegger who offers him a bottle marked 'Wood Alcohol! Poison!' Frost spends the second act in an alcoholic delirium during which he is elected President and nearly destroys America, bringing the nation to the brink of war and bankruptcy with cronyism, corruption and incompetence. As sobriety returns with the end of the play, he renounces any desire to be President; he will aspire to nothing more than being a postman. 'Art invariably grows out of a period when in general the artist admires his own nation and wants to win its approval,' Fitzgerald remarked later. 'This fact is not altered by the circumstances that his work may take the form of satire for satire is the subtle flattery of a certain minority in a nation. The greatest artists grow out of these periods as the tall head of the crop.' While mocking American politics in general, Fitzgerald also took aim at some sacred cows. He even poked fun at the beloved tale of Abraham Lincoln's journey from log cabin to White House.

Edmund Wilson was uncharacteristically enthusiastic about *The Vegetable*; he declared it 'no doubt, the best American comedy ever written', and wondered whether Fitzgerald's alcoholic fantasy sequence had been inspired by the similar hallucinatory scene at the end of Joyce's *Ulysses*. If not, the resemblance 'must take its place as one of the great coincidences in literature'. It was indeed a coincidence, but few producers shared Wilson's view of its greatness. Over the next year, Fitzgerald continued to revise the play, finally deciding to arouse interest, and make some money, by publishing it as a book. Indeed, he told Max Perkins, it was more like 'a book of humor ... than like a play – because of course it is written to be read'. *The Vegetable* certainly reads better as a book than as a play: Fitzgerald put most of his writing energy into the stage directions, for one thing. When the

*Scene in front of Scribner's windows: Fanny Brice, with a copy of 'The Vegetable' under her arm, and F. Scott Fitzgerald, looking at the collection of Conrad manuscripts.*

bootlegger enters Fitzgerald tells the reader 'I wish I could introduce you to the original from whom I have taken Mr Snooks.' If his audience had heard this aside, perhaps they might have appreciated the copy more.

Scribner's published *The Vegetable* in early 1923, with another dust jacket by John Held, Jr. Fitzgerald's popularity was sufficient for the book to be reviewed widely; some readers, including Burton Rascoe, who called it 'gorgeously funny', were charmed, but by and large *The Vegetable* was dismissed as a trivial work. In May, the *Tribune* ran a cartoon featuring

Scott Fitzgerald in front of Scribner's bookstore window, next to popular novelist Fannie Hurst, who is clutching a copy of *The Vegetable* and peering at Joseph Conrad manuscripts; Fitz saved the image in his scrapbook.

In the summer of 1923 the producer and Great Neck resident Sam Harris agreed to stage the play at last. Fitzgerald spent the next six months revising and working in rehearsals, as he also began intermittently drafting his new novel. They shared similar themes: *The Vegetable* satirizes unthinking faith in the American success story, the same mistake in judgement that *The Great Gatsby* treats more tragically. The thrust of the play's satire is away from *Gatsby*'s faith in grandeur, however. *The Vegetable* is about knowing one's place, accepting one's limitations, ridiculing the American shibboleth that everyone has the potential for greatness. Nick Carraway cheerfully cops on the first page of *Gatsby* to being snobbish, but it is a snobbishness that values 'a sense of the fundamental decencies' over money or social status.

*The Vegetable* is now treated as an impertinent text, read only by Fitzgerald completists and ignored even by most scholars. But without the lessons he learned from *The Vegetable*'s failure, Fitzgerald probably could not have written *The Great Gatsby*. And in the beginning, at least, he may have toyed with the idea of including topical political satire in *Gatsby* too: throughout 1922, a senator named Caraway had been rising to national prominence, becoming famed as 'modest and self-contained', the only honest senator in America. *Gatsby* opens with Nick Carraway protesting that he was unjustly accused of being a politician at Yale: in the novel's earliest drafts Nick's last name was spelled 'Caraway'.

### CARAWAY DEVOTED TO DUTY.

#### A Modest Man, His Is the Shortest Sketch in Congressional Directory.

# New York's After-Midnight "Clubs"

Another reason for choosing Great Neck as the place to unsettle that autumn was its proximity to the nightlife of New York. At the beginning of 1922 the *New York Times* had reported on a new concept known as 'night clubs', 'though no club membership is required for admission'. In New York at least, prohibition speakeasies were often less clandestine than modern imagination suggests. The 'City on a Still' had become a national symbol for resistance to prohibition, famed for its estimated thirty thousand or more speakeasies and nightclubs, where the Volstead Act was enthusiastically flouted. Not until the autumn of 1922 did they begin to camouflage their drinks. In October, O. O. McIntyre dolefully observed, 'Two months ago they were serving cocktails openly in deli-cate glasses and wine in silver buckets. Now the cocktails are served in bouillon cups and wine is taboo.'

Some speakeasies were deluxe, with silk-festooned interiors and doormen, but most were crowded, noisy, smoke-filled basement or back-room dives, cheaply decorated with magazine pictures shellacked onto the walls, where they served lethally astringent cocktails. Many enterprising establishments, marked by discreet signs such as 'Chez Robert' or 'Fernando, Interior Decorator', set up boutique drinking salons on the higher floors of brownstone apartments. In his 1930 novel *Parties*, Carl Van Vechten described a typical bootlegger's apartment, 'furnished with a sufficient number of chairs and tables of Grand Rapids manufacture, a piano, a radio, a phonograph, a few cheap rugs, and some framed lithographs of nude women. The seven rooms of the apartment were arranged on a corridor so that it was possible, when desirable, to keep the customers more or less apart', although usually they happily mingled in the front room.

Speakeasy, cocktail and bootlegger were not prohibition terms, although they would become synonymous with the era. Cocktail was first recorded in 1803; Dickens uses it in *Martin Chuzzlewit* ('He could drink more rum-toddy, mint-julep, gin-sling, and cocktail, than any private gentleman of his acquaintance'). The term bootleg was first recorded in 1889 and is supposed to have derived from the American Civil War, when soldiers secreted whisky flasks in the tops of their boots. The origins of 'speakeasy' are obscure; it might be Irish slang or American, a place to speak of quietly, or 'easy'. There were various codes in operation. In early 1923 Van Vechten wrote to Theodore Dreiser, sharing the details of a bootlegger: 'When you want something, tele-phone him, mentioning my name ... Over the telephone one is discreet and calls gin *white* ... mention the number of bottles you want. Scotch is *gold*.' For a password, often a name would suffice: '32 West Eighty-second, ask for Charles; 425 East Seventy-third, Mr Bailey; 298 West Forty-seventh, mention Mr Gray; 207 East Forty-fifth, by divine revelation' suggests a knowledgeable butler in Zelda's play *Scandalabra*. Cellar doors were hidden in the shadows, unmarked; but if a patron hesitated, unsure of a blind pig's location, a ragged boy lin-gering nearby would shout, 'Here it is, right down those steps.' Given a dime, the boy would demand a quarter: it was the boom, after all.

Membership cards, easier for drunken clientele to preserve than hazy memories of passwords, were preferred by speakeasies and boot-leggers alike, who printed business cards and matchbooks with slogans: 'Don't Throw Me Away: You May Need Me Some Day', or 'When You Are Blue and Dry, Don't Sit There And Sigh, Just Call Digby'. Cards were printed announcing a new shipment of unspecified 'merchandise' of 'the highest quality and guaranteed'. Others promised that all their merchandise was tested by registered chemists. On the back of speakeasy cards were printed cocktail recipes, or pornographic cartoons. Fitz saved three among his papers: Louis & Armand, at 46 East 53rd Street, Ye White Horse Tavern at 114 West 45th Street and Club Des Artistes, 'always open' at Broadway and 64th. A folding card offered recipes for a range of drinks including Bronx Cocktails, Manhattan Cocktails and North and South Cocktails; they also explained how to make a Kentucky, a Miami and a New York. Prohibition was drawing a spiritous map of America.

Lois Long, who wrote a column as 'girl about town' for the *New*

*Yorker*, remembered being 'loaded down with the cards you were supposed to have, although the doorkeepers quickly came to know you'. Having been told that a bootlegger couldn't fake the smell and taste of cognac, young women all thought brandy was safe, but safety was relative: 'You were thought to be good at holding your liquor in those days if you could make it to the ladies' room before throwing up. It was customary to give two dollars to the cabdriver if you threw up in his cab.'

Some of the stories about prohibition drinking are exaggerated, but the idea that bootleg liquor frequently blinded its drinkers is not. The papers reported daily of people turning up at hospitals or police stations, screaming that they couldn't see. In 1921 the Prohibition Enforcement Agency ordered druggists to poison hair tonics and other toiletries containing alcohol, to render them undrinkable. But basic economics provided sufficient incentive for bootleggers to add cheap, often toxic chemicals such as paint thinner to 'denatured' or wood alcohol. Chemists working for the New York police analysed the liquor brought by those turning up at the hospitals and found industrial alcohol, sometimes with traces of disinfectants such as Lysol and carbolic acid, or kerosene, or mercury. In the Bowery they drank a lethal concoction called 'Smoke' – water mixed with fuel alcohol. Drinking illegal liquor was becoming a game of Russian roulette, but only the poor were gambling with their lives, an outrage that would eventually help lead to prohibition's repeal.

Raids were daily occurrences, to which owners and clients alike took violent exception. On 17 October 1922 the police raided the White Poodle on Bleecker Street, one of the most popular cabarets in the Village. The same night the police also raided a cellar speakeasy at 160 East Fourth Street, where they were met with a shower of cups, saucers, plates and cooking utensils thrown at them by staff. The owner's wife knocked one agent out cold with a rolling pin. Ten days later, as a frost threatened, prohibition agents 'were stoned by angry residents' when they tried to raid a winery in the Bronx.

Within a few years, the US government had begun deliberately poisoning denatured liquor to act as a deterrent; it didn't, and soon hundreds of Americans were dying, poisoned by their own government.

Citizens began to accuse the government of murder; defenders insisted that the bootleggers removing the poison labels were the real killers, but deaths continued to mount.

# GOVERNMENT WON'T DROP POISON ALCOHOL POLICY; DEATHS HERE 400 IN YEAR

The public backlash helped sweep politicians against prohibition into power at the end of 1932; they would repeal the 18th Amendment in 1933. But back in the optimistic days of the early 1920s the 'Drys', as Volstead supporters were known (anti-prohibitionists were 'Wets'), thought they simply needed to crack down on illicit drinking, which helped the little cellar speakeasies make huge profits from skyrocketing black-market prices. By the mid-1920s, there were more speakeasies in the brownstones lining the West 50s than residents, many of them catering to increasingly upscale clientele.

In the speakeasies, cocktails, jazz rhythms and 'wild' Harlem dances, as well as the growing popularity of cocaine, combined to provoke customers to ever more riotous behaviour – as did the illicit nature of the establishments themselves. Jazz may have put the sin in syncopation, as the *Ladies' Home Journal* declared in 1921; but it was drinking the 'devil's candy' that made them feel beautiful and damned. All rules were suspended: so Zelda danced naked on table-tops and Scott dropped his trousers to display 'his gospel pipe', as Mencken once put it.

Nor did most of the prohibition agents try very hard to uphold it; a British newspaper sardonically referred to the American 'enforcement' of prohibition. It was said that if you needed a good bootlegger, you should ask the nearest policeman. In October 1922 New York reported that 'the intoxication of policemen had increased under prohibition to the extent that it was responsible for a murder a week', and hypocrisy was already brazen. The New Jersey Democratic candidate for governor, running on a Dry platform, gave a speech about the importance of enforcing the law at a dinner where 'wine enough flowed to float a battleship'.

Ted Paramore told of a night at the Montmartre or the Rendezvous in Greenwich Village, when a 'soused' policeman went round all the tables threatening to close the place, but accepting drinks from every table as a bribe. When he got to Paramore's table and demanded a drink, they confessed they had nothing left. In outrage, the policeman announced with his hat on the back of his head, 'Well I've a good mind to run yez in!'

In late October 1922, as temperatures hovered just above freezing, the story of the murders of Hall and Mills veered wildly again. Five weeks into the investigation, as a special prosecutor named Wilbur A. Mott was appointed, a new character entered the tale, who would soon be known to America as the 'Pig Woman'.

Mrs Jane Gibson, described as a widow who kept pigs near De Russey's Lane, suddenly announced that she had witnessed the murders of Hall and Mills. On the fatal night, she claimed, she saw a shadowy figure leave her property. Fearing robbery, 'she mounted one of her mules and set off', following him toward the Phillips farm, where she witnessed two men and two women 'silhouetted' against a crab-apple tree. She saw the 'flash of a pistol and heard a shot and saw one of the figures drop. Then she heard a woman's voice cry out, "Oh Henry!", and then, "Don't! Don't! Don't!"' Mrs Gibson's mule 'backed away' in fear. She heard some more shots, but could not recall how many, then she saw 'another figure fall'. Deciding she'd seen enough, Mrs Gibson dug her heels into the mule's flanks and went home. The mule was named Jenny, a detail that delighted the press.

*The Phillips farm, New Brunswick's house of silence*

Phillips Farm

There were discrepancies between this account and the few known facts: the angle of the bullet wound in the rector's head suggested that he was shot from above, for example. But Mrs Gibson's story fanned the flames of interest in the case. That Sunday so many sightseers visited the Phillips farm that they caused a traffic jam. 'The curiosity seekers took everything they could get their hands on as souvenirs', including the denuded crab-apple tree, which had been reduced to 'a spectral line against the sky'. All this madness was good for local enterprise, however, as 'Fakers from New Brunswick flocked to the scene with balloons, pop corn, peanuts and soft drinks.' New York had developed a thriving industry in what they called 'rubberneck tours', helping Americans enjoy 'the marvels of a nation that finds it easy to marvel'. New Jersey would provide some marvels of its own.

Meanwhile, a policeman had finally been detailed to the Phillips Farm – to direct traffic.

----

# October's Bright Booze Weather

Since moving to Great Neck Zelda had 'unearthed some of the choicest bootleggers (including Fleischman)'; which bootlegger she meant is unclear, although (perhaps coincidentally) the Fleischmann Yeast Company was under investigation throughout 1922. A self-styled 'gentleman bootlegger' named Max Fleischman who 'lives like a millionaire' appears in Edmund Wilson's first play, *The Crime in the Whistler Room*, which he wrote in 1923. It features a celebrated, attractive but 'dissipated and haggard' young writer, a man of 'disarmingly childlike egoism' who tends to get boiled and start brawls and is the author of a story called 'The Ruins of the Ritz' (he is planning a book called 'The Skeleton in the Taxi').

By this point Fitzgerald had already told Wilson his idea for a novel about a gentleman bootlegger, and Wilson's portrait of Fleischman reads like a crasser James Gatz:

> Fleischman was making a damn ass of himself bragging about how much his tapestries were worth and how much his bath-room was worth and how he never wore a shirt twice – and he had a revolver studded with diamonds that he insisted on showing everybody. And he finally got on my nerves – I was a little bit stewed – and I told him I wasn't impressed by his ermine-lined revolver: I told him he was nothing but a bootlegger, no matter how much money he made ... and that it was torture to stay in a place where everything was in such terrible taste.

Wilson saw only the gaucherie ('Bunny appreciates feeling after it's been filtered through a temperament,' Fitzgerald once explained, 'but his soul is a bit *sec*'); it took Fitzgerald to register the poignancy of someone trying to be a connoisseur, and failing.

Fitzgerald and Wilson were not the only ones to see that black-market booze provided a quick route to the prosperity that might purchase an entrée into the leisure class; bootlegging was becoming indistinguishable from bootstrapping. In early 1922 a satirical *New York Times* piece explained that illicit profits were enabling bootleggers 'to acquire works of art, go to the opera, patronize the best tailors ... enjoy in elegant leisure all the purchasable luxuries' and meet 'our best citizens' socially, 'on equal terms as fellow law-breakers'. Drinking was a great leveller, not because it made everyone equally drunk but because it made everyone equally guilty.

'The hangover became a part of the day as well allowed-for as the Spanish siesta,' Scott wrote later. Wilson noted that Ted Paramore's favourite hangover cures were veal cutlets in sauce Veronal – a popular and easily obtained opiate – or sweetbreads smothered in aspirin. 'Most of my friends drank too much – the more they were in tune to the times the more they drank.' Fitzgerald published a 'Short Autobiography' in the *New Yorker*, offering a summary of each year of his drinking life, beginning when he was seventeen and bringing his career up to date: '1929: A feeling that all liquor has been drunk and all it can do for one has been experienced, and yet – "*Garçon, un Chablis-Mouton 1902, et pour commencer, une petite carafe de vin rose. C'est ça – merci.*"' The entry for 1922 reads: 'Kaly [Kalman]'s crème de cacao cocktails in St Paul. My own first and last manufacture of gin.' This brief foray into bathtub gin was most likely also in St Paul, and almost certainly in a spirit of fun. (Making gin didn't require a bathtub; the name originated from the size of the jar used, which people tended to fill from the tap in the bath.)

Part of Gatsby's business, we learn, was selling grain alcohol over the counter from drugstores, which most Americans used to make their gin. Burton Rascoe explained the system in his 1947 autobiography: given the well-publicized risks of buying from bootleggers, the safest way was to make synthetic gin oneself. 'A great many drugstore proprietors ... dispensed bonded whisky on prescription and grain alcohol without it.' It was easy to find a doctor who would write such a prescription, but it cost a fortune, as one had to bribe the doctor in addition to paying a hefty premium for real whisky. 'Most druggists, however, seemed to have an unlimited supply of grain alcohol in gallon cans, tested and guaranteed to be pure', and far more affordable. Nearly everybody who drank used synthetic gin until bootlegging became well organized, in around 1926, said Rascoe, helpfully sharing the recipe.

Preserved among Fitzgerald's papers is his handwritten recipe for bathtub gin, which was almost the same as Rascoe's. If 1922 was indeed Fitzgerald's first and last manufacture of gin, then this undated recipe may come from the year in which *Gatsby* is set.

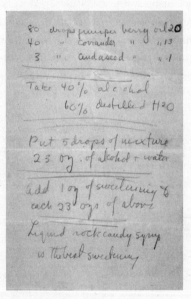

'80 drops juniper berry oil; 40 drops coriander oil; 3 drops aniseed oil // Take 40% alcohol; 60% distilled H²O // Put 5 drops of mixture 23 oz of alcohol + water // Add 1 oz of sweetening to each 23 ozs of above // Liquid rock candy syrup is the best sweetening.'

The Fitzgeralds were also acquainted with a bootlegger named Max Gerlach. Zelda would tell one of Fitzgerald's earliest biographers that Jay Gatsby was 'based on a neighbor named Von Guerlach or something who was said to be General Pershing's nephew and was in trouble over bootlegging'. When Gerlach became Gatsby he lost his American uncle and acquired a more villainous German one: 'One time he killed a man who had found out that he was nephew to Von Hindenburg and second cousin to the devil.' There is little reason to believe that Max Gerlach's noble predicate 'von' was any more authentic than his use of the aristocratic affectation 'old sport', but his improvement of his name may be mimicked in James Gatz's transformation into Jay Gatsby.

Fitzgerald preserved a small cutting in his scrapbook, a newspaper photograph of himself, Zelda and Scottie. Later, another cutting of the same photo was found, on which a note had been scrawled: 'Enroute from the coast – Here for a few days on business – how are you and the family old sport? 7/20/23 – Gerlach.'

Max Gerlach has haunted Fitzgerald scholars for decades, and some years ago a few hired a private detective to run him to ground. A man named Max Gerlach ran a garage in Flushing in the 1930s and attempted suicide by shooting himself in the 1950s. When Gerlach joined the US Army in 1917 he was required to give character references; two of his references were Judge Ariel Levy and George Young Bauchle. Levy was known as a fixer for a gangster named Arnold Rothstein and Bauchle was an attorney and the front man for a floating gambling club run by Rothstein, called the Partridge Club.

Fitzgerald's first biographer, Arthur Mizener, was contacted by a man named Gerlach in the 1950s, who identified himself as 'the real Gatsby', but Mizener declined the invitation to meet. Perhaps he was uninterested in anyone capable of the category error of declaring himself a 'real' fictional character, or of believing that a catchphrase and a history of black-market dealings suffice to define one of literature's most popular inventions. Maybe Mizener was also remembering a bootlegger named Larry Fay, who was famous for the trunkloads of brightly coloured shirts he boasted of having shipped from England, or the extravagant parties of a bootlegger named George Remus. Perhaps he was remembering how much of himself Fitzgerald later said he had shared with Gatsby. Years later Fitzgerald inscribed a copy of *Gatsby* with what he perceived at the time to be its failings: 'Gatsby was never quite real to me. His original served for a good enough exterior until about the middle of the book he grew thin and I began to fill him with my own emotional life. So he's synthetic – and that's one of the flaws of the book.' Max Gerlach may have believed that he was the real Jay Gatsby, but for Scott Fitzgerald he was merely the original – assuming Gerlach is indeed the man to whom he referred.

But Gatsby was always synthetic; lying is how he makes himself up and how he reinvents himself. And even amid his lies, some of what Gatsby tells Nick on their trip into New York is true. As Nick and Gatsby drive across the bridge into the 'wild promise' of New York, a dead man passes them in a hearse. The comedy of human pretension is underscored by *Gatsby*'s second instance of casual racism – once again used to make a point about social mobility, as Nick laughs aloud when 'three modish Negroes' driving past roll 'the yolks of their eyeballs ... toward us in haughty rivalry'.

And then they meet the gangster Meyer Wolfshiem, Gatsby's partner, in a cellar speakeasy. The caricature of the dishonest Jew that defines his cartoonish portrayal is as disillusioning as the easy racism of laughing at the 'Negroes' in the fancy automobile with pretensions to 'haughty rivalry' with the privileged white men in Gatsby's Rolls-Royce. Racist humour was common and casual in 1920s America; when she finished

*Gatsby* Edith Wharton praised Wolfshiem as a 'perfect Jew', an anti-Semitic caricature that was her favourite part of the novel. Reading *The Waste Land* and noting the 1922 poem's anti-Semitism, William Empson observed, 'A writer had better rise above the ideas of his time, but one should not take offense if he doesn't.' True enough, and one should also not be surprised. But any novel's greatness is partly measured by its wisdom, and in a story that claims to believe in judging people by conduct rather than by condition it is disenchanting to find some characters limited by the most inescapable social conditions of all, race and ethnicity. At the very least it's a failure of imagination, just when the story has promised us that anything could happen, anything at all.

It is also its own kind of aesthetic category error, a jarring moment of dissonance in a novel mostly characterized by remarkable tonal control: these flickers of racism are the only moments in *The Great Gatsby* when Fitzgerald mistakes for comedy what was, in fact, a vast historical tragedy.

---

As the nation's front pages continued to remark on 'five weeks of inexpert investigation' into the Hall–Mills murders, the papers all carried the extraordinary story of Charles Buckley, whose drunken driving had killed a four-year-old girl. As reparation, Buckley 'offered to give his own child, Isabel, aged 5', to the bereaved parents. Buckley's wife, who was in the car when the accident occurred, 'was willing to join in . . . "if it would sufficiently compensate that other mother for what she has lost."' Evidently it wouldn't: the victim's mother declined their offer.

That same day Carl Van Vechten recorded another encounter with modern violence in New York:

*Sunday, 22 October 1922*

I dine at Avery [Hopwood]'s ... We visit The Jungle, 11 Cornelia Street in the Village, a tough gangster resort. Avery loses his overcoat. On way to police station to report loss we run into a murder.

The murder didn't seem to warrant further comment; the entry ends there, and what happened to the overcoat remains a mystery. Three days later, Van Vechten was enjoying the story enough to repeat it in a letter: 'New York suddenly became *very* brilliant – so brilliant that I broke my arm at a party – but it was soon bandaged up and I continued to go to parties and saw a man shot at one of them – or shortly after. He lay in the street quite bloody.'

The Hall–Mills investigation was offering much more brilliant entertainment than a mere shooting. New theories were constantly adduced. One detective suggested that the careful placement of the victims' bodies, the scattering of letters and covering of their faces, 'hints at a sort of charitable regret or sorrow on the part of the murderer'. Perhaps because they were so convinced that one of the murderers was a woman, they seemed unable to relinquish the belief that the killer would prove to be kind-hearted in the end.

Meanwhile, the Mills family had been receiving letters from around the country: one note told Charlotte that if she sent the writer a dollar, she would learn who had killed her mother. Charlotte also received several letters purporting to be from the Ku Klux Klan: 'If you do not stop your silly activities and keep on exploiting your foolish ideas, the Klu [*sic*] Klux Klan will give you a taste of the same medicine we gave to Mrs Mills, so beware or you will see the fiery cross some night and get your due reward. [Signed] K.K.K.'

Gossip had been swirling for weeks that the murders might have been committed by the Klan. The prosecutor said no evidence existed to support these persistent rumours, but the idea that a white couple might have been killed by the Klan was less bizarre than it may sound today. In the early 1920s the Klan was enjoying a resurgence across America, not just in the South; it was active in New Jersey, New York

City and Long Island, and it did not restrict itself to racially motivated violence. Swope had just commissioned a pioneering and prize-winning series of articles investigating this resurgence, while the *New York Times* published 275 stories on the Klan in 1922 alone. The new Klan used modern media and recruitment tactics to persuade unprecedented numbers of 'middle Americans' to join them, as well as the kind of cere-monial spectacle and eugenicist theories that were becoming the hallmark of European fascists at the same time.

These are the ideas that Tom Buchanan lectures Nick about at their first dinner party, when he insists that scientific books have proven that the Buchanans and their friends are 'Nordics', the 'dominant races' who need to protect Western civilization from coloured hordes. Nick feels sorry for Tom, clinging to his pathetic theories of supremacy, 'as if his complacency, more acute than of old, was not enough to him any more'. But Tom is prepared to use violence – or to incite it – to defend what he views as the prerogatives of his class and race. His violence is more discreet than the Klan's, but no less effective.

The Klan saw itself as the gatekeeper of a broadly reactionary defini-tion of 'decency': Catholics, Jews and even white Protestants transgressing against the Klan's ideas of morality were frequently the victims of violence. In the autumn of 1922 the *Times* reported the story of a white man in Maryland who had both cheeks and his forehead branded in acid with the letter K, and was beaten and left for dead; he said that his attack-ers told him it was because he 'mistreated' his wife, although his wife denied the charge.

People having interracial relationships were particular targets for Klan violence, but stories of adulterous white couples being attacked by the Klan were also becoming familiar. Women were tarred and feathered if found in bed with men who weren't their husbands; the men might be beaten, branded, castrated or even lynched. The prosecutor could deny it all he liked, but people kept asking whether the Klan had killed Hall and Mills, and the papers kept reporting the rumours.

Meanwhile, James Mills offered a novel suggestion to the police: 'What should have been done was to arrest the whole Mills family and the whole Hall family and then let us fight our way out.' A universal presumption of guilt might make for an inefficient system of justice, but no one remarked on the meek Mr Mills suddenly showing such gladiatorial spirit.

----

# Stock Market Manipulation

As the temperate weather bloomed its last, headlines on Tuesday 17 October announced the brief postponement of the first of four trials in what would prove one of the biggest financial scandals of the decade. The indictment of a Great Neck resident named Edward M. Fuller for larceny and 'bucketing' frauds became one of the first dominoes to fall in the run that would bring Wall Street crashing down seven years later.

The so-called 'bucket shops' stretched back to the days after the Civil War, when financiers like Jay Gould sold railroad securities to artificially created markets at manipulated prices, all of which was perfectly legal in the days of nineteenth-century profiteering. By the 1920s, bucket shops had developed a simple system of betting against the market: brokers chose stocks to lose value and sold them to customers, but never purchased the stocks. They pocketed the money and informed customers that their stocks had devalued; if the bucketeers were unlucky and the stocks rose, they usually had sufficient cash on hand to cover the difference. Bucketeers were at the heart of the 1920s economic boom – they would finally be outlawed by the financial regulations enacted in the early 1930s in the wake of the Wall Street Crash. The bucket shops operated not on the New York Stock Exchange, but on the Consolidated Stock Exchange; E. M. Fuller and William F. McGee operated the largest house on the Consolidated. In 1922 the bucket system began to fall apart for the simple, self-cancelling reason that the boom of the 1920s had begun in earnest. Suddenly even worthless stocks were rising, and Fuller's brokerage firm collapsed in June 1922, announcing debts of up to five million dollars.

Over the course of Fuller's trials, documentary evidence disappeared, witnesses were bribed and even kidnapped; eventually Fuller served only one year of a five-year prison sentence.

## What goes on
## inside a large bank?

Soon rumours were circulating that America's most notorious gangster, Arnold Rothstein, was connected to Fuller's business. While awaiting indictment, Fuller reportedly hid out at Rothstein's estate on Long Island.

Arnold Rothstein was infamous as the gangster widely believed to have fixed the 1919 World Series. He was implicated in most major criminal conspiracies of the day, linking narcotics to newspapers to policemen to politicians. He was the liaison between New York's underground economy and its official one, involved at a very high level in labour-union racketeering, and he helped give Legs Diamond, Dutch Schultz and Lucky Luciano their criminal starts. He owned and protected a wide variety of shady financial endeavours, including a number of bucket shops; he was also widely rumoured to be fencing stolen bond securities. Nothing was ever proven: Rothstein was indicted repeatedly, but never convicted. He was murdered in 1928, shot in the back as he left a poker game. A compulsive gambler, Rothstein would bet on anything, and was reputed to have fixed most of his bets. He was also, by no coincidence, a close acquaintance of Herbert Bayard Swope, who supplemented his income with high-stakes gambling. Swope played regularly at the Partridge Club (which also included impresario and Great Neck resident Florenz Ziegfeld).

While Scott Fitzgerald was living like Swope, he was being regaled by the tales that made Swope America's first star reporter. In 1912 Swope had revealed that Herman 'Rosy' Rosenthal, a small-time hoodlum in a gambling ring, would testify to the corruption of a policeman named Charles Becker. Before Rosenthal could testify, he was gunned down in front of the Hotel Metropole in Times Square. Becker was eventually tried, convicted and executed for conspiracy to murder Rosenthal, and the story catapulted Swope to the top of America's press corps. One of Rosenthal's cronies, implicated in the gambling ring, was none other than Arnold Rothstein. For obvious reasons Swope downplayed his long association with Rothstein, but in fact Swope and his wife Margaret were the only witnesses at Rothstein's wedding in 1909. Rothstein probably tipped Swope off about the Rosenthal–Becker story in the first place; some even argue that Rothstein used Swope to set Becker up, and that Becker was innocent.

These are the murders about which gangster Meyer Wolfshiem becomes misty-eyed when he meets Gatsby and Nick Carraway at roaring noon in a well-fanned cellar speakeasy on West 42nd Street in July 1922. 'I can't forget so long as I live the night they shot Rosy Rosenthal,' Wolfshiem sighs. 'Four of them were electrocuted,' Nick remembers. 'Five with Becker,' Wolfshiem corrects him. After Wolfshiem leaves, Gatsby 'coolly' informs Nick that Wolfshiem is the man who fixed the World Series – because he 'saw the opportunity'. The idea 'staggers' Nick: 'It never occurred to me that one man could start to play with the faith of fifty million people – with the single-mindedness of a burglar blowing a safe.' What staggers him is the scale of such a betrayal of faith. Faith, hope and charity are at the centre of *Gatsby*'s moral universe; Fitzgerald's Catholicism may have lapsed, but it never expired completely.

In December 1924, in response to Max Perkins's suggestion that Gatsby's shady underworld dealings should be given more texture, Fitzgerald wrote: 'After careful searching of the files (of a man's mind here) for the Fuller McGee case & after having had Zelda draw pictures until her fingers ache I know Gatsby better than I know my own child.' Facts, or the illusion of facts, create the necessary conviction to produce a persuasive fiction.

Years later, reflecting on the composition of *Gatsby*, Fitzgerald said he chose material 'to fit a given mood or "hauntedness" … rejecting in advance in *Gatsby*, for instance, all of the ordinary material for Long Island, big crooks, adultery theme and always starting from the small focal point that impressed me – my own meeting with Arnold Rothstein for instance'. Some of us are haunted by the story Fitzgerald never told, of the circumstances of that remarkable meeting. The only remnant we have, other than this epistolary trace, is Meyer Wolfshiem himself, the venal but sentimental gangster who backs Gatsby and sighs over bullet-riddled friends. Arnold Rothstein has forged his way into hundreds of footnotes on *The Great Gatsby* because he was the prototype of the comically sinister Meyer Wolfshiem. In fiction, Wolfshiem is haunted by the murder of Rosy Rosenthal; in fact, he is haunted by Arnold Rothstein, whose copy he is.

The cheating Black Sox, Rosy Rosenthal and Charles Becker are all transposed directly into the fictional world, where they anchor *The Great Gatsby* in an actual American history of murderous corruption. He divagated over Gatsby's various vices, but Fitzgerald always knew that his central character was a gangster: this is a story about cheating. Gatsby admits to Nick that he has been in the drug business and the oil business: by 1925, both enterprises were notoriously corrupt. The oil industry was at the heart of the scandal that would bring President Harding's administration crashing down in 1923. Gatsby is implicated in the era's widespread financial swindles as well: eventually Nick learns that he was fencing stolen bonds. In the drafts of *Gatsby*, Nick reports hearing that Wolfshiem was later 'tried (but not convicted) on charges of grand larceny, forgery, bribery, and dealing in stolen bonds'.

Gatsby's crimes are not merely an array of prohibition-era get-rich-quick schemes, although they are that. They are swindles, frauds, and deceptions, suggesting fakery and dishonesty. Everything about Gatsby is synthetic, including his gin – everything except his fidelity.

All of America had become 'aroused over this double murder', wrote *Town Topics* on 26 October. 'Had it not been for the publicity given to the affair by the New York press it would long ere this have been allowed to lapse into oblivion' by embarrassed officials, but it was too late for that now, especially while the papers had the Pig Woman – who kept improving her tale.

Asked how she had seen the murders on a moonless night, Mrs Gibson suddenly recalled a car fortuitously appearing round the bend at just the right moment. Its headlights revealed 'a woman in a light gray coat and a stocky man with a dark mustache and bushy hair', a description that perfectly matched the photos of Willie Stevens that had graced the front pages for weeks. Then Mrs Gibson remembered that she'd returned to the scene around 1 a.m., where she found the woman in the light-grey polo coat kneeling and sobbing by the rector's side. This image was felt to be 'in harmony with the loving care that some one took in arranging the position of the rector's body ... The authorities believe that such touches were the work of the woman who knelt beside his body at 1 o'clock in the morning', a remorseful woman who was now being accepted as fact. Mrs Gibson next revealed that Mrs Mills had 'fought terribly' and been dragged along the ground before she was killed, a claim the papers said 'was verified' by the autopsy, which showed long deep cuts on her right arms and wrist. But the results of the autopsy had been in the papers for weeks; like the repentant woman in grey, these reports were now being used to 'verify' the stories they seemed to have inspired.

At the end of October Sir Basil Thomson, the former chief of

Scotland Yard who was visiting New York, was asked to comment on the Hall–Mills investigation, as they 'had never seen so much publicity given to any crime nor so much interest taken all over the United States as there was in this celebrated case'. Thomson declined to discuss the case in detail, but offered a helpful suggestion that was widely shared in the press: 'I have found that there are many persons who seem to take delight in the publicity of being an identifier,' he pointedly observed.

Meanwhile the press suddenly announced that James Mills's accounts of his movements the night that his wife was murdered were, in fact, uncorroborated. But New Brunswick's officials were untroubled, for his claim that he was home all night, except when he went to the church to look for his wife, had not been disproven either. Although they had only his word for his actions during the hours when the murder had most likely taken place, between approximately 8.30 and 11 p.m., and having 'commented on the lack of corroboration for Mills's account of his movements', they also 'pointed out, however, that there was no proof that he was not telling the truth. If there was no one to corroborate, they said, there was no one to deny what he said was true. The same was said of Mrs Hall's accounts of her movements.'

Unfortunately, the inability to disprove something is not a very good justification for believing it. By that line of reasoning, the law of New Brunswick admitted almost limitless imaginative possibility – a 'hint of the unreality of reality, a promise that the rock of the world was founded securely on a fairy's wing', as Nick says of Gatsby's dreams.

For the first time the press were permitted to see the victims' clothing: Eleanor Mills had been wearing a blue velvet hat, which now had a three-inch blood stain; her dress, dark blue with red polka dots, was edged with cheerful red ribbon and 'saturated with blood'. The *Times* noted that 'the clergyman's expensive garments contrasted sharply with the cheap material of which Mrs Mills's garments was made'.

The papers were making much of 'the contrast between the social status of the rector and Mrs Mills'. Witnesses thought Eleanor's adultery was motivated, at least in part, by aspiration, her 'dissatisfaction' with life in her 'drab apartment'. Eleanor Mills had tried to seize the day, to find something more romantic in life than an unprosperous existence with a grey, inadequate husband on the second floor of a dreary frame house at the edge of town.

'Mrs Mills' home was on the second floor of this house'

When Nick Carraway meets Myrtle Wilson she is wearing 'a spotted dress of dark blue crepe-de-chine'; he senses an 'immediately

perceptible vitality about her as if the nerves of her body were continually smouldering. She smiled slowly and walking through her husband as if he were a ghost shook hands with Tom, looking him flush in the eye. Then she wet her lips and without turning around spoke to her husband in a soft, coarse voice.' Myrtle knows that you can't live forever; Eleanor Mills found in romance her only possibility for escape, and would die trying to leave her origins behind.

## ILLUSION ESSENTIAL

At the end of October, a young woman from the Midwest made the nation's front pages when she was acquitted of murdering her 'sheik lover'. Although her defence was temporary insanity, this was recognized as a euphemism for the so-called 'unwritten law', which held that juries would condone violence provoked by sexual infidelity: 'ACQUITTAL OF PEGGY BEAL FOR SLAYING "SHEIK LOVER" INVOKES NEW UNWRITTEN LAW' shouted the *World*. Peggy Beal had been lured by the 'professional sheik' to a hotel room with promises of marriage, but after he had seduced her Frank Anderson told her he had no intention of marrying her, adding that he had lied 'because I am a devil'. Beal shot Anderson dead before shooting herself in the heart. The papers did not explain why she had brought a gun to a romantic tryst, nor how she survived, but they did explain her inspiration: Beal 'had been reading a passage in a romantic novel in which a woman killed her lover'. Books kept leading women astray, it seemed.

As Jordan tells Nick the story of Daisy's romance with Gatsby at the end of Chapter Four, they are driving through Central Park in a Victoria cab. Floating past the apartments of the movie stars in the West Fifties comes the sound of a hit song in the twilight:

> I'm the Sheik of Araby,
> Your love belongs to me.
> At night when you're are asleep,
> Into your tent I'll creep –

'Sheik' – after Rudolph Valentino's immensely popular film character – was one of the most popular American slang terms of the early 1920s for a playboy or 'gigolo' (a word first introduced to English in 1922). Listening to the song, Nick feels relieved that he has 'no girl whose disembodied face floated along the dark cornices and blinding signs' to haunt him: without any inconvenient promises or illusions curbing his behaviour, he kisses Jordan.

Nick is not oleaginous enough to be called a sheik, but his treatment of women is certainly opportunistic. There is a girl in the Midwest under the illusion that they might be engaged, and that summer he has an 'affair' with a girl in Jersey City whose brother makes it clear he thinks Nick is treating her badly. Jordan's aunt considers Nick 'an ill-intentioned young man', and she may be right. Nick is with Jordan that night from sunset until 2 a.m., which is when he tells us he returned to Great Neck at the beginning of the next chapter. Cabs had been famous ever since *Madame Bovary* for the privacy they afforded for what Jordan calls 'amour'; perhaps Nick seized his chance. Fitzgerald doesn't say.

According to the *Man's Hope* outline, the inspiration for Jordan's story of her 'white girlhood' with Daisy in Louisville that ends this chapter was a wedding Fitzgerald never attended. In his scrapbook he preserved a wedding invitation, captioned THE END OF A ONCE POIGNANT STORY. It came from his first love, Ginevra King, a wealthy young woman from Lake Forest outside Chicago, and a famous debutante whose father owned a string of polo ponies. Tom Buchanan will hail from the same affluent town, his string of polo ponies measuring his vast wealth. Ginevra rejected Fitzgerald before he met Zelda; his conviction that she'd discarded him because he was poor was later confirmed, he thought, by her engagement to an equally wealthy young man from her own circle. Ginevra married on 4 September 1918. Three days later Fitzgerald noted in his journal, 'Fell in love on the 7th', with Zelda.

Ginevra King had been known as one of the 'Big Four' debutantes in pre-war Chicago. One of the other four was her close friend Edith Cummings, who was becoming a famous golfer; her matches had made headlines by the summer of 1922 and she won the US Women's Amateur title in 1923. Dubbed 'The Fairway Flapper' by the press, Cummings would be the first sportswoman on the cover of *Time* magazine in the summer of 1924 – just as Fitzgerald was creating her copy.

In a letter to Max Perkins as he finished *Gatsby*, Fitzgerald explained: 'Jordan of course was a great idea (perhaps you know it's Edith Cummings) but she fades out.' And Ginevra King became one of the prototypes for Daisy Buchanan.

Gatsby thinks that Daisy rejected him because he was poor – and perhaps he's right: the $350,000 strand of pearls that Tom gives Daisy as a wedding gift is not an incidental detail. Jordan tells Nick enough to make it clear that Daisy did care, in her careless way, for Gatsby. Her wild plans to elope and drunkenness just before her wedding show that she was not indifferent to him. But in the end she marries Tom 'without so much as a shiver', and when Nick talks with her three years later in her garden he registers her 'basic insincerity': 'I waited, and sure enough, in a moment she looked at me with an absolute smirk on her lovely face as if she had asserted her membership in a rather distinguished secret society to which she and Tom belonged.'

Before she inspired Daisy, Ginevra King had inspired another flapper *belle dame sans merci* in Fitzgerald's fiction. Just as he and Zelda left St Paul in September 1922, Scott finished 'Winter Dreams', which would be published that December. Fitzgerald would later call this story a 'sort of 1st draft of the Gatsby idea'; it shows his deepening understanding of the poignancy of loss and its artistic power, a personal loss that becomes an aesthetic gain.

A poor young man, Dexter Green, who is casually working on a golf course as a caddy, falls in love with a beautiful, wealthy, hollow young woman named Judy Jones. Resenting her assumption of superiority, he is spurred to ambition. Dexter grows prosperous from a specialist cleaning service for the wealthy, symbolically hinting that he takes care of their dirty laundry, a legal business anticipating Gatsby's shadier underworld dealings. Hard-working Dexter understands that 'carelessness was for his children', for carelessness 'required more confidence than to be careful'. Judy toys with Dexter before rejecting him to marry a richer man; years later he hears that her husband drinks and is unfaithful, and she has lost her looks. For Dexter, Judy's degradation means the world has lost its promise of beauty and glory.

In the story Judy's waning appeal is Dexter's tragedy, not her own. Her squandered promise symbolizes Dexter's lost illusions, and his frightening revelation that he will never feel so intensely again. 'Winter Dreams' closes with Dexter's realization that the loss of love is much easier to bear than the loss of illusions: 'Even the grief he could have borne was left behind in the country of illusion, of youth, of the richness of life, where his winter dreams had flourished.'

A dozen years later, in his lovely jazz-age reminiscence 'My Lost City', Fitzgerald wrote of the moment of shocking recognition that a dream realized is a dream destroyed: only deferral and frustration can keep it alive. He dates the realization between 'trying to disrobe' at the *Scandals* in 1921 and punching a policeman in 1923. Some time in that period of trafficking in scandal, he discovered that he would never be so happy again, that, as Zelda said, you can't be swept off your feet indefinitely. 'At last we were one with New York, pulling it after us through every portal,' Fitzgerald wrote:

> Even now I go into many flats with the sense that I have been there before or in the one above or below – was it the night I tried to disrobe in the Scandals, or the night when (as I read with astonishment in the paper next morning) 'Fitzgerald Knocks Officer This Side of Paradise'? Successful scrapping not being among my accomplishments, I tried in vain to reconstruct the sequence of events which led up to this denouement in Webster Hall. And lastly from that period I remember riding in a taxi one afternoon between very tall buildings under a mauve and rosy sky; I began to bawl because I had everything I wanted and knew I would never be so happy again.

He was right: happiness was no sooner grasped than it began to dissolve. He would never recover it fully again. Fitzgerald was driven by desire, he came to see, 'because as a restless and ambitious man, I was never disposed to accept the present but always striving to change it, better it, or even sometimes destroy it'. 'The Sensible Thing', a story written in the summer of 1924 and which Fitzgerald told Perkins was 'about Zelda & me. All true', also ends with the recognition that even gaining what one desires is itself a loss, the loss of the sustaining, driving desire itself. 'She was something desirable and rare that he had fought for and made his own – but never again an intangible whisper in the dusk, or on the breeze of night ... Well, let it pass, he thought; April is over, April is over. There are all kinds of love in the world, but never the same love twice.'

------------

# Where Is the Real Man?

The *New York Times* reviewed *Tales of the Jazz Age* on 29 October 1922, declaring Fitzgerald 'a writer whom it is a joy to read', and defending his right to 'paint with startling vividness and virility the jazz aspect of the American scene', valuable if only because it was so 'astonishingly sincere and unself-conscious'. As a collection, the reviewer found the book patchy and uneven, but filled with 'hints, promise and portents' of Fitzgerald's genius: 'there are flashes of wings and sounds of trumpets mingled with the tramp of feet and casual laughter'. The main question the book prompted was: 'What will this man do next?'

The answer to the reviewer's question was that next Fitzgerald would write his greatest failure, *The Vegetable*, and then he would write his masterpiece, the book that imagined angels' wings and trumpets in the very midst of tramping feet and casual laughter.

After *The Great Gatsby* was published, Fitzgerald wrote to John Bishop, saying he feared that perhaps it was a flaw in the book that he hadn't defined Gatsby more clearly: 'You are right about Gatsby being blurred and patchy. I never at any one time saw him clear myself – for he started as one man I knew and then changed into myself – the amalgam was never complete in my mind.' But to which man that he knew is he referring: Max Gerlach, or someone else? We will probably never know. Gatsby borrows many qualities from many people, including Scott Fitzgerald's romantic aspirations, boundless hope, and charm – but he is no more Scott Fitzgerald than he is Max Gerlach or any of a collage of other bootleggers.

'Desire just cheats you,' laments Anthony Patch in *The Beautiful and Damned*. 'It's like a sunbeam skipping here and there about a room. It stops and gilds some inconsequential object, and we poor fools try to grasp it – but when we do the sunbeam moves on to something else, and you've got the inconsequential part, but the glitter that made you want it is gone.' There is no real Jay Gatsby to grasp behind the glittering one we love: history may help us understand the world he inhabits, but it was fiction that produced him.

The artist, wrote Joseph Conrad, 'speaks to our capacity for delight and wonder, to the sense of mystery surrounding our lives'. That was the art that Scott Fitzgerald would find, reminding us that a mirage may be more marvellous in its way than an oasis in the desert. Gatsby's great error is his belief in the reality of the mirage; Fitzgerald's great gift was his belief in the mirage as a mirage. 'Splendor', Fitzgerald came to understand, 'was something in the heart'.

# NOVEMBER 1922

It was the hour of a profound human change, and excitement
was generating on the air.

## V. THE MEETING ALL AN INVENTION. MARY

When I came home to West Egg that night I was afraid for a moment that my house was on fire. Two o'clock and the whole corner of the peninsula was blazing with light which fell unreal on the shrubbery and made thin elongating glints upon the roadside wires. Turning a corner I saw that it was Gatsby's house, lit from tower to cellar. At first I thought it was another party, a wild rout that had resolved itself into 'hide-and-go-seek' or 'sardines-in-the-box' with all the house thrown open to the game. But there wasn't a sound. Only wind in the trees which blew the wires and made the lights go off and on again as if the house had winked into the darkness. As my taxi groaned away I saw Gatsby walking toward me across his lawn.

*The Great Gatsby*, Chapter 5

## Misdirected Inventions.

'The tendency of intelligent men is to approach nearer and nearer the truth, by the processes of rejection, revision and invention,' wrote H. L. Mencken in his 1908 book *The Philosophy of Friedrich Nietzsche*, a work that greatly influenced the young Scott Fitzgerald. The processes of rejection and revision were sometimes invisible, but inventions accumulated in the *Man's Hope* outline as Fitzgerald mused on the origins of his novel: 'the meeting all an invention', he said of the central scene in Chapter Five, the reunion of Gatsby and Daisy. But this need not imply that the novel begins at this point to leave history behind. Invention, after all, means literally to 'come upon', and in its earliest English uses invention was synonymous with discovery, before it came to mean contrivance or fabrication.

When Gatsby and Daisy meet again, it is the result of much contrivance and fabrication – and a heroic effort at self-invention. Gatsby spent five years turning himself into the person he thought Daisy wanted, sustaining his beautiful illusions, and then bought a house as close to her as he could get. At the end of the previous chapter, after Jordan tells Nick that Gatsby and Daisy had once been in love, Nick finds it 'a strange coincidence' that Gatsby should have ended up so near to the woman he had known five years earlier in Louisville. 'But it wasn't a coincidence at all,' Jordan explains. 'Gatsby bought that house so that Daisy would be just across the bay.' This conversation is a sleight of hand, distracting our attention from the real coincidence: that the house next door to Gatsby's had earlier chanced to be rented by Daisy's cousin. That is an authorial manipulation, which is what we mean by 'coincidence' in fiction, and why coincidences in fiction are far less beautiful than coincidences in fact.

Facts can be beautiful, and illusions can be ugly. Scott Fitzgerald loved Keats more than any other writer, and learned a great deal from him – much of the best writing in *Gatsby* riffs on Keats – but by 1922 he had decided that a romantic intoxication with life's beauty could only be sustained through chemical intoxication. Faith in the truth of beauty was a necessary illusion, but an illusion all the same, he wrote in *The Beautiful and Damned*:

There was a kindliness about intoxication – there was that indescribable gloss and glamour it gave, like the memories of ephemeral

and faded evenings. After a few high-balls there was magic in the tall
glowing Arabian night of the Bush Terminal Building – its summit
a peak of sheer grandeur, gold and dreaming against the inaccessible
sky. And Wall Street, the crass, the banal – again it was the triumph
of gold, a gorgeous sentient spectacle; it was where the great kings
kept the money for their wars … The fruit of youth or of the grape,
the transitory magic of the brief passage from darkness to darkness –
the old illusion that truth and beauty were in some way entwined.

Fitzgerald may have loved the Romantic poets more, but like the rest
of his generation he grew up reading Symbolist poets, Rimbaud,
Verlaine, Mallarmé. Beauty, said the Symbolist Remy de Gourmont,
does not exist in itself. There are only beautiful things, waiting to be
invented or discovered.

------------

## People Do Love to See Their Names in the Paper

Next to headlines reporting that Mussolini's Black Shirts had seized
power in Rome, with 'ITALY FIRMLY IN GRIP' of the Fascisti, America's
front pages announced on Wednesday 1 November: 'MRS GIBSON'S
STORY WILL STAND FIRE, PROSECUTOR SAYS.' Special prosecutor
Wilbur Mott told reporters 'in an offhand manner that the case eventually would go to the grand jury, as all murder cases do sooner or later'.
Mrs Gibson had given another affidavit, an 'astonishing, rambling
statement'. Mott didn't believe some of what Mrs Gibson now claimed,
but felt that he was 'forced to believe [her] in other aspects', namely the
parts of her story in which he already believed: the grey-coated woman,
the bushy-haired man, the marks on Eleanor Mills's wrists. In fact Mott
had not been forced to believe anything: the willing lies of fiction
depend upon willing believers. Like love, belief is an act of volition.

Mrs Gibson had already sold her life story to the papers and was repeating her tale to anyone who would listen, all the while loudly deploring the publicity she was receiving. Her tale grew ever more literary as she embellished it: now a woman at the murder scene screamed 'in a towering rage' at Mr Hall, 'Explain! Explain! You must explain these letters!' An abrupt pistol shot burst out. From 'the stillness which followed, came the poignant, remorseful, frightened scream of a woman crying in protest. "Oh Henry! Please – please – please!"' This touching appeal was answered by 'four more shots' – one shot too many, but no one cared. Meanwhile, local officials started looking for fingerprints and photographing the murder scene, seven weeks after the killings. Their efforts were somewhat hampered by all the sightseers milling about.

That Mrs Gibson was finding inspiration for her fictions in the newspapers was obvious to everyone but the investigators. On 2 November *Town Topics* printed a satiric comment on 'the disgusting Hall–Mills affair': having 'sold the story of her life for a tidy sum' and with her obvious talent for publicity, Mrs Gibson and her mule ('yclept Jenny') should seek greener pastures in Hollywood, now that America was 'consumed with interest in everything she has to say'. Thanks to her facility for invention, Mrs Gibson could 'tell a new and entirely different story every day in the week'; the article ended by caustically observing that her 'latent literary taste' was disclosed by the 'quantities of newspapers piled high near her favourite window, from which she viewed her vast estates and watched her pigs at play'.

Her facility for invention was not the only entertainment Mrs Gibson provided. Much satire was directed at her poverty, as the papers described the tumble-down 'shack' in which she lived surrounded by farm animals. Against Mrs Gibson's indigence and the Mills family's 'humble dwelling' was pitted the growing local belief that the Halls' wealth was enabling them to evade justice. The homes of the principals in the case offered a simple, graphic way to convey the economic divide: papers across America printed pictures of the Halls' house, described as 'The Palatial Home', next to drawings of the Millses' clapboard apartment, captioned 'Embittered by poverty'.

As the *World* announced that Inspector Mott 'SEEKS FLAWS IN MRS HALL'S STORY' – rather than in the more obviously flawed stories of Mrs Gibson – the rector's widow reluctantly agreed to be interviewed, hoping that if she gave reporters what they wanted, they would stop besieging her house. She was calm, controlled, unforthcoming – a demeanour that completely backfired. The press decided that such 'poise' and 'perfect self-control' were unnerving, 'an inexplicable phenomenon' that deserved study in 'medical annals for some time to come'. Comparing Mrs Hall to Boadicea and 'murderous queens' of ancient lore, the *Tribune* insisted that her 'extraordinary' composure could not be accounted for by her patrician upbringing: 'Not even the tutoring of a lifetime in that strata of society, where to betray the feelings is to indulge an unpardonable faux pas, can satisfactorily explain away Mrs Hall's stoical composure.' She was like a matron of ancient Rome, they felt, ready to kill to protect her pride.

Although it was clear to everyone that the press was trying the Hall–Mills case, without any evidence at all, that didn't stop them. The media commented on their own prejudicial practices even as they kept loading the dice. *Town Topics* declared itself speechless at media bias and in the same breath implied that Mrs Hall was a sociopath: 'There has been so much criticism here, and especially abroad, about our alleged practice of trying criminal cases in the newspapers ... that one scarcely knows what to say of the extraordinary [interview with] Mrs Hall, the widow of the murdered clergyman.' This protest was immediately followed by a description of Mrs Hall in the stock terms of a dime-novel killer: 'the principal impression which she made upon the inquisitors of the press was that of cleverness, coolness and unemotional poise, astonishing on the part of one who has been a central figure in the tragedy'.

Before it finished, *Town Topics* returned to *Simon Called Peter*, pointing out that although it 'has been called all sorts of names' and 'placed upon the Index of Public Libraries', the novel 'only tells much the same story in fiction which the daily papers have been relating every day *ad nauseam* and as fact'. The *New Republic* (for which Edmund Wilson was writing) similarly linked the Hall–Mills murder to Sumner's efforts to proscribe the *Satyricon*: 'Petronius is Sunday School literature as compared with the press reports of the Hall–Mills murder case, so far as its command over the imagination is concerned.' The difference was that in the press reports of the murder 'illicit words' were not used, although 'the illicit meanings are adequately conveyed'; but Sumner was 'after words, not meanings'.

Telling the same story in fiction that the papers have been relating daily as fact might be a sign of the meretriciousness of a bad novel like *Simon Called Peter*, or it might be the start of a masterpiece, one as interested in meanings as in words.

---

## Signs and Portents.

Fitzgerald's ledger entry for November 1922 begins: 'More Ring Lardner'. Lardner would come over to the Gateway Drive cottage, and the two writers would sit up all night talking (and drinking). Still talking (and drinking) as the sun rose, they would wander into the kitchen and order some breakfast (and possibly a drink); at which point, the story goes, Lardner would stretch and announce: 'Well, I guess the children have left for school by now – I might as well go home.'

On 2 November Zelda wrote to Ludlow Fowler, who had been best man at their wedding, offering an extravagant apology for what she, at least, felt had been their recent boorish behaviour. 'Dearest Lud – I'm running wild in sackcloth and ashes because Scott and I acted like two such drunks the other night. Aside from the fact that you were horribly bored, I am sorry because we saw nothing of you. It's been years since we three spent a satisfactory evening together – so won't you please come back Sat or Sunday or whenever you will so we can astound you with our brilliant conversation and splendid example of what is known as tee-totalers?'

Some have speculated that the ill-omened occasion to which Zelda refers might have been the party in the Fitzgerald's living room that was photographed, as they say that Ludlow Fowler stands in the corner of the image, unsmiling (and thus bored, goes the reasoning) – but Zelda continues in the letter to offer to introduce him to someone else who is in the photograph. Fowler had become 'a legendary figure', Zelda assured him, with neighbours of theirs called the Bucks: 'I told them you were richer than God and lived in this 12-story house with 30 Nubian slaves ... So jam a million ruble note in your pants and come along with some prestige for Fitzg House!' It would seem that Lud did not avail himself of her offer of hospitality on Saturday 3 November, for that night Scott and Zelda stayed up until five playing poker with members of the Algonquin Round Table, according to Algonquinite Franklin Pierce Adams (F.P.A.), who reported the game in his column for Swope's *World*. Although not always a fan ('think of that horse's ass F.P.A. coming around to my work after six years of neglect. I'd like to stick his praise up his behind,' Fitzgerald wrote to Perkins after *Gatsby* was published), Fitz still saved the item in his scrapbook. Posterity was calling.

## Lucky Charms

As Zelda was writing to Fowler, the *Tribune* ran a full-page advertisement from the *Saturday Evening Post*, declaring that it had hired Lothrop Stoddard, 'whose brilliant books', *The Rising Tide of Color* and *The Revolt Against Civilization*, had been a publishing sensation over the last few years. Achieving, as a later critic aptly put it, the dubious distinction of being the most popular racist of the American 1920s, Stoddard was the model for 'this man Goddard', the author of *The Rise of the Colored Empires*, the white-supremacist screed that so impresses Tom Buchanan.

Opposite the tribute to Lothrop Stoddard was an advertisement for a taxi company: 'Look for the Fay Cab, It's A Gray Cab'. Passengers should remember to 'ride in the taxi with the swastika trade mark on the doors'.

Larry Fay's grey taxis with inlaid black swastikas were a common sight in Manhattan in 1922. Having forcibly acquired a monopoly of the taxi ranks at Grand Central Terminal and Pennsylvania Station, Fay had a fleet of 450 cabs when he sold out to the Yellow Taxi Corporation at the end of 1923. The swastikas were not the only notable features of Fay's 'distinctive' vehicles; they also had blinking lights and horns offering a flamboyant burst of melody – like the three-noted horn of Jay Gatsby's gaudy motor car.

A small-time hoodlum from Hell's Kitchen, Larry Fay had placed a lucky bet on a horse with a swastika on its blanket and bought a taxi with his winnings. Soon after prohibition began, he was hired by a bootlegger to drive to Montreal and back, learning along the way how easy it was to smuggle liquor in a cab. A quick study, Fay expanded his taxi fleet by laundering bootlegging profits through it. Taxi drivers were often bootleggers, for the reasons Larry Fay had serendipitously discovered. A current joke had a cab driver asking if a passenger needed help getting his case, and being told, 'You're too late, I just bought three cases from the fellow down the street!'

Once he could afford to customize his cars, Fay adorned them with the swastikas he'd adopted as a good-luck charm. Popularized by Heinrich Schliemann's discoveries of swastika-decorated artifacts at Troy, swastikas could be either left- or right-facing. Ancient traditions may have assigned symbolic meanings to the different directions, but when they became fashionable at the turn of the twentieth century they were used interchangeably. The Nazi Party adopted the right-facing swastika as their symbol in 1920 (Hitler was nothing if not unoriginal), but throughout the 1920s most Americans saw the Nazis as a radical European fringe group – objectionable, but not important enough to alter the meaning of a common emblem from good luck to bad. That toxic power was emerging: in July 1922, a *New York Times* editorial denounced the 'Nordic' race theories being espoused by 'the societies which rally under the Swastika', which are 'open only to blond Aryans', but there were far more examples of benign swastikas in the media at the time. The swastika continued to be used by Americans as a generic name throughout the 1920s: in 1926, the grandson of Giuseppe Garibaldi, the 'liberator' of Italy, bought a ten-acre estate in Connecticut named Swastika, while on 3 July 1922 the general manager of a California wholesaler called the Swastika Fruit Company, rumoured to be a bootlegging front, was found murdered with his mistress, in a story reported around the country.

Soon Fay had opened his own nightclub, the 'El Fey', also decorated with swastikas, and hired the cabaret star Texas Guinan to be the club's hostess; one of his backers was none other than Arnold Rothstein. As Fay's profits increased, he began to indulge a taste for sartorial extravagance, becoming known as an aspiring dandy. He famously boasted that he had trunk-loads of tailored coloured shirts shipped to him every year from London, claiming never to wear the same shirt twice.

When Gatsby takes the woman who was named Daisy Fay when he fell in love with her on a tour of his 'incoherent failure' of a house, through rooms decorated haphazardly in symbolically classy styles, they end in Gatsby's bedroom. Explaining, 'I've got a man in England who buys me clothes. He sends over a selection of things at the beginning of each season, spring and fall,' Gatsby pulls out a rainbow of shirts and begins throwing them one by one onto the table 'in many-colored disarray'. Daisy suddenly bursts into tears: '"They're such beautiful shirts," she sobbed, her voice muffled in the thick folds. "It makes me sad because I've never seen such – such beautiful shirts before."'

Perhaps Daisy is having an authentic aesthetic reaction to the splendour of Gatsby's wardrobe; more likely, Fitzgerald is implying that Daisy and Gatsby are both thrilled by enchanted objects. Like the house, the shirts become a good-luck charm, a kaleidoscopic emblem of magical thinking. Daisy is amazed, and moved, by the exquisiteness of Gatsby's wealth – but not moved far enough to forget her position.

All symbols – from trademarks to brands to lucky charms – are enchanted objects, icons imbued with mystical significance. Gatsby has an array of symbolic objects, but Nick has his totemic volumes of Morgan, Maecenas and Midas, even Meyer Wolfshiem has his molar cufflinks – and when Nick seeks Wolfshiem after Gatsby dies, he finds him fronting the 'Swastika Holding Company'. This small, crooked symbol has had the power to complicate the meanings of the Jewish gangster Meyer Wolfshiem for many readers, to perplex them into wondering what, exactly, his swastika company might be holding.

Fitzgerald may have had no way of predicting what the swastika would come to mean, but by the end of 1924, as he completed *The Great Gatsby* at the Hôtel des Princes in Rome, he certainly knew that Jay Gatsby's chromatic array of bright shirts provided a marked contrast to the Black Shirts in control of the city where he was putting the final touches to his masterpiece.

---

## Cheese, Royalty and Americanisms.

On the same rainy Thursday in November that Zelda wrote to Ludlow Fowler, Carl Van Vechten recorded in his diary a gathering of noteworthy New Yorkers at the Algonquin Hotel for 'a particularly brilliant day'. Among those attending the star-studded lunch were Douglas Fairbanks, Mary Pickford, Anita Loos, Heywood Broun, Alec Woollcott, Robert Benchley, George S. Kaufman and Horace Liveright, as well as the actress Tallulah Bankhead, who had grown up in Montgomery with Zelda. (Tallulah also shared Zelda's penchant for taking off her clothes: on 25 September Van Vechten had thrown a party, during which Tallulah 'stood on her head, disrobed, gave imitations, and was amusing generally'.) Frank Case, the owner-manager of the Algonquin, had added 'Onion Soup with Cheese, Rascoe' to the menu, but Burton Rascoe was, for once, conspicuous by his absence.

Two days later, celebrities gathered again at the Algonquin, joined this time by Rascoe. 'All the literary, theatrical and cinema world seemed to be there,' he reported in his Day Book column, listing many of the same stars and adding matinée idol Richard Barthelmess, actress and singer Peggy Wood (who would appear decades later as the Mother Superior in *The Sound of Music*), Mary Blair and F. Scott Fitzgerald, come to join the fun. After a front-page *Tribune* story catching the reader up on the latest in the Hall–Mills investigation ('MAN IN HALL CHURCH CALLED AN EYEWITNESS: STATE CLAIMS PROOF HE WAS AT PHILLIPS FARM WITH WOMAN NIGHT RECTOR AND SINGER WERE SHOT'), Fitzgerald found Rascoe's mention of their lunch and saved it in his scrapbook.

At the lunch, Rascoe learned how he had come to be named a big cheese by the Algonquin. Two weeks earlier, Rascoe had written of lunching there with Tallulah Bankhead. 'The food was execrable,' he'd declared, but Tallulah had been laughing so hard that Heywood Broun, the *World*'s dramatic critic, had complained – on the basis that nothing Burton Rascoe 'could say would be funny enough to cause such laughter'. Although 'Mr Case never reads the papers,' Rascoe went on, 'Tallulah Bankhead had read my review of his food and had thought the word "execrable" meant something awfully complimentary, and had so reported. Mr Case wanted to show his appreciation for the ad, and put my name to two of the best dishes', so that 'rivaling Melba and Napoleon, I got onto the menu for two days running', until at last he had arrived to appreciate the joke of being termed 'Cheese Rascoe'.

As it happens, Scott Fitzgerald was also named a big piece of cheese that year by someone who didn't appreciate his jokes and wrote to tell him so. Having read 'The Curious Case of Benjamin Button' in *Collier's* magazine, a reader informed him, 'I want to say that as a writer you are a good lunatic. I have seen many big pieces of cheese in my time, but you are the biggest, and I don't know why I waste this paper and my time on you, but I will. Sincerely, Your Friend and Constant Reader.' Fitzgerald found the letter so funny he included it in the Table of Contents when he put 'Benjamin Button', first published 27 May 1922, into *Tales of the Jazz Age*.

Food has always been a source of slang, but the jazz age had a special fondness for food jokes. 'Yes, we have no bananas', from a 1923 novelty song, was one of the most enduring catchphrases of the 1920s; by the end of the decade 'baloney' had come to mean nonsense, while 'American as apple pie' was first recorded in 1924. The Frigidaire was almost as revolutionary a machine as the motor car in the 1920s, and American recipes were being reinvented as cooks puzzled over how to add flavour to food that could no longer include alcohol. Great quantities of sugar and salt were the most common solution, and the sweetening of American food would continue apace throughout the twentieth century.

At the end of 1923, Fitzgerald met Max Perkins for lunch at the Hotel Chatham, on Vanderbilt Avenue in Manhattan, to discuss publishing a collection of Ring Lardner's stories. Lardner, always self-deprecating, was hesitant, so Fitzgerald and Perkins were taking matters into their own hands. Fitzgerald jotted down ideas for titles on the back of a menu, which he saved. In the early 1920s, food in New York was Francophilic, as a symbol of cultural cosmopolitanism, and not only in expensive establishments; speakeasies, too, featured 'chicken fricassee, family style' or 'bouillabaisse marseillaise'. On 9 November 1922, American caterers called for menus to be written in 'One hundred per cent Americanism'. Demands for one hundred per cent Americanism would only grow louder as the century progressed.

The menu Fitzgerald saved is valuable not because of what it teaches us about food, however, but because it is a relic, a trace of the past. A love of enchanted objects often leads us astray, as Jay Gatsby will learn; but it is also instinctive, clutching at the palpable for evidence of a life before us that otherwise is only storied. Without the things that survive us, there would be no history.

## FOOLS' PARADISE

On Sunday 5 November Carl Van Vechten attended a cocktail party that appeared to be hosting 'all the kept women & brokers in New York'. One of the other guests was twenty-four-year-old George Gershwin, who entertained the party by playing his hit song from *The Scandals of 1922*, 'I'll Build A Stairway to Paradise'. It could have been the theme song of Jay Gatsby, who would see a stairway to paradise on the streets of Louisville as he kissed Daisy Fay for the first time. The bandleader Paul Whiteman, who recorded 'Stairway to Paradise' in 1922, would commission Gershwin two years later to compose a serious, full-length jazz composition; the result was 'Rhapsody in Blue', which premiered in February 1924, two months before the Fitzgeralds quit New York for the blue Mediterranean.

Gershwin's invention was inspired, he said, by the daily rhythms and noises of urban life, sounds of modern America being born: 'It was on the train, with its steely rhythms, its rattle-ty bang, that is so often so stimulating to a composer – I frequently hear music in the very heart of the noise ... I heard it as a sort of musical kaleidoscope of America, of our vast melting pot, of our unduplicated national pep, of our metropolitan madness.' Gershwin's original title for the composition about metropolitan madness was 'American Rhapsody', until his brother Ira suggested that he model himself on the titles of James McNeill Whistler's paintings, such as *Nocturne in Black and Gold*.

At Gatsby's first party, as the moth-like women flutter through whisperings with yellow cocktail music rising above them, they are entertained by a performance of the 'Jazz History of the World'. In the *Trimalchio* drafts, Fitzgerald wrote a long description of the musical kaleidoscope played for Gatsby's guests, before he decided to leave it to the reader's imagination. Nick's description is a meditation on cyclicality and coherence:

> It started out with a weird, spinning sound, mostly from the cornets. Then there would be a series of interruptive notes which colored everything that came after them until before you knew it they became the theme and new discords were opposed outside. But just as you'd get used to the new discord one of the old themes would drop back in, this time as a discord, until you'd get a weird sense that it was a preposterous cycle after all. Long after the piece was over it went on and on in my head – whenever I think of that summer I can hear it yet.

Let the preposterous cycle be a symbol, then, for the weird sense that all of the spinning themes and discordant interruptions are connected after all. It is worth listening for the music in the very heart of the noise.

---

# THE ADVANTAGES OF POETIC LICENSE

As Gershwin was building a stairway to paradise for all the kept women in New York and their brokers, the *New York Times* reported on 5 November that Mrs Gibson had admitted telling different versions of her tale: '"The story I told the authorities and the story I told you reporters are two different things," she said. "And when I get on the stand, I will give you a better story than you have had yet."' The reporter pointedly observed that Mrs Gibson held 'stacks of newspapers' as she spoke, but special prosecutor Mott remained marvellously untroubled by his star witness's admission that she was making up her story as she went.

Arrests were being postponed until after the governor's election in three days, leading to increased murmurs of corruption and carelessness in New Jersey. Rumours spread that the authorities planned to drop the whole case after the election; Mott was alleged to have said he was a 'good waiter' and was biding his time for the papers to lose interest in the story.

Meanwhile, Mrs Gibson continued telling the story of her life to avid listeners. She claimed to have an aristocratic background, her ancestors came over on the *Mayflower*, and she was a college graduate. She was raised on a horse farm in Kentucky, where she rode to hounds ('which accounts for her agility at midnight on the back of her saddle mule'). After that, she was for a time a bareback rider in a circus and then she'd married her husband, a minister who had drowned seventeen years before.

But not a word of it was true. Even the Pig Woman's name was an invention: 'It has been established to the satisfaction even of the officials', noted the press sardonically, that she had adopted the name Gibson from the previous owner of her farm. There was no romantically perished minister, she had not gone to college, her family was not *Mayflower* stock. Her current husband was a local factory worker named Easton; asked to comment on his estranged wife's tale, he remarked, 'It's an amazing story ... She has a brilliant mind.' But local authorities insisted that Gibson's story of the murders was not made less credible by 'romantic inaccuracies in her story of her past life'.

Asked to explain herself, Gibson grew increasingly pugnacious: 'I know they say I was a figure in the Piper murder case some years ago. I know everyone wonders why I said I was the widow of a clergyman named Gibson who died seventeen years ago, and why I have not revealed the full story of my life.' She did not answer any of these questions. The Piper case was a five-year-old unsolved murder near New Brunswick; a student named John Piper had disappeared and a witness, described as 'an elderly woman', and whose name no one could now remember, 'gave a vivid account of hearing a man's voice cry, "My God!

Don't shoot me!'" No one commented publicly on the stories' pronounced resemblance.

'Well I don't care,' Mrs Gibson declared defiantly. 'What difference does it make whether I have had a past or not? My past is my own business.'

WILLIAM GIBSON and MRS. JANE GIBSON
Copyright, 1922 (New York Evening World) by Press Publishing Co.

Mrs Gibson with her son William and two pigs

When Nick asks Gatsby 'what business he was in', Gatsby answers abruptly, 'That's my affair,' before realizing 'that it wasn't the appropriate reply' in the circles to which he aspires. Romantic inventors of new and improved selves remained convinced that their past was their own business: 'What better right does a man possess than to invent his own antecedents?' asks Nick in the drafts of *Gatsby*. The inventive Jane Gibson would doubtless have endorsed this sentiment, even as her story might seem to suggest that some antecedents are not invented, but discovered.

# The Vicious Circle.

On the chilly, rainy Monday evening of 6 November, most of the writers of the Algonquin Round Table gathered at the première of a musical revue they had written with Ring Lardner. *The '49ers* played for a grand total of fifteen performances, until 18 November, when it fell flat on its face.

Otherwise known as 'The Vicious Circle', the Algonquinites were among the most famous writers in America in the 1920s, renowned equally for their repartee and self-promotion, using their journalism to publicize each other's – and their own – witticisms. Most of them would end up writing for the *New Yorker* when Harold Ross launched it in February 1925, where Dorothy Parker reviewed books as 'Constant Reader', Alec Woollcott invented the 'Shouts and Murmurs' column and all of them contributed reviews, fiction and comic sketches. By 1922 the Algonquinites were already writing freelance for the same magazines (*Vanity Fair*, the *New Republic*), as well as for Swope's *World*, which would publish Dorothy Parker's most famous poem, 'Résumé', in 1925. One of the peripheral members of the group was Deems Taylor, Swope's music critic, as was Swope himself. Another was Scott Fitzgerald.

All of the Algonquinites frequented Swope's house parties, frolicking for long weekends on Long Island. Swope's wife Margaret called their Great Neck home 'an absolutely seething bordello of interesting people'. Deems Taylor's wife recorded in her journal that Swope 'filled his house at this time with everybody who was talked about or working on important jobs. To be left out of Swope's list was to argue yourself unknown. He was fond of us. Deems was his direct antithesis – quiet, shy, small voiced, but always standing up to him and giving him what he adored, a chance for intelligent conversation.' She called Swope 'one of the most forceful men I have ever met ... a loud talkative man with a mop of red hair and a big, active body. He was inexhaustible and ... stored in his big frame the loudest vocal sounds ever exploded by any human being.'

Dorothy Parker was also a regular guest at the Swopes'; supposedly one of the perpetual games at their parties inspired one of her more often-repeated jokes. Told that some of the guests were ducking for apples, Parker quipped, 'there, but for a typographical error, is the story of my life'. Like Fitzgerald offering the year 1922 as an 'exhibit' of the jazz age, or Willa Cather declaring that 'the world broke in two in 1922 or thereabouts', Dorothy Parker also commemorated the spirit of their age, in poems such as '1922' and 'The Flapper', which ended:

> All spotlights focus on her pranks.
> All tongues her prowess herald.
> For which she well may render thanks
> To God and Scott Fitzgerald.

Parker became good friends with Scott, and seems to have been, at least in the beginning, slightly infatuated with him. She was 'beglamored by the idea of Scott Fitzgerald', wrote Wilson, but Parker always thought 'there was something petulant' about Zelda, she later said. (It is decidedly possible that Zelda might have returned the compliment.) For most of 1922, Parker was having an affair with playboy playwright Charlie MacArthur, unaware for some time that this did not place her in as select a company as she'd have liked. In late 1922 Parker became pregnant with MacArthur's child and had an abortion, describing the thirty dollars that MacArthur contributed to the operation as 'Judas making a refund'; this is also supposed to have been the experience that prompted her famous wisecrack, 'Serves me right for putting all my eggs in one bastard.' The *New Yorker* columnist Lois Long wrote that she and her friends shared a woman doctor who would perform safe abortions; the doctor took holidays at Christmas to rest up for the 'rush after New Year's Eve'.

In March 1922, when Scott and Zelda came to New York to celebrate the publication of *The Beautiful and Damned*, Fitzgerald launched into what he called an 'interminable party': 'I couldn't seem to get sober enough to tolerate being sober,' he wrote. 'In fact the whole trip was largely a failure.' Zelda had accompanied him, but her reason for making the trip may have been less festive than his. At least six biographies, beginning with Nancy Milford's influential *Zelda* in 1970, have repeated the story that, having just had Scottie four months earlier, Zelda had discovered she was pregnant again. They claim that on page 176 of Scott's ledger, in the entry for March 1922, he does not mention the publication of his second novel or their trip to New York, recording instead only four ominous words: 'Zelda and her abortionist.'

However, Scott's entry for March 1922, which is indeed on page 176 of his ledger ('Twenty-five Years Old'), doesn't say anything of the kind. After noting the publication of *The Beautiful and Damned* in February, it lists the trip to New York in March, partying with Engalitcheff, quarrelling with Alec McKaig (which ended their friendship), meeting celebrities such as Constance Bennett and Marilyn Miller, and visiting Selznick's film studio (in New York), but nothing about Zelda or an abortionist.

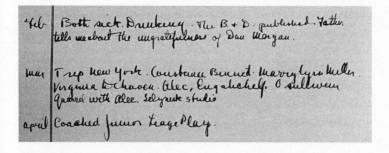

Nowhere in Scott's ledger or published notebooks does he write 'Zelda and her abortionist', but the claim about the March 1922 entry has been repeated in almost every biography of the pair since Milford's. The only exception is Matthew J. Bruccoli's 1981 *Some Sort of Epic Grandeur* (but he doesn't mention this recycled mistake, either).

This doesn't mean that Zelda couldn't have had an abortion during the March trip – just that there's no evidence that she did. She most likely did have at least one abortion during their marriage, probably in New York (Scott wrote in his notebooks of a son being flushed down a toilet in a hotel, after 'pills' were prescribed by an unnamed doctor), but it is not easy to date when it occurred. If Zelda did indeed have an abortion during this visit she may not have entirely sympathized with Scott's frailties while she coped with the most likely painful effects of pills given to her by one Dr Lackin, a doctor to whom she alluded in a later letter to Scott, remembering these early years.

Regardless of whether they were dealing with a traumatic situation or just 'Both sick. Drinking', as Fitzgerald's February 1922 ledger entry actually does read, Scott spent the March trip to New York heroically drinking himself under the table. Bunny Wilson wrote to John Bishop: 'We find them both rather changed – particularly Zelda, who has become matronly and rather fat (about which she is very sensitive)', as well she might be, less than six months after giving birth; she had lost her baby weight by the time they returned to New York in September. 'Much of her old jazz has evaporated', Wilson continued, 'and, as she becomes more mellowed, I like her better.' As for Scott, he looked 'like John Barrymore on the brink of the grave ... but also, somehow, more intelligent than he used to ... He arrived this morning in a hansom, after an all-night party of some kind, and wanted to take me for a drive in the park.'

Around the same time, Wilson was finishing a long essay on Fitzgerald's writing, and sent Scott a draft that said the greatest influences on Fitzgerald's work were the Middle West, Irishness and liquor; Fitzgerald responded by asking him to cut the public references to his drinking (it was perfectly true, Fitzgerald ingenuously admitted, but it would make him look bad). Scott added: 'Your catalogue is not complete ... the most enormous influence on me in the four and a half years since I met her has been the complete, fine and full-hearted selfishness and chill-mindedness of Zelda.'

## Waste Lands

Early November brought big literary news, an epochal event that, combined with the publication of *Ulysses*, has continued to define 1922 as the *annus mirabilis* of modernist literature. T. S. Eliot's long-awaited poem, *The Waste Land*, appeared with much fanfare in the November issue of the *Dial* magazine, and would be published in book form by Horace Liveright that December. Its fragmentary, elliptical obscurity baffled most of its first readers, but a handful of astute critics, including Burton Rascoe and Edmund Wilson, could see the thematic unity behind the poem's apparently discordant themes and disjointed narratives.

It was a poem about the chaos of the present day, that much was clear, concerned with the relationship of modern life to historical origins, and the artist's search for sources of creativity and inspiration. The poem shows that meaning changes, dissipates, is lost, but it is also a quest for the origins of meaning and of art, and *The Waste Land*'s influence on Fitzgerald's ideas about the novel he was mulling has long been acknowledged.

Burton Rascoe recorded his first impressions of *The Waste Land* – 'a thing of bitterness and beauty' – in his Day Book column on 5 November 1922. Interested in the poem's 'erudite despair', Rascoe listed some of Eliot's many sources, from the *Satyricon* to modern jazz songs. This 'highly elliptical' poem played with 'all the shining verbal toys, impressions and catch lines' of a poet who was endlessly alert to the life around him. The poem was an 'etching of modern life'.

Later that month, Wilson published a joint review of *The Waste Land* and *Ulysses*, arguing that Joyce and Eliot were the writers who best 'reflect our present condition of disruption. We are all tumultuous fragments ... And no one makes any attempt to pick up the scattered pieces.' In order to make his point more explicit, Wilson added 'a quotation from a more conventional author', one whose conventionality did not prevent him from catching 'something of the spirit of the time': "'I know myself but that is all,'" cries one of Scott Fitzgerald's heroes, who has 'grown up to find all gods dead, all wars fought, all faiths in men shaken'. And that is precisely the point of the modern novelist or poet: "'I know myself but that is all.'" Fitzgerald saved Wilson's mention.

'It will be said that [Eliot] depends too much upon books and borrows too much from other men,' Wilson correctly predicted. *The Waste Land*'s first readers were unconvinced that a poem so dependent on familiar stories and external ideas could be an original work of art. Eliot seemed merely to quote other writers: wasn't this little better than plagiarism? The originality, argued Wilson, was in the composition: not in invention, but in discovery and order. In any event, 'Mr Eliot's trivialities are more valuable than other people's epics,' Wilson concluded.

Fragments of meaning culled from past and present and then composed into something new was a modern kind of originality, and T. S. Eliot was not the only writer making art from what he saw around him. When Scott Fitzgerald published *The Great Gatsby*, he sent a copy to Eliot, inscribed to the 'Greatest of Living Poets from his enthusiastic worshipper'. Fitzgerald had written a homage to Eliot's poem in one description of the ash heaps: 'We walked back a hundred yards along the road under Doctor Eckleburg's persistent stare. The only building in sight was a small block of yellow brick sitting on the edge of the waste land, a sort of compact Main Street ministering to it and contiguous to absolutely nothing.' For some scholars, this lone allusion suffices to explain Fitzgerald's decision to set his book in 1922: the date is a tribute to the year of *The Waste Land*, signalling Fitzgerald's aspirations toward high modernism, they argue. Eliot's poem probably helped Fitzgerald discover what he was looking for, but the resonances of 1922 in *The Great Gatsby* far exceed this passing salute – and Fitzgerald's ambitions for his novel similarly exceeded merely translating into prose what Eliot had said in poetry.

After reading *The Great Gatsby* Eliot returned Fitzgerald's compliment. He had read the novel three times: it 'interested and excited me more than any new novel I have seen, either English or American, for a number of years', he wrote to Fitzgerald. 'In fact, it seems to me the first step that American fiction has taken since Henry James.' The two writers had more in common than a shared metaphor for the sterility of modern life: both were playing with 'shining verbal toys' redeemed from the ash heaps of history, searching for definitive beauty. But Fitzgerald could see more than Eliot's waste land. He could also see the delights of the gorgeous, riotous island next door.

# 'THE LOVE NEST.'

One of the modern jazz songs that *The Waste Land* plays is a burst of ragtime: 'O O O O that Shakespeherian Rag – / It's so elegant / So intelligent.' Many readers assume that T. S. Eliot invented this line, but the credit belongs to a team of songwriters who composed 'That Shakespearian Rag' in 1912. It was a big hit, nearly forty years before Cole Porter's more famous 'Brush Up Your Shakespeare'.

One of the composers of 'That Shakespearian Rag' was Gene Buck, who had, by 1922, been writing songs and producing hits for the Ziegfeld Follies for years; he also promoted the dancer Joe Frisco, among other ventures. Buck was rich, successful, smiling and vain. He was also one of the show business luminaries of Great Neck. He and his wife lived on Nassau Drive, around the corner from Ring Lardner, in a vast house of remarkable ostentation. Lardner, who collaborated with Buck on a few plays, described Buck's living room as 'the Yale Bowl, with lamps'; Buck also liked throwing extravagant parties. His Great Neck friends included his boss, Florenz Ziegfeld, and producer Sam Harris, who would stage *The Vegetable*.

Gene Buck and his wife Helen, a former showgirl, became friends with the Fitzgeralds, although at some point friction developed between Scott and Zelda over Helen. In one of her first letters urging the Kalmans to come east for the Princeton–Yale game in November, Zelda had described life in Great Neck. 'We have been having a hell of a time,' she wrote. 'We have been gotten drunk with three times by the Ring Lardners and various others.' Lardner was 'a typical newspaperman', whom at first she didn't 'find particularly amusing', although her opinion of Ring would quickly improve. 'His wife is common but I like her. He is six feet tall and goes on periodical sprees lasting from one to X weeks. He is on one now, which is probably the reason he called on us. He plays the saxophone and takes us to Mr Gene Buck's house – Mr Gene Buck originates Ziegfeld's Follies and lives in a house designed by Joseph Urban. It looks like a lot of old scenery glued together – Mr Buck says "seen" where he should say "saw" and is prob-ably a millionaire ... I like Mr Buck,' she added, explaining that he'd married a 'chorus girl who has lovely legs and consequently a baby'. Fitzgerald may have admired Helen Buck rather more; such, at any rate, was Zelda's eventual accusation: 'in Great Neck there was always dis-order and quarrels ... about Helen Buck, about everything'.

But at least some of the time, Zelda and Helen were also drinking companions. Bruccoli reports a story of Zelda and Helen Buck drink-ing a pitcher of orange blossoms during a lunch at Gateway Drive, before heading off with a thermos of cocktails to the golf club, 'where Zelda and Helen became drunk on the course, with Zelda singing, "You can throw a silver dollar down upon the ground, And it'll roll, because it's round ..."' Eventually Ring Lardner helped them get home.

Whatever their quarrels, the Fitzgeralds and the Bucks were frequent companions during the months at Great Neck. Scott inscribed several books to them: a 1922 edition of *This Side of Paradise* is signed 'For Helen and Jean [*sic*] – whose courtesy and kindness to the pilgrims, the Fitz will never forget. From theirs, The Bowing Fitz' (most of the inscription is in such a drunken scrawl that it is illegible), and he gave a copy of *The Vegetable* to 'Helen – not of Troy but of Great Neck – a lovely girl who is so sweet as to sing for us, now and then – F. Scott Fitzgerald'.

He also inscribed a copy of Joseph Conrad's *Youth*, 'For Gene Buck from Joseph Conrad', adding 'F. Scott Fitzgerald, middle-man', below. Some readers have concluded that Conrad must have given Fitzgerald the copy to present to Buck, but this is missing the joke with a vengeance. In fact, Fitzgerald never met Conrad, much to his disap-pointment, although he and Lardner did drop by during Conrad's stay at the nearby Doubleday estate in May 1923, paying homage to their idol by singing and dancing on the lawn outside the mansion in the middle of the night. Some say the dance they chose was the hornpipe, in honour of the old sea captain; everyone says they were drunk. The only people who saw the tribute performance were the night watchmen who forcibly removed the pair from the Doubleday grounds.

Perhaps Fitzgerald's manifold literary gifts to the Bucks were a hint that they might benefit from some culture. In 1926 Ring Lardner published a story called 'The Love Nest', lampooning the Bucks, in which a journalist named Bartlett drives through 'an arc de triomphe of a gateway' to a 'white house that might have been mistaken for the Yale Bowl', where he interviews a publicity-seeking film director. The director's wife, a former showgirl, joins them as the husband leaves for an appointment. The wife, it emerges, spends her life bitterly drunk, exclaiming "'I never did love him! ... He wanted a beautiful wife and beautiful children for his beautiful home. Just to show us off ... I'm part of his chattels ... like his big diamond or his cars or his horses."' The next morning she pretends again to be a happy housewife, a pose as fraudulent as the director's insistence that his grandiose mansion is just a 'love nest'. When the story was published, Lardner wrote to Fitzgerald in Paris: 'Gene didn't make any comment on "The Love Nest", but evidently had no suspicion. Anyway, we are still pals.'

After Gatsby achieves his dream of impressing Daisy with his lavish house that looks like a lot of scenery glued together, he ushers Daisy and Nick into the music room. Klipspringer, the eternal boarder, plays the piano, beginning with 'The Love Nest', a popular song from 1920. Fitzgerald doesn't reprint the lyrics, but his audience would have known them:

> Just a love nest
> Cozy with charm,
> Like a dove nest
> Down on a farm ...
> Better than a palace with a gilded dome,
> Is a love nest
> You can call home.

The other song Klipspringer plays is no less ironically chosen, no less sharply pointed: 'Ain't We Got Fun', with its chorus emphasizing the ruthless passage of time – 'morning', 'evening', 'meantime', and 'between time' – and its verse joking about the class divide: 'the rich get rich and the poor get ... children'.

Knowing that life can provide the same grace notes as art, Fitzgerald might well have used another chorus from a Gene Buck tune as a refrain in *Gatsby*: 'Wasn't it nice? Wasn't it sweet? Wasn't it good?'

---

# OUR INVESTMENT.

The artist, wrote Conrad, shines 'the light of magic suggestiveness' on 'the commonplace surface of words: of the old, old words, worn thin, defaced by ages of careless usage'. Beauty fires us with the faith to search for hidden meanings; old words burn through stories like new gold.

In June 1924, as he settled down on the Riviera into serious work on *The Great Gatsby*, Fitzgerald decided to cut a long section delineating Jay Gatsby's back story, 'because it interfered with the neatness of the plan' for his novel. Thriftily, he revised that section into an independent short story, called it 'Absolution' and sent it to the magazines. One of Fitzgerald's finest stories, 'Absolution' tells of an eleven-year-old boy's avowal of beauty and rejection of religion. Young Rudolph Miller is sent to the family priest for a routine confession; as he is confessing to sins of pride (he believes his parents are too inferior to him to be his real parents), disobedience and his emerging erotic desires, he ends up lying during confession, a mortal sin. But the priest is even more at sea than the boy: Fitzgerald implies that he is breaking down from sexual repression. Listening to the child confess, the priest suddenly 'cries wildly': 'You look as if things went glimmering ... Did you ever go to a party? ... My theory is that when a whole lot of people get together in the best places things go glimmering all the time.'

The priest recommends abruptly that Rudolph go to an amusement park: '"It's a thing like a fair, only much more glittering ... A band playing somewhere, and a smell of peanuts – and everything will twinkle ... But don't get up close," he warned Rudolph, "because if you do you'll only feel the heat and the sweat and the life.'" The unnerving experience confirms the boy's faith in beauty: 'Underneath his terror he felt that his own inner convictions were confirmed. There was something ineffably gorgeous somewhere that had nothing to do with God.' This was to have been Jay Gatsby's prelude, the origins of his quest for something ineffably gorgeous in life and his faith in enchanted objects. Most of the 'catholic element' that Fitzgerald initially thought would characterize his novel didn't survive into the final draft, but Gatsby's faith in the meaning of symbols remains Catholic, and he chooses a catholic array of symbols to represent his secular faith. He is particularly fond of symbolic light: when it stops raining during his reunion with Daisy, Gatsby smiles 'like a weather man, like an ecstatic patron of recurrent light'.

Only in the imagination does every truth find an undeniable existence, Conrad also said. 'Imagination, not invention, is the supreme master of art as of life.'

---

# THE WONDERS OF RELATIVITY

On Thursday 9 November 1922, Albert Einstein was awarded the Nobel Prize for his theories about space, time and recurrent light. The idea of relativity began, Einstein famously said, with a metaphor: he imagined himself riding on a beam of light, and wondered what he would be able to see. If light were a wave, one could imagine sweeping along its peaks and valleys. But if he were simultaneous with light, would the light stand still? Would time halt? Could he ride that beam of light forever, a frozen moment that could never fade? If he travelled faster than light, perhaps he could even repeat the past. Eventually, Einstein would explain relativity using symbolic clocks positioned at every point in the universe, each one running at a different speed.

When Daisy comes to Nick's house and finds her old flame waiting for her, Fitzgerald offers a symbol to suggest the awkwardness of the reunion: a small 'defunct mantelpiece clock' that Gatsby nearly knocks over and then puts back on the mantel. Some readers think the defunct clock is too contrived a symbol – Gatsby wants time to stand still, to start over again with Daisy – but it also suggests that things are not synchronized, and that Gatsby is trying desperately to keep time, as literally as he can. Gatsby knows exactly how long it's been since he and Daisy last met ('Five years next November'), a response so reflexive that it is a dead giveaway of how carefully he's kept track. 'The automatic quality of Gatsby's answer set us all back at least another minute,' Nick wryly observes, keeping time himself; he has already jotted his list of Gatsby's party guests on a timetable. Even Gatsby's green light might have suggested time-keeping in the New York of 1922: the traffic towers being built that autumn on Fifth Avenue were also equipped with 'synchronized clocks on the north and south faces and 350-pound bronze bells' that tolled the hours. It has been said that Fitzgerald, 'haunted by time', wrote as if he were surrounded by clocks and calendars; maybe he was.

Gatsby's longed-for meeting with Daisy ends with a hint of the disillusionment to come. Reality could not possibly live up to his overwrought expectations: 'He had been full of the idea so long, dreamed it right through to the end, waited with his teeth set, so to speak, at an inconceivable pitch of intensity. Now, in the reaction, he was running down like an overwound clock.' As they tour through Gatsby's house they pass through a pastiche of history, like a diorama in a museum, including a Marie Antoinette music room, an upscale echo of Myrtle Wilson's Versailles sofas. 'I think he revalued everything in his house', Nick observes, 'according to the measure of response it drew from her well-loved eyes.'

But before the chapter closes, the beat of Gatsby's disappointment begins to shift away from time and toward light, an anticipation of the failures in relativity that await. He shows Daisy the green light at the end of her dock, visible across the bay from his gilded 'love nest', and then pauses. 'Possibly,' Nick thinks, 'it had occurred to him that the colossal significance of that light had now vanished forever ... Now it was again a green light on a dock. His count of enchanted objects had diminished by one.'

A scholar once counted how often time is referred to in *The Great Gatsby* (nearly five hundred times: once every hundred words); mention time, and people start counting. So here's another enumeration: if you subtract title, numbered chapter headings and epigraph, *The Great Gatsby* is 48,885 words long. The magic of modern computers counts for us, making it easy to pinpoint the centre of a novel that Fitzgerald wrote in longhand. The sentence at the novel's precise midpoint, its fulcrum (words 24,434 to 24,457, while we're counting), is a description of Nick, Daisy and Gatsby passing through Gatsby's facsimile of a library as they take their tour of his proud, gilt-domed mansion: 'As Gatsby closed the door of "the Merton College Library" I could have sworn I heard the owl-eyed man break into ghostly laughter.'

The owl-eyed man haunts the dead centre of the novel, a trace of life finding its way, ghostily, into fiction's facsimile of a library. 'We do love the centre of things', wrote Zelda eight years later. 'You feel the motion so much less.'

---

# TYRANNY OF GRANDEUR

Bunny Wilson invited Fitz to a party on Wednesday 8 November, at the Washington Square Book Shop on West 8th Street, starting at 6.30: 'Can't you come? Dos Passos, Sew Collins, Elinor Wylie, and others are going to be there. The idea is to make *Playboy* [a literary magazine] a sort of mouthpiece for all the bizarre and scurrilous things which people can't publish elsewhere'. History does not record whether Fitz attended, but it is hard to imagine him declining the offer to discuss the bizarre and scurrilous over drinks at a bookstore. As they partied, if they partied, and gossiped about the bizarre and scurrilous, the papers were reporting that the Swopes and Heywood Broun, the *World*'s dramatic critic, were in a car crash in Great Neck. Mrs Swope's injuries were 'painful' but not serious; the two men and the Swopes' chauffeur escaped unhurt. Swope told reporters that the worst part of the accident was that several oil paintings they were taking to New York from their Great Neck house had been damaged.

They were changing the channels of their avidity, Fitzgerald remarked later. When the word 'class' came into common currency in the sixteenth century it largely superseded 'order', as in the lower and upper orders, from peasants to the ruling class. Musing on the relationship between wealth and taste in his notebooks, Fitzgerald observed that bad taste among the bourgeoisie is called vulgarity when found among the proletariat. The vagaries of such ideas about taste and money interested him, he added, 'because it shows classes in movement'.

When Daisy and Gatsby meet at his cottage Nick beats a tactful retreat for half an hour (as he did during the parallel scene in Myrtle's apartment, when he reads *Simon Called Peter*), occupying himself by staring at Gatsby's house 'like Kant at his church steeple'. Gatsby's house becomes a symbol of inspiration, an object of worship, and an emblem of futility and death:

A brewer had built it early in the 'period' craze, a decade before, and there was a story that he'd agreed to pay five years' taxes on all the neighboring cottages if the owners would have their roofs thatched with straw. Perhaps their refusal took the heart out of his plan to Found a Family – he went into an immediate decline. His children sold his house with the black wreath still on the door. Americans, while occasionally willing to be serfs, have always been obstinate about being peasantry.

The brewer's dreams of aristocratic grandeur are as vain as Gatsby's. Nick lives in a tiny cottage that has not yet been razed by developers, a vestigial trace of the old fishing village that will soon disappear altogether in the rush to build ever more grandiose homes. 'Like so many

Americans,' Fitzgerald wrote a few years later, 'he valued things rather than cared about them.'

To compensate Nick for arranging his reunion with Daisy, Gatsby clumsily offers remuneration: 'You might pick up a nice bit of money. It happens to be a rather confidential sort of thing.' Nick understands that the opportunity, involving bonds, must be dishonest: 'I realize now that under different circumstances that conversation might have been one of the crises of my life. But, because the offer was obviously and tactlessly for a service to be rendered, I had no choice except to cut him off there.'

In other words, Nick might have been tempted by financial inequality into contemplating a swindle, but he couldn't consider payment for organizing an adulterous afternoon with his married cousin. Nick's objection seems primarily focused on the fact that the offer is too 'obvious' and 'tactless' – perhaps he would have been open to a transaction less crass, less banal. So Nick arranges the rendezvous, but high-mindedly refuses compensation. He might occasionally be willing to be a panderer, but he is obstinate about being a pimp.

---

# Another Lost Lady

Playing 'Who Am I?', like one of Swope's party guests, we may be stumped by Fitzgerald's uncommunicative note of 'Mary' in the *Man's Hope* outline as one of the imaginative sources for the reunion scene. Who is the Mary about whom Fitzgerald remembers thinking as he tried to invoke the 'fire and freshness' of Daisy? Some have conjectured that Mary may refer to an actress named Mary Hay, who lived in Great Neck with her husband, the matinée idol Richard Barthelmess.

In February 1921 the *World* published a tribute to Mary Hay from a reader who felt she 'deserved immortalization in rhyme':

Look at the style of her,
Gaze all the while at her,
At that sweet smile of her,
Miss Mary Hay!
My, how real sweet she is!
And how petite she is!
What a real treat she is!
Miss Mary Hay!

It goes on, but it doesn't improve.

Fitzgerald made various observations about Mary Hay over the years – if this is the Mary to whom his note refers. In his 1935 essay 'My Lost City', he said that in New York in the early 1920s, 'You danced elbow to elbow with Marion Davies and perhaps picked out the vivacious Mary Hay in the pony chorus.' Envisioning Rosemary in *Tender is the Night*, Fitzgerald described her as being like 'Mary Hay – that is, she differs from most actresses by being a lady, simply reeking of vitality, health, sensuality'.

In April 1930 Zelda published a sketch called 'The Girl with Talent', which Fitzgerald said was based on Mary Hay, the story of a young dancer with 'physical magnetism' (what her managers call 'hot stuff') who drinks too much gin and avoids her young husband and small child, until eventually she sails for Paris without them. When a friend asks if her husband knows that she's 'raising Cain over here', the dancer responds incredulously that she is living so chastely as to make a nun look like a nymphomaniac. A week later she runs off with a man; 'I never saw her again until after her divorce', says the narrator, by which point the dancer is ready to run off with someone else. By the time Zelda wrote this sketch, Mary Hay had left Richard Barthelmess and their daughter for another man.

But 'Mary' may not be Mary Hay at all. Deems Taylor's wife was named Mary, and in May 1923 Fitzgerald noted in his ledger a visit with a Mary Armstrong, who may have been the same Mary Armstrong who was married to Ben Hecht. Even Mrs Rumsey was named Mary, although it's unlikely that the Fitzgeralds were on a first-name basis with her (Fitzgerald and his agent, Harold Ober, worked together for seven years before they used each other's first names in correspondence, and Nick Carraway thinks it is worth remarking that after their first drinks he and Myrtle Wilson called each other by their first names). Someone the Fitzgeralds knew better was Mary Blair, whom Edmund Wilson married in February 1923.

Just before the Fitzgeralds returned to Manhattan in September 1922, a *Tribune* article used Mary Hay as an example of the versatility of New York, 'the skyscraper city', contrasting her against a well-known suffragist with a very similar name: 'imagine the divergent New Yorks', it suggested, of 'Mary Hay, and Mary Garrett Hay'. Together, the two Mary Hays symbolized the impossibility of ever comprehending reality: 'New York is like The Truth – an absolute concern in theory, yet so intricate and extensive as to be comprehended by no one ... This Manhattan scope, this versatility, this enswirling of the individual is part of the city's peculiar charm.'

And *The Great Gatsby* is a novel that considers it a subtle tribute to be interested in someone whose origins you don't know. Fitzgerald's note of 'Mary' is everything we can't know, this divergence, this scope, this versatility, these enswirled individuals who laugh, flicker and vanish.

Over the first weeks of November, the press continued to wonder whether Mrs Gibson's 'statements and romantic stories of a past adventure, culture and refinement' might give Inspector Mott pause. But as New York and New Jersey went to the polls, and the papers reported the failure of a proposed mandatory equal wage for women (the court ruled that 'no greater calamity could befall workers than to have pay fixed by law'), headlines announced that an indictment of 'one woman and two men' was expected in the Hall–Mills murder case.

Just as a grand jury was finally summoned, however, sentiment in New Brunswick was turning away from a trial. The community, reported the *World*, had already judged the killers 'in the court of public opinion and have acquitted them out of regard for the "unwritten law"', which held that violence was a justifiable response to adultery. The citizens of New Brunswick regarded 'a formal court trial as a rank extravagance', one which they were beginning to mutter against paying for.

On Saturday 11 November Mott announced that Mrs Gibson had identified the murderer of Hall and Mills. She had selected Henry de la Bruyère Carpender, a stockbroker who was Mrs Hall's first cousin and lived two doors down from the Hall mansion in New Brunswick. The Carpenders had frequently been mentioned in the coverage of the case, and Henry de la Bruyère Carpender shared a first name with Mrs Hall's brother. It was during the papers' initial discussion of Henry Stevens's whereabouts on the day of the murder that Mrs Gibson had suddenly appeared, announcing she'd heard a woman cry out 'Henry! Henry!' as shots rang out. Unfortunately for Mrs Gibson, Henry Stevens had an alibi his lawyer described as 'copper-riveted', but then it turned out there was another Stevens relative named Henry. Mistakes in identity can sometimes be extremely convenient, a fact Tom Buchanan will ruthlessly exploit at *Gatsby*'s end. In the case of the Henrys, Mrs Gibson could keep changing her mind about which Henry she had seen.

Meanwhile a 'negress' named Nellie Lo Russell, who lived near Mrs Gibson and frequently quarrelled with her, came forward saying that Mrs Gibson had been with her on the night of the murder, 'at the hour the pig-raising Amazon says she was astride her mule watching the double killing'. But Mott decided once again to ignore questions about Mrs Gibson's credibility, focusing this time on Mrs Russell's credibility. A farmer who lived nearby claimed Mrs Russell 'talks in bunches. I don't think she's reliable.' She wouldn't be the only unreliable narrator in the story, but Mott defended Mrs Gibson: 'Why should any woman tell a story like that unless she had some real foundation for it?' Clearly, Mr Mott was not au fait with current slang: the phrase 'publicity hound' was first recorded in 1920, and 'publicity-driven' would appear in 1925.

The question of whether there was anyone to corroborate James Mills's alibi for the period of the murder had, it seems, been entirely lost amid the narrative mayhem.

---

# Novel Models

On Sunday 12 November 1922, a bright autumnal day, as the *Tribune* printed a story on the new science of quantum mechanics and its 'Quest for the Atom', Burton Rascoe declared that American literature was, for the first time, 'being treated with seriousness and respect by English critics', who were praising modern novelists including Scott Fitzgerald; Fitzgerald saved the mention in his scrapbook. The same day, the *New York Times* published an article on '"Americanism" in Literature' ('when American writers come before us, it is only natural that we should ask what it is that they have which is peculiar to themselves'), and the *Morning Telegraph* printed a long interview with F. Scott Fitzgerald with the overblown headline 'Juvenile Juvenal of the Jeunesse Jazz'.

The article began by noting that Fitzgerald was named for his 'ancestor' (in fact a distant cousin) Francis Scott Key, author of the poem 'The Star-Spangled Banner'. In 1922 America did not have a national anthem, but had begun to debate the possibility of adopting one. 'The Star-Spangled Banner' was a candidate, but was meeting with violent opposition. Earlier in the year an advertisement in the *Tribune* insisted 'the Star-Spangled Banner can never become our national anthem' as its 'violent, unsingable cadences' could never express 'the spiritual ideals upon which the nation was based'. The music had not been composed by an American; worse, it was 'a ribald, sensual drinking song'. 'Never has Congress, and never will Congress, legalize an anthem which sprang from the lowest qualities of human sentiment,' declared the advertisement. 'God forbids it.' Congress would make the 'The Star-Spangled Banner' America's national anthem in 1931, two years after the market crashed, when Americans needed a renewal of faith.

But as the debate over the anthem continued in 1922, Francis Scott Key's relation, no stranger to drinking songs, was reading about himself in the *Morning Telegraph*: 'The critics, one and all, from Mencken to Broun and from Burton Rascoe to Hildegarde Hawthorne, have acclaimed F. Scott Fitzgerald as a genius.' Fitzgerald observed humorously to the interviewer that most of his readers were convinced his 'novels of jazzing young America' were 'biographical' – that he was drawing on life for his art. Nor did Fitzgerald deny that he was. Although some readers deplored the fact that most of Fitzgerald's characters 'are rotters or weaklings, base or mean', remarked the interviewer, this also seemed a perfectly valid representation of their modern Babylon.

The article ended with a list of F. Scott Fitzgerald's favourite things: he 'prefers piquant hors d'oeuvres to a hearty meal. He is also fond of Charlie Chaplin, Booth Tarkington, real Scotch, old-fashioned hansom cab riding in Central Park and the "Ziegfeld Follies."' A loyal New Yorker, he 'prefers Fifth Avenue to Piccadilly and the Champs Elysees'. And then Fitzgerald closed the interview by offering a jocose list of famous couples he also admired: 'Mencken and Nathan, Park & Tilford [whisky], Lord & Taylor, Lea & Perrins, the Smith Brothers, and Mrs Gibson, the pig lady, and her Jenny mule'.

Fitzgerald cut out the interview and saved it in his scrapbook. Behind us, the owl-eyed man laughs, ghostily.

> F. Scott Fitzgerald prefers piquant hors d'oeuvres to a hearty meal. He also is fond of Charlie Chaplin, Booth Tarkington, real Scotch, old-fashioned hansom cab riding in Central Park and the "Ziegfeld Follies." He admires Mencken and Nathan, Park & Tilford, Lord & Taylor, Lea & Perrins, the Smith Brothers, and Mrs. Gibson, the pig lady, and her Jenny mule.

# VI. BOB KERR'S STORY.
# THE 2ND PARTY.

About this time an ambitious young reporter from New York arrived one morning at Gatsby's door and asked him if he had anything to say. 'Anything to say about what?' inquired Gatsby politely. 'Why, – any statement to give out.' It transpired after a confused five minutes that the man had heard Gatsby's name around his office in a connection which he either wouldn't reveal or didn't fully understand. This was his day off and with laudable initiative he had hurried out 'to see.' It was a random shot, and yet the reporter's instinct was right. Gatsby's notoriety, spread about by the hundreds who had accepted his hospitality and so become authorities on his past, had increased all summer until he fell just short of being news. Contemporary legends such as the 'underground pipe-line to Canada' attached themselves to him, and there was one persistent story that he didn't live in a house at all, but in a boat that looked like a house and was moved secretly up and down the Long Island shore. Just why these inventions were a source of satisfaction to James Gatz of North Dakota, isn't easy to say.

*The Great Gatsby*, Chapter 6

# THE POWER OF SUGGESTION.

Although Nick Carraway is not a journalist, he is a reporter, as well as Gatsby's biographer and publicist. The other reporter in *The Great Gatsby*, who tries to interview Jay Gatsby at the beginning of Chapter Six, seems incidental, but when he comes rushing in following his instincts, Gatsby's story takes a decided turn for the worse. The reporter doesn't know quite what he's looking for, so he asks his quarry if he has anything to say. Gatsby responds, politely and logically, 'Anything to say about what?' But Nick tells us that Gatsby, too, likes being talked about. He may not be a 'publicity hound' – he needs secrecy to protect his illicit activities – but he finds the inventions about himself a source of obscure satisfaction.

Perhaps one reason he enjoys these inventions is that they echo his own self-creation: the pleasure of an impresario finding an audience. But Gatsby never says; he gives the reporter no statement. Or, rather, Nick gives us no statement. This is one of Nick's most characteristic lapses, his occasional bouts of silence and aphasia. At key moments Nick is liable to declare himself at a loss for words, and announce that Gatsby's visions are 'unutterable' or that his own memories are 'uncommunicable'. Some might consider this rather unhelpful on the part of a reporter, and Nick has certainly become one of literature's better-known unreliable narrators. The problem is less that the accuracy of Nick's narration cannot be relied upon than the fact that he cannot always be relied upon to narrate. On the nights when he is a *flâneur* strolling through the enchanted metropolitan twilight, Nick tells us of his pleasure in hearing laughter from unheard jokes, joy imagined in unintelligible gestures. Nick is a romantic in the Keatsian sense: he thinks untold stories are lovelier.

This is a conjuring trick, enabling Fitzgerald to have it both ways. The insufficiency of language becomes, in his hands, not a tragedy of human inarticulacy, but a romance of possibility. Most of *The Great Gatsby* remains forever fixed in a single, gorgeous moment of potential, ideas that are described as 'unheard', 'unintelligible', 'uncommunicable', 'unutterable', 'unfathomable', 'indefinite', 'ineffable', 'incalculable' – and yet hover in the margins. The characters, too, are suggestions rather than declarations: they have strong physical presences, and yet they are strangely featureless. Fitzgerald offers only impressions: Buchanan's bulk and power, Gatsby's charm and ecstatic smile, Daisy's thrilling voice. By no coincidence, Jordan is the most physically defined (she has hair the colour of a yellow autumn leaf, is small, athletic, a trifle androgynous, with tanned skin and grey, sun-strained eyes); she is also the person Nick calls 'limited'. The rest of them are limited only by our imaginations, and by Fitzgerald's evocative, bold strokes of colour and form.

As Nick begins to ponder the pleasure to be derived from invention, he shares with us the secret of Gatsby's origins, the tale of how young James Gatz created his ideal personality through an act of sheer will. Part of the mystery is solved, just as more mysteries begin to accumulate. Gatsby has the imagination of an artist, but his desires have been shaped by a country that channelled those desires into climbing social ladders rather than imaginative ones. 'The thing which sets off the American from all other men,' wrote Mencken in 1922, 'and gives peculiar color not only to the pattern of his daily life but also adds to the play of his inner ideas, is what, for want of a more exact term, may be called social aspiration.' But Fitzgerald also recognized that social aspiration could involve an aesthetic process: the invention of the self as work of art.

There were only two things left for a genuine artist in America to do, Burton Rascoe observed in the summer of 1922 – stay drunk or commit suicide.

---

## JUST REWARDS OF INVENTION

On the cold, bright Thursday of 16 November, Carl Van Vechten lunched at the Algonquin with Tom Smith, Horace Liveright and Tallulah Bankhead. Van Vechten was preparing to attend the première of John Barrymore's *Hamlet*, the theatrical event of the season; a writer named Thomas Beer had asked him 'some time ago', Van Vechten noted in his diary irritatedly, 'but he is unable to get seats & calls it off today. Very Tom Beerish!' Tom Beer had published his first novel in 1922, *The Fair Rewards*, about a naive young dreamer from the provinces who idealizes a deceitful woman . Beer inscribed a copy of the novel: 'For Scott Fitzgerald from Thomas Beer. τοῖἐς ἔμπροσθεν ἐπεκτινόμενος', which translates as 'reaching forward to what lies ahead'. It comes from the Bible, ending a passage that reads: 'Brethren, I do not regard myself as having laid hold of it yet; but one thing I do: forgetting what lies behind and reaching forward to what lies ahead.' When Fitzgerald came to write his own novel of an idealist in 1922, who persistently reaches forward to what lies ahead, he would make his hero unable to forget what lies behind. Jay Gatsby remains convinced that what he has lost is always lurking nearby, 'just out of reach of his hand'.

Four days after Beer stood him up, Van Vechten invited round a poet named Wallace Stevens, who brought the manuscript for *Harmonium*, his first collection of poems, which Van Vechten had helped persuade Alfred Knopf to publish; it would come out in early 1923 and become one of the defining events of American modernism, including such now-classic poems as 'Thirteen Ways of Looking at a Blackbird' and 'Anecdote of the Jar'. 'I do not know which to prefer,' Stevens famously wrote in *Harmonium*, 'the beauty of inflections or the beauty of innuendoes.'

In life, however, it seemed that Stevens had less difficulty identifying his preferences. After drinking 'half a quart of my best bourbon', Van Vechten reported, 'Wallace told me he didn't like me' and left. So much for the beauty of innuendoes.

---

# Biography as Fiction

The Fitzgeralds travelled with Gene and Helen Buck to New Jersey on Saturday 18 November, a journey of a few hours by train, to watch the

Yale–Princeton football game. Swope's *World* was Fitzgerald's preferred paper for sports in those days, and he faithfully followed the Princeton Tigers throughout his life. On that November Saturday the *World* put the Princeton game on its front page.

Immediately to the left of the big game was the latest update on the Hall–Mills investigation in New Brunswick. 'SURE STRONG CASE IS BUILT UP FOR HALL GRAND JURY', ran the headline. 'Investigators Hint Mystery of Double Killing is Near Solution.' As it happens, the last stop before Princeton on the commuter train from New York is New Brunswick: they had to travel right past the scene of the year's most notorious crime to get to their football game.

The game, as Zelda told the Kalmans, who had not made it east, 'was very spectacular and very dull', and all she remembered was the score: Princeton won 3–0. Afterwards they went round to the university's clubs to drink with the undergraduates, which made her feel like Methuselah; it was 'a sad experience'. But generally life in Great Neck was like 'Times Square at the theatre hour. It is fun here.' Scott and Ring stayed up all night drinking together, and wrote Kalman another letter about their excursion, undated, but timed: it was 5.30 a.m. and they were 'not so much up already as up still'. Although the game was 'punk' the Kalmans would still have been amused: 'This is a very drunken town full of intoxicated people and retired debauches & actresses so I know that you and she to who you laughingly refer to as the missus would enjoy it … Everything is in its usual muddle.'

Zelda added a tidbit of gossip to her letter that she was sure would amuse the Kalmans: a girl they knew had visited the Fitzgeralds recently and 'lured John Dos Passos back to New York when he was expected to stay overnight' with them in Great Neck. 'This was astonishing as he looks like an elongated squirrel.' Zelda's surprise was primarily because the girl was 'so partial to the arrow collar brand'; Dos 'is attractive tho', Zelda admitted.

The day after the Princeton game, Marcel Proust died in Paris (which would not be reported in America for some weeks). If the Fitzgeralds read the Sunday *New York Times* on their train journey home to Great Neck they would have seen an article in the book section by the English writer John Cournos, whose novel *Babel* was enjoying a vigorous marketing campaign, complete with an endorsement from Scott Fitzgerald: 'Beautifully written … The author's graphic atmospheres in London and Paris and New York are flawless.'

In his *Times* article that Sunday, 'Biography as Fiction', Cournos argued that the best art was produced when 'realities themselves are used as symbols'. In fact, Cournos was prepared to go further and say that the only fiction that deserved to be called art was 'fact in the light of imagination'. This is the difference between art and documentary reportage, being debated in the pages of the *New York Times* that rainy mild Sunday in November as the Fitzgeralds trained back to Long Island, trailing a hangover.

---

# Relics and Curios.

Over the weekend as the Fitzgeralds and Bucks travelled to Princeton, the papers discussed the forthcoming grand jury trial in the Hall–Mills case, which was finally going to be convened on Monday. Witnesses would include the hapless Pearl Bahmer and Raymond Schneider, still awaiting trial for the misdemeanours that followed their finding the bodies; the maids in the Hall residence; the doctors and detectives who'd been at the scene when the bodies were discovered; and, of course, Jane Gibson. Mr Mott intended to argue that Mrs Hall was behind the crimes: 'The motive accepted by Mr Mott for proof before the grand jury was that Mrs Hall's intense desire for the preservation of the conventions, outraged by the furtive spooning of her husband and the singer, led up to anger which caused the situation which got beyond her control and brought about the murders,' explained the *World*, in what was possibly the first and last instance of 'furtive spooning' being cited as a motive for murder.

The Hall–Mills story was beginning to be defined by women, a novel and somewhat disturbing development, said the *Tribune*. 'A jury will decide between the two women – one throughout her life a symbol of exclusive respectability in New Brunswick; the other a turbulent character, who in recent years has made a living transmuting New Brunswick's garbage into pork' – and its swinishness into garbage. Charlotte Mills was reported to be 'aggrieved' at not having been called to testify, complaining that Prosecutor Beekman had cut her off when he deigned to question her at all, saying, 'That's all right, little girl. That's all we want to know.'

American women had finally won the vote two years earlier, in a constitutional amendment that followed hard on the heels of the Volstead Act. The question of women's role in public and professional life was now urgent, and much debated: suddenly something called the 'woman's vote' was taken into account in elections and treated as very different from the normal vote made by people who were not women. Equally concerning was the idea that women were beginning to sit on juries, a development much discussed that autumn. The women who would join the Hall–Mills grand jury were named by the press, which speculated on their likely attitudes toward the case. That October the American ambassador to Britain had given a talk asking if women had souls; if they did, he said, they would need their own set of commandments. The speech caused a small storm in America: asked for comment, Ring

Lardner said there was no point in writing new commandments for women, as they would only break them. He recommended that all the women in the world be killed or sent to New Jersey.

On 18 November, as the Fitzgeralds and Bucks made their merry way to Princeton, the *Saturday Evening Post* featured a woman golfer on the cover, viewing her club with a certain amount of dismay – or confusion.

As America waited with mounting anticipation for the New Brunswick grand jury to convene, two new witnesses came forward, strengthening the state's case. Another hog farmer, named George Sipel – promptly dubbed the 'Pig Man' – was said to have corroborated Mrs Gibson's statement, claiming he was the owner of the truck that drove past the crime scene, illuminating the murder with its headlights just in time for Mrs Gibson to witness it. Another witness was claiming to have been the confidant of Edward Hall. Paul Hamborszky was a Hungarian minister in New Brunswick who had recently been relieved of his ministerial duties after complaints of his drinking, and had since become a used-car salesman. Although Hamborszky's statement was hearsay, vague and did not actually deal with the crime, and thus could not be put before the grand jury, 'the authorities do not consider this a fatal defect in the Hamborszky story'.

In the meantime, an enterprising local had opened a 'murder museum' at the Phillips Farm, charging admission and serving 'soda water, sandwiches, peanuts and pop corn as refreshments'. The crab-apple tree had disappeared, torn down by souvenir-seekers, so sightseers brought shovels and dug up earth from the crime scene; those who had forgotten containers could purchase paper bags to carry their dirt home.

The *Tribune* sardonically suggested a route for Sunday drives. Given the rise of tourism as a pastime, the crowds that 'burned up New Jersey roads to the scene of the Hall–Mills murder ... [and the] bits of houses, trees and furniture' that now 'have a wide distribution on mantles and bureaus in homes', perhaps America should consider organizing 'Ideal Crime Tours': 'On left, turf field in which motorists may search for new evidence or souvenirs ... Large excavation dead ahead. On that spot the crime was committed. Entire spot has been carried away by souvenir hunters. Drive on.'

One woman wrote to the *World*, describing such an excursion: 'having read much about the Hall–Mills murder, we decided to visit the Phillips farm. We drove along till we came to a sign reading: "This is the way to the tragedy." Then we came upon another sign, reading: "This is the spot." But the crab apple tree has disappeared, taken away by souvenir hunters. However, there is a stick with a black string tied about it to show where it was.'

What is the difference between the historian and the souvenir-hunter? Both are in search of relics, of sacred objects; both tend to linger over scenes of carnage and tragedy. Ideally, historians do less damage to the source material, but this cannot always be guaranteed. The same is true of their search for meaning. The tour guide is not morally superior to the tourist, only more familiar with the route.

This is the way to the tragedy. But when you get there, instead of an historical relic, a sacred object, the totemic tree itself, all you may find is a stick with a black string tied to it by someone who got there first. History makes rubbernecks of us all.

De Russey's Lane, autumn 1922

## AMERICA AS A PIONEER.

On their journey home that Sunday, the Fitzgeralds would have had time to read a large illustrated feature in the *New York Times* on the 'romance' of 'Border Rum Runners'. Although there's no evidence that they did, there is a reason for us to read it, as it explains something that the Fitzgeralds knew but is now largely forgotten. For the previous three years, outlaws had been running whisky on the border states between Canada and the American Middle West: rum-running was America's last frontier romance. By 1922 such romance was already doomed: alcohol was beginning to make its way across the country by means of rapidly organizing crime, 'from Chicago by the dirty channels of bribed politicians and "fixed" garages'. What would become the National Crime Syndicate was gathering force. Soon rapacious men like Arnold Rothstein would be obliterated in the public memory by celebrity gangsters such as Al Capone – who in 1922 was manager and part-owner of a speakeasy and brothel in Chicago, and looking for bigger things.

Although the 'dashing rascals of the romantic novel type' who first ran the whisky trail were already disappearing, said the *Times*, 'the spirit of adventure still lingers in the lake lands of Northern Minnesota', where 'the whiskey was running' from Canada across Lake Superior, or in a 'four-hour dash across the border' to Minot, North Dakota, the gangster capital of the west in the 1920s. The crossing from the Canadian border to North Dakota was called 'Whiskey Gap'. North Dakota became the pipeline for bootleg alcohol travelling to the Twin Cities of Minneapolis and St Paul – which Scott and Zelda had just left. At first, public sentiment in North Dakota had been disposed toward bootleggers: any business was welcome in a state that had gone bankrupt before prohibition was enacted. But now, in 1922, rum-running in North Dakota had become déclassé: 'there are too many common people who have managed to climb into it ... There's taint in the blood of the people who have fallen to the lure of the easy money of the bootleg industry.'

After the reporter comes calling on Jay Gatsby, Nick Carraway reveals that he is really – or at least originally – James Gatz, the son of shiftless farm people in North Dakota, who grew up convinced that he was destined for greater things. Although seventeen-year-old James Gatz's departure from North Dakota in 1907 pre-dates prohibition,

Gatsby is constantly associated with images suggesting bootlegging – including the state from which he hails. The investigative reporter is drawn to Gatsby by 'contemporary legends such as the "underground pipe-line to Canada," [which] attached themselves to him, and there was one persistent story that he didn't live in a house at all, but in a boat that looked like a house and was moved secretly up and down the Long Island shore' – like a boat in Rum Row. The truth, we are about to learn, is that Gatsby got his start from a 'yachtsman' – another common euphemism for bootlegger, because of the flotilla of boats running rum up from the West Indies.

After leaving North Dakota, Gatz drifted to Minnesota, where he spent a year wandering along the south shore of Lake Superior. One day he saw a yacht drop anchor in a dangerous part of the great lake and rowed out to warn the owner. Recognizing the young man's 'extravagant ambition' and his promise, the yachtsman Dan Cody brings him on board as a general factotum. James Gatz, meanwhile, has availed himself of the opportunity to become the more aristocratic-sounding Jay Gatsby. His climb up America's social ladder has begun.

Dan Cody, Gatsby's mentor, is a self-made man, a millionaire whose fortune came from the west: 'the pioneer debauchee, who during one phase of American life, brought back to the eastern seaboard the savage violence of the frontier brothel and saloon'. He was produced, Nick tells us, by the Nevada silver fields, Yukon gold, Montana copper, 'every rush for metal' since 1875. His name suggests American folk heroes of westward expansion: Daniel Boone, Buffalo Bill Cody. But it also suggests Daniel Drew, known as 'Uncle Dan Drew', a nineteenth-century robber baron who teamed up with Jay Gould and Jim Fisk to try to outmanoeuvre Cornelius Vanderbilt for control of the Erie Railroad in 1866. Together, the three are said to have milked the Erie line for as much as nine million dollars; when a warrant was issued for Drew's arrest, they retreated to Jersey City and began systematically plundering Wall Street. Banks nearly collapsed and America's national credit was jeopardized. Drew himself was finally hoist with his own petard, ruined in the Panic of 1873. Years later Fitzgerald included *The Book*

*of Daniel Drew*, an 'imaginative memoir' by Bouck White, on a long list
of books he recommended.

Dan Cody had a clearer model than Dan Drew, however. Another
of the Fitzgeralds' neighbours in Great Neck during their fateful sojourn
there was a man named Robert C. Kerr, who told Fitzgerald a story in
the summer of 1923 (when 'Scott and I were "buzzing" one evening,'
Kerr told the *Great Neck News* in 1929). As a fourteen-year-old boy
living in Brooklyn in 1907, Kerr had been in Sheepshead Bay one day
and seen an expensive yacht drop anchor where it would be damaged
when the tide ran out. He had rowed out to warn the owner, a man
named Edward Robinson Gilman, who hired the young Kerr to join his
staff for twenty-five dollars a week. The *Great Neck News* reported that
it was 'regular Horatio Alger stuff . . . "From Rags to Riches" for fair'.

Edward Gilman, the yacht's owner, was the general manager of the
Iron Clad Manufacturing Company, owned by Robert L. Seaman, an
elderly millionaire. Seaman had married Nellie Bly, the most famous
female reporter in America, in 1895, when he was seventy and she was
thirty-one. Within a few years of the wedding, rumors that Bly and
Gilman had begun an affair were being reported in the tabloids. In
1905 Seaman died and Bly inherited his companies. Gilman died in
1911, at which point it was discovered that he and others had embez-
zled almost half a million dollars from Iron Clad; one of the purchases
he'd charged to the company was the twenty-five-thousand-dollar
yacht that Robert Kerr had seen drop anchor in dangerous shallows.
Nellie Bly lived another ten years; her death in January 1922 was
reported in all the national papers. Her old paper the *World* placed Bly
in the 'front rank of women journalists', in part because of her trip
around the world in seventy-two days back in 1889; she had stopped
in France to meet Jules Verne. Bly had first become famous for her
courage in feigning insanity and being admitted to Blackwell's insane
asylum in New York in order to expose abuses there, in what remained
her most celebrated piece of investigative journalism. When Robert
Kerr had told Fitzgerald about Edward Gilman, he'd implied that Nellie
Bly was not only his mistress, but also grasping and acquisitive.

In the summer of 1924, while writing *The Great Gatsby*, Fitzgerald sent a letter to Kerr, headed 'Great Neck – I mean St Raphaël, France, Villa Marie', telling Kerr that his stories were figuring in the novel: 'The part of what you told me which I am including in my novel is the ship, yacht I mean, & the mysterious yachtsman whose mistress was Nellie Bly. I have my hero occupy the same position you did & obtain it in the same way. I am calling him Robert B. Kerr instead of Robert C. Kerr to conceal his identity. (This is a joke – I wanted to give you a scare. His name is Gatsby.)' After the book came out, Fitzgerald sent a copy of *Gatsby* to Kerr with the inscription: 'Dear Bob, Keep reading and you'll finally come to your own adventures which you told to me one not-forgotten summer night.'

Being imported wholesale into a work of fiction would give anyone a scare; as soon as Bob Kerr's name is changed, however, it becomes a simple case of mistaken identity, a funny joke to play on a friend. It also, as an added bonus, provided a way for Fitzgerald to get even with Nellie Bly, whom he had reason to dislike. In his scrapbook, Fitzgerald clipped an article Bly wrote in 1922 urging that readers 'not praise a book like that beautiful and damned thing just because a smart and undesirable lot of young nobodies call it literature. It is a pitiful thing to see a young man like Fitzgerald, with a wonderful talent, going as he has, but it is not too late for him, and here is hoping that he will do the great thing which he can and write a book which people would not fear to read aloud to their mothers and other decent folk.' Fitzgerald had his revenge, writing Bly into literary history as the unscrupulous, greedy Ella Kaye, who takes up with Dan Cody after years of riotous living.

Nellie Bly didn't live long enough to read *The Great Gatsby*, although it isn't clear that she would have recommended it to decent folk and their mothers, either. Bly was not alone in her distaste. In March 1922 the editor and critic Constance Lindsay Skinner wrote to the historian Frederick Jackson Turner, the man famous for recognizing the 'significance of the American frontier', thanking him for permission to reprint his landmark essay, in which he celebrated the self-made pioneer individualist as the great product of American life. Skinner apologized for not being able to secure two columns for a review of Turner's new book: 'If an author wants 2 cols. he must write some such hectic twaddle as "The Beautiful and the Damned" [*sic*] on the principle that midnight supper parties are "American Life" – and history isn't!'

The significance of the American frontier was becoming clearer to Americans in the early 1920s; as the country began to write the story of its life, divisions between east and west started to overtake the nineteenth century's preoccupation with divisions between north and south. On 12 November the *Tribune* noted the commonplace understanding that prohibition had divided America between the 'dry West' and the 'wet East'. In the spring of 1922, in 'The Wild West's Own New York', the *New York Times* asked whether the Midwest's ideas about New York were any more accurate than New York's ideas about the Midwest. The article ended with prescience and some elegance:

> New York is megalomaniac; so is America. New York is rushing, restless, formless, strident, sensational, credulous, vulgar. What American city is not? It is cluttered with ugliness, the irretrievable ugliness of the temporary in decay. It has impulses of beauty, sudden and splendid, intimations of its power, its imagination, its hurried and interrupted dreams. It is friendly and valiant and generous, careless and young, sure of its capacities, unsure of its judgments. It is a little like the New Poetry, difficult to scan, unamenable to reason and tradition, trailing off indifferently into the baldest and most jerry-built prose, but with a robust and magnificent intention, sometimes justified by clear new images and by occasional vivid evocations of beauty and of truth. And that, also, is it not America?

'I see now that this has been a story of the West, after all – Tom and Gatsby, Daisy and Jordan and I, were all Westerners, and perhaps we possessed some deficiency in common which made us subtly unadaptable to Eastern life,' Nick muses at the end of *The Great Gatsby*. The perspective of all the characters is shaped, in different ways, by vagabonds and pioneers; by bringing in Dan Cody, the last tycoon who made a fortune from mining, Fitzgerald begins to pull the history of the frontier into his account of modern American life, which until then had seemed to consist primarily of frivolous 'midnight supper parties' in the wild west of New York. A story about careless, young America begins to emerge: its sudden and splendid intimations of power, its hurried and interrupted dreams of magnificent intention.

After an unseasonably warm weekend, dramatic thunderstorms broke in New York on Monday 20 November, bringing heavy downpours as the grand jury finally convened in New Brunswick to consider evidence from the Hall–Mills murder. The nation's front pages went into overdrive: 'GRAND JURY IN SESSION', 'PIG WOMAN'S STORY IS STATE'S HIGH CARD'. The *World* reported that the courthouse was crowned with a statue of justice, blindfolded. No one remarked on the irony of how blind justice in New Jersey was proving.

The press could see other ironies in the saga, however. Announcing 'FICTION PUT TO SHAME BY GROUP OF WOMEN TANGLED IN HALL CASE', the *Tribune* presented the six women in paired types, some more familiar than others: 'Widow With Fierce Pride Of Family And Slain Singer Of Romantic Mind; "Mule Woman" And Negress; Salamander Flapper And Slum Waif'. Their 'stories are stranger than fiction'; the six women were 'not like the normal people of everyday life'. Some might think this begs a question about what defines normal people, or everyday life: unlike fiction, reality has no obligation to be realistic.

All six women were symbolized by their homes, said the article. Against Eleanor Mills was pitched the rich widow, described as 'the cold, proud woman of Southern blood', reminding readers that Mrs Hall came originally from South Carolina. Eleanor Mills had been 'sickened by sordid surroundings and a colorless life', but her 'deeply implanted instinct for self-development' had 'found expression in her romantic attachment' to Hall, and in her home, where one room revealed her desire for splendour, its furnishings 'indicating her pathetic strivings for some of the finer things of life'. After enjoying some comedy at the expense of Jane Gibson and Nellie Lo Russell, both pictured as poor and grotesque, the article ended with Charlotte Mills and Pearl Bahmer. Pearl was 'dazed and stupid and uncomprehending', while Charlotte was 'a pathetic little salamander who has emerged from her chrysalis since her mother died'. 'Salamander' was slang for a flirt: *The Gilded Lily*, a 1922 film, was billed as the tale of 'a glittering salamander', while a magazine story published that June explained that some women can, 'like the salamander', 'pass unscathed through the fire that would destroy' more 'sensitive' women. The salamander liked 'perilous adventures' and 'new excitements', playing with men 'for the sheer fun of it'.

Ten years later Zelda Fitzgerald looked back on her life and remarked that in the early 1920s she had 'believed I was a Salamander'. The term confused her earlier biographers: Nancy Milford speculated that perhaps Zelda was referring to the mythical salamander, which could survive fire. This was evidently the source of the slang, probably originating with a 1914 novel, but it was more specifically a jazz-age image of glittering, powerful, careless women.

As the Hall–Mills grand jury convened that Monday, the *Evening World* printed a parodic notice of a new play they had invented: 'Seats selling eight weeks in advance for Hall–Mills murder mystery. Management claims farce will run for full year.' It would run longer than that.

# INSULT TO OUR IDEALS.

The first woman senator in American history was sworn into office on Tuesday 21 November 1922. Her name was Rebecca Felton, she was eighty-seven years old and she served the state of Georgia for only one day: the appointment was an honorary one. Whether she deserved the honour is another question; although Felton was a prominent supporter of women's suffrage she was an equally prominent supporter of lynching. A former slave-owner (holding the dubious distinction of being the last slave-owner on the floor of the US Senate), Felton was an avowed white supremacist who defended the 1899 lynching of Sam Hose, a black man accused of raping a white woman. After lynching Hose, his murderers carved up his body and sold the pieces as souvenirs. Felton said any decent man would have done the same.

Two weeks before Felton's appointment to the Senate, New York police had to rescue a black man from a mob of two thousand white people in Manhattan. The mob had beaten the man senseless and was preparing to lynch him for having allegedly kissed a white woman.

Immediately after Mrs Felton was sworn in and out, the National Association for the Advancement of Colored People bought a full-page advertisement in the *New York Times*, seeking support for the Dyer Anti-Lynching Bill, which was debated throughout 1922, and disputing several canards about lynching that persist to this day. The first was that lynching was restricted to the South, when the threat was alive and kicking on the streets of Manhattan. The second was that 'lynching' always, or usually, meant hanging: more often it meant

> **CHURCHGOERS SEEK ROPE FOR A NEGRO**
>
> Police, With Revolvers Drawn, Rescue Prisoner From Crowd in Hell's Kitchen.
>
> ———
>
> KISSED A WHITE WOMAN
>
> ———
>
> Her Son Gives Chase to Negro, Who Defends Himself With Knife and Wrench.

burning at the stake and other modes of torture including dismemberment. The ad also challenged the white supremacist myth that revenging rape was the motivation behind lynching, accurately reporting: 'Of 3,436 people murdered by mobs in our country, only 571, or less than 17 per cent, were even accused of the crime of rape. 83 women have been lynched in the United States: do lynchers maintain that they were lynched for "the usual crime?"' (In fact, history has shown that more often than not black people were lynched for economic competition against whites, rather than supposed sexual crimes; the ad lists some of the other excuses and ostensible reasons, including 'jumping a labor contract' and 'being a relative of a person who was lynched'.) The NAACP advertisement didn't work: the Dyer Anti-Lynching Bill failed again that autumn, and would continue to fail until it disappeared altogether.

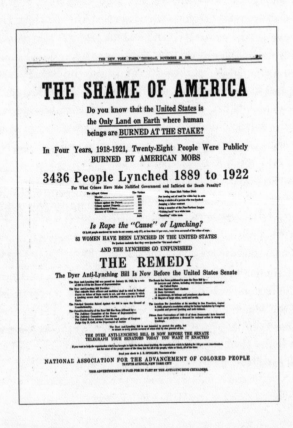

The same day that Felton took her seat in the Senate, the *New York Times* front page reported a new 'popular idol' on the rise in Europe, its first mention of a man it said the Germans referred to as 'Der Hitler' and whose followers they called 'Hakenkreuzlers' – swastika-wearers. There is nothing socialist about the National Socialism' being preached in Bavaria, warned the *Times* reporter; indeed, Hitler 'probably does not know himself just what he wants to accomplish'. However 'the keynote of his propaganda' is 'violent anti-Semitism'.

**NEW POPULAR IDOL RISES IN BAVARIA**

Hitler Credited With Extraordinary Powers of Swaying Crowds to His Will.

FORMS GRAY-SHIRTED ARMY

Armed With Blackjacks and Revolvers and Well Disciplined, They Obey Orders Implicitly.

LEADER A REACTIONARY

Is Anti-Red and Anti-Semitic, and Demands Strong Government for a United Germany.

If Mrs Felton shows the dangers of idealizing the past, it is also wise to avoid patronizing it. Despite the era's widespread anti-Semitism, the *New York Times* recognized Hitler's threat from its first mention of him. The next day the paper followed up with a report that 'sophisticated politicians' in Germany believed Hitler's anti-Semitism might have been a mere ploy to manipulate the ignorant masses. Because the general population can never be expected to appreciate the 'finer real aims' of statesmen, said one German politician, 'you must feed the masses with cruder morsels and ideas like anti-Semitism' rather than the higher 'truth about where you are really leading them'.

Alas for sophisticated politicians and where they really lead people: similar arguments had led latter-day Puritans in America to drag the nation back into a state of counterfeit innocence by banishing the demon liquor. Empty promises and national myths would continue to mislead people, including those convincing themselves that they were leading their nation toward higher truths rather than toward cataclysm.

# WHAT'S IN A NAME?

In January 1923 Scott Fitzgerald wrote a story that begins: 'Parts of New Jersey, as you know, are under water, and other parts are under continual surveillance by the authorities.' He sold it to Hearst's *Metropolitan* magazine, which published it under the heading 'A Typical Fitzgerald Story'. 'Dice, Brass Knuckles & Guitar' is another tale of an outsider, a young man named Jim Powell, who falls in love with a debutante. Attired in the outlandish costume of bell-bottom trousers that were a fad among very young men in the early 1920s, he hits on a scheme for teaching society girls how to protect themselves using brass knuckles, how to play jazz guitar and how to shoot craps ('I protect pocketbook as well as person'). Shooting craps had become a popular pastime at high-society parties, as part of the decadent, modern metropolitan world: Alec Woollcott and Margaret Swope shot craps at the Paris Ritz, and the party scenes in DeMille's *Manslaughter* feature satin-gowned sophisticates crouched on marble steps shooting craps.

Fitzgerald's story begins by describing the 'last-century landmarks' that could still be found in the New Jersey countryside, including gracious old Victorian homes, which the modern tourist driving past would lack the taste to appreciate: 'He drives on to his Elizabethan villa of pressed cardboard or his early Norman meat-market or his medieval Italian pigeon-coop – because this is the twentieth century.' Jay Gatsby is a son of the twentieth century, confident that the early Norman meat-market he has purchased will impress – but Scott Fitzgerald was less convinced.

Jim Powell's 'Jazz School' is a great success, but he remains excluded from Long Island high society: 'he lay awake many nights in his hotel bed and heard the music drifting into his window from the Katzbys' house or the Beach Club, and turned over restlessly and wondered what was the matter. In the early days of his success he had bought himself a dress-suit, thinking that he would soon have a chance to wear it – but it still lay untouched in the box in which it had come from the tailor's.

Perhaps, he thought, there was some real gap which separated him from the rest.' When he confronts the rich, snobbish villain of the tale, Jim is informed, 'Ronald here'd no more think of asking you to his party than he would his bootlegger.'

Unlike many of Fitzgerald's heroines, the debutante in this tale loves the hero; she informs him, 'You're better than all of them put together, Jim.' But Jimmy Powell remains an outcast. At the story's end he hits the road in his jalopy (with his black 'body-servant' Hugo – it is one of the most carelessly racist of Fitzgerald's works), as the girl returns to the aristocratic world of the Katzbys. Less than two years later, Fitzgerald would have Nick Carraway tell Jay Gatsby virtually the same thing: 'You're worth the whole damn bunch put together.' As it happens, both Jim Powell and the girl he loves pretend to be people they aren't: masquerade may be the favourite game of romantic comedy, but it is also at the heart of the game of fiction, whether your name is Katzby or Gatz or Gatsby.

---

## ASKS 'CLEAN BREAST' IN HALL-MILLS CASE

As the grand jury hearings progressed, 'the number of feminine witnesses called' made for 'lively' days in court, reported the *Tribune*. James Mills also took the stand, 'a thin, emaciated drooping man, with a perpetually apologetic expression on his face', wearing 'a cheap suit of clothes'. He'd spent the morning wandering the streets in front of the courthouse, eating doughnuts. In the afternoon, 'James Mills sat stonily across the hall, his face as white and set as marble, his hands twitching nervously with his hat ... He had a hangdog air, and such dejection that he was noticeable amongst all the witnesses.' There was no mention of the lingering question of his alibi. As soon as Mills finished testifying, he requested his witness fee. Four days later the *Tribune* reported that Mills was 'as lugubrious as usual, pitying himself for his sad domestic state'. A few pictures of Jim Mills survived the media circus, including one of him praying beside his dead wife's freshly dug grave, in which he appears to be smiling.

Meanwhile, said the *World*, 'the "woman in gray" and one man may be charged with the crime', but no evidence had been found against a third person. Instead, Mott's 'whole case will have to stand or fall on the story of Mrs Jane Gibson', who had identified 'the woman in gray' as Mrs Hall but had named three different men as the 'man with the bushy hair' whom she claimed to have seen. At least two of these men were understood to have strong alibis, which was awkward for the prosecution.

Throwing themselves on the mercy of the killer, Mott and the other state officials announced that they were 'hoping for a "break" in the form of a confession'. A confession is certainly one kind of a break – and possibly nothing less than having the solution handed to them on a silver platter would have enabled the New Brunswick authorities to make any progress. No wonder they wanted to believe the killer had a tender heart.

## *DELUSION OF DEMOCRACY*

It should not be surprising that Gatsby's second party does not go as well as the first – and the first ended in mayhem. Having grown perturbed by the idea of his wife running around alone, although unaware of the fact that she's begun an affair with Gatsby, Tom decides to accompany Daisy one night to Gatsby's house. For the first time, Nick doesn't enjoy himself at one of Gatsby's revels. Despite the 'same profusion of champagne, the same many-colored, many-keyed commotion', Nick feels 'an unpleasantness in the air'. Perhaps, he thinks, the change comes from his suddenly looking at West Egg 'through Daisy's eyes', instead of through Gatsby's. Nick has become accustomed to West Egg 'as a world complete in itself', which has no idea of being inferior to anywhere else, because it is unconscious of its own crassness – but its vulgarity becomes clear in Tom and Daisy's affronted reaction to it.

Covering her discomfort with brittle gaiety, Daisy offers to hand out green cards to young men who might want to kiss her – her card colour-coded by Fitzgerald to match Gatsby's green light. Daisy spends the party protesting too much but abandoning her protests ('I'm having a marvelous – '), while Tom makes cutting remarks that Gatsby misunderstands. He innocently tells Tom that he will see many celebrated people, people he's heard about, and Tom replies, underscoring the Buchanans' social exclusivity, that they 'don't go around very much ... In fact I was just thinking I don't know a soul here.'

It is at this point that they see another of *Gatsby's* enduring images, the gorgeous, scarcely human orchid of a woman, a movie star sitting in state under a white plum tree, with her director bending over her. 'Tom and Daisy stared, with that peculiarly unreal feeling that accompanies the recognition of a hitherto ghostly celebrity of the movies.' The movie star and her director remain in this tableau for the rest of the party, as Fitzgerald offers an art deco update of Keats's lovers on the Grecian urn, forever young, forever beautiful, frozen in time. In the *Trimalchio* drafts Daisy draws the line at sharing her hairdresser with the movie star, although Gatsby tells her 'impressively' that it will make her 'the originator of a new vogue all over the country'. Daisy responds, 'Do you think I want that person to go around with her hair cut exactly like mine? It'd spoil it for me.' In the final version Fitzgerald has eliminated this exchange, allowing the aristocrat to stand silently bewitched by the star.

When Daisy and Gatsby dance, they do no wild Charleston, but instead 'a graceful, conservative fox-trot' that Nick finds as surprising as will readers whose expectations have been created by film adaptations. Meanwhile, Tom amuses himself with a young woman whom Daisy dismisses as 'common but pretty', as she mockingly offers Tom a 'little gold pencil' to take down phone numbers of the women he picks up. Nick and Gatsby both realize that Daisy is not having fun; they are at a 'particularly tipsy table', with people whose company Nick had recently found amusing. But now these people's behaviour has turned 'septic' – the tawdriness is showing: 'When she's had five or six cocktails she always starts screaming like that.' Doc Civet has stuck a drunken girl's head in the pool to sober her up, and got her dress all wet. 'Anything I hate is to get my head stuck in a pool,' Miss Baedeker says, and begins to mumble about death in New Jersey.

Daisy is offended by this 'place' so unlike hers that it must be marked by sceptical inverted commas, so appalled by a society that has liberated itself from any constraints of decorum that Fitzgerald repeats the offence to her pride: 'But the rest offended her – and inarguably, because it wasn't a gesture but an emotion. She was appalled by West Egg, this unprecedented "place" that Broadway had begotten upon a Long Island fishing village – appalled by its raw vigor that chafed under the old euphemisms and by the too obtrusive fate that herded its inhabitants along a short cut from nothing to nothing. She saw something awful in the very simplicity she failed to understand.' Daisy is playing at love – she offers only gestures, not emotions. She was raised among the same aristocracy that Edith Wharton described as a world in which people with emotions were not visited, sharing Jordan Baker's urbane distaste for the concrete. The raw vigour of West Egg is also the raw vigour of Gatsby – and, indeed, of the jazz age.

Daisy's banter reveals her distaste for it all. 'I've never met so many celebrities!' she exclaims. 'I liked that man – what was his name? – with the sort of blue nose.' When she insists that she found Gatsby's guests 'interesting', Tom laughs and asks Nick, 'Did you notice Daisy's face when that girl asked her to put her under a cold shower?' Tom is no more impressed than Daisy by 'this menagerie', demanding suddenly who Gatsby is: 'Some big bootlegger? … A lot of these newly rich people are just big bootleggers, you know.' Both Daisy and Nick are indignant at the slur. Daisy declares that Gatsby earned his money from a chain of drugstores, adding suddenly, as it occurs to her, that all of these vulgar people must be gatecrashers, not his friends: 'That girl hadn't been invited. They simply force their way in and he's too polite to object.' She's right, in one sense: they are not his friends, for Gatsby has no friends – just uninvited guests.

As the party unravels to its disillusioning end, 'a neat, sad little waltz of that year' called 'Three O'clock in the Morning' is playing, one of the biggest hits in recent memory. The song was recorded by Paul Whiteman, whom Scott and Zelda often heard play at the Palais Royal on Broadway. Zelda tended to hear the ripple of music throughout life; her memories were often washed deep in musical images. 'Paul Whiteman played the significance of amusement on his violin,' said Zelda later. 'Three O'clock in the Morning' was recorded at least

Palais Royal, 1920

once more that year, and advertised in the pages of the *New York Times* on Saturday 18 November 1922, as the Fitzgeralds took the train through New Brunswick to the football game.

'In the real dark night of the Soul,' Fitzgerald wrote much later, 'it is always three o'clock in the morning.' Perhaps this is the waltz Zelda was asking him to save: she found her novel's title, she said, in the Victor Record Catalogue. Music measured life into beats: 'Listen,' David tells Alabama, 'you're not keeping time.'

## Gold and Cocktails.

An American industrialist was asked by a women's college to consider making a donation to support women's education. He responded that he thought that all women's colleges should be burned, and those studying there sentenced to hard labour. The story made the front pages on 23 November; Americans could peruse it at their leisure, for it was Thanksgiving Day. If they kept browsing the *Times*, they would also have seen the story of a seventy-year-old 'spinster' who had been released from police custody after threatening to shower eggs upon a young woman selling birth-control pamphlets outside Grand Central Terminal.

Neither Scott nor Zelda left any record of how they spent the day, or what cooking – if any – was attempted, but some years later Fitzgerald offered some useful thoughts on what to do with leftover Thanksgiving turkey. A recipe for a turkey cocktail was his first suggestion: 'To one large turkey add one gallon of vermouth and a demijohn of angostura bitters. Shake.'

The day after Thanksgiving, the *New York Times* reported the indictment of a 'Bootleg King' named Mannie Kessler. He was only the latest
in a long line of Bootleg Kings crowned by the press in 1922. Far and
away the most notorious 'bootleg king' of 1922 was a lawyer from
Cincinnati named George Remus, who had begun selling alcohol from
drugstores as soon as the Volstead Act came into force; some credit
Remus with singlehandedly transforming drugstores into a byword for
bootlegging. In just two years Remus became fabulously rich, building
a lavish mansion with a marble pool and a solid-gold piano. For the
previous New Year's Eve he had thrown a party at which it was reported
that champagne 'flowed like the Rhine', and a hundred girls, 'garbed in
Grecian robes of flowing white', served a midnight banquet graced by
'water nymphs' who gave a diving exhibition. Remus was arrested in
May 1922. Over the summer the papers were filled with tales of the
flamboyant parties he was supposed to have thrown. Swope's *World* ran
a full-page story saying Remus 'Ruled Like a King, Lived in A Palace,
Scattered Huge "Overnight" Fortune in Revelry and Largess'. The story
was accompanied by novelistic illustrations of Remus's revels:

Remus was eventually sentenced to two years in a federal penitentiary. While he was serving time his wife began an affair with a prohibition agent. When he was released, his wife filed for divorce; Remus shot and killed her, claiming temporary insanity on the grounds of her adultery. The 'unwritten law' was invoked and after deliberating for less than twenty minutes the jury found Remus not guilty of murder by means of temporary insanity. He was committed to a mental hospital, but three months later the hospital discharged him because he was not insane. Temporary insanity, indeed.

A few months before Remus murdered his wife the first film version of *The Great Gatsby* was reviewed in the *New York Times*, headlined 'Gold and Cocktails'. It described a few scenes from the film: Daisy is seen 'assuaging her disappointment in life by drinking absinthe. She takes enough of this beverage to render the average person unconscious. Yet she appears only mildly intoxicated, and soon recovers.' Indeed, the review noted, 'Cocktails are an important feature in this picture'. Even 'the girls in a swimming pool [are] snatching at cocktails, while they are swimming'. Gatsby, a 'man of sudden means', displays his profligacy by carelessly tossing gold pieces into the water so his guests can dive for them.

This 1926 version of *Gatsby* has been lost; all that survive are a few such descriptions and the film's trailer, featuring party scenes that bear a striking resemblance to the newspapers' illustrations of the bash George Remus threw to welcome in 1922:

## Unreliable Information on Important Problems.

Two days before Thanksgiving in 1922 Burton Rascoe found himself in an embarrassing situation. Carl Van Vechten had presented to him (doubtless with some unholy glee) a copy of a Boston paper in which a well-known writer denied that she had lunched with Rascoe, as he had recently reported in his Day Book column. Rascoe was forced to admit that he had fabricated the encounter: 'My mentioning our having had lunch together last week was merely a wish-fulfillment on my part, for I have long wanted to meet her; but I haven't had that pleasure, I must confess.' Rascoe, however, hastened to deny that his entire column was an invention: 'And let me on my part deny her flattering assumption that I invent the whole "Daybook" and actually see no one. That would be an ideal way, I suspect, to do the thing; but, except for this one instance, I have had to exercise only memory.' In fact, Rascoe was often accused of inaccuracy, especially in the way that he rendered conversation. Nonetheless, his defenders maintained, he usually didn't make things up. 'The substance of the conversation is generally characteristic,' said the *Bookman*; 'he conveys the speaker's personality, though it be by means of an imaginary dialogue.' Sometimes this technique is described as fiction.

The day before Van Vechten had confronted him with telltale evidence of unreliability, Rascoe had lunched with Edmund Wilson and discussed *The Waste Land*. (Unless, of course, we no longer believe him.) It seems the lunch signalled a rapprochement. Two months earlier, on the day that *Tales of the Jazz Age* came out, Wilson had written to John Bishop to tell him about visiting the Fitzgeralds at the Plaza the previous evening, adding as an aside that he'd stopped seeing Rascoe because he was so unreliable a narrator: 'he quoted me so much and so inaccurately that it finally got on my nerves and I ceased to see him at all (though other causes contributed to this, too) for almost a month ... Everybody began to give him the laugh about it and it is true that he wrote some of the most exquisitely silly things I have ever seen.' A few months later, Edmund Wilson was writing to Fitzgerald with some amusement about Rascoe's report of Fitzgerald's 'Dog, Dog, Dog' song. 'I enclose Burton Rascoe's report of a conversation with me, which speaks for itself. Ted Paramore and I have extracted almost as much amusement from it as from the initial pleasantries.'

Wilson didn't mention what the other reasons were that had led to his avoiding Rascoe, but Wilson admitted to having gone to bed with Burton's wife Hazel at least once. A former nightclub dancer with 'the most obvious sex appeal of any woman I have known', Wilson wrote in his journals, Hazel Rascoe had suddenly phoned Wilson up one night: 'I told her, full of hope, to come right around. But in spite of the fact that I performed the at that time for me heroic feat of carrying her into the bedroom, it turned out that she only wanted to tell me how worried she was about [Burton's] drinking.' She also wanted to talk about her 'latest passion': 'when she felt an interest in someone, she would apparently simply go to bed with him till her appetite had worn off. It was no wonder her husband drank,' Wilson added.

At a party one night around this time Wilson and Rascoe got into a drunken fight, which neither of them remembered afterwards. Bystanders offered different accounts. The fight may have occurred 'at a gathering at Edmund Wilson's, in the course of which several of the guests fell to brawling in various corners of a rambling apartment he had in the Village', which he rented in late November 1922. Wilson became 'engaged in combat with Mr Burton Rascoe and bit him in the calf'. Another witness, however, claimed that Rascoe bit Bunny Wilson on the nose when he was 'overadmirous' of Hazel. Despite this

Burton Rascoe, 1928

contretemps, and regardless of who was biting whom, the two men remained close enough friends that in 1927 Wilson's first will left bequests to Rascoe, and thirty years later Wilson wrote to Hazel Rascoe that her late husband 'never gets full credit now for all he did in the twenties and before. In his best days, he was worth a dozen of the so-called New Critics.'

The problem with unreliable narrators is that sometimes they tell the truth – it's just difficult to know when.

----

# SEES MODERNISTS AND FOES IN ERROR

As the *Tribune*'s literary editor was admitting his unreliability on 26 November, the *New York Times* published a feature on the books that had come out in the course of a remarkable literary year, in which popular idols and shibboleths had fallen foul of the rage for the modern. The piece opened, as did the year, with the publication of Joyce's landmark *Ulysses*; the year had also brought the first English translation of Marcel Proust's *Swann's Way* ('another subjective rendering of a man's mind'), which the *Times* reviewed a few pages later. And then there was T. S. Eliot's *The Waste Land*, due to hit the local bookstores any day.

The 'Books of the Year' feature made much of *Babbitt*, Willa Cather's *One of Ours*, Rebecca West's *The Judge* and *Cytherea* by Joseph Hergsheimer. Buried in a long list of also-rans, nearly all forgotten today, was 'Young Mr Scott Fitzgerald', who 'continued his flippant mood in *The Beautiful and Damned*'. The article ignored *Tales of the Jazz Age* altogether, as well as Virginia Woolf's *Jacob's Room*, Katherine Mansfield's *The Garden Party and Other Stories*, Elizabeth von Arnim's *Enchanted April*, Jean Toomer's *Cane*, Walter Lippmann's *Public Opinion*, D. H. Lawrence's *Studies in Classic American Literature* and *England, My England*, and the first of Ezra Pound's *Cantos*. They also overlooked the less lofty but more influential first edition of *Reader's Digest*, as well as the auto-suggestion of the immensely popular Emile Coué, the father of self-help, who taught Americans that all ills could be cured by repeating the simple formula, 'Every day, in every way, I'm growing better and better.' Self-improvement had never been easier.

A few months later, Fitzgerald contributed to a newspaper feature titled '10 Best Books I Have Read'. He cited Conrad's *Nostromo* as 'The great novel of the past fifty years, as "Ulysses" is the great novel of the future.' It was from Conrad's character Marlow, who narrates *Heart of Darkness*, *Lord Jim* and *Youth*, among others, that Fitzgerald discovered how an unreliable narrator might improve his novel. For most story-tellers, Conrad wrote, a tale 'has a direct simplicity, the whole meaning of which lies within the shell of a cracked nut'. But when Marlow told a story, 'the meaning of an episode was not inside like a kernel but outside, enveloping the tale which brought it out only as a glow brings out a haze'. Learning from Conrad, Fitzgerald would create in Nick Carraway a narrator who could discern lambent meaning in the haze surrounding his story.

Fitzgerald's appreciation of *Nostromo* put him ahead of his contemporaries, but they were all certain that *Ulysses* was the book of the future – and they were right, up to a point. None of them would have believed, however, that a hundred years later readers would consistently vote the two greatest novels in English of the twentieth century to be *Ulysses* and a novel that F. Scott Fitzgerald was about to write, called *The Great Gatsby*. The two novels have more in common than might at first appear, and not just their hinging, in their different ways, on the year 1922. The Irish critic Mary Colum told Rascoe that one eminent critic had lectured her on the meaning of a figure in *Ulysses*, a character whom the critic was confident was a symbolic invention. But in point of fact, she'd informed him, 'it is an exact portrayal of a very notorious, quaint man everybody knows' in Dublin. *Ulysses* contained, Colum said, 'every resident of Dublin one would be likely to encounter

ten years ago in an afternoon's walk ... There are satirical allusions in
the book,' her husband added, 'that no one outside of Dublin would
recognize.'

'Fiction is history, human history,' said Conrad, 'or it is nothing.'

As the grand jury hearing continued through late November, Mrs
Hall's maid, Louise Geist, was called as an unwilling witness. On the
stand the 'pretty maid' suddenly corroborated Mrs Hall's alibi for
the time of the murders: 'until today her movements had been
accounted for only until 9:30', but Geist said Mrs Hall was at home
during the hours the murders were thought to have taken place.
A married vestryman and choir singer took the stand; several witnesses had seen his green car parked on De Russey's Lane that
night, a car that was destroyed by fire not long after the murders.
He claimed it was just a coincidence. Eleanor Mills's sister Elsie
Barnhardt also testified, insisting that her sister had not been in any
trouble. The final witness on the final day was the prosecutor's
trump card, Mrs Gibson, who testified for almost two hours on
28 November. She told once more the story that had been repeated
so often in the press, of the woman in the grey polo coat, the man
with the bushy hair, the shouts of 'Henry!', Eleanor Mills dragged
through the undergrowth, and returning to the scene hours later
to find the woman in the polo coat weeping by the body of the
rector. The grand jury withdrew in mid-afternoon, returning in less
than an hour, as wild rumours began to race around the courthouse.

The jury brought back no indictments, a result that was an anticli-
max but not a surprise. If the authorities acquired new evidence within

the month they could present it to the same grand jury and seek a new indictment. But public opinion was veering strongly toward dropping the investigation, to avoid 'the expense of a trial that might end in easy acquittal'. Mott told reporters that for the time being investigators would remain 'in suspended animation', which wouldn't, on the evidence, have made much of a change.

The case had become such a debacle, said the *World*, that it had found its way into the debate over the Dyer Anti-Lynching Bill on Capitol Hill. It was clear to the entire nation that vigilante justice was being condoned in New Brunswick: even if the grand jury had indicted Mrs Hall and her relatives, 'there was not the remotest possibility of a conviction by a petit jury which would always see the unwritten law inscribed on the wall of the courtroom'. Gleefully attacking the New Jersey senator who was attempting to build a case against lynching, a Southern senator 'razzed' his colleague 'for the failure of the State of New Jersey to take action in the Hall–Mills case'.

**HALL-MILLS JURY REFUSES TO INDICT IN MURDER MYSTERY**

Does Not Call Rector's Widow, Who Keeps All-Day Vigil in Court House.

FUTURE OF CASE IS IN DOUBT

Foreman Gibb Says That Action by Present or Subsequent Jury Is Not Precluded.

"IN SUSPENDED ANIMATION"

Prosecutor Mott Thus Describes His Own Status and That of the Investigation.

The prosecution had entirely failed to construct a plausible explanation for the events of 14 September. The jury rejected the consoling, corrupted fictions offered by Jane Gibson and applauded when the vote was announced. Someone was going to have to improve the story, to lie better than the truth.

---

## EMPTY PARTY BOTTLES.

At the end of Chapter Six, Nick and Jay Gatsby walk out among the debris, a 'desolate path' of fruit rinds and discarded party favours and crushed flowers, exposing the waste and decay. Gatsby admits that Daisy didn't enjoy herself and Nick warns him against asking too much of her. 'You can't repeat the past,' he tells Gatsby. 'Can't repeat the past?' Gatsby cries incredulously. 'Why of course you can!'

Nick concludes that what Gatsby wanted to recover was 'some idea of himself perhaps, that had gone into loving Daisy'. As the waste begins to show, so does the projection, the solipsism of Gatsby's great devotion. It is single-minded, determined, in its way hugely creative; but it is also colossally self-absorbed. The chapter ends with Nick's first meditation on Gatsby's dream of Daisy, his feeling that he could climb to the top of the world, finding a Jacob's ladder to heaven (or a social ladder to riches) on the streets of Louisville 'if he climbed alone'. But Daisy is with him, and Gatsby succumbs to temptation, although he knows it will limit his dreams and possibilities: 'He knew that when he kissed this girl, and forever wed his unutterable visions to her perishable breath, his mind would never romp again like the mind of God.' He hears a sound as if a tuning fork has been struck against a star and kisses Daisy Fay, at which point 'the incarnation was complete'. He has entered the tender night, where, says Keats, the Queen-Moon is on her throne clustered around 'by all her starry Fays'.

Nick distances himself from this 'appalling sentimentality', but finds that he too is reminded of something by Gatsby's words, 'an elusive rhythm, a fragment of lost words, that I had heard somewhere a long time ago. For a moment a phrase tried to take shape in my mouth and my lips parted like a dumb man's, as though there was more struggling upon them than a wisp of startled air. But they made no sound and what I had almost remembered was uncommunicable forever.'

Five days after *The Great Gatsby* came out, Carl Van Vechten reviewed it for *The Nation*. What defined the novel, he felt, was the character of Jay Gatsby, 'who invented an entirely fictitious career for himself out of material derived from inferior romances . . . His doglike fidelity not only to his ideal but to his fictions, his incredibly cheap and curiously imitative imagination, awaken for him not only our interest and suffrage, but also a certain liking.' Van Vechten also singled out the novel's 'gargantuan drinking-party, conceived in a rowdy, hilarious, and highly titillating spirit'.

Van Vechten began his own novel about gargantuan drinking parties a few years later: *Parties* centres on the mutually destructive love of a couple named David and Rilda Westlake, who bear a striking resemblance to Scott and Zelda. He is the golden boy, a talented painter who charms everyone while he drinks himself into oblivion; she is his beautiful, desperate wife, alternately driving him to jealous rages and clinging to him. They constantly threaten each other with murder and suicide. The novel opens with David drunkenly arriving at a friend's apartment, announcing, 'I've killed a man or he's killed me.' Rilda soon rings, shouting that she has committed suicide. Before long she is sending telegrams declaring that she murdered her lover and so did their bootlegger. David goes to bed with various women, but tends to say venomous things like, 'I'll be too drunk to do *you* any good.' The story ends in a tale of violent stabbing and accidental death, but the Westlakes and their friends '"fix" the police', 'the newspapers with thin copy to go ahead on growled for a few days about "imminent investigations"' and 'the inquest was a farce'. Everyone gets off scot-free. When *Parties* came out in August 1930, it was met with 'filthy notices', recorded Van Vechten in his diaries. Even his devoted wife, Fania Marinoff, hated it.

In 1922, Fitz drew up a household budget that allotted eighty dollars a month to 'House Liquor' and one hundred to 'Wild Parties'. Not all parties were wild, of course. Rascoe wrote in 1924 of a story he'd heard from John Bishop, lately returned from two years in Europe. Bishop had attended a 'literary and artistic tea party' thrown in London by Lady Rothermere, to which she'd invited T. S. Eliot as guest of honour. An American guest, much impressed, asked Eliot if he didn't find the party extremely interesting. '"Yes," he'd replied, "if you concentrate on the essential horror of the thing."'

There is a reason why the word 'decadence' comes from the Latin for 'falling down'. All the sad young men were going to pieces, as Fitzgerald had told Rascoe that warm autumn night in 1922. Even in the midst of paradise, loss assumes a shape. *Et in arcadia ego*: beauty is not alone in the garden. Death is waiting there too.

# DECEMBER 1922

Only the dead dream fought on as the afternoon slipped away, trying to touch what was no longer tangible.

# VII. THE DAY IN NEW YORK

It was when curiosity about Gatsby was at its highest that the lights in his house failed to go on one Saturday night – and, as obscurely as it had begun, his career as Trimalchio was over. Only gradually did I become aware that the automobiles which turned expectantly into his drive stayed for just a minute and then drove sulkily away … the whole cara-vansary had fallen in like a card house at the disapproval in her eyes.

*The Great Gatsby*, Chapter 7

## ACCIDENT, NOT FATE.

Meaning can be salvaged from the wreckage of experience: accidents may reveal a pattern, a composition of sorts, if we look closely enough. It is only since the advent of cars that one meaning of the word 'acci-dent' has pushed itself to the front of the conversation so violently; accident has not lost its ability to mean chance, of course, although it tends now to mean mischance. But because the accidental also means the contingent, Catholic theologians used the word 'accidental' to describe the inessential bread and wine left behind after the ritual of communion had turned them into mystical symbols. At story's end, Gatsby finds himself left only with accidentals, the inessential objects that once had glittered for him, disenchanted things made ordinary again. The accidental is the merely material, once its mystical promises have been abandoned. It is no accident that Fitzgerald uses an accident – and the word 'accident', repeatedly – to bring about this turn in a carefully composed final three chapters about accidents and disenchantment, for the accidental is what we are left with once we have lost our illusions.

## The Importance of Being Thrilled

The December 1922 entry in Fitzgerald's ledger reads: 'A series of parties – the Boyds, Mary Blair, Chas & Kaly. Charlie Towne.' It is likely another of his retrospective entries, a hazy sense of parties blending

one into another. His memory of that December stretched out into a steady silvered roar, a catalogue of parties as a list of names. 'Nobody knew whose party it was,' Zelda wrote later. 'It had been going on for weeks. When you felt you couldn't survive another night, you went home and slept and when you got back, a new set of people had consecrated themselves to keeping it alive.' She took a picture of their Great Neck house in the snow and decorated it with spring flowers.

Scott and Zelda drew up a list of 'Rules For Guests At the Fitzgerald House':

1. Visitors may park their cars and children in the garage.
2. Visitors are requested not to break down doors in search of liquor, even when authorized to do so by their host and hostess.
3. Week-end guests are respectfully notified that the invitations to stay over Monday, issued by the host and hostess during the small hours of Sunday morning, must not be taken seriously.

Once the guests had arrived the rules of the Fitzgerald house were invoked. Everyone slept till noon – including the baby, whom, it was said, they used to slip some gin so she would sleep through the racket. Guests would pass out in the hammock in the backyard, or on the sofas and the floors; others wrote of hiding in the cellar to get away from the noise. More than once their houseman found both Fitzgeralds asleep on the front lawn when he awoke in the morning: by the time they left Long Island, Scott was said to have slept on every lawn from Great Neck to Port Washington. Zelda told an interviewer in 1923 that their meals at Gateway Drive were 'extremely moveable feasts', which sometimes seemed to mean moving away from the idea of providing food at all.

'The remarkable thing about the Fitzgeralds', Bunny Wilson later explained, 'was their capacity for carrying things off and carrying people away by their spontaneity, charm and good looks. They had a genius for imaginative improvisations.' Like Gatsby's ostentatious parties, the Fitzgeralds' parties were theatrical and spectacular – and it's no good being theatrical without an audience. A decade later Scott reminded Zelda that they had been 'the most envied couple' in America in the early 1920s. She replied, 'I guess so. We were awfully good showmen.' For Gatsby, the cost of being a showman is that audiences are indistinguishable from witnesses; he must end his career as Trimalchio when he needs to protect the secret of his affair with Daisy, to keep the servants from gossiping. As for the Fitzgeralds, Scott later wrote, 'we had retained an almost theatrical innocence by preferring the role of the observed to the observer'. Gatsby's ostentation is similarly innocent, although he prefers to observe its effects from the margins.

Zelda so enjoyed being observed that she continued to punctuate their parties with 'exhibitionism', to use the new psychoanalytic term. George Jean Nathan wrote in his memoirs years later of instances of Zelda 'divesting herself' of her clothes, once in the middle of Grand Central Station, he claimed, and another time standing on the railroad tracks in Birmingham, Alabama. According to Nathan, Scott told him that Zelda stood naked on the tracks, waving a lantern and bringing the train to a halt; 'Scott loved to recount the episode in a tone of rapturous admiration.' Nathan sounded testy when he wrote this account, but in the golden years he had written Zelda several notes in flirtatious admiration: 'Nothing about you ever fades,' he told her in April 1922, after seeing her in New York that March.

Nathan also claimed that during the planning of *Gatsby* Fitzgerald asked for his help in meeting various bootleggers upon whom he could model his 'fabulously rich Prohibition operator who lived luxuriously on Long Island'. And so, Nathan recalled, 'I accordingly took him to a house party on Long Island at which were gathered some of the more notorious speakeasy operators and their decorative girl friends.' One might have thought that Fitzgerald didn't require Nathan's assistance in meeting bootleggers and their clients on Long Island, but perhaps Nathan had his own underground pipeline. Or perhaps his memory was deceiving him.

Others were convinced that Fitzgerald's fondness for bourgeois revels was symptomatic of a more fundamental philistinism. Edmund Wilson's 1923 essay 'The Delegate from Great Neck' imagines Scott as a fledgling Rockefeller enthusiastically preaching the gospel of wealth:

Can't you imagine a man like [E. H.] Harriman or [James J.] Hill feeling a certain creative ecstasy as he piled up all that power? Think of being able to buy anything you wanted – houses, railroads, enormous industries! – dinners, automobiles, stunning clothes for your wife – clothes like nobody else in the world could wear! – all the finest paintings in Europe, all the books that had ever been written, in the most magnificent editions! Think of being able to give a stupendous house party that would go on for days and days, with everything that anybody could want to drink and a medical staff in attendance and the biggest jazz orchestras in the city alternating night and day! I must confess that I get a big kick out of all the glittering expensive things.

Wilson can't have been paying attention to such stories as 'The Diamond as Big as the Ritz', in which Fitzgerald had already shown his contempt for tycoons who clutched at glittering expensive things – even if he admired the glittering things themselves.

Wilson uses (an equally ventriloquized) Van Wyck Brooks in the essay to voice an older, more puritanical tradition in American letters; Wilson's Brooks fears that Fitzgerald and his generation are permitting 'art to become a business', surrendering to 'the competitive anarchy of American commercial enterprise', which would create only 'money and hollow popular reputations', bringing 'nothing but disillusion and despair'.

The fictional Fitz ends the dialogue by urging Brooks to come to a Great Neck party:

Maybe it would bore you to death – but we're having some people down who ought to be pretty amusing. Gloria Swanson's coming. And Sherwood Anderson and Dos Passos. And Marc Connelly and Dorothy Parker. And Rube Goldberg. And Ring Lardner will be there. You probably think some of those people are pretty lowbrow, but Ring Lardner, for instance, is really a very interesting fellow: he's really not just a popular writer: he's pretty morose about things. I'd like to have you meet him. There are going to be some dumb-bell friends of mine from the West but I don't believe you'd mind them – they're really darn nice. And then there's a man who sings a song called, *Who'll Bite your Neck When my Teeth are Gone?* Neither my wife nor I knows his name – but his song is one of the funniest things we've ever heard!

Wilson's portrait is deeply patronizing, his Fitzgerald little more than a buffoon, but it also suggests the cheerful exuberance with which his friend greeted the lunatic energy of the world around him. Wilson did not understand until much later – until it was, in a sense, too late – that another part of Fitzgerald was always standing aside, holding tight to a devout faith in art and viewing their debauchery with hard, cold eyes. Fitzgerald could see that materialism led to disillusion and despair, and debased ideals, as clearly as Wilson or Brooks. When he conceived of his fourth novelistic alter ego, Dick Diver in *Tender is the Night*, Fitzgerald called him a 'natural idealist, a spoiled priest' – not an indulged priest but a corrupted one, ruined by the glittering expensive things, the heat and the sweat and the life of the carnival he is running.

As it happens, Van Wyck Brooks offered his own memory of the Fitzgeralds, far less censorious than Wilson's imaginary debate. Brooks wrote of a dinner party at Ernest Boyd's apartment on East 19th Street, to which both Fitzgeralds arrived an hour late, after everyone had finished eating. Sitting at the dinner table, they 'fell asleep over the soup that was brought in, for they had spent the two previous nights at parties. So Scott Fitzgerald said as he awoke for a moment, while someone gathered Zelda up, with her bright cropped hair and diaphanous gown, and dropped her on a bed in a room near by. There she lay curled and asleep like a silky kitten. Scott slumbered in the living-room, waking up suddenly again to telephone an order for two cases of champagne, together with a fleet of taxis to take us to a night-club.'

At least one contemporary could see that Fitzgerald's gift for pleasure was not incommensurate with his gift for art. In 1924 Ernest Boyd wrote a book called *Portraits*, which included a depiction of Scott and Zelda. Fitzgerald told John Bishop that he rather liked Boyd's portrait of 'what I might ironically call our "private" life'. Scott Fitzgerald was 'a character out of his own fiction, and his life a series of chapters out of his own novels,' Boyd declared. 'Zelda Fitzgerald is the blonde flapper and her husband the blonde philosopher of the Jazz Age.' Here was a man who 'combines the most intellectual discussion with all the superficial appearances of the wildest conviviality ... He is intensely preoccupied with the eternal verities and the insoluble problems of this world. To discuss them while waiting for supper with Miss Gilda Gray is his privilege and his weakness.' Boyd may have seen Fitzgerald's love of glamour as a weakness, but it did not tempt him into underestimating the shrewdness of his views: Fitzgerald 'is one of the few frivolous people with whom one can be sure of having a serious conversation'. (In fact, history would prove, Fitzgerald was one of the few serious people who was capable of so much frivolity.) In particular, 'upon the theme of marital fidelity his eloquence has moved me to tears,' said Boyd, 'and his stern condemnation of the *mores* of bohemia would almost persuade a radical to become monogamous. There are still venial and mortal sins in his calendar.'

Fitzgerald's natural milieu was on Broadway, in the 'Roaring Forties' or in Harlem cabarets, Boyd continued; a typical night consisted of 'music by George Gershwin, under the baton and rhythmically swinging foot of Paul Whiteman; wines and spirits by special arrangement with the Revenue Department', followed by a wild drive back to Long Island in their second-hand red Rolls-Royce, 'the most autonomous automobile in New York'. After a night during which they wandered from cabarets like the Palais Royal to the Plantation Club, from the Rendezvous to Club Gallant, with many a detour en route, finally would commence a miraculous departure for Great Neck. Scott would pull out his chequebook 'for the writing of inexplicable autographs in the tragic moments immediately preceding his flight through the weary wastes of Long Island', and a madcap drive home would ensue. 'By an apparently magic, and certainly unexpected, turn of the hand', the car would suddenly swing round, 'dislodging various friends who have been chatting confidently to the occupants', while standing on the running boards. After summarily dispensing with extra passengers, Scott would begin the erratic journey back to Long Island. 'When it is a moral certainty that one is miles off the true course', Fitz would suddenly turn over the wheel to some passenger who had never driven a car before and climb into the back to join the sleeping party, confident that they'd be carried home. Eventually, after 'consulting' with various policemen who were willing to overlook the Volstead Act when presented with evidence of a fiduciary trust, the car would glide graciously to their front door in Great Neck.

Boyd ended his portrait of the Fitzgeralds by noting that after rising at midday, and finding some party to while away the afternoon, 'the evening mood gradually envelops Scott Fitzgerald'. Another 'party must be arranged. By the time dinner is over, the nostalgia of town is upon us once more. Zelda will drive the car.'

Glowing lights scintillate and vanish into the darkness. We are trying to find what Henry James called 'the visitable past', to revisit Babylon – but it isn't easy to discern the route to the lost city.

---

## NEW YORK IS CALLED A 'MODERN BABYLON'

Charlotte Mills announced on Friday 1 December that she was 'disgusted' by the prosecution's failure to bring anyone to trial for her mother's murder. A resourceful girl, she had decided to solve the mystery herself – by speaking to her mother's ghost. She had been inspired by recent press reports of Arthur Conan Doyle's experiments with séances and his well-publicized insistence that science supported his investigations. 'If what I read is true,' Charlotte explained, 'I shall certainly be able to communicate with my mother and learn the truth.' Unfortunately for Charlotte, what she read wasn't true, but she insisted that she would continue to 'fight for a real investigation'. A week later Conan Doyle wrote to the New York Times to protest against a large reward recently offered by Scientific American magazine for any proof of the claims made by spiritualists. Such a reward,

Conan Doyle argued, would 'stir up every rascal in the country', inciting fakers, frauds and publicity seekers.

That Sunday, a New Jersey minister preached about the Hall–Mills 'fiasco', inveighing against the widely held opinion that local citizens had 'put the question of expense ahead that of justice and the protection of society'. 'There is a trend,' the minister observed, 'toward a luxurious and vicious form of life, exceedingly wicked and corrupt, and the use of violent power to obtain advancement. This constitutes our modern Babylon and it will assuredly be destroyed as was the Babylon of old, not leaving a vestige of its greatness behind.' Their Babylon would disappear, it is true – but another would rise in its stead.

If revisiting Babylon is difficult, even visiting Babylon was a dangerous enterprise. On Tuesday 5 December 1922 the *Tribune* reported with palpable amusement that a monkey had been killed in the town of Babylon, Long Island, for 'hugging the postmaster's wife': a small monkey, which might have been the 'bootlegger's baboon' that had escaped and terrorized Babylon a few weeks earlier ('though those who saw the latter animal emphatically deny it'), was shot when it leapt into the open horse-drawn surrey of Mrs Samuel Powell. She was on her way to buy a goat when the monkey 'dropped right into Mrs Powell's lap and embraced her fervently'. Her passenger, Henry Kingsman, was an expert on goats, the reporter noted, but knew nothing about monkeys; however, as Mrs Powell screamed at Kingsman to help her he 'obediently detached the monkey and flung it to the road'. A hunter emerged from the side of the road, as if in a modern fairy tale. The hunter's 'specialty' was neither goats nor monkeys, but rabbits; however, 'being a somewhat less ethical savant than Mr Kingsman', the hunter aimed his gun and 'blazed away' at the monkey. 'The charge struck the monkey, and the monkey bit the dust.' The hunter refused to give his name to Mrs Powell, but he 'presented the defunct monkey to her', which it seems she kept as a souvenir. Mrs Powell drove home 'with a dead monkey and a live goat and an anecdote that will brighten the winter for Babylon'. The

*World* was also amused enough to share the story, hinting that the monkey might have been a victim of the unwritten law: 'A monkey was shot near Babylon, L.I. for hugging a married woman. Monkey business of this kind is always dangerous', as the murders of Hall and Mills had shown.

---

## DEEPENING THE MYSTERY.

Murder mysteries creep into Chapter Seven almost immediately. When Nick and Gatsby arrive together for lunch at the Buchanans' on the last day of the summer, Nick imagines that the butler roars at them from the pages of a detective novel: 'The master's body! ... I'm sorry Madame but we can't furnish it – it's far too hot to touch this noon!'

On this climactic day Daisy inadvertently reveals that she is in love with Gatsby by telling him how cool he always looks – Tom suddenly hears an inflection in her 'indiscreet voice', that voice full of money, and realizes that she and Gatsby have been having an affair. The realization sets the plot into motion and all five main characters drive into New York. Tom insists on driving Gatsby's yellow 'circus wagon' of a car and Gatsby grows angry, his anger as revealing as Tom's. Nick observes a look on Gatsby's face that he declines at first to characterize, but that he sees two more times before the episode is finished: 'an indefinable expression, at once definitely unfamiliar and vaguely recognizable, as if I had only heard it described in words'. Near the chapter's end Nick will finally tell us what it was: Gatsby looks like a killer.

Meanwhile Tom says repeatedly that he's been making an 'investigation' into Gatsby's affairs. Insisting that he's not as dumb as they think, he claims to have a kind of 'second sight' and begins to say that science has confirmed such phenomena, before realizing that he can't explain how. Abruptly abandoning another of his pseudoscientific theories (when 'the immediate contingency overtook him, pulled him back from the edge of the theoretical abyss'), Tom settles for repeating that he's been making an investigation, and Jordan jokes: 'Do you mean you've been to see a medium?' The jest merely confuses Tom, while Jordan and Nick laugh at the idea of Tom as a Conan Doyle using séances to solve the mystery of Gatsby's identity.

They stop for gas at the garage among the ash heaps, as grey, ineffectual Wilson emerges from the dark shadows of the story's margin. He looks sick, telling them as he gazes 'hollow-eyed' at the yellow car that he 'just got wised up to something funny the last two days' and wants to go west, the place of fresh starts and frontiers, along with his wife.

As Nick looks up and sees the giant eyes of T. J. Eckleburg keeping their composed vigil, he also notices another set of eyes, discomposed, peering out at their car from an upstairs window above Wilson's garage. It is Myrtle, and she too has 'a curiously familiar' expression on her face (her symmetry with Gatsby subtly recurring), an expression that seems 'purposeless and inexplicable' until Nick realizes that 'her eyes, wide with jealous terror, were fixed not on Tom but on Jordan Baker, whom she took to be his wife', as they drive off in their expensive car to New York. Scholars have asked why Nick finds this expression 'curiously familiar', and speculated that perhaps he recognizes it from the movies. But expressions are also phrases, and a woman with jealous terror in her eyes would be a curiously familiar expression to anyone who had been following the Hall–Mills case, as well.

When the party from Long Island arrives at the Plaza, Tom forces a confrontation over the affair by calling Gatsby's relationship with Daisy a 'presumptuous little flirtation'. The *Trimalchio* drafts are rather more explicit, as they often are: Nick says he and Jordan wanted to leave, for 'human sympathy has its curious limits and we were repelled by their self absorption, appalled by their conflicting desires. But we were called back by a look in Daisy's eyes which seemed to say: "You have a certain responsibility for all this too."' Nick's responsibility remains, but his acknowledgement disappears in the final version, an implication of his culpability to which he never admits.

It is as Gatsby grows more betrayed by Daisy's admission that she loves him 'too', instead of with the singular devotion he has brought to her, that Nick realizes Gatsby 'looked – and this is said in all contempt for the babbled slander of his garden – as if he had "killed a man." For a moment the set of his face could be described in just that fantastic way.' How murderous is Gatsby? Fitzgerald will not tell us, preferring to 'preserve the sense of mystery', as he later wrote in a letter, but he carefully makes the insinuation, even if it's a conditional one.

Daisy and Gatsby leave in Gatsby's car to return to Long Island, while Tom, Jordan and Nick drive the blue coupé back across the ash heaps. Nick suddenly remembers it is his thirtieth birthday and begins to reflect on ageing as they drive 'on toward death through the cooling twilight'. By placing this remark just after Nick's meditation on mortality, Fitzgerald cushions its barb. We may be lulled on first reading into thinking that they drive toward death in the general human sense, as if Tom's wheeled chariot hurries them toward it. But there are more imminent, and more violent, deaths waiting. When Daisy and Gatsby leave the hotel, Fitzgerald hints at what will come: 'They were gone, without a word, snapped out, made accidental, isolated like ghosts even from our pity.' People can become accidental, too, material accessories – in this case, to murder.

---

# THE PONZI LESSON.

During the first week of December 1922 a swindler named Charles Ponzi was making headlines across America. The 'get-rich-quick financier' and Boston-based 'exchange wizard' who'd promised his victims 50 per cent profit in forty-five days had two years earlier given his name to a particular form of financial fraud: a Ponzi scheme. Ponzi was indicted for one of the biggest swindles in American history, broken by the investigative journalism of the *New York Post*. Ponzi had been in jail since 1920; by early 1922, financial swindlers across the country were labelled a 'Chicago "Ponzi"' or an 'East Side "Ponzi"' as other 'Ponzi schemes' quickly followed in the press, and the nation exploded in protest at his willingness to help so many Americans try to get something for nothing. When the Ponzi story first broke in 1920, the *New York Times* ran an editorial on 'The Ponzi Lesson', a lesson America would spend the rest of the century forgetting.

While serving time, Ponzi continued to be arraigned for other aspects of his mail-order fraud: Massachusetts brought charges of larceny in 1922, putting Ponzi back in the news. When the latest trial began that autumn, the judge warned the jury 'against being swayed by popular clamor in reaching a verdict'. The public was still enraged and baying for more of the swindler's blood.

Ponzi declared during his trial that he hadn't kept a cent of his spoils, insisting that he had always believed his business was legitimate – thanks to the simple expedient of not enquiring into the law. 'I didn't go into the ethics of the question,' he said. 'I decided to borrow from the public and let the public share the profit I made ... I got my first returns in February [1920] and from that time it grew and grew as people got their returns. Each one brought ten others.' In the early months of 1920 Ponzi began by taking in two thousand dollars a day; by the end of the first month he was making two hundred thousand dollars a day – at least two million in today's money. On 2 December 1922 headlines across the country reported that Ponzi had been found not guilty of the additional charges and sent back to jail. Eventually he would be deported to Italy.

The big stories of the early 1920s were unforgettable, Burton Rascoe later wrote, for anyone who read the daily newspapers, whether the hysteria over Valentino's funeral or 'the Snyder–Gray and Hall–Mills murder cases'. Although early popular histories of the 1920s all relied upon 'the headlines of the more sensational stories in the press', this didn't mean that everyone actively participated in the scandals and fads of the era. But they all knew about them. 'I did not sit on a flag-pole, participate in a marathon dance ... try to get 1,000 per cent on an investment with the swindler Ponzi, nor did I know of anybody, personally, who did.' But everyone followed the scandals: everyone participated in them vicariously, and they were all busily speculating. The twenties were marked by speculation, Rascoe recalled, not just in finance, but as a way of life: 'the world seemed to have gone mad in a hectic frenzy of speculation and wild extravagance and I was interested in the phenomenon, especially since nearly all the other values of life had been engulfed by it. To retreat from it was to retreat from life itself.'

Ponzi was only the latest in a long line of American speculators, one article about him suggested. The rush to believe in Ponzi's promises of vast, easy wealth was no different from the California Gold Rush – or indeed from the discovery of America itself: 'get-rich-quick promises' had always lured 'venturesome souls ... from the days of Columbus, who sought a shorter route to the fabled wealth of the Indies, down to the days of Ponzi'.

---

## BEAUTIFUL, BUT IS IT ART!

On Monday 11 December 1922 Fitzgerald's agent, Harold Ober, received a story from Scott entitled 'Recklessness'. It was never published and, rather fittingly, may have been lost, but we can't be certain. It is possible that it changed its name to something more aristocratic.

The day before, the film version of *The Beautiful and Damned* opened in New York at the Strand Theater, a première which Scott and Zelda seem to have attended. Fitzgerald would have been in his dinner-coat, perhaps recollecting his objection to Scribner's illustration for the dust jacket of *The Beautiful and Damned*, which he had disliked. He told Perkins, 'The girl is excellent of course – it looks somewhat like Zelda. But the man, I suspect, is a sort of debauched edition of me.' It was a close enough copy to be recognizable, and a distorted enough copy to be distasteful. Fitzgerald complained that the illustrator had drawn the picture 'quite contrary to a detailed description of the hero in the book', for Anthony Patch was tall, and dark-haired, whereas 'this bartender on the cover is light haired ... He looks like a sawed-off young tough in his first dinner-coat.' Not unlike Jay Gatsby then, whom Jordan calls 'a regular tough underneath it all'.

The 'movieized' version of *The Beautiful and Damned*, as the papers described it, had received much advance publicity. Fitzgerald clipped

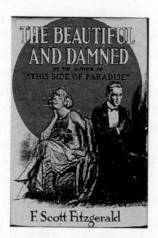

out a newspaper advertisement for the film ('Beginning Sunday'), as well as all the New York reviews – the *Tribune*, the *World*, the *Times*, and the New York *Review* – and saved them in his scrapbook.

The *Evening World* recommended the 'screenic version' – for its superficiality: 'We thoroughly believe that if you liked the book you will like the screen edition of this best seller because it does not delve quite so deep into flappers as one might suspect.' When the *World* reviewed the film in early 1923 it suggested that art was copying life: 'Quite a lot of the frenzy that is poured out of the silver cocktail shaker gets into this picture at the Strand. We have a suspicion that a good camera man could slip into the living room of a great many young homes around New York almost any Saturday night and grind out reproductions of several of its scenes from real life.' The novel 'merely presented a little bit of life as it is being lived by the sweet and carefree'. While 'not a profound picture play (if there is such a thing)', the review added, the film was 'interesting by virtue of its success in clinging closely to reality'.

Like so much else, the film has been lost, but another review Fitzgerald saved in his scrapbook gives a startling glimpse of the ending. At the conclusion of the novel, Anthony and Gloria Patch inherit a fortune, which is the final push over the edge into dissipation and damnation; they have been ruining themselves for some time, and Fitzgerald makes it clear that riches will complete their degradation. In the film, by contrast, the Patches were evidently redeemed by wealth. Their 'sudden wealth takes on a religious aspect', wrote *Life*. 'It serves to purge the hero and heroine of their manifold sins and wickednesses, and in the final subtitle, Anthony says, "Gloria, darling, from now I shall try to be worthy of our fortune and of you."' They should have changed the film's title to *The Beautiful and Blessed*, a sentiment more consonant with the simple faith that God must love rich people more.

Fitzgerald was not impressed. A day or two after seeing the film, he told the Kalmans: 'it's by *far* the worst movie I've ever seen in my life – cheap, vulgar, ill-constructed and shoddy. We were utterly ashamed of it.' He added buoyantly, and somewhat inconsistently, 'Tales of the Jazz Age has sold beautifully', closing the letter with a signature boxed in by a dotted line, so that it could be cut out as an autograph. It was a gag Fitzgerald enjoyed. He had sent a similar autograph to Burton Rascoe earlier in the year with the suggestion, 'clip for preservation on dotted line':

Fitzgerald would doubtless have been relieved to learn that the film of *The Beautiful and Damned* was lost: he clearly thought it less worth preserving than his signature. But he would have been delighted to know that he is the reason we feel its loss.

## AMERICA FINDS HER VOICE.

The winter's first serious snowstorm fell on Thursday 14 December, leaving three inches of crisp white snow all over the city and causing a sharp increase in traffic accidents. Careless drivers were not helped by the snow and icy rain that followed in its wake. 'That winter to me is a memory of endless telephone calls and of slipping and sliding over the snow between low white fences of Long Island, which means that we were running around a lot,' Zelda wrote in a story later.

The *Times* reported that on the same Thursday in December President Harding had told the Senate, 'When people fail in the national view-point and live in the confines of a community of selfishness and narrowness, the sun of this Republic will have passed its meridian, and our larger aspirations will shrivel in the approaching twilight.' It is possibly the only wise statement Harding made during his presidency – until he supposedly confessed just before he died under the pressure of the corruption scandals that engulfed his administration in the summer of 1923, 'I am not fit for this office and never should have been here.'

A new America was pushing its way up through the approaching twilight, mushrooming into life. In November, a New York woman had sued her daughter for injuries sustained in a car crash, testifying that 'her daughter was driving fast, and just before the accident she had cautioned her to drive more slowly'. The aptly named Mrs Gear was seeking fifty thousand dollars from her daughter as the price of ignoring a back-seat driver. A week later, a woman in Missouri successfully sued a railroad company for causing her to gain 215 pounds after, she claimed, an accident made her endocrine glands cease to function; she sought fifty thousand dollars and was awarded one thousand in damages. 'Gains Weight, Gets Damages,' jeered the *Times*. 'Missouri Woman Declared Railway Accident Trebled Her Avoirdupois.'

Two years earlier, an article in the *Times* feared that it saw 'American Civilization on the Brink', lamenting: 'As I watch the American Nation speeding gayly, with invincible optimism, down the road to destruction, I seem to be contemplating the greatest tragedy in the history of mankind.'

## WRITERS OF QUEER LETTERS ADD TO HALL CASE MYSTERY

While the temperature in New York continued to drop and winter settled in, the *Tribune* offered some thoughts on 'Murder and the Quiet Life'. Conclusions were beginning to be drawn – not about who had murdered Edward Hall and Eleanor Mills, but about the 'historic collisions' that produce the best stories. Recent public interest in the New Brunswick murder case had crossed class boundaries and made writers of everyone. No one was immune from guesswork, and the entire nation was absorbed in the case, speculating over the dinner table about who had committed the crimes. 'Everybody followed it. Persons of the palest, most rarefied refinement watched the divagations of the authorities and made shrewd guesses. The mystery maintained itself on the front pages for a length of time probably unparalleled, under similar circumstances, in the annals of newspaperdom ... A good mystery is, after all, a good mystery; which is to say that it embraces surprise, suspense, illusion; yea, reader, all the constituents of pure romance.'

The investigation into the New Brunswick murders was slowing down, but the nation was unwilling to relinquish the story. Without an official version, readers were writing their own endings. Thousands of people, 'shielded by the cloak of anonymity', had offered their theories and opinions about the case: 'probably never before in all the history of crime have so many letters been written'. Charlotte Mills decided to share them with the press.

One of her letters came from the ubiquitous John Sumner, of the Society for the Suppression of Vice, asking for information about 'certain books' her mother had read. Charlotte wouldn't tell reporters what her response had been, but shared Sumner's reply: 'I note what you say with reference to your mother having made quite a few criticisms on both books. These criticisms would be of interest if available. I am glad that you feel that such books never influenced your mother in any way. That is the way you should feel in the matter and indicates a degree of faith in the wisdom of your mother which would be fortunate if all young girls could feel.' Reserving judgement may be a matter of infinite hope, but Charlotte had some reason to have lost faith in the wisdom of her mother.

James Mills received a letter on the stationery of a 'leading' country club, demanding: 'Who said this country is a democracy? That's a lie! A country where money controls everything, even justice, the most sacred of human institutions, cannot be a true democracy! Isn't there anybody who has nerve enough and backbone enough to take a hand in this? . . . What about fingerprints? What a comedy throughout!' And a woman wrote to Charlotte: 'Imagine that doctor not reporting that your mother's throat was cut. My husband is a young conscientious doctor, and he says it is a crime the way some doctors are influenced.'

Under pressure, New Brunswick officials insisted that they were doing more 'than the public suspect'. Officers Lamb and Dickman had been replaced by New Jersey state police, who were 'conducting an investigation into New Brunswick's underworld'. New evidence had suggested they should 'delve into New Brunswick's lower social strata in their search for the murderer'.

Almost everyone had theories, Zelda later observed: that the Longacre Pharmacies carried the best gin in town; that anchovies sobered you up; that you could tell wood alcohol by the smell; that you would be drunk as the cosmos at the end of the night and discover that there were others besides the desk sergeant in the Central Park Police Station. Unfortunately, she added, none of her theories worked.

---

## POLICE SEEK DEATH CAR.

As Daisy and Gatsby drive home in the cooling twilight, Myrtle Wilson rushes out into the street and is struck down by the car that symbolizes Gatsby's wealth. Her thick, dark blood pools into the ashes and dust of the road; her breast is torn open and her mouth ripped, as if she died choking on her own vitality. She expires under the faded eyes of T. J. Eckleburg, the billboard her husband mistakes for God.

Nick is able to reconstruct what happened from the testimony in the newspapers, legitimating Fitzgerald's sudden shifts in perspective to what George Wilson's neighbour Michaelis observed at the ash heaps. Nick is now narrating as a reporter and so can tell us of things that he didn't see at first hand. The jump to Michaelis's point of view begins with the news that he was the 'principal witness at the inquest', suggesting that Nick reconstructs this account of George Wilson's movements from the inquest itself and from the newspapers' reports.

While Tom, Nick and Jordan were also driving back through the twilight toward Long Island, Wilson was telling Michaelis of his determination to take his wife west. Michaelis was astonished at Wilson's sudden vigour: 'Generally he was one of these worn-out men: when he wasn't working he sat on a chair in the doorway ... when anyone spoke to him he invariably laughed in an agreeable colorless way. He was his wife's man and not his own.' When Myrtle Wilson breaks out of the room where Wilson has locked her, she taunts him, daring him to stop her ('Throw me down and beat me, you dirty little coward!'), and rushes into the road as a car races toward her in the gloom. It doesn't stop, even after it's struck her down; newspapers called it 'the death car', Nick tells us. Michaelis is unsure of its colour, but thinks it might have been light green – the fateful inverse of Gatsby's hopeful green light.

On 8 December 1922, the *Evening World* reported after a hit-and-run killing in New York that 'the police have sent out a general alarm for the driver of the death car'. Given the number of accidents on the roads, newspaper reports of killings involving a 'death car' were all too common. It was becoming so familiar that there were jokes about it. *Town Topics* reported that the new motor-car would come 'with springs so perfectly adjusted that the occupants feel no discomfort when the car runs over a pedestrian'. In mid-November the New York police had sought another 'death car' after a reckless driver killed an officer; in July, a Mrs Mildred Thorsen had been killed by a 'death car' that continued at high speed after it ran over her. That summer the American papers all reported the sensational story of Clara Phillips, a Los Angeles woman who'd heard that her husband was having an affair with an acquaintance named Alberta Meadows. He was not: rumour had lied again. But Mrs Phillips believed the rumours and so she'd bashed in Alberta Meadows's head with a hammer. '"GOSSIP" REAL MURDERER OF MRS MEADOWS' shouted the *Evening World*. The victim had been found in a pool of blood in her own car; it was promptly labelled 'the death car'.

When Tom, Jordan and Nick return to the Buchanans' after discovering Myrtle's body, Nick encounters Gatsby, lurking outside the house. Under the misapprehension that Gatsby was driving the car that killed Myrtle, Nick half expects to see Wolfshiem's thugs lurking in the shrubbery. But then Nick guesses the truth: the death car was driven by a woman. Daisy is the culprit; devoted Gatsby is watching over her to ensure that Tom doesn't try 'any brutality'. Nick goes back to the house, where he sees Daisy and Tom by the window, talking urgently: 'there was an unmistakable air of natural intimacy about the picture and anybody would have said that they were conspiring together'. Nick leaves them to their conspiracy, and Gatsby stays all night at his sacred vigil, still hoping.

Commit No Murders
on These Premises.

This Means YOU.

On the cold, dry, bright day of Saturday 16 December the *World* ran a satirical feature on modern murder, in which a fictional character – who owes a debt to Ring Lardner's collection of semi-literate rustics and jazzy rude mechanicals – opines on the wide gap between the unrealistic competence of fictional 'detecatives' and the incompetence of real ones: 'The Government might just so well issue shooting licenses for bootleggers and declare open seasons on rectors in Jersey, because the way it is now, murder ain't a crime in this country. It's a sport.' In fact, the character suggested, 'if they want to make an arrest in a case like this here New Jersey murder', they should 'arrest the witnesses, the widow, the executors and the owner of the property where the crime was committed upon the ground that he failed to put up a notice reading: "Commit No Murders on These Premises. This Means YOU."'

Having been mined for all it was worth, the rich vein of the Hall–Mills story seemed to be petering out. Mrs Gibson was still panning for gold, however. She announced that she wanted to make a new statement 'supplementing her former story', but the prosecutor declined to meet her. A private investigator claimed to have found new eyewitnesses, but readers around America scoffed loudly at the idea that yet another person might have witnessed the murders. 'If they could just get the fellow who sold the tickets to that affair, they might find out something,' quipped the *Cleveland Plain Dealer*, a joke that was picked up around the country.

Meanwhile a justice in the New Jersey Supreme Court announced that there was no longer any reason for haste in pursuing the investigation, offering a masterful summation of the facts: 'The crime was committed. It did not commit itself. The murderer is still unpunished ... But in my judgment anything like fervid haste to discover the criminal seems now no longer to exist,' said the *Times*. (The *World* quoted him as saying 'fevered haste', which seems more likely; either way, he was in no rush to solve the murders.) 'There is nothing mysterious in the fact that the murderer has not been caught,' insisted Justice Parker. 'Sometimes they are never discovered and often it has taken years to find them.' He then comfortingly listed a number of recent unsolved murder cases to bolster his argument in defence of the New Jersey justice system.

# TRIAL  IS· HIGHBALL  EPIC

As 1922 drew to a close, yet another farcical trial was under way, eight miles from Great Neck. That summer, the actress and singer Reine Davies had held a party at her weekend house on Long Island. During the party a prosperous contractor named Wally Hirsch was shot in the face; the force of the blast knocked his false teeth out of his mouth. The teeth were admitted into evidence when the state accused Hirsch's wife Hazel of attempted murder.

The story had made headlines in June and not only because of its macabre comedy. Celebrity played its role, too, for Reine Davies was the sister of the movie star Marion Davies. Reine Davies had already featured in another trial that January, when she was thrown from her car on Long Island after a collision, and sought half a million dollars in damages from the other driver for head injuries she'd sustained when she almost hit a cow.

## Reine Davies Nearly Hit Cow When ˈHurled From Auto, Says Sheriff.

A constable was 'leading a cow near where the collision happened' and 'Miss Davies narrowly missed hitting the cow when she was thrown out'. The constable 'dropped the cow's leash, put on his badge, and charged [Davies'] chauffeur with driving recklessly'. Davies was awarded $12,500 in damages for her hazardous encounter with nineteenth-century arcadia.

That summer Davies made headlines again for the party she'd thrown in her 'rathskellar' (basement bar). Although her famous sister had not attended, their magistrate father had, seeming untroubled by the bibulous atmosphere. As the party was ending guests heard shots. Hirsch was found sitting on a bench outside, drunk and dazed, shot in the face. His wife, running away, began screaming that he made her do it before throwing herself on the ground and drumming her heels hysterically.

Witnesses testified that Hirsch shouted that his wife had shot him, adding that he called her 'an offensive name', which the papers declined to reprint. Davies's 'negro chauffeur', however, claimed that Hirsch said someone named 'Luke McLuke' shot him. When the police arrived, Hirsch told them the same thing, 'that Luke McLuke shot him'. They found an automatic and followed a bloody trail from the pistol to the porch, encountering 'three sections of false teeth' along the way. Two officers testified that Hirsch told them 'Luke McLuke, or something like that, shot him'; 'the State then put the teeth in evidence, on the ground that they had been shot out of Hirsch's mouth'.

'Luke McLuke' was the pen name of popular syndicated humorist S. J. Hastings, and 'Luke McGlook, the Bush League Bearcat', also spelled Luke McGluke, was a popular cartoon using the semi-literate baseball humour popularized by Ring Lardner. In 1923 Fitzgerald was interviewed by *Picture-Play* magazine, and used an imaginary person called 'Minnie McGluke' to represent filmmakers' idea of the average moviegoer: 'This "Minnie McGluke" stands for the audience to them who must be pleased and treated by and to pictures which only Minnie McGluke will care for.' To blame Luke McLuke, in other words, was to blame everyone and no one, as if claiming that Hirsch had been shot by John Doe.

When Hirsch and his wife sobered up, both insisted she would never have shot him; perhaps she found him holding a gun and tried to wrestle it from him, but neither could remember what happened. At the trial, witnesses testified that Hirsch had drunk at least twenty whiskys, snatching cocktails from other guests (who still sounded aggrieved six months later). Everyone was too drunk to remember what happened and Hazel was acquitted.

The *World* was highly amused, saying that if the story had a 'moist beginning', it had 'a very wet ending': both Hirsches 'sobbed together and separately' upon hearing the verdict. Witnesses described Reine

Davies's party in such a way as 'to create a thirst even in a hardened Volsteadian': Davies had 'a regular bar, tended faultlessly by a "professional bartender" who dispensed Scotch whisky, highballs, cocktails and beer while a Negro orchestra added jazz'. The reporter sounded distinctly envious. Even the comparatively staid *New York Times* called the story a 'Highball Epic'.

Reine Davies's sister Marion lived with William Randolph Hearst – the man who, in four years' time, would initiate the final phase of the Hall–Mills murder investigation.

---

# WANT TRUER HISTORY BOOKS

American writers including Fitzgerald, Wilson, Rascoe, Boyd and Bishop had been energetically debating the status of American letters throughout 1922. Van Wyck Brooks wrote, 'Our literature seemed to me, in D. H. Lawrence's phrase, "a disarray of falling stars coming to naught."' In the spring of that year Wilson had observed: 'Things are always beginning in America. We are always on the verge of great adventures . . . History seems to lie before us instead of behind.' Americans' sense of defensive inferiority in regards to European culture was diminishing. Industrial economic might was booming; the arts could not be far behind. 'Culture follows money,' Fitzgerald wrote to Wilson in the summer of 1921, during his and Zelda's first trip to Europe. 'You may have spoken in jest about N.Y. as the capitol of culture but in 25 years it will be just as London is now. Culture follows money & all the refinements of aestheticism can't stave off its change of seat (Christ! what a metaphor). We will be the Romans in the next generation as the English are now.' As usual, Fitz was guessing right. That autumn he wrote, 'Your time will come, New York, fifty years, sixty. Apollo's head is peering crazily, in new colors that our generation will never live to know, over the tip of the next century.'

By the end of 1922, it seemed to many that American culture was consolidating its position. On Christmas Eve, Rascoe reported that a friend recently returned from abroad had found the English 'terribly keen about American literature', 'eager to hear all about it, read it and discuss it'. In particular, he'd been surprised to find the English 'less snobbish than the Americans'. At home social distinctions ruled, but in England he'd found that just writing 'An American' on his card meant he was asked everywhere. He'd been impressed by such democratic egalitarianism, but in *Gatsby* Fitzgerald suggested another, far more cynical, reason for the warm welcome Americans were receiving in postwar Europe. Scattered among Gatsby's parties are a number of Englishmen, 'all well dressed, all looking a little hungry and all talking in low earnest voices to solid and prosperous Americans. I was sure that they were selling something: bonds or insurance or automobiles. They were, at least, agonizingly aware of the easy money in the vicinity and convinced that it was theirs for a few words in the right key.'

Liking American money was one thing, liking American literature another. After a trip to Britain that summer, Ernest Boyd told Rascoe: 'They don't know whether to begin to regard American literature seriously and they are much upset about it … anxious to be reassured that American literature is a joke, so they won't have to bother about reading it.' And many British writers remained unshakeably confident in their inherent right to determine the language: Hugh Walpole read Carl Sandburg's Chicago poems, and complained: 'If this fellow Sandburg will use slang why will he not endeavour to be just a bit more comprehensible. He speaks here, for instance, of an engine's being "switched" when he might just as easily have used "shunted."' American slang was so incomprehensible that British editions of Sinclair Lewis's *Babbitt* were being printed with a helpful glossary, including:

Darn — puritanical euphemism for the word damn.
Gee — puritanical euphemism for God.

Guy — fellow.

Heck — familiar for Hecuba, a New England deity.

Highball — tot of whiskey.

Hootch — drink.

Jeans — trousers.

Junk — rubbish.

Liberal — label of would-be broadminded American.

Lounge-lizard — man hanging about in hotel lobbies for dancing and also flirting.

Mucker — an opportunist whose grammar is bad.

To pan — to condemn.

Peach of a — splendid.

To root for — to back for support.

Roughneck — antithesis of highbrow.

Slick — smart.

Spill — declamatory talk.

Tux — Middle-western for Tuxedo, American for dinner jacket.

Weisenheimer — well-informed man of the world.

The errors in translation must have been a source of much amusement to American readers; within a few years, no definitions would be required for jeans, junk or tux. The American century was at hand, and America was getting ready for a revolution in literature. By 1930 America would see the publication of Ernest Hemingway's *The Sun Also Rises* and *A Farewell to Arms*, John Dos Passos's *Manhattan Transfer*, the plays of Eugene O'Neill, the works of Langston Hughes and the other writers of the Harlem Renaissance, and William Faulkner's *The Sound and the Fury*, among others.

The endless conversations about the validity of American art necessarily also begged the question of what defined America. Discovering an authentic American literature requires knowing what is authentically American, and American history was similarly accelerating its production. 'America is a hustling nation even in accumulating a history,' wrote the *New York Times* that same Christmas Eve in 1922. 'The story of our national life [recently] seemed to be almost pitifully small compared with the ample and anciently rooted histories of European countries. But we have been making up for lost time at a great rate.'

Accelerating the 'speed production' of American history also inevitably accelerated debates over the truths of that history. Appalled to find American textbooks teaching a version of American history they considered untrue, veterans of the Great War announced in December that they would seek elimination of 'un-American ideals' from schools. One way to pretend to define authentic Americanism is by the simple expedient of labelling other things 'un-American'. Thirty years later, America would poison itself in the futile effort to stop 'un-American activities'. For now, self-appointed guardians of American culture were urging the revision of American textbooks, to expunge 'foreign propaganda', although no one elaborated upon what this dangerous propaganda actually said. A committee was formed 'with a view to eliminating propaganda and to see that the histories teach nothing but American ideals'. Foreign values are propaganda, but American values are ideals. 'Want truer history books', the veterans' committee insisted. Don't we all.

---

## The Raw Material of History.

For Christmas 1922, Ring Lardner sent a poem to Zelda that reads in part:

> Of all the girls for whom I care,
> And there are quite a number,
> None can compare with Zelda Sayre,
> Now wedded to a plumber.

> I read the World, I read the Sun,
> The Tribune and the Herald,
> But of all the papers, there is none
> Like Mrs Scott Fitzgerald.

The poem also made reference to other Great Neck couples, including the Farmer Foxes, who figure more than once in Scott's ledger and in the Fitzgeralds' later correspondence. 'In Great Neck there was always disorder and quarrels: about the Golf Club, about the Foxes, about Peggy Weber, about Helen Buck, about everything. We went to the Rumseys, and that awful night at the Mackeys when Ring sat in the cloakroom.'

The Mackays were an immensely wealthy family with an estate in nearby Roslyn, Long Island. Fitzgerald's ledger records a party there in June 1923; Zelda saved an invitation from the Mackays for Sunday 8 July 1923. Clarence H. Mackay's daughter Ellin was a famous heiress who rejected her debutante lifestyle, and in 1926 shocked the nation and her family by marrying a Jewish immigrant, fifteen years her senior, named Irving Berlin, the most famous composer in America. Her Catholic father threatened to disinherit Ellin, but they were reconciled some years later; as fate would have it, Irving Berlin would bail out his father-in-law during the Great Depression. Within twenty years, people in 'the show business' were buying up the older American aristocracy.

In 'My Lost City', Fitzgerald uses Ellin Mackay's marriage as a milestone that defined the twenties' union of high and low culture. By 1920, 'there was already the tall white city of today, already the feverish activity of the boom', he wrote, but 'society and the native arts had not mingled – Ellin Mackay was not yet married to Irving Berlin'. But then over the next two years, 'just for a moment, the "younger generation" idea became a fusion of many elements in New York life . . . The blending of the bright, gay, vigorous elements began then . . . If this society produced the cocktail party, it also evolved Park Avenue wit, and for the first time an educated European could envisage a trip to New York as something more amusing than a gold trek into a formalized Australian bush.'

Why Ring Lardner hid in the cloakroom at the Mackays' estate one summer night has been lost to history, however.

Five years later, Lardner sent the Fitzgeralds another Christmas poem:

> We combed Fifth Avenue this last month
> A hundred times if we combed it onth,
> In search of something we thought would do
> To give to a person as nice as you.
> We had no trouble selecting gifts
> For the Ogden Armors and Louie Sifts,
> The Otto Kahns and the George E. Bakers,
> The Munns and the Rodman Wanamakers
> It's a simple matter to pick things out
> For people one isn't wild about,
> But you, you wonderful pal and friend, you!
> We couldn't find anything fit to send you.

The following Christmas, Scott responded in kind:

> You combed Third Avenue last year
> For some small gift that was not too dear,
> – Like a candy cane or a worn out truss –
> To give to a loving friend like us
> You'd found gold eggs for such wealthy hicks
> As the Edsell Fords and the Pittsburgh Fricks,
> The Andy Mellons, the Teddy Shonts,
> The Coleman T. and Pierre duPonts.
> But not one gift to brighten our hoem
> – So I'm sending you back your Goddamn poem.

It seems the Fitzgeralds spent Christmas Day 1922 in Great Neck; Zelda wrote to Xandra Kalman in early January saying they'd had 'astounding holidays' which began 'about a week before

Christmas' and didn't end until 5 January, when she was writing her letter.

If Fitzgerald managed to read the book section of the *New York Times* that Christmas weekend, he would have seen an editorial on fiction writing and the facts, as he mused over his new novel: although 'fiction writers have emancipated themselves from many restraints, as to both form and content', they still had to come up with their own plots. 'They are, of course, at liberty to use so much material from real life as can be incorporated without danger of libel; but such material needs so much working over before it can become plausible fiction that it entails about as much effort as inventing plots offhand.'

What if invention is not a question of effort, however, but of meaning? When *The Great Gatsby* was reissued in 1934, Fitzgerald wrote a preface, saying that he had never tried to 'keep his artistic conscience as pure' as during the ten months he spent writing the novel in 1924. 'Reading it over one can see how it could have been improved – yet without feeling guilty of any discrepancy from the truth, as far as I saw it; truth or rather *equivalent* of the truth, the attempt at honesty of imagination. I had just re-read Conrad's preface to *The Nigger* [*of the "Narcissus"*], and I had recently been kidded half hay-wire by critics who felt that my material was such as to preclude all dealing with mature persons in a mature world. But, my God! it was my material, and it was all I had to deal with.'

The aim of art, wrote Conrad in the preface, is 'by the power of the written word, to make you hear, to make you feel – it is, before all, to make you see ... If I succeed, you shall find there according to your deserts: encouragement, consolation, fear, charm – all you demand; and, perhaps, also that glimpse of truth for which you have forgotten to ask.'

Fitzgerald often had this passage in mind as he wrote; in 1923, he quoted it in a letter: 'As Conrad says in his famous preface, "to make you hear, to make you feel, above all to make you see ..."' He had reread the preface again as he wrote *Gatsby*. Fitzgerald was thinking about his materials, what he had to work with, as he tried to offer a glimpse of the truth for which his audience had forgotten to ask. Critics told him that his material was inessential, scarcely created – but facts are always merely material, until someone shines what Conrad called a light of magic suggestiveness on them. When he sailed for France in 1924, Fitzgerald had decided that his project would be to 'take the Long Island atmosphere that I had familiarly breathed and materialize it beneath unfamiliar skies'. He materialized it, made it material and made it real – and then he made it matter.

By the time he wrote 'How to Waste Material – A Note on My Generation' in 1926, Fitzgerald had begun to think of a writer's material as capital; later he said that he'd made 'strong draughts on Zelda's and my common store of material'. Their life together was like a joint bank account, upon which only one of them could afford to draw. But thinking about his life as capital for art proved a dangerous business. As Fitzgerald, of all people, should have understood, Mammon is a treacherous god. 'There is no materialist like the artist,' wrote Zelda later, 'asking back from life the double and the wastage and the cost on what he puts out in emotional usury. People were banking in gods those years.'

The sculptor Théophile Gautier once said that his sculptures became more beautiful if he used a material that resists being sculpted – marble, onyx or enamel. The same may be true for writers, sculpting their own resistant material, struggling to release the angel from the rock. Near the end of his life, Fitzgerald wrote that once he had believed that his writing should 'dig up the relevant, the essential, and especially the dramatic and glamorous from whatever life is around. I used to think that my sensory impression of the world came from outside. I used to believe that it was as objective as blue skies or a piece of music. Now I know it was within, and emphatically cherish what little is left.' He no longer thought that his material was capital, but that his artistry was – and he had wasted it.

# USED AUTO TO KILL A SUPPOSED ROBBER

### Gillen Admits He Ran Down Man Who Blocked His Road Near Mackay Estate.

---

### HIS STORY IS ACCEPTED

---

### District Attorney Is Satisfied With Explanation of Puzzling Death.

---

Christmas over, the *New York Times* reported in late December 1922 that 'the puzzling death' of Phillip Carberry, a car salesman 'whose bruised body was found on the road near the Clarence H. Mackay estate', was solved the day after Christmas. A man named Lester J. Gillen admitted 'he had run down a man standing in the road, presumably Carberry, in the belief that he was a robber who was trying to hold him up'. So he had accelerated and deliberately run him over. The district attorney 'indicated his satisfaction' with the story, reported the *Times*. Gillen explained that he and his passenger 'did not stop, because we believed our lives in danger', and that seemed to be sufficient justification for running Carberry over.

In March 1924 Fitzgerald published an article about young people in America, in which he noted that a rich young American 'thinks that when he is arrested for running his car 60 miles an hour he can always get out of trouble by handing his captor a large enough bill – and he knows that even if he has the bad luck to run over someone when he's drunk, his father will buy off the family and keep him out of jail'. He seems to have had good reason for drawing this conclusion.

When George Wilson begins to mutter that his wife was deliberately run down in the road by the gaudy yellow Rolls-Royce, Michaelis tells him, 'You're morbid, George . . . This has been a strain to you and you don't know what you're saying.' George repeats, 'He murdered her.'

'It was an accident, George.'

Wilson shook his head. His eyes narrowed and his mouth widened slightly with the ghost of a superior 'Hm!'

'I know,' he said definitely, 'I'm one of these trusting fellas and I don't think any harm to nobody, but when I get to know a thing I know it. It was the man in that car. She ran out to speak to him and he wouldn't stop.'

Michaelis had seen this too but it hadn't occurred to him that there was any special significance in it.

Maybe George isn't nourishing morbid pleasures, or deluded, after all. Perhaps he has just been reading the papers, and begins to see special significance where others don't.

Wilson tells Michaelis that when he got 'wised up' to Myrtle's affair, he'd marched her over to the window, where they could see the pale, enormous eyes of T. J. Eckleburg staring down at them, and confronted her with her guilt: 'I told her she might fool me but she couldn't fool God. I took her to the window . . . I said, "God knows what you've been doing, everything you've been doing. You may fool me but you can't fool God!"' 'God sees everything,' Wilson adds.

'That's an advertisement,' Michaelis assures him.

---

# NOSTALGIA.

Burton Rascoe declared in December 1922 that nostalgia 'is one of the oldest of fallacies'. Even Aristotle, he pointed out, was lamenting that the 'the theater is no longer what it used to be, that standards are being trodden upon, that the rabble is being catered to'. And so, in forty more years, Rascoe predicted, perhaps 'Scott Fitzgerald will be flooding his whiskers with tears of sorrow over the decline of morals since the Jazz Age.' Such a prospect was not so 'chimerical' as some might think, he insisted. The Fitzgeralds had already begun their holiday celebrations by the time the article appeared, which may account for Fitzgerald missing this mention: it is not in his scrapbooks.

As *The Great Gatsby* draws to a close, Nick Carraway remembers returning home to the Midwest for Christmas from his schools in the east. In Chicago, he changed trains for St Paul. 'When we pulled out into the winter night and the real snow, our snow, began to stretch out beside us and twinkle against the windows, and the dim lights of small Wisconsin stations moved by, a sharp wild brace came suddenly into the air. We drew in deep breaths of it as we walked back from dinner through the cold vestibules, unutterably aware of our identity with this country for one strange hour before we melted indistinguishably into it again.'

'That's my Middle West,' Nick says, 'not the wheat or the prairies or the lost Swede towns but the thrilling, returning trains of my youth and the street lamps and sleigh bells in the frosty dark and the shadows of holly wreaths thrown by lighted windows on the snow.' The thrill is in the return. This requiem to the dark fields of the snowy republic is the moment when *The Great Gatsby* begins to converge with the emotion that drives the great Gatsby and destroys him: nostalgia, the wistful longing to recapture the past, the expelled Adam seeking a route back into Paradise. A nation so fixed on progress will always be pulled, Nick begins to see, back into nostalgia, reaching for what lies ahead yet longing for what lies behind. This is what it means to be American, Nick concludes: to sense our identity with this country even as we lose our place in it. Before we even grasp it, it is gone, leaving us buffeted by a deep wave of nostalgia, rippling through us like the cold night air. If its faith in progress represents America's hope in the future, then nostalgia is its hope in the past.

For all its sparkling modernism, *The Great Gatsby* is coloured with nostalgia, peopled with characters carrying well-forgotten dreams from age to age. Although Gatsby is more driven by nostalgia than anyone else, he is by no means the novel's only nostalgic character. Even Tom wistfully seeks 'the dramatic turbulence of some irrecoverable football game'. Only thoroughly modern Jordan is immune to it.

Fitzgerald never became a whiskered old man, although he certainly managed some pungent remarks on the decline of standards as he grew older. In 1940 he sternly wrote to his daughter about her projected course of study at Vassar. He hated to see her spend tuition fees 'on a course like "English Prose since 1800"', he told her. 'Anybody that can't read modern English prose by themselves is subnormal – and you know it.'

To Scott Fitzgerald's contemporaries he was the voice of the eternal present, but now he is the voice of nostalgic glamour: lost hope, lost possibility, lost paradise. Rascoe guessed right, but for all the wrong reasons: Fitzgerald would become the American twentieth century's greatest elegist. Nostalgia is a species of faith. 'Like all your stories there was something haunting to remember,' Zelda told Scott later, 'about the loneliness of keeping Faiths.'

Gatsby is left at the end of the chapter, watching over nothing. Dawn breaks jaggedly, like a crack in a plate.

# JANUARY 1923–
# DECEMBER 1924

One night I did hear a material car there and saw its lights stop at his front steps. But I didn't investigate. Probably it was some final guest who had been away at the ends of the earth and didn't know the party was over.

# VIII. THE MURDER (INV.)

I couldn't sleep all night; a fog-horn was groaning incessantly on the Sound, and I tossed half-sick between grotesque reality and savage frightening dreams. Toward dawn I heard a taxi go up Gatsby's drive and immediately I jumped out of bed and began to dress – I felt that I had something to tell him, something to warn him about and morning would be too late. Crossing his lawn I saw that his front door was still open and he was leaning against a table in the hall, heavy with dejection or sleep. 'Nothing happened,' he said wanly. 'I waited, and about four o'clock she came to the window and stood there for a minute and then turned out the light' ... It was this night that he told me the strange story of his youth with Dan Cody – told it to me because 'Jay Gatsby' had broken up like glass against Tom's hard malice and the long secret extravaganza was played out.

*The Great Gatsby*, Chapter 8

## MEMORIES OF THE FUTURE

It was most likely at the end of 1922 that Fitzgerald found a newspaper offering him a 'Flappy New Year': 'To Scott Fitzgerald, flapper king / A Flappy New Year do I sing.' He preserved the tiny clipping in his scrapbook, but as usual didn't bother to note its origins – and yet it mattered enough to save the floating scrap, yellowed now and darkening like old champagne.

> II.
> To Scott Fitzgerald, flapper king,
> A Flappy New Year do I sing.

Fitzgerald wrote to his agent on the last working day of the year that he didn't think his new novel, still unnamed, would be suitable for serialization, which suggests it was starting to take shape in his mind, if not yet on the page. Meanwhile Zelda saved two snapshots of herself in the snow at Gateway Drive, sitting down and laughing, and then, standing in her ankle-length dress, dissolving into the past:

Burton Rascoe observed on New Year's Eve: 'Life is not dramatic; only art is that. Life is melodramatic, with elements of low comedy relief; and to be a good journalist, a good reporter, one must recognize this truth.' A good reporter was one who could 'see events in a cynical, cool light as a spectacle, amusing, pathetic, ephemeral – as ephemeral as last year's great murder mystery'. Fitzgerald saw the melodramatic, amusing, pathetic spectacle around him, but he bathed it in the warm glow of lost ideals, rather than in a cool, cynical light. Last year's murder mystery proved ephemeral, but the art in which it entangled itself would endure.

A long article about the end of 1922 by the renowned writer and progressive William Allen White appeared in the *Tribune* just after Rascoe's review. Famous for an 1896 editorial entitled 'What's the Matter with Kansas?', White was widely perceived by the early 1920s as a spokesman for Middle America; he would win the Pulitzer Prize in 1923. 'For America,' White began, 1922 'has produced prosperity, which, according to our outward religion, is the chief aim of man'. But White was among those who were unconvinced that its faith in business, the religion of success, would take America forward. As for faith in progress, 'it may be a great delusion', the great progressive spokesman admitted. 'Perhaps all this fidgeting that we call change is circular, and not forward; maybe the twilight's purple rim toward which we are going is only a vicious circle and we are getting nowhere.' He had a point.

White's faith in progress was not quite as shaken as he thought, however, for he did have one confident prediction for 1923: 'we realize now that we have been asleep while the grafters and boodlers and amiable agents of special privilege have been taking the shingles off the roof and the stones out of the foundation of the Republic'. But America had awakened to the ways it was being dismantled, and that was one change White was certain would come: the nation would no longer acquiesce to special interests. In the brave new world of the twentieth century, Americans would unite against entitlement and crony capitalism; special privilege would be stamped out, corruption halted.

Instead, the Teapot Dome Scandal was about to burst forth, bringing down the Harding administration as widespread graft, bribery and fraud were revealed. Within eight months Harding would be dead and the vicious circle would continue spinning. 'The new world couldn't possibly be presented without bumping the old out of the way,' wrote Fitzgerald later – but the new world tends to look peculiarly like the old.

Scott and Zelda spent that New Year's Eve at what she considered a 'dull party'; Zelda livened it up 'by throwing everybody's hat into a centre bowl-shaped light. It was very exhilarating.' On 3 January John Dos Passos held an exhibition of his paintings in Greenwich Village, jotting on his invitation to the Fitzgeralds: 'Come and bring a lot of drunks.' Two days later, the beaming Fitz pitched up at Famous Players Studios, in Astoria, to watch the filming of Edith Wharton's *Glimpses of the Moon*, directed by Allan Dwan. Scott had been paid five hundred dollars to write film titles that were never used; he saved a clipping that said the titles had been rejected for being 'too flippant'. As the year turned, Zelda was amazed to find that they had been in Great Neck for only three months: 'it seems so much longer'.

Two weeks later Carl Van Vechten went to a literary party at Theodore Dreiser's with Ernest Boyd; Burton Rascoe was there too. The gathering became legendary, recorded by many of those present and repeated in biographies ever since. Its fame, Rascoe said, arose because of its 'abject failure': Dreiser neglected to provide his guests with alcohol. As they all sat in a semicircle, 'gazing with disconsolate incredulity at a table covered with bottles of near-beer', Boyd reported, Scott Fitzgerald suddenly walked in, a trifle 'dazed', clutching bottles of champagne in either hand. He was late, he explained, because it had been difficult to locate the champagne: 'it had taken him much time, going from speakeasy to speakeasy, and in his colloquies with the bartenders in each as to where he might pick up a good bottle of vintage wine, he acquired quite an edge'. Fitzgerald presented his tribute to the older writer, who took the champagne from Fitzgerald and carefully put it in his refrigerator, to the outrage of all his guests.

---

# Voyage of Discovery

Although Gatsby's dead dream fights on as the story draws to an end, even he must confront the dismal truth that Daisy and Tom will stay together. Every other couple will be destroyed or divided, but old money survives intact, untouched and untouchable. Trying to hang on to the shreds of his illusions, Gatsby tells Nick the morning after Myrtle dies of his romance with Daisy, and we begin to understand that Daisy represents more than a love affair: Gatsby's romance is with a way of life. Daisy's house enchants Gatsby first, and he knows he is in it 'by a colossal accident'. This is presumably why he is so determined for her to see his house in West Egg. He wants to fix the accidental into destiny, make the material transcendent: 'There was a ripe mystery about it, a hint of bedrooms upstairs more beautiful and cool than other bedrooms, of gay and radiant activities taking place through its corridors and of romances that were not musty and laid away already in lavender but fresh and breathing and redolent of this year's shining motor cars and of dances whose flowers were scarcely withered.'

A few months earlier, the *Times* had noted that 'Scott Fitzgerald and his contemporaries' thought they inhabited a world in which 'passion is the fashion'. That may be true, remarked the journalist, 'but it is fashionable only as Rolls-Royces and ermine coats are fashionable. Aspiration is general, capacity is limited.'

------

# THE DISINTEGRATING PARTY

Some time in the future, looking back on his twenty-sixth year as it stretched from his birthday in September 1922 to August 1923, Fitzgerald scribbled a summary on the top of his ledger page: 'The repression breaks out. A comfortable but dangerous and deteriorating year at Great Neck. No ground under our feet.'

The series of parties strewn across December 1922 would dissipate rapidly into a longer series of parties across 1923, recorded in Fitzgerald's ledger, interspersed with many brief hops onto the wagon and long falls off of it, and punctuated by brawls: 'February: Still drunk ... March: Kalmans in New York. Party with the Boyds. Bunny marries. April: Third anniversary. On the wagon. Joined club here. Party with Barthelmess – another fight. Tearing drunk. May: Met Mrs Rumsey & Tommy Hitchcock & went to parties there ... Fight with Helen Buck's brother-in-law. June: Party at Clarence Mackays. Began my novel. Squabble at Ring's. Party in New York with Mencken and Nathan.' Drunkenness floated across the months, making it harder for Fitz to date his memories accurately: still drunk, tearing drunk, roaring drunk.

He began to feel, too, as if his popularity was waning. In New York, he suddenly found, 'we were no longer important. The flapper, upon whose activities the popularity of my first books was based, had become passé by 1923 – anyhow in the East.' He was accused of racketeering his signature, as they called it. In March, *Town Topics* sniped, 'As a boy and youth Fitzgerald was always ready to give to those that were older than himself the full benefit of his inexperience, and as a grown-up he has not changed his spots, they say. The only difference seems to be that instead of talking gratuitously, he now sells his opinions for many shekels.' Scott was probably annoyed by the criticism – but not annoyed enough to keep from preserving it, unattributed, in his scrapbook.

Their epic drinking sprees meant that over these months he was on average writing only about a hundred words a day, he would realize with horror at the end of the year. One Thursday in June, Zelda sent a letter to the Kalmans, who had visited New York, apologizing for missing their friends: she and Scott had been drunk for an entire week, like Owl-Eyes without a library to sober him up. 'Dearest and Most Colossal Eggs (as my husband would say),' Zelda wrote. 'First of all I feel perfectly awful about not seeing you on Monday – or whatever day it was. Everything beginning Friday and ending today has lost itself in the dimness and shadiness of my past and the Gregorian Calendar has lost all significance to me.' After a weekend in 'regions unmentionable because unknown', Zelda had received a message to call the Kalmans at the Ritz. She 'had some faint difficulty with the clerk', because she was so drunk: 'I'm not sure that I told my right name but if I did, did you get word?' She and Scott were berating themselves for missing their friends, she added: 'but Scott now has a flash of clairvoyance and informs me that I rode out of your room in a laundry wagon – and that Sandy became very high hat about it – so maybe you hope you will never see us again'. The letter concludes with twenty-two-year-old Zelda's insouciant remark: 'O well! – I was young once.'

A month later, Zelda told the Kalmans that they were turning over a new leaf, as Scott had started his third novel at last, 'and retired into strict seclusion and celibacy. He's horribly intent on it and has built up a beautiful legend about himself which corresponds somewhat to the old fable about the ant & the grasshopper. *Me* being the grasshopper.' Great Neck was 'razzle-dazzling a hundred fold' in the heat of the summer: 'all the pools and even the Sound reek of gin, whiskey and beer, to say nothing of light wines. I am afraid to say we have moved to a place of very ill repute.'

Before they knew it the summer of 1923 had drifted past, and Scott's resolution to work on his novel in strict sobriety had gone the way of prior grand resolves. 'It was an exquisite summer and it became a habit with many world-weary New Yorkers to pass their week-ends at the Fitzgerald house in the country. Along near the end of a balmy and insidious August I realized with a shock that only three chapters of my novel were done,' he said. 'We drank always,' Zelda remembered, 'and finally came to France because there were always too many people in the house.' Fitz told Ring Lardner that they left New York because people seemed to think their home in Great Neck was a roadhouse, a quip that Burton Rascoe repeated in his column, and which perhaps Scott was remembering when he had Nick initially dismiss Gatsby as 'simply the proprietor of an elaborate roadhouse next door'.

At one of their Great Neck house parties that summer, a friend of Zelda's found a large roll of cash casually stuffed in the door of their Rolls and forgotten. Anita Loos, whose *Gentlemen Prefer Blondes* would be a bestseller the year after *Gatsby* appeared, joined them one day at the Plaza, where Fitzgerald was so drunk the waiter refused to serve them. That seemed no reason for him not to drive home, however, so they piled into the car, waving bottles of warm champagne in the air as they wended their way back to Great Neck, where they ordered cocktails from the servants. A woman suddenly showed up at the door, who seemed to be making a play for Scott; he got rid of her, but Zelda made a remark and soon it deteriorated into a shouting match. Scott swept all the china off the table in a rage; the women daintily picked their way across the broken fragments on the floor and had coffee in the living room, while Scott passed out under a tree outside. When Anita Loos told the story years later she said they had run across to Ring Lardner's house for safety, which would have been a long run. None of their stories was losing anything in the telling. At midnight on 9 July, Scott and Zelda joined a party with Burton Rascoe, during which 'Fitzgerald showed us some card tricks he had learned from Edmund Wilson, Jr.,' Rascoe reported, and 'told us the plot of "the great American novel" which he is just writing (and asked me not to give it away)'. If only Rascoe had given it away, we might know more about how Fitzgerald's conception of the great American novel changed over the course of the fifteen months that he worked on it.

Reading Fitzgerald's ledger, it is difficult to see how he completed as many as three chapter drafts that summer: 'July: Tootsie [Zelda's sister Rosalind] arrived. Intermittent work on novel. Constant drinking. Some golf. Baby begins to talk. Party at Allan Dwan's. Gloria Swanson and the movie crowd. Our party for Tootsie. The Perkins arrive. I drive into the lake. August: Tootsie again. More drinking.' And so on, through the opening and disastrous tryout of *The Vegetable* in Atlantic City that November, to December: 'Still on the wagon. Fell off Xmas. Party Goldberg. Deterioration.' In the wake of *The Vegetable*'s humiliating failure, Fitzgerald settled down at last to some serious work on short fiction to earn some money. Meanwhile, Zelda wrote to the Kalmans, 'Ring is drinking himself to an embalmed state so he'll be all ready for the grim reaper. I don't think he'll have long to wait, if he keeps on. His wife is worried sick. At Atlantic City he was certainly the man about town at Evelyn Nesbit's café. She doesn't take dope any more. Isn't that too sweet of her?' In his 'Short Autobiography' for the *New Yorker* in 1929, Scott wrote that 1923 consisted solely of 'oceans of Canadian Ale with R. Lardner in Great Neck, Long Island'.

On 14 December, Burton Rascoe correctly guessed that an anonymous *Vanity Fair* sketch he'd seen called 'The Invasion of the Sanctuary' had been written by Scott Fitzgerald, and took the opportunity to accuse Fitzgerald of superficiality: 'he has a saving quality of wit, malice and fantastic drollery,' Rascoe observed bitingly; 'otherwise his books would be Robert W. Chambers all over again, only not so well written'.

Robert W. Chambers's romances of the 'delightful idle rich' epitomized vacuous, sentimental fictions of high society; Chambers was generally dismissed, said the *New York Times* in 1921, 'as a creator of a cheap type of fiction, a sort of housemaid's delight'. Fitzgerald's earliest books had been compared to Chambers with infuriating regularity: *This Side of Paradise*, *Flappers and Philosophers* and *The Beautiful and Damned* had all been likened to Chambers by various reviewers, often more than once. A book serialized in *Cosmopolitan* in the autumn of 1922 had been belittled by its reviewer as 'Just one more great wealth-and-high-society novel. The Chambers formula, not the Fitzgerald one.' At least someone could tell the difference; Fitzgerald saved the clipping in his scrapbook. He would not have been pleased by Rascoe's jibe.

The Fitzgeralds spent their last Christmas in Great Neck throwing another house party, which Bunny Wilson described to John Bishop: 'Scott's play went so badly on the road that it was taken off before it got to New York, thereby causing them a great deal of chagrin. Since then, Fitz has entered upon a period of sobriety of unexampled duration, writing great quantities of short stories for the popular magazines. He is also doing a new novel. Esther Murphy, [Gilbert] Seldes, Dos Passos, Mary [Blair Wilson] and I had Christmas dinner with them at Great Neck. I like Zelda better and better every year and they are among the only people now that I'm always glad to see.'

One Wednesday afternoon in late January 1924, Carl Van Vechten was home working ('not very hard'), when Scott phoned up. He was at Ernest Boyd's apartment: 'I went over there,' wrote Van Vechten, '& found him & Zelda with Ernest, later Madeleine. Cocktails ...' The midweek afternoon deliquesces into an ellipsis that says it all.

Their months in Great Neck began to melt away behind them. 'There were many changing friends,' wrote Zelda of Long Island, 'and the same old drinks and glamour and story swept their lives up into the dim vaults of lobbies and stations until, as one said, *evenements* accumulated. It might have been Nemesis incubating.' They thought Bacchus was presiding over the festivities, until Nemesis appeared – the retributive goddess whom the Romans aptly called Invidia. Nothing would survive but the stories, the tales of a quest for lasting pleasure, which left a trace of beauty: the disarray of falling stars didn't come to naught after all.

---

# UNSOLVED MURDER MYSTERIES ELUDE POLICE LIKE SPECTRES

As 1923 passed, the murders of Hall and Mills drifted away from America's collective attention. Memory is as unreliable as narration, and there was always a new story. But every now and then the ghosts returned to haunt the nation's press and its readers, a spectral reminder that justice was being undone.

In April 1923 the *New York Times* reviewed the story of the Hall–Mills murders in the context of several other recent, unsolved homicides, including Joseph Browne Elwell, who was found shot in a locked room without a gun, and William Desmond Taylor. 'No detective story ever written,' the article declared, 'had more to excite the imagination than such cases as the Elwell and the Hall–Mills mysteries. Day after day for months on end they appeared on the front pages of the newspapers. They were read as detective stories are read – the thrills outweighing the horror. But the concluding chapters are missing.' Before it finished, the article brought readers up to date on Jane Gibson: the 'picturesque pig woman' was appearing 'with Jenny her mule in a circus, profiting by the publicity the Hall–Mills case brought her'. A month later, the investigation showed faint signs of life, as detectives turned their attention to a 'certain man who was questioned early in the case and who at the time gave what was then considered a satisfactory alibi. His manner, too, convinced us he was clear.' Now they were less convinced. But Mrs Gibson had been thoroughly discredited: 'it is probable,' surmised an investigator brilliantly, that the Pig Woman had been 'inspired by a desire to make some money out of the murders. She sold her story to newspapers, received money for posing for photographs, and lately capitalized her alleged connection with the case by appearing with her mule at a carnival in New York.'

James Mills swiftly responded to these reports, 'bitterly' complaining 'I know who they're driving at when they talk about alibis.' Feeling that suspicion was shifting to him, he reiterated his story: 'My wife left the house that night at 7.30, refusing to tell me where she was going and saying that I'd have to follow her if I wanted to find out her destination.' He stayed home until 'late at night', he said, 'not leaving the house until I went to the church to look for my wife in the early morning. The murder hour has been placed at around 9.30. At that time I was in the house and I can prove it by two witnesses, a man I work with and a woman neighbor. The man saw me in the house at 8 o'clock. The woman told the detectives the last time she saw me was 10 o'clock and I was in the house.' She also saw him in the house at 8.30, he claimed. 'And if anybody had come to the door after that they would have found me in.' Only they hadn't.

Four months later, the first anniversary of the murders was noted, but there was little to report. Mrs Hall had gone abroad; her brother Willie had recently returned to the Hall home from a sojourn in Florida and spent his days running from fire station to fire station, hoping for a conflagration. Louise Geist, the Halls' servant 'and an attractive figure in the case', had married. Charlotte Mills had graduated from high school and was eager to turn eighteen, complaining of her father's refusal to allow her to accept a vaudeville agent's offer for $750 a week, 'just to show yourself on the stage without singing or saying a word'. She would go on stage as soon as she was legally independent, if the offer still stood, she said.

All tragedy, Fitzgerald had written in *This Side of Paradise*, has that strain of the grotesque and squalid – so useless, so futile.

---

## Self-Made Man Is a Myth

After Myrtle's death, Nick and Gatsby talk as dawn arrives in his strangely dusty mansion. It seems even emptier than usual, as if it is hollowing out from the inside, like the dreams it symbolizes. Images of ghosts drift in: Nick stumbles on the keys of a 'ghostly' piano, and as the sun rises 'ghostly birds' begin to sing among the blue leaves. Gatsby is 'clutching at some last hope', Nick realizes, but 'I couldn't bear to shake him free.' It is at this point that Gatsby finally tells Nick the truth about his humble origins.

Much of Gatsby's masquerade had come about by accident. Although he believed that life should be a splendid pageant, he had not started out with claims of 'phantom millions'. When he met Daisy he thought only to deceive her in the most commonplace way, letting her believe that he came from the same social stratum as she, so that he could seduce her. He had intended, 'unscrupulously', to take what he could from her under false pretences and leave. But then the story turns, and it is Gatsby who feels betrayed and abandoned when she vanishes back into her rich life after they sleep together. He feels married to her, and his intense fidelity means that such a spiritual union can never be dissolved.

Gatsby hangs suspended between chasing the future and longing for the past: the present means nothing to him. But Daisy is defined by the present. She needs immediacy, for she dwells in the shallows of time, drifting unrestfully and without purpose from moment to moment. And Daisy is very young: she was eighteen when they fell in love, twenty-three when the action of *Gatsby* takes place. As she was trying to wait for Gatsby to return from Europe after the war, Tom Buchanan arrived in Louisville, a present force 'of love, of money, of unquestionable practicality': 'doubtless there was a certain struggle and a certain relief'. Daisy marries Tom; the choice is made. Gatsby will spend the rest of his life in the futile effort to unmake it, to reverse time and put himself in Tom's place. And so upon returning to America after the war he built a fortune unscrupulously, to win Daisy back, to make a fresh start.

But just as he thinks he has achieved his dream of Daisy and the aristocratic life she represents, his hopes are brought crashing down by the real aristocrat, her husband. The illusion of 'Jay Gatsby' shatters like glass against Tom's hard malice, arrogance, and social power, his insistence that Gatsby will remain Mr Nobody from Nowhere. And so 'the long secret extravaganza was played out'.

Gatsby's tale ends with a journey he took back to Louisville while Daisy was on her honeymoon, his attempt to relocate the past in the place where it was located, the magical thinking of relativity that space and time are conjoined after all: 'He stretched out his hand desperately as if to snatch only a wisp of air, to save a fragment of the spot that she had made lovely for him. But it was all going by too fast now for his blurred eyes and he knew that he had lost that part of it, the freshest and the best, forever.' He will never recover it, but he will never stop trying.

---

## LEAVING NEW YORK BEHIND.

In May 1924 the Fitzgeralds sailed for Europe, to put the temptations of the new world behind them, with the conviction that they had left their old selves behind forever. Along with their seventeen pieces of luggage and *Encyclopedia Britannica*, the Fitzgeralds carried with them the true dream of America: that if you go to a different place, you can become a different person, that identity is just an accident.

Their voyage was 'a weird trip', Zelda said, haunted by tunes including 'Horsey, Keep Your Tail Up, Keep the Sun Out of My Eyes'. Fitzgerald sent a telegram from the ship to Max Perkins, introducing him to a young English actor named Leslie Howard, whom they had befriended in Great Neck and who would become world-famous when he played Ashley Wilkes in *Gone with the Wind*. Howard was a 'great friend of mine', Fitzgerald told his editor, and 'has a considerable writing talent'. On board there was 'nearly a scandal about Bunny Burgess', Zelda recalled, an incident memorable enough that both Scott and Zelda continued to refer to it, without ever explaining it. In his ledger for May Scott noted: 'Sailed. Bunny Burgess. The Captain's table'; later, in his notebooks, he remembered 'Bunny Burgess episode of glass and wife'. It's not clear who the wife in the episode was: the passenger list for the *Minnewaska* suggests that Frederick Burgess, a Long Island stockbroker, sailed alone, perhaps to join his wife Olive, who was in Paris that summer. The wife in the near-scandal on board the *Minnewaska* may well have been Scott's.

At Cherbourg they caught a boat train promising to carry them to Paris in around seven hours. They stayed at the Hôtel des Deux Mondes, where they hired a nurse for Scottie at twenty-six dollars a month ('my God!' Fitzgerald told a friend, 'we paid $90 in New York'). They bathed Scottie in the bidet, and when she drank a gin fizz thinking it was lemonade, the two-year-old 'ruined the luncheon table next day'. Nevertheless, Zelda wrote to Perkins triumphantly that their stay in Paris was 'a complete success': they'd 'found a good nurse and resisted the various temptations that beset our path – to some extent – '.

While in Paris they saw some old friends including John Peale Bishop, and probably met Sara and Gerald Murphy, whose sister

Esther they'd partied with during the previous Christmas at Great Neck. The Murphys planned to summer on the Côte d'Azur; the Fitzgeralds decided to go there too. In Paris they 'boarded the train for the Riviera, the hot, sweet South of France', meandering down through a profusion of colour, blending hues and shadows to Provence, 'where people do not need to see unless they are looking for the nightingale'.

They stopped first at Hyères, the oldest resort on the Riviera, 'the loveliest piece of earth I've ever seen without excepting Oxford or Venice or Princeton or anywhere', Fitzgerald wrote to a friend. 'Zelda and I are sitting in the cafe l'Universe writing letters (it is 10:30 P.M.) and the moon is an absolutely *au fait* Mediterranean moon with a blurred silver linen cap & we're both a little tight and very happily drunk.' They were 'going to look at a villa that has a butler & cook with it for the summer & fall ... on the whole it looks like a gorgeous working summer'.

Zelda said that Scott was revealing 'the most romantic proclivities' on the Riviera, reading nothing but lives of Byron and Shelley. She feared he might even drown in the Mediterranean, she joked: 'I shall be obligated to snatch a heart from a burning body – which I should hate.' The villas they saw at Hyères were unsuitable – too impractical for Zelda to run (she said), too unromantic for Scott to write (he said), or too expensive, and the aptly named Grimm's Park Hotel appeared to have nothing but goat on the menu.

So they made their way to St Raphaël, where they rented the Villa Marie, and Scott finally settled down into writing his novel. For Zelda, whiling away curving Provençal hours as Scott remembered jazzy New York, the afternoons grew 'long and still and full of a consciousness of night long before evening falls'. Days began to stretch in front of her, hot and empty. 'What can I do with myself?' Alabama wonders restlessly in *Save Me the Waltz* when she finds herself on the Riviera; soon she is blaming her artist husband 'for the monotony'.

In the nearby town of Fréjus was an air base, and Zelda befriended a group of young French aviators. They danced, gambled and drank in a beach casino; as evening fell the Fitzgeralds would wander through the dusty pink twilight to join the flyers. René Silvé and Bobbé Croirier were 'very nice boys', Zelda wrote, perhaps hinting that they were more interested in each other than in her. They 'protruded insistently from their white beach clothes and talked in undertones of Arthur Rimbaud'. René had eyes of 'cold fire', as if painted by Tintoretto. An officer named Edouard Jozan had the 'head of the gold of a Christmas coin', with 'broad bronze hands' and 'convex shoulders'; he was 'slim and strong and rigid' in his dazzling white uniform.

During the days Zelda relaxed with her aviators on canvas mats stretched over the sand. Scott was pleased that Zelda was occupied; Zelda was pleased that she was the centre of attention again. The flyers flirted with her, flattered her and kept her company while her husband brooded over his memories of Long Island. On the beach 'we warmed our sunburned backs and invented new cocktails,' she recalled; their avant-garde cocktails do not survive.

In July, Scott took a quick break from his novel to compose 'How to Live on Practically Nothing A Year', which earned some fast money from the *Saturday Evening Post*. Describing expatriate life in France, he wrote of keeping up with the news from home by means of the *New York Times*. 'It is twilight as I write this,' he ended; as the sun set, the people around him, 'like the heavy roses and the nightingales in the pines, will seem to take an essential and indivisible part in the beauty of this proud gay land'. Becoming a stranger had prompted Fitzgerald to think more consciously about national identity, what it meant to be from one land or another, as he watched people melt indistinguishably into the background that absorbed them.

As his novel progressed, Fitzgerald had changed its title, but not its theme. It would still concern the arrivistes among New York's ash heaps and millionaires, but now he thought he would call it 'Trimalchio'. Zelda didn't like the new title, but Scott's confidence in the book was growing; his prose was deepening, tightening, stretching.

They swam in hope like the midnight-dark sea, buoyed by good fortune. It seemed that life was a simple affair after all. They were not just happy once, he wrote; they were happy a thousand times.

---

## TWO RICH STUDENTS CONFESS TO KILLING FRANKS BOY IN CAR

America's front pages were consumed that summer with the sensational story of two intelligent, well-educated young men from Chicago named Nathan Leopold and Richard Loeb, who murdered a boy they knew merely 'for the thrill of it', convinced that their high IQs would enable them to commit the perfect crime. They were mistaken: having left a trail of evidence implicating themselves, they quickly confessed. Leopold and Loeb demonstrated the 'perils of precocity', it was felt: intelligence-testing had been much debated for several years, and Leopold and Loeb reminded experts that precocity 'often leads to perversion'. The prosecution charged that the pair's murderous 'phantasies' came from a book. Loeb reportedly announced: 'I have money; my people have money; don't you suppose we will have a smart lawyer to get us out?' Leopold and Loeb had overweening confidence in their own brilliance, but perhaps they also had reason to doubt the intelligence of those who would be assigned to investigate their crimes.

Fitzgerald followed the story avidly; a year later he was writing to Perkins that, after *Gatsby*, his next novel would be about 'several things, one of which is an intellectual murder on the Leopold–Loeb idea. Incidentally it is about Zelda and me and the hysteria of last May and June [1924] in Paris.' If not about Leopold and Loeb, he told Harold Ober, his next novel might concern 'such a case' as Dorothy Ellingson, 'that girl who shot her mother on the Pacific coast last year'.

The novel that would eventually become *Tender is the Night* went through many permutations, but for some years it was about a headline murder case. As he continued to mull over tabloid murders, Fitzgerald wrote a story called 'Jacob's Ladder' that would feed into *Tender is the Night*. It opens with 'a particularly sordid and degraded murder trial', a case that makes the protagonist feel 'he had childishly gobbled something without being hungry, simply because it was there. The newspapers had humanized the case, made a cheap, neat problem play out of an affair of the jungle.'

In late June headlines blared that Leopold and Loeb had been found guilty of murder; turning the pages of the *New York Times*, a reader would also have been confronted with a reminder of another brutal murder that had recently dominated the nation's news.

## HALL-MILLS CASE RECALLED

### Woman Who Was a Witness Beaten, Another Is Arrested.
#### *Special to The New York Times.*

Mrs Jane Gibson, 'the "pig woman" in the Hall–Mills murder mystery at New Brunswick', had been found 'badly beaten', and Nellie Russell, 'the negro woman who contradicted Mrs Gibson's story' at the time of the murder investigation, had been arrested and charged with 'atrocious assault'. 'The two women have quarreled many times since the murder case made them widely known characters'; this time, in a dispute over a horse, Russell 'attacked' Mrs Gibson, throwing her to the ground and knocking out four teeth. 'Hall–Mills Case Recalled,' noted the small headline. It didn't take much to recall the case for anyone who had lived through its grotesquerie.

# FITZGERALD CONFOUNDS THE GOSSIPS

The summer burned on as Fitzgerald wrote. Keeping it brief, condensed, lyrical, he forced the novel through draft after draft. He was reading Byron and Milton, a biography of Shelley in French, and he was always reading Keats. Poetry mingled in his head with the cynical slang of modern America. That spring, just before they sailed, Fitzgerald had explained to a magazine editor that *The Beautiful and Damned* had been led astray by the literary theories of H. L. Mencken: 'I am so anxious for people to see my new novel which is a new thinking out of the idea of illusion (an idea which I suppose will dominate my more serious stuff) much more mature and much more romantic than This Side of Paradise. The B&D was a better book than the first but it was a false lead . . . a concession to Mencken . . . The business of creating illusion is much more to my taste and my talent.'

While Scott consorted with the New York ghosts who haunted him, Zelda concentrated on the present. Alone with his manuscript over the phantom wash of the Mediterranean, Scott did not notice that Zelda and the aviator Edouard Jozan were becoming closer; but everyone else on the Riviera did. Rumour began to quicken and race, as her oblivious husband remained lost in the pages of his novel.

But oblivion, like love, can't be trusted to last forever. 'The Big Crisis' came on 13 July, Scott wrote in his ledger. Two weeks after the papers recalled the Hall–Mills case, matters appear to have come to a head over Zelda's feelings for Jozan. Stories differ, as they always do. Some say that Zelda asked Fitzgerald for a divorce, telling him that she wanted to chase her chance for happiness; others that Scott confronted her and demanded that she end whatever was happening. Gossip has been speculating about what exactly that was ever since. Zelda's romance with Jozan may have been a serious affair, or as insubstantial as a flirtation and a moonlight kiss. But it is clear that for Scott and Zelda, the affair, whatever its particulars, was deeply damaging; Zelda genuinely cared for Jozan, it seems, and Scott did not forgive easily.

But it's also true that the Fitzgeralds enjoyed being protagonists in a melodrama, still preferring the role of the observed to the observer. Zelda wrote to Bunny Wilson that summer that she felt 'picturesque', and her pleasure would only be complete if it gave rise to gossip back home: 'Everything would be perfect if there was somebody here who would be sure to spread the tale of our idyllic existence around New York.' By the end of the summer, she'd shown that Scott wasn't the only one who could create a story. They both told others later that Fitzgerald had locked Zelda in her room over the Jozan affair, in some versions for as long as a month.

After the 'Big Crisis', Fitzgerald's ledger notes a 'sad trip to Monte Carlo' in July. He also recorded, cryptically, 'Wire Olive Burgess', but whether the wire was to her or from her, or why it was worth remembering, he doesn't say. He kept an undated letter from Olive Burgess, written on Paris hotel stationery, among his papers. 'Dear Mr Fitzgerald,' she wrote, 'Can you come to see me tomorrow at my hotel? I can arrange any time that suits you. Please don't mention even to the members of your household that you are calling on "Bunny Burgess' wife" – I sound exactly like a shilling shocker – I'm sorry. It's rather important to you. Would you telephone or send me a line today, so I can know when you're coming? Cordially, Olive Moore Burgess.' The nature of the clandestine matter that was so important to Scott Fitzgerald was as lost as what Bunny Burgess did with a glass and someone's wife, but it's tempting to guess.

Meanwhile, Scott continued to note trips and parties over the summer of 1924 in his ledger. The Fitzgeralds went to Monte Carlo, gave at least one dinner and went down the coast to Sainte-Maxime more than once. 'Zelda swimming every day. Getting brown,' he observed prosaically later in July. They went often to Antibes to visit the Murphys, and Fitzgerald read drafts of his work in progress to John Dos Passos, Donald Ogden Stewart and Gilbert Seldes, who were all on the Riviera. Scott lists more dinner parties – it's not easy to see when they might have fit the month of Zelda's incarceration into their busy social schedules.

Looking back, Fitzgerald remembered 'the going to the Riviera' in his notebooks. 'The table at Villa Marie ... The aviation field. The garden in the morning. The Seldes. Night in St. Maxime. Feeling of proxy in passion strange encouragement. He was sorry, knowing how she would pay. Bunny Burgess episode.' Adultery seems to be the line that connects the dots: in May 1926 Olive would divorce Bunny Burgess in Paris, and remarry within months. Fitzgerald's entry is so gnomic that we can only guess what he meant, but it is at least possible that what he felt as a proxy in passion was a strange encouragement to translate his feelings into the proxy characters of fiction.

'I've been unhappy but my work hasn't suffered from it,' Fitzgerald wrote to Perkins when his novel was finished. It was true: he had suffered, but the book hadn't. Indeed, his suffering probably improved it. The flippancy that had jarred in his first two novels was entirely in abeyance in the third: it is threaded throughout with satirical, wry humour, but there is nothing light-hearted in the novel concerned with the tragic consequences of misplaced fidelity, about a man who is destroyed by the colossal vitality of the illusion that has sustained him.

Life is always there waiting to be transfigured into a splendid fiction, however sad or sordid its origins. A story of adultery ends in the violent extinction of a woman of tremendous vitality. A dreamer keeps faith with the faithless, and a double shooting draws closer in the cooling twilight, as the writer tries to determine whether what he holds in his hand is the past, or the future.

---

## PROXY PLOT.

As Nick returns to Long Island after an abortive day trying to sell stocks on Wall Street, and an even more abortive conversation with Jordan Baker, who tells him that she's left the Buchanans' house and complains that Nick wasn't nice to her after Myrtle was run over, the commuter train takes him past the ash heaps. The accident is already being turned into a story for gawkers and thrill-seekers, he imagines: 'there'd be a curious crowd around there all day with little boys searching for dark spots in the dust and some garrulous man telling over and over what had happened until it became less and less real even to him and he could tell it no longer and Myrtle Wilson's tragic achievement was forgotten'.

Then Nick returns to his reconstruction, from the newspapers, of the actions of Michaelis and George Wilson the night before. As Michaelis kept him company, Wilson grew distracted and began to mutter that he had ways of tracing the owner of the yellow car that killed his wife, in which he had seen Tom Buchanan driving to town that afternoon. Dawn approaches and the two men are still talking among the ash heaps, mirror images of Nick and Gatsby talking at the same moment in Gatsby's dusty mansion. Both pairs of men are discussing parallel cases of unfaithful women. One unfaithful woman is a killer, the other is killed; the men sit amid the ashes and the dust to which they will all return.

Wilson leaves the garage in late morning, while Nick sleeps uneasily in his chair on Wall Street; Wilson begins to make his way toward West Egg, searching for the owner of the car that ran down his wife. The police concluded that Wilson must have walked from garage to garage, enquiring after a yellow car, but as Nick points out, no garage men reported seeing him, and Wilson had an 'easier, surer way of finding out what he wanted to know'. Wilson knows Tom Buchanan by name, after all; he just doesn't suspect that Buchanan is the man who was having an affair with his wife. 'By half past two he was in West Egg where he asked someone the way to Gatsby's house. So by that time he knew Gatsby's name.'

The 'mistaken identity' that will kill Gatsby – that is, George Wilson's blaming Gatsby for the crimes of Tom and Daisy Buchanan – is set in motion by Gatsby's own desire. Gatsby's aspiration to Tom's life could be said to be the story's original sin, the first case of mistaken identity: he is a usurper, a pretender in both senses of the word. When Tom realizes that Gatsby wants to supplant him, he gives Gatsby precisely what he thought he wanted: Gatsby is put in Tom's place, taking the fall for both Buchanans' crimes, Daisy's careless driving and Tom's affair with Myrtle. But although Gatsby's death is often described as George Wilson's mistake in identity, it is actually Tom Buchanan's lie. He turns Gatsby into his and Daisy's proxy, much as Nick Carraway's great-uncle sent a substitute to the Civil War to die for him. Wilson holds the gun that shoots Gatsby, but it is Tom Buchanan who pulls the trigger – or so we believe until the novel's final pages, when Fitzgerald turns the screw one last time.

## Perfecting the Plan.

When Fitzgerald had finished drafting his novel and was completing his final revisions, he wrote to Ludlow Fowler. 'We've had a quiet summer and are moving in the fall either to Paris or Italy,' he said. 'I remember our last conversation and it makes me sad. I feel old, too, this summer – I have ever since the failure of my play a year ago. That's the whole burden of this novel – the loss of those illusions that give such color to the world that you don't care whether things are true or false as long as they partake of the magical glory.'

He was nevertheless writing in his ledger that August, 'Zelda and I close together', and in September, 'The novel finished ... Trouble clearing away.' He told Perkins that the novel wouldn't reach America before October: 'Zelda and I are contemplating a careful revision after a week's complete rest.' After a few notes about business, he added, 'I think my novel is about the best American novel ever written.' In early September, he wrote to Perkins that the novel was nearly finished and 'It is like nothing I've read before.' His letters throughout September remained cheerful, and he was proud of what he had accomplished, confident that his novel was marvellous. But the disintegration that had begun could not be stopped so easily. He would write in his notebooks later, 'That September 1924, I knew something had happened that could never be repaired.' It was exactly two years since the Fitzgeralds had returned to New York as the murders of Eleanor Mills and Edward Hall began to consume America.

On 27 October 1924, Scott Fitzgerald wrote to Max Perkins: 'Under separate cover I am sending you my third novel, *The Great Gatsby*.' He was certain that 'at last I've done something really my own', although 'how good "my own" is remains to be seen'. (He also scrawled a postscript down the right-hand side of the letter's margin, asking Perkins to send him the New York *World* for its accounts of the Princeton games against Harvard and Yale.) Ten days after sending Perkins the manuscript, Fitzgerald sent him a letter from the Hotel Continental in St Raphaël, oscillating between different possible titles and saying he'd like to add a new scene. 'I have now decided to stick to the title I put on the book. Trimalchio in West Egg. The only other titles that seem to fit it are Trimalchio and On the Road to West Egg. I had two others, Gold-hatted Gatsby and the High-bouncing Lover but they seemed too light.' He and Zelda were leaving St Raphaël in two days to spend the winter in Rome, as soon as he finished 'Love in the Night', his story based on Val Engalitcheff.

In November, they said goodbye to René Silvé and travelled to Rome, where there was 'ill feeling with Zelda', he noted in his ledger. They stayed at the Hôtel des Princes, in the Piazza di Spagna, across the golden square from where John Keats had lived his final months, dying at the age of twenty-six – the age Fitzgerald had been when he had begun thinking about the novel he had just finished. Looking at the Spanish Steps, he wrote, his spirit soared before the flower stalls and the house where Keats had died. But the Fitzgeralds both hated Rome, and they spent a captious winter there as he corresponded with Perkins about revising the manuscript. Zelda had an 'operation to enable [her] to become pregnant' which led to a lingering infection. 'Dr Gros said there was no use trying to save my ovaries,' she remembered. 'I was always sick and having *picqures*' (injections). They kept quarrelling, and Fitzgerald got so drunk that he picked a fight with a plainclothes policeman and was badly beaten and jailed, a traumatic experience that he would write into *Tender is the Night*.

Perkins read the manuscript immediately, responding quickly and with characteristic insight: 'I think the novel is a wonder ... It has vitality to an extraordinary degree, and glamour, and a great deal of underlying thought of unusual quality. It has a kind of mystic atmosphere at times ... It is a marvelous fusion, into a unity of presentation, of the extraordinary incongruities of life today. And as for sheer writing, it's astonishing.' However, he added that his colleagues didn't like the title 'Trimalchio in West Egg', although Perkins himself felt that 'the strange incongruity of the words in it sound the note of the book'. But he feared the Trimalchio title would not help them sell the novel, and Fitzgerald continued to vacillate over the title right up to publication, frantically cabling Perkins at the last minute: 'Crazy about title under the red white and blue what would the delay be.' Possibly Perkins was less crazy about the title 'Under the Red, White and Blue', although it might have helped its first readers understand that this was a novel about all of America. But it was too late. For better or worse, Fitzgerald's novel would be called *The Great Gatsby*.

Perkins especially admired Fitzgerald's handling of Carraway: 'In no other way could your irony have been so immensely effective, nor the reader have been enabled so strongly to feel at times the strangeness of human circumstance in a vast heedless universe.' His main criticism of the *Trimalchio* draft was that he felt Gatsby was too vague a character; other readers at Scribner's had agreed. Suggesting that Fitzgerald amplify his protagonist's biography, Perkins wrote: 'He was supposed to be a bootlegger, wasn't he, at least in part, and I should think a little touch here and there would give the reader the suspicion that this was so.' Fitzgerald agreed, but decided that the problem was not Gatsby's vagueness on the page, which was deliberate, but his vagueness in Fitzgerald's head:

*I myself didn't know what Gatsby looked like or was engaged in* & you felt it. If I'd known & kept it from you you'd have *been too impressed*

*with my knowledge to protest.* This is a complicated idea but I'm sure
you'll understand. But I know now – and as a penalty for not having
known first, in other words to make sure I'm going to tell more.
It seems of almost mystical significance to me that you thought he
was older – the man I had in mind, half unconsciously, *was* older
(a specific individual) and evidently, without so much as a definite
word, I conveyed the fact.

Or rather, he immediately corrected himself, 'I conveyed it without a
word that I can at present and for the life of me, trace.'

In order to define Gatsby better in his own mind, so as to withhold
that knowledge convincingly from the reader, he had spent much time
in 'careful searching of the files (of a man's mind here) for the Fuller
McGee case & after having had Zelda draw pictures until her fingers
ache I know Gatsby better than I know my own child. My first instinct
after your letter was to let him go & have Tom Buchanan dominate the
book (I suppose he's the best character I've ever done . . .) but Gatsby
sticks in my heart. I had him for a while then lost him & now I have
him again.'

On 20 December he wrote to Perkins again, outlining some of his
worries about the novel: 'I'm a bit (not very – not dangerously) stewed
tonight & I'll probably write you a long letter.' He did, explaining that
he had some more changes planned, although they were already getting to the stage of page proofs, which would make it pricey: 'I can now
make it perfect but the proof . . . will be one of the most expensive
affairs since Madame Bovary.' The comparison is not inapt: Flaubert's
novel also concerns a protagonist whose dreams are distorted by the
books she reads, and who is driven by a desire that never quite distin-
guishes status from sex. In particular, Fitzgerald had lingering doubts
about the confrontation between Tom and Gatsby at the Plaza, the
scene leading to the accident that kills Myrtle. But by January 1925
he had resolved them: 'The Plaza Hotel scene (Chap VII) is now
wonderful and that makes the book wonderful,' he told Perkins, before
writing to Ober that he'd spent three further weeks on the novel,

'clearing up that bum Plaza Hotel scene and now it's really almost perfect of its kind'. He remained convinced, however, that the novel's 'title is bad', and feared that 'it may hurt the book's popularity that it's a *man's book*. Anyhow I think (for the first time since The Vegetable failed) that I'm a wonderful writer.'

Two months later the Fitzgeralds left Rome for Capri to await publication of *The Great Gatsby*. Fitzgerald wrote to Bishop from the bright white sunshine of the Mediterranean, heading the letter: 'I am quite drunk I am told that this is Capri, though as I remember Capri was quieter', and then merrily hailing his friend's latest missive as proof that an authentic American literature was finally emerging:

I am glad that at last Americans are producing letters of their own. The climax was wonderful and the exquisite irony of the 'sincerely yours' has only been equaled in the work of those two masters Flaubert and Ferber ... Oh Christ! I'm sobering up! Write me the opinion you may be pleased to form of my chef d'oeuvre & others' opinion. *Please!* I think it's great but because it deals with much debauched materials, quick-deciders like Rascoe may mistake it for Chambers. To me it's fascinating. I never get tired of it ... PS I am quite drunk again ...

The fear that his new novel would once again be classified with Chambers was continuing to grow.

That spring he wrote to Ernest Boyd as well, telling him of his novel. It 'represents about a year's work', Fitzgerald said, 'and I think it's about ten years better than anything I've done. All my harsh smartness has been kept ruthlessly out of it – it's the greatest weakness in my work, distracting and disfiguring it even when it calls up an isolated sardonic laugh. I don't think this has a touch left. I wanted to call it *Trimalchio* (it's laid on Long Island) but I was voted down by Zelda and everybody else.'

And he wrote to Bishop once more, as the book was about to come out, asking for news. In jokey Franglais, he commended his friend for '*cherching*' the past:

I read your article (very nice too) in Van. Fair about cherching the past. But you disappointed me with the quality of some of it (the news) – for instance that Bunny's play [*The Crime in the Whistler Room*] failed ... I've done about ten pieces of horrible junk in the last year though that I can never republish or bear to look at – cheap and without the spontaneity of my first work. But the novel I'm sure of. It's marvelous ... Is Dos Passos's novel any good? And what's become of Cummings's work ... Do you still think Dos Passos a genius? My faith in him is somehow weakened. There's so little time for faith these days.

Still he mustered up some more cheer and more chat. 'Is Harlock (no connection) dead, or was that Leopold and Loeb,' he asked, thinking about newspaper murder mysteries. 'The cheerfulest things in my life are first Zelda and second the hope that my book has something extraordinary about it. I want to be extravagantly admired again. Zelda and I sometimes indulge in terrible four day rows that always start with a drinking party but we're still enormously in love and about the only truly happily married people I know.' It is possible that Scott was putting on a brave face for John Bishop, married to a woman whom none of his friends liked; or perhaps Fitzgerald's novel had become so tangled with his feelings about marriage that hope in the one brought a resurgence of hope and faith in the other – that the two had become adulterated.

'Like Gatsby I have only hope,' Fitzgerald wrote to Gertrude Stein, as he waited to learn if the world would share his sense of wonder at the book he had created. Fact and fiction so easily become adulterated too, especially when we are cherching the past.

---

## THE PURSUIT OF BEAUTY.

He sometimes thought, Keats once said, that the value of poetry was created only by 'the ardour of the pursuer – being in itself a nothing'.

Even such nothings, however, can become magnificent when they are 'dignified by an ardent pursuit'.

As he tells of his love affair with Daisy, Gatsby confesses that 'it excited him too that many men had already loved Daisy', for 'it increased her value in his eyes'. But as Gatsby finishes telling Nick the story of his ardent pursuit of Daisy, even he has to concede that Daisy might have loved Tom: 'just for a minute, when they were first married – and loved me more even then, do you see?' Presumably Nick does not see, but then Gatsby adds 'a curious remark': 'In any case,' he says, 'it was just personal.' Nick does not know what to make of this, except 'to suspect some intensity in his conception of the affair that couldn't be measured'. Intensity is what transforms romance into ardour: Gatsby's love for Daisy is as symbolic for him as it is for readers, a universal dream of love that exceeds the merely personal. This is what makes Gatsby's side of the affair transcendent, giving it the mystical cast, the sense of glorious destiny whose current pulls him forward. 'Premature success,' wrote Fitzgerald later, 'gives one an almost mystical conception of destiny as opposed to will-power – at its worst the Napoleonic delusion. The man who arrives young believes that he exercises his will because his star is shining.' The ardent pursuit is all.

When they have finished talking, Nick leaves for work, bestowing upon Gatsby his valediction: 'They're a rotten crowd,' he shouts. 'You're worth the whole damn bunch put together.' Nick tells us he's glad he said this: 'it was the only compliment I ever gave him, because I disapproved of him from beginning to end'. Gatsby's face breaks into his radiant smile, 'as if we'd been in ecstatic cahoots on that fact all the time'. He's still in his luminous, 'gorgeous pink rag of a suit', and Nick leaves the house remembering the first time he'd met Gatsby three months before, when his lawn 'had been crowded with the faces of those who guessed at his corruption – and he had stood on those steps, concealing his incorruptible dream'.

Some read Nick as priggish for insisting upon his disapproval, but Fitzgerald needs the censure to undercut Gatsby's romantic heroism, to remind us that he is a crook: the kind of crook that built America.

His dream may be incorruptible, but Fitzgerald thought he had made Gatsby's material corruption quite plain. He wrote to Perkins as the novel was in its final revisions: 'This is very important. Be sure not to give away *any* of the plot in the blurb. Don't give away that Gatsby *dies* or is a *parvenu* or *crook* or anything. It's part of the suspense of the book that all these things are in doubt until the end.' Which presumably means that Fitzgerald considered these things no longer in doubt by the end, that readers would finish the novel with no illusions left about Gatsby, just as Gatsby finishes with no illusions left about life.

When Gatsby realizes that Daisy will not come to him, his disillusionment is complete: he sees reality for the first time. The truth isn't pretty, thinks Nick: Gatsby 'must have felt that he had lost the old warm world, paid a high price for living too long with a single dream. He must have looked up at an unfamiliar sky through frightening leaves and shivered as he found what a grotesque thing a rose is and how raw the sunlight was upon the scarcely created grass. A new world, material without being real, where poor ghosts, breathing dreams like air, drifted fortuitously about . . . like that ashen, fantastic figure gliding toward him through the amorphous trees.' All the old symbols of romance and hope – roses, sunlight, fresh grass – are turned into symbols of horror. They are the merely material, the accidental stuff of life that doesn't matter.

When Nick returns home that afternoon, he has a premonition that something is wrong and runs up the steps of Gatsby's house. 'With scarcely a word said', he rushes with three servants to the pool, where Gatsby has gone for a swim. Looking in the pool Nick describes what he sees: a body revolving slowly in the water, 'tracing, like the leg of compass, a thin red circle in the water'. When Fitzgerald first submitted his manuscript to Perkins he had written that Gatsby's body on the pneumatic raft was like 'the leg of a transept', the cross-section of a church floor. Perkins queried the word, and Fitzgerald changed it, saying that what he really meant was the leg of a compass, like Donne's faithful lover in 'A Valediction: Forbidding Mourning'. This is Gatsby's valediction and mourning is required, but the religious metaphor of the transept was not inapt, for Gatsby dies when he loses his faith.

'A small gust of wind that scarcely corrugated the surface was enough to disturb its accidental course with its accidental burden.' Gatsby has been snapped out, made doubly accidental, material without being real – like the poor grey ghost, the secret sharer who floated toward him out of the ashes and shot him dead.

## SIFTING THE TRUTH.

This is a story in which everyone is guilty.

'VIII. The Murder (inv.)' jotted Fitzgerald at the end of *Man's Hope*. The murder that ends Chapter Eight is, indeed, Scott Fitzgerald's invention. Under the triple misapprehension that Jay Gatsby was driving the car that killed his wife, that Gatsby was his wife's lover and that these two untruths were causally related, George Wilson shoots Gatsby at the end of the chapter, as he's floating in the swimming pool he never used, and then Wilson shoots himself. 'The holocaust was complete,' Nick tells us, although few remember any more that holocaust has not always meant genocide, or even massacre: in the 1920s, its primary meaning was a sacrificial offering. This is the climax of *The Great Gatsby*: Myrtle run over by a careless driver; Gatsby shot in error, in what is often described as a case of mistaken identity; and Wilson's suicide to cheat the electric chair, in the expression of the day. The rest will be denouement.

However, the story's end can also be described, no less accurately, in slightly different terms. It is a double shooting in September 1922. The person who pulls the trigger is a little, grey, ineffectual man, anaemic and apparently pusillanimous, who lives in a ramshackle structure on the edge of town; he works at menial jobs, and generally is known as his wife's man and not his own. His wife was called pushy, officious and vulgar; she aspired to finer things in life and was trying to acquire them by having an affair with a man who came from a higher social stratum.

She wore a spotted dark-blue crêpe de chine dress and loved the novel *Simon Called Peter*. Class-consciousness and envy run through the story: people are symbolized by the homes in which they live, from poverty to grandeur. One of the suspects feels enjoined by the honour of his family to silence; another of the culprits may be a rich, aloof wife with Southern blood. Mistakes in identity thread through the tale: they live in a world of fabulists and frauds, gossip and violence, romantics who invented the kind of past they believed they ought to have had – not just the impostor Jay Gatsby, but also the sad pretensions of Myrtle Wilson and her friends, and even the 'honest' Carraways, whose family line starts with a deception, a mythical ducal ancestry that shares a name with the place where the real woman was killed. Indeed, one synthetic name (Jay Gatsby) sounds much like another (Jane Gibson).

At the end of *The Great Gatsby*, there are three explanations for the deaths that litter the Long Island stage, all motivated by adultery: the aristocratic Southern wife did it; the inadequate working-class husband did it; and it was a case of mistaken identity. These are also the three possible explanations that were offered for the murders of Eleanor Mills and Edward Hall. Fitzgerald's story about possibility is capacious enough to grasp all three possibilities. The creative process makes the murders of Hall and Mills look unneeded: the story has been set free to fly into fiction, transposed into a different key, but audible in echoes and harmonic shifts, transfigured from the wretched to the beautiful. Fiction is not a reassembling of concrete facts, a jigsaw puzzle to solve. It is a palimpsest country of inklings and hunches, echoes and traces. Impressions that Fitzgerald registered, with the seismic sensitivity to life's vibrations that he attributes to Jay Gatsby, ripple through his story, shading it with waves of dark life.

The murders of Hall and Mills are a story that can be detected behind the novel, a phantom double, not an exact correspondence: a nightmare version of grotesque reality, unrelieved by the consolations of art. *The Great Gatsby* is certainly not a true story, nor is it in any meaningful way based on a true story. It might better be regarded as an untrue story, one that took myriad facts and unmade them. The murder is invented, as Fitzgerald said, but it is also discovered – and once upon a time, these meant the same thing.

The story of the murders of Edward Hall and Eleanor Mills reminds us that if *The Great Gatsby* has become our favourite book about what we now call the American dream, it is also a story about knowing your place. It is about the brutality of forcing people back into their places, the cruelty of being found out.

*The Great Gatsby* is the great American novel of hope and longing, and it is one of the handful of novels in which American history finds its figurative form. *Gatsby* is history, and it is about history. But the sordid, sad tale of the murders of Edward Hall and Eleanor Mills is also a story of America: competing romantic fictions driven by envy and jealousy on both sides, riven by questions about money and status and power, erupting into a brutality that is met with incompetence and corruption. It is a story of violence triumphant, of chaos and disappointment. The story of Hall and Mills tells not of America's romantic past, but of its invidious future.

Fitzgerald always felt a strong sense of American history at his back: he was buoyed by it, as it streamed past him. 'I look out at it,' he wrote in his notebooks near the end of his life, 'and I think it is the most beautiful history in the world. It is the history of me and of my people. And if I came here yesterday,' he added, 'I should still think so. It is the history of all aspiration – not just the American dream but the human dream and if I came at the end of it that too is a place in the line of the pioneers.' Aspiration is general, but capacity is limited. Fitzgerald's tale of a fraudster and the shallow, careless woman he loves would become a story about all of America.

# 1925–1940

It was all very careless and confused. They were careless people, Tom and Daisy – they smashed up things and creatures and then retreated back into their money or their vast carelessness or whatever it was that kept them together, and let other people clean up the mess they had made ...

# IX. FUNERAL AN INVENTION

After two years I remember the rest of that day, and that night and the next day, only as an endless drill of police and photographers and newspaper men in and out of Gatsby's front door. A rope stretched across the main gate and a policeman by it kept out the curious, but little boys soon discovered that they could enter through my yard and there were always a few of them clustered open-mouthed about the pool. Someone with a positive manner, perhaps a detective, used the expression 'mad man' as he bent over Wilson's body that afternoon, and the adventitious authority of his voice set the key for the newspaper reports next morning. Most of those reports were a nightmare – grotesque, circumstantial, eager and untrue. When Michaelis's testimony at the inquest brought to light Wilson's suspicions of his wife I thought the whole tale would shortly be served up in racy pasquinade ...

*The Great Gatsby*, Chapter 9

## "Success Story"

Our faith in possibility may be glorious, but it's easy to forget that one possibility is always failure.

As he awaited the publication of *The Great Gatsby*, Fitzgerald's expectations were keyed even higher than usual. The book was marvellous: at last he had done something better than he was capable of. That spring he began work on 'The Rich Boy', a long story inspired by Ludlow Fowler, which opens, 'Begin with an individual, and before you know it you find that you have created a type; begin with a type, and you find that you have created – nothing . . . When I hear a man proclaiming himself an "average, honest, open fellow," I feel pretty sure that he has some definite and perhaps terrible abnormality which he has agreed to conceal.' If any readers prefer to believe Nick Carraway when he proclaims his own honesty, 'The Rich Boy', begun only weeks after *Gatsby* was finished, should give them second thoughts.

'The book comes out today,' Fitzgerald wrote to Perkins on 10 April 1925, 'and I am overcome with fears and forebodings. Supposing women didn't like it because it has no important woman in it, and critics didn't like it because it dealt with the rich and contained no peasants borrowed out of *Tess* in it and set to work in Idaho? . . . In fact all my confidence is gone.' But the book's now iconic cover art by Francis Cugat, the gas-blue night with a woman's eyes dancing out over the jewelled red and yellow of carnival lights, was, he said, 'a delight'; Zelda, too, was 'mad about it'. Before long Perkins cabled the initial news: 'Sales situation doubtful excellent reviews.' In fact, reviews would be decidedly mixed, and the first edition of twenty thousand sold slowly. Fitzgerald's hopes of selling eighty thousand copies would prove wildly optimistic; in August Scribner's printed another three thousand copies, which would never sell out in Fitzgerald's lifetime. Nor was he able to serialize *Gatsby* in a respectable magazine. One editor explained: 'It is too ripe for us . . . we could not publish this story with as many mistresses and as much adultery as there is in it.' On 25 April Scribner's ran an advertisement for the novel captioned, 'F. Scott Fitzgerald, Satirist', which set the tone for much of what would follow. No one yet recognized the transformation Fitzgerald had achieved.

The book gradually garnered qualified praise amid mostly uncomprehending responses. Swope's *World* headlined an anonymous review 'F. Scott Fitzgerald's Latest A Dud', declaring, 'with the telling of the plot, *The Great Gatsby* is, in newspaper parlance, covered'. The review so infuriated Fitzgerald that he referred to it ten years later: 'one woman, who could hardly have written a coherent letter in English, described it as a book that one read only as one goes to the movies around the corner'. But many critics could see in *Gatsby* merely a book that was covered in newspaper parlance, one that borrowed from reality in ways that obscured, for them, its deeper meanings.

One review described it as 'a strange mixture of fact and fancy'; another said Fitzgerald oddly blended 'melodrama, a detective story, and a fantastic satire, with his usual jazz-age extravaganza adding his voice to the mental confusion ... Altogether, it seems to us this book is a minor performance.' Heywood Broun's wife, Ruth Hale, wrote that the jacket's description, promising 'magic, life, irony, romance and mysticism', was either 'completely mad' or a cynical exercise in marketing. (Fitzgerald later called this 'a snotty (and withal ungrammatical)' review.) Another said that *Gatsby* was 'most decidedly, not a great novel ... neither profound nor imperishable ... [but] timely and seasonable'. That emphasis on the book's seasonality would linger. Another declared, '"The Great Gatsby," certainly, is written in the style of 1925. [But] the 1925 model, in literature or automobile, is likely to be supplanted by a later model. Genuinely good writing ... does not reflect the fads of the season's conversation.'

Even appreciative reviews glimpsed the novel's meanings only peripherally: the *New York Times* called it 'a curious book, a mystical, glamorous story of today'. Fitzgerald saved an undated clipping that defended *Gatsby* against accusations that its plot was implausible: 'Fitzgerald has been criticized for the Hamlet ending, with three deaths. We cannot concur ... The fact is that every newspaper recounts events as bizarre, as absurd and as tragic.' William Rose Benét also saw newspapers in *Gatsby*'s inception: writing 'out of the mirage', Fitzgerald 'surveys the Babylonian captivity of this era unblinded by the bright lights. He gives you the bright lights in full measure, the affluence, the waste, but also the nakedness of the scaffolding that scrawls skeletons upon the sky when the gold and blue and red and green have faded, the

ugly passion, the spiritual meagerness, the empty shell of luxury ...
Gatsby is a mystery saliently characteristic of this age in America.' If
the story had grown from the fertile ground of newspapers, it had flowered in unexpectedly beautiful ways, Benét realized: 'As for the drama
of the accident and Gatsby's end, it is the kind of thing newspapers
carry every day, except that here is a novelist who has gone behind the
curt paragraphs and made the real people love and breathe in all their
sordidness.'

Fitzgerald was deeply disappointed and frustrated, but the critics did
not change his assessment of the novel. They were oblivious to what
he had achieved, but he would be vindicated eventually, he told
Perkins: 'Some day they'll eat grass, by God! ... I think now that I'm
much better than any of the young Americans *without exception*.'

Not until his friend Gilbert Seldes, who had heard Fitzgerald read drafts
over the previous summer, gave the book a glowing review that August
did anyone seem to grasp that Fitzgerald was saying something about
America, about faith, illusions and cupidity. With *Gatsby*, wrote Seldes,
Fitzgerald had finally 'mastered his talent and gone soaring in a beautiful
flight, leaving behind him everything dubious and tricky in his earlier
work, and leaving even farther behind all the men of his own generation
and most of his elders'. Fitzgerald was conveying the 'spirit' of American
life, distilling the nation's substance and insubstantiality: 'Fitzgerald has
ceased to content himself with a satiric report on the outside of American
life and has with considerably irony attacked the spirit underneath.'

But Seldes was in a minority. Mencken dismissed *Gatsby* as a 'glorified anecdote', a book in which 'the story is obviously unimportant',
and peopled with 'false' characters; it was 'certainly not to be put on the
same shelf with, say, *This Side of Paradise*'. Mencken, too, could see only
present reality in the novel: 'The Long Island [Fitzgerald] sets before
us ... actually exists. More, it is worth any social historian's study, for
its influence upon the rest of the country is immense and profound ...'
Fitzgerald responded angrily to Bunny Wilson: 'Without making any
invidious comparisons between Class A and Class C, if my novel is an
anecdote so is *The Brothers Karamazov*. From one angle the latter could

be reduced into a detective story ... Of all the reviews, even the most enthusiastic, not one had the slightest idea what the book was about.'

Burton Rascoe's colleague Isabel Paterson reviewed *Gatsby* for the *Tribune*; her piece has become notorious, ranking with 'HERMAN MELVILLE CRAZY' as one of literary history's worst guesses. Because its subject was 'the froth of society', *The Great Gatsby* was 'an imponderable and fascinating trifle', which had not 'gone below that glittering surface, except by a kind of happy accident'. One of Paterson's pronouncements has become especially subject to retrospective ridicule: 'What has never been alive cannot very well go on living; so this is a book of the season only, but so peculiarly of the season, that it is in its small way unique.' For Paterson, too, the ghosts of newspaper headlines drifted through the book: 'He gets the exact tone, the note, the shade of the season and the place he is working on; he is more contemporary than any newspaper, and yet he is (by the present token) an artist.' They could only see Fitzgerald's shimmering reproduction of their world's surface, not the way he had also plunged past it, foretelling a nation that would be adulterated by success. Fitzgerald had shown that a belief they treasured (which in six years they would learn to call the American dream) was a myth – but they were far too deep within the myth to hear him. Isabel Paterson would later champion Ayn Rand and become one of the founding voices of modern American libertarianism; she was the last person to appreciate a book warning against the corrupting force of wealth.

Another depreciative review was written by Burton Rascoe himself, who had left the *Tribune* at the end of 1924 and gone into syndication. A clipping of his review had been sent to Fitzgerald, who wrote to Seldes about it, seething: 'Burton Rascoe says *The Great Gatsby* is just Robert Chambers with overtones of *Nedra* by Harold Nigrath. So I think I'll write a "serious" novel about the Great Struggle the Great American Peasant has with the Soil. Everyone else seems to be doing it. Burton will be the hero as I'm going to try to go to "life" for my material from now on.' Fitzgerald told Perkins that Rascoe's 'little tribute is a result of our having snubbed his quite common and cheaply promiscuous wife'.

Still fuming, he wrote to Perkins again that Rascoe 'has never been known to refuse an invitation from his social superiors – or to fail to pan them [...] when no invitations were forthcoming'. By 1927 his anger at Rascoe had become entrenched. He told Hemingway that 'God will forgive everybody – even Robert McAlmon and Burton Rascoe.' God might, but it was evident that Fitzgerald had not: that year Fitzgerald also described him (adopting Hemingway's favourite insult) as 'that cocksucker Rascoe'. It was the same year that Bunny Wilson would leave bequests to Rascoe in his first will, but for Scott Fitzgerald, forgiveness would take much longer.

Rascoe's review of *Gatsby* was lost; when Matthew Bruccoli edited Fitzgerald's *Life in Letters* in 1995 he added a footnote to this series of letters, explaining that Rascoe's piece, which so infuriated Fitzgerald, has never been identified. Some scholars speculated that Fitzgerald confused it with Paterson's review, but he saved Paterson's review with her byline in his scrapbook so he was perfectly clear about who authored which piece. It is perhaps natural to assume that after almost a century scholars must have found all the extant evidence pertaining to *The Great Gatsby*, but there are still missing pieces.

The gap into which Rascoe's *Gatsby* review had slipped, it turns out, is a small arts magazine, long forgotten. And hidden within Rascoe's

I HAVE a letter from F. Scott Fitzgerald, inclosed with a copy of "The Great Gatsby" which he was gracious enough to have his publishers send me. In part it reads: "I give you my word of honor this isn't a moral tale—nor has it any more resemblance to Chambers because it deals with the rich than has 'The Twelve Little Peppers' to 'My Antonia' because it deals with the poor. It happens to be extraordinarily difficult to write directly and simply about complex and indirect people. And I should prefer to fail at the job ridiculously as James often did than to succeed ignobly. . . .

misplaced review is a tiny, heart-stopping treasure: a long-lost letter from Scott Fitzgerald about his intentions in *Gatsby* that has apparently never been read or reprinted since its publication in 1925. Rascoe's review copy of *Gatsby* had arrived with a cover letter from Fitzgerald explaining his novel, and Rascoe opened his review by quoting from it – a letter that refers to Robert Chambers, and Fitzgerald's persistent fear that he would always be compared to him.

> I give you my word of honor this isn't a moral tale – nor has it any more resemblance to Chambers because it deals with the rich than has 'The Twelve Little Peppers' to 'My Antonia' because it deals with the poor. It happens to be extraordinarily difficult to write directly and simply about complex and indirect people. And I should prefer to fail at the job ridiculously as James often did than to succeed ignobly ... Dostoyefski said that people's motives are much simpler than we think by [sic] any uncorrupted motive has an average life of six hours or less.

The 'by' is presumably a typo for 'but' – and Dostoevsky said that people's motives are usually more complicated than we think, an idea that is certainly borne out by the exchange between Fitzgerald and Rascoe. Although Rascoe saved half a dozen letters from Fitzgerald, this one is not among his papers; Fitzgerald's letter may only survive as this abridged quotation in Rascoe's lost review.

What did Rascoe say about *Gatsby* that so enraged Fitzgerald? He'd shown 'greater technical brilliance', Rascoe felt, 'than even his warmest champions knew him capable of', but the novel

> triumphs by technique rather than by theme ... I must confess to a minority opinion that the novel is not as good in substance as it is in technique. There are some superbly drawn scenes, and the tragic overtones are managed with great economy and skill; but the point of view is wavering, the characters dissolve too readily, my feeling is that it is more a comment upon a situation than a statement of it,

and that comment is not as well reasoned as it might be. But the novel shows that Fitzgerald is maturing in the right direction.

The review damns with faint praise, and shows that Fitzgerald's anxieties about being mistaken for Chambers were so great that he tried to pre-empt the comparison by introducing it into the conversation; Fitzgerald seems to have remained convinced that any reservations about the novel's 'substance' were derived from its subject matter.

Some friends were more perceptive. In July 1925 Deems Taylor, still the music critic for Swope's *World*, wrote to Fitzgerald: 'It's just four o'clock in the morning, and I've got to be up at seven, and I've just finished "The Great Gatsby", and it can't possibly be as good as I think it is. What knocks me particularly cold about the book is not so much the fact that it's a thoroughly adult novel – which it is, and which so few Americans seem to be able to write – as the much more important fact that it's such a glamorous and moving one. You've got [the] gift of going after the beauty that's concealed under the facts; and goddammit, that's all there is to art.' Everyone else was blinded by the facts, but Taylor could see that Fitzgerald had found in them a latent beauty. The art was in the discovery, and in shaping those facts into something more beautiful than their incongruous, natural chaos would suggest to others, realizing that the beauty of the facts was an unheard melody waiting to be heard.

Scott carefully pasted the two pages of Taylor's letter into his scrapbook. He did not keep Rascoe's clipping, which is one of the reasons why it was lost until now.

---

## "Every Day, in Every Way, I'm Growing Better and Better."

The final chapter is a nocturne, Fitzgerald's American Rhapsody. It is a tribute to what America promises, and a denunciation of what it delivered: not people discovering their finest selves, but blind hedonists racing along a shortcut from nothing to nothing.

One of the many patterns to which its first readers were blind, aptly enough, is Fitzgerald's careful linking of vision to the meanings of America. From T. J. Eckleburg's gigantic eyes to Nick's 'eyesore' of a cottage next to Gatsby's mansion, from Owl-Eyes to Myrtle Wilson's little dog who views the party with 'blind eyes through the smoke', vision is distorted, obscured; appearance comes to substitute for the truth. At the story's end Nick calls the newspaper reports of the car accident and double shooting 'a nightmare – grotesque, circumstantial, eager and untrue. When Michaelis's testimony at the inquest brought to light Wilson's suspicions of his wife I thought the whole tale would shortly be served up in racy pasquinade.'

But instead of telling the truth, to control the nightmare Nick connives in lying about it. At the inquest, Myrtle's sister Catherine 'looked at the coroner with determined eyes under that corrected brow of hers and swore that her sister had never seen Gatsby, that her sister was completely happy with her husband, that her sister had been into no mischief whatever. She convinced herself of it and cried into her handkerchief as if the very suggestion was more than she could endure.' Nick declares that Catherine 'showed a surprising amount of character' in lying to the coroner – one of the moments that makes readers doubt Nick's pious claims of honesty. But Nick is adhering to the patrician code that says aristocrats are above the law and must keep out of newspapers at all costs. And so 'Wilson was reduced to a man "deranged by grief" in order that the case might remain in its simplest form.' If Daisy and Tom looked like they were conspiring after Myrtle's death, Nick colludes with that conspiracy, withholding evidence to keep the story from becoming a scandal. Given that Daisy is his second cousin, some might think that Nick chose to protect the honour of his family in covering up a double murder.

When Nick returns to West Egg he tries to locate Gatsby's family to inform them of his death, but the only antecedent he can find is 'the picture of Dan Cody, a token of forgotten violence staring down from the wall'. Gatsby's father has seen the story in the newspapers, however, and soon Henry C. Gatz arrives at the house, bringing with him other forgotten tokens of pioneer violence, including a ragged old copy of *Hopalong Cassidy* that Gatsby had loved when he was a boy.

In the back of the book, the importance of time culminates: on the last fly-leaf of the western is printed the word SCHEDULE, and the date 'September 12th, 1906'. And underneath:

Rise from bed  . . . . . . . . . . . . . . . . . . . . . . . . . . . . . .6.00 A.M.
Dumbbell exercise and wall-scaling  . . . . . . . . . . . .6.15-6.30 "
Study electricity, etc  . . . . . . . . . . . . . . . . . . . . . . . . .7.15-8.15 "
Work  . . . . . . . . . . . . . . . . . . . . . . . . . . . . . . . . . . . .8.30-4.30 P.M.
Baseball and sports  . . . . . . . . . . . . . . . . . . . . . . . . .4.30-5.00 "
Practice elocution, poise and how to attain it  . . . . .5.00-6.00 "
Study needed inventions  . . . . . . . . . . . . . . . . . . . .7.00-9.00 "

GENERAL RESOLVES

No wasting time at Shafters or [a name, indecipherable]
No more smokeing or chewing
Bath every other day
Read one improving book or magazine per week
Save $5.00 [crossed out] $3.00 per week
Be better to parents

Gatsby's schedule has garnered nearly as much attention as his green light. His determination to improve himself unites two favourite American mythologies, the autobiography of Benjamin Franklin and a dime-novel western. Together they define ideals of American individualism. Fitzgerald carefully parallels Gatsby's schedule for self-improvement with Franklin's famous 'scheme of employment' from his autobiography: Gatsby, too, awakens early, reminding himself to wash, to read, to work. But he does not try to improve the inner man; he forgets to ask Franklin's daily questions: 'What good shall I do this day?' and 'What good have I done today?' The moral of the story is that there must be morals in the story. Nick, the man who prides himself on reserving all judgement, begins to see that judgements must be made.

'I come across this book by accident,' Gatz tells Nick, as he shows him the schedule. 'It just shows you, don't it?' Accidents keep showing us what we need to see, if we pay attention. Gatz is so impressed by his son's industry that he 'was reluctant to close the book, reading each item aloud and then looking eagerly at me. I think he rather expected me to copy down the list for my own use,' Nick remarks. 'Gatsby's life seemed to have had the same accidental quality as his death,' he adds in the *Trimalchio* drafts, suggesting that anyone who is self-made can be unmade too. Gatsby is a modern Faust, who makes a fortune and in the process loses what once would have been called his soul.

The distortion is not just of vision, but of visionaries. America was inventing a country that would be unable to distinguish wonder from wealth, while telling itself that every day, in every way, it was growing better and better.

---

## EXPATRIATES
### *THE GILDED CARAVAN.*

In the end, initial reviews of *The Great Gatsby* were not so much negative as unseeing: Fitzgerald's novel that had undone the facts also appeared to have been undone by them. Fitzgerald was left defensive and uncertain by the novel's commercial failure and often obtuse reviews, although he was cheered by praise from writers he admired, including T. S. Eliot, Edith Wharton and Gertrude Stein, who was one of the most acute of the novel's early readers, telling Fitzgerald that he was 'creating the contemporary world'. A few months after *The Great Gatsby* appeared, the *New Yorker* published a 'suggested bookplate' for the library of F. Scott Fitzgerald: like William Rose Benét, the cartoonist Herb Roth also saw Fitzgerald scrawling skeletons across the New York sky.

*Suggested Bookplates*

The day after *Gatsby* appeared, Bunny Wilson wrote to Fitzgerald that the novel was 'full of all sorts of happy touches', but objecting to the 'unpleasant' characters. They made the story 'rather a bitter dose ... Not that I don't admire Gatsby and see the point of the whole thing, but you will admit that it keeps us inside the hyena cage.' John Bishop also concentrated on the novel's resemblance to life: 'Gatsby is a new character in fiction, and, as everyone is now saying, a most familiar one in life.' Edith Wharton focused on the role of tabloid news, writing to Fitzgerald that she admired the novel, but adding: 'My present quarrel with you is only this: that to make Gatsby really Great, you ought to have given us his early career ... instead of a short résumé of it. That would have situated him, & made his final tragedy a tragedy instead of a "fait divers" for the morning papers.' Within a month of its publication, Fitzgerald was writing: 'Gatsby was far from perfect in many ways but all in all it contains such prose as has never been written in America before. From that I take heart. From that I take heart and hope that some day I can combine the verve of *Paradise*, the unity of

*The Beautiful & Damned* and the lyric quality of *Gatsby*, its aesthetic soundness, into something worthy of [...] admiration.'

In May, Scott and Zelda returned to Paris, where Fitzgerald made the acquaintance of an aspiring young writer named Ernest Hemingway. Fitzgerald urged Perkins to publish Hemingway, and over the next months helped him edit *The Sun Also Rises* while also acting as his unofficial agent with Scribner's, with whom Hemingway soon signed. Fitz and Hemingway went to Lyons to recover a broken-down car that the Fitzgeralds had abandoned on their journey back to Paris from Capri; the episode became one of the anecdotes in Hemingway's *A Moveable Feast*, written more than thirty years later, in which Fitzgerald is rendered as a pathetic drunk, a ridiculous hypochondriac and a fool. At the time, however, Hemingway cheerfully wrote to Perkins of their excursion: 'We had a great trip together ... I've read his The Great Gatsby and I think it is an absolutely first-rate book.' Hemingway's memoir also seems to notice only when Fitzgerald was drinking, but Hemingway told Ezra Pound at the time that they had both drunk enormous quantities of wine, which is far more likely.

That Paris summer, Fitzgerald wrote in his ledger, consisted of '1000 parties and no work'. Later in the summer the Fitzgeralds returned to the Riviera with the Murphys and Dos Passos for a visit, after which Gerald Murphy wrote that they were much missed: 'Most people are dull, without distinction and without value [... but] you two belong so irrevocably to that rare race of people who are *valuable*.' Zelda wrote to Madeleine Boyd: 'We went to Antibes to recuperate but all we recooped was drinking hours. Now, once again, the straight and narrow path goes winding and wobbling before us and Scott is working.' Back in Paris, they took a family picture holding hands with Scottie under their Christmas tree, smiling in a chorus kickline. Fitzgerald was toying with ideas for his next novel, about a boy who murders his mother, based on the Leopold–Loeb case. But what work he completed was commercial magazine fiction to pay the bills.

'The Rich Boy', one of his finest stories, was finished in late 1925. It contains one of Fitzgerald's most famous, and most misquoted, passages: 'Let me tell you about the very rich. They are different from you and me. They possess and enjoy early, and it does something to them, makes them soft where we are hard, and cynical where we are trustful, in a way that, unless you were born rich, it is very difficult to understand. They think, deep in their hearts, that they are better than we are because we had to discover the compensations and refuges of life for ourselves.' These are not the words of a man in thrall to riches, but of one making a study of power and corruption.

The following year *Gatsby* was staged, to Fitzgerald's pleasure (its success partially compensated for the failure of *The Vegetable*), and it was adapted into the first of four Hollywood film versions to date. The Fitzgeralds lived off the income from those adaptations and he made little progress on his new novel. He published another story collection, *All the Sad Young Men*, in February 1926, and dedicated it to the Lardners; it included 'The Rich Boy' and three other classic stories that emerged from the gestation of *Gatsby*, 'Winter Dreams', 'Absolution' and 'The Sensible Thing'. Around this time, twenty-six-year-old Zelda began to express an interest in resuming the ballet dancing she had loved as a girl. That spring they went to Juan-les-Pins, on the Riviera, where the usual Murphy ménage at Antibes was joined by Ernest Hemingway, his first wife Hadley, and Pauline Pfeiffer, who was well on her way to becoming his second wife. It was a summer, Zelda wrote to Max Perkins at the time, coloured by a 'sense of carnival and impending disaster'. Fitz wasn't the only one who could make predictions.

The antics that had once been amusing, if sophomoric, were acquiring a vicious edge. One evening with the Murphys they met the dancer Isadora Duncan, who began flattering Scott; Zelda responded by flinging herself silently down the wide stone steps of the terrace. The Murphys thought it a miracle she wasn't killed; Zelda rose a moment later, wiping blood from her knees and her dress. The year was, wrote Fitzgerald in his ledger, 'Futile, shameful useless but the $30,000 rewards of 1924 work. Self disgust. Health gone.' Europe was not saving them. Fitzgerald's drinking was accelerating as fast as their spending, and dissipation was becoming frighteningly literal: 'he suddenly realized the meaning of the word "dissipate'", Fitzgerald wrote in 'Babylon Revisited' a few years later – 'to dissipate into thin air; to make nothing out of something'.

On 10 December 1926, the Fitzgeralds sailed back to America to put the temptations of the old world behind them. On board the SS *Biancamano* were Ludlow Fowler and his new wife, who came from Winnetka, Illinois, a few miles south of Lake Forest, the home of real Ginevra King and fictional Tom Buchanan, the place Fitzgerald had once thought 'the most glamorous place in the world'. Zelda told their friend: 'Now Ludlow, take it from an old souse like me – don't let drinking get you in the position it's gotten Scott if you want your marriage to be any good.' They sat at an uproarious table every night. Scott demanded, 'Is there any man present who can honestly say he has never hit his wife in anger?' and then led a jocular discussion about the precise definition of anger. When they landed, Fowler provided his friend with a recommendation for a speakeasy, scrawling on his calling card, 'Dear Adolph, Please let Mr Fitzgerald have the privileges of your establishment.'

They found themselves, said Zelda, 'back in America – further apart than ever before', returning to a country that was falling into the vortex as fast as they were. The America they rediscovered was consumed by a restlessness that 'approached hysteria', wrote Fitzgerald. 'The parties were bigger ... The pace was faster ... the shows were broader, the buildings were higher, the morals were looser, and the liquor was cheaper; but all these benefits did not really minister to much delight.' Everything was intensified, but the perpetual party was growing strained and frantic.

---

## CALLS US A JADED NATION.

### Have to Rake Up Hall-Mills Case for a Thrill, Dr. Young Says.

They arrived home just in time to catch the final chapter of an unfinished story. The previous year, America had been reminded of the

Hall–Mills murders by a popular film called *The Goose Woman*, about a famous former opera singer who lost her singing voice while giving birth to an illegitimate son (why this medical mystery occurred is not explained). Bitter and resentful, she descends into alcoholism and a life of squalid poverty. When a murder is committed next door, she decides to put herself back in the spotlight; all the goose woman cares about is 'seeing my name in print again'. The film was a big hit, its marketing campaign and reviews all depending on its use of the Hall–Mills case.

A year later a man named Arthur Riehl filed to annul his marriage to Louise Geist, on the grounds of misrepresentation. Although such requests frequently graced the nation's papers, this one was attention-grabbing: Louise Geist had been the Halls' maid, testifying before the 1922 grand jury, and her husband's justification for requesting the annulment was his claim that Louise lied to him about her role in the murders. The story might have disappeared, but William Randolph Hearst had recently purchased the *New York Daily Mirror*, starting a circulation war with the *Daily News*. He had been searching for a headline-creating campaign, preferably an unsolved murder. Now, thanks to Riehl, Hearst had his story.

According to Riehl, Geist had told him that she warned Mrs Hall that the rector intended to elope with Eleanor Mills. Geist and the Halls' chauffeur had driven Mrs Hall and her brother Willie to Buccleuch Park, to confront the pair. The two servants had been paid five thousand dollars to keep quiet, Riehl alleged, adding that Geist had claimed Willie Stevens was a fine shot and kept a pistol in the Hall library. The *Mirror* ran the story for all it was worth, driving the national headlines for weeks. Louise Geist insisted Riehl's story was nonsense, but the New Jersey governor ordered a review, and in July 1926 Frances Stevens Hall was arrested for the murders of her husband and Eleanor Mills. No one doubted the cynicism of Hearst's motives, the *New Yorker* reporting that it was obvious Hearst had reopened the case only 'to increase his paper's circulation'.

In the four years since the botched investigation, most of what little evidence the state had acquired had been lost or damaged, but the new grand jury was made of sterner – or more imaginative – stuff than the last. They voted to indict Mrs Hall, both her brothers, and their cousin Henry Carpender. All four pleaded not guilty and the papers went wild. The carnival mood rapidly returned to New Brunswick; locals again sold refreshments and souvenirs. The township brought in a special switchboard for the journalists wiring copy across America. More than three hundred reporters descended, including one named Damon Runyon, who would become famous for his stories of the New York underworld, featuring a gangster named 'The Brain', modelled closely on Arnold Rothstein. The trial lasted just under a month, during which time twelve million words went out over the wires, enough to fill 960 pages of newspapers, or make a shelf of books twenty-two feet long.

Another autopsy was ordered, and the abused corpses of Eleanor Mills and Edward Hall were exhumed once more. A further surprise awaited: Eleanor's tongue and larynx had been cut out, which no one had noticed during any of the previous autopsies. The trial of Mrs Hall and her two brothers began on 3 November 1926; Henry Carpender successfully petitioned to be tried separately at a later date. The evidence was circumstantial at best: Willie's smudged fingerprint, which may have been found on the rector's calling card (expert witnesses on both sides argued that it was and wasn't his fingerprint), was no more persuasive than Riehl's hearsay report of Mrs Hall allegedly bribing his soon-to-be ex-wife.

The prosecution's star witness, however, was none other than Mrs Jane Gibson, Pig Woman. The whole story would be invented once more. Suffering from terminal cancer, Mrs Gibson was carried into the courtroom on a hospital bed. She would not die until 1930, however, and was strong enough to testify; some say she melodramatically exaggerated her illness. Whatever the true state of her health, the redoubtable Pig Woman put on quite a show. Photographed by reporters from the gallery, she might have been a drunken woman on a stretcher, covered all in white with one hand dangling by her side. The whole country knew the woman's name – it was the wrong name, but no one cared.

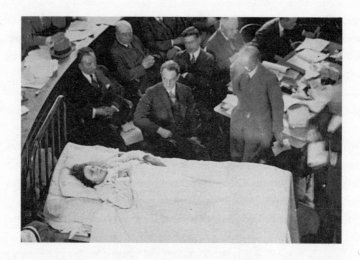

Her story had improved over the years: she had refined its details and added a number of artistic flourishes. The dramatic effect was somewhat spoiled, however, when her own mother, wonderfully named Salome Cerenner, denounced her daughter in court, muttering: 'She's a liar! Liar, liar, liar! That's what she is, and what she's always been!' Cross-examination showed that Jane Gibson could not remember when or whom she had married over the years, which also rendered her narrative somewhat unreliable.

Frances Hall and Willie Stevens both denied all knowledge of the crimes; the supposedly 'simple' Willie Stevens delighted reporters by proving a shrewd, quick-witted witness, whom the prosecution failed to outwit, parrying the state's questions with ease. The jury heard 157 witnesses in just under a month, and on 3 December 1926 deliberated for five hours, before acquitting all three defendants. The case against Henry Carpender was dismissed, and the Stevens family joined forces in suing Hearst and the *Mirror* for libel; they settled out of court. The next day, the week before the Fitzgeralds sailed back to the US, the *New Yorker* offered a hypothesis: 'After reading pages of testimony as voluminous as Wanamaker's advertisements, everyone has voiced an opinion on the Hall–Mills case. Of all the theories advanced to date our favorite follows: Senator Simpson was carrying the "Pig Woman's" Rifle when Willie threw a bluefish at him and the gun went off, leaving a finger-print on the defendant's calling card.'

Charlotte Mills appeared at the Hoboken Rialto Theatre on 27 December 1926, where a play based on the murders called *Who is Guilty?* was playing to a packed house. 'My mother was a good woman,' Charlotte told the audience. 'Please try not to think badly of her.'

Who was guilty? Everyone, it appeared, was guilty of something. Failure was endemic; only the killer (or killers) triumphed. Carelessness had proven as powerful in life as it was in fiction.

## WHO IS GUILTY?

In January 1927 the Fitzgeralds took their first trip to Hollywood, where Scott worked on a film that was never made, and became deeply infatuated with a seventeen-year-old actress, Lois Moran, who would inspire

Rosemary in *Tender is the Night*. Fitzgerald later referred to his 'affair' with Moran, although few biographers think it was consummated. But his sentiments were barely concealed and Zelda was furious, later reproaching him for having 'engaged in flagrantly sentimental relations with a child. You said you wanted nothing more from me in all your life, though you made a scene when Carl [Van Vechten] suggested that I go to dinner with him . . .'

The Fitzgeralds were quarrelling constantly. That spring, as the papers were flooded by the story of the Ruth Snyder murder on Long Island, they moved to Delaware, renting a large house called Ellerslie; they threw lavish parties and Zelda started taking daily ballet lessons. She wrote some magazine pieces; to her annoyance they were accepted only if Scott's name was added to hers or replaced it entirely. In 1928 Zelda wrote an essay called 'Looking Back Eight Years', anticipating Fitzgerald's more famous retrospective essays on the jazz age. 'Success was the goal for this generation and to a startling extent they have attained it,' she wrote, but 'nine in ten would confess that success is only a decoration they wished to wear: what they really wanted is something deeper and richer than that'. Everyone she knew 'still hope[d] wistfully that things will again have the magic of the theater', but suspected things wouldn't.

Zelda had little time to write, however: dance was increasingly consuming her days while her husband increasingly spent his days consuming alcohol. He continued to write brilliantly, but more sporadically; his behaviour was deteriorating. After one party, he apologized for being 'the world's worst bore': 'I was in the insistent mood – you know the insistent mood? . . . It's all very dim to me . . . I can be almost human when sober.' They returned to France, and Zelda continued dancing, practising compulsively, nine, ten hours a day. She was suddenly overtaken by a fierce determination that no one knew she had, to leave idleness behind and prove that she too could achieve success, creating the magic of theatre. She danced constantly, in the futile hope that, having begun serious training at the age of twenty-seven, she could become a professional dancer. Her frantic ballet reminded one old friend of the dancing madness of the Middle Ages.

Fitzgerald increasingly resented Zelda's dancing, complaining that she neglected him and the house, that she was becoming a stranger. But he understood perfectly well how basic her motivation was: she 'wanted to have something for herself, be something herself'. In the autumn of 1928, the peripatetic Fitzgeralds sailed back to America, renting Ellerslie again. Then, in spring 1929, it was back to Paris, then to the Riviera for the summer, then Paris again.

Although progress on his novel had slowed, Fitzgerald continued to write stories to support the family. On 19 October 1929 he published 'The Swimmers', a story about the destruction of America by a crass belief in material prosperity, which also uses sexual infidelity to symbolize every betrayal of faith. At one point an unfaithful wife, who is French, complains about American women on the Riviera: 'Great ladies, bourgeoises, adventuresses – they are all the same.' She points to one girl: 'That young lady may be a stenographer and yet be compelled to warp herself, dressing and acting as if she had all the money in the world.' Told that perhaps the girl will be rich someday, she retorts: 'That's the story they are told; it happens to one, not to the ninety-nine. That's why all their faces over thirty are discontented and unhappy.' Four days after 'The Swimmers' was published, Wall Street crashed: the eternal carnival shuddered to a halt. Fitzgerald's gift for guessing right had not abandoned him.

The Fitzgeralds stayed in Europe, and friends grew concerned about Zelda's behaviour. When the Kalmans visited Paris, Kaly said to Scott he thought something was seriously wrong. At a flower market in Paris Zelda told Scott the flowers were speaking to her. On 23 April 1930, after almost exactly a decade of marriage, Zelda was admitted to the Malmaison clinic outside Paris 'in a state of acute anxiety', continually repeating: 'This is dreadful, this is horrible, what is going to become of me, I have to work, and I will no longer be able to, I must die, and yet I have to work. I will never be cured, let me leave.' She insisted on seeing her dance teacher: 'she has given me the greatest joy that can exist, it is comparable to the light of the sun that falls on a block of crystal, to a symphony of perfume, the most perfect chord from the greatest composer in music'. Ten days later Zelda discharged herself, against doctors' advice. Before long she was hearing terrifying voices, haunted by nightmares, and kept fainting. She was calmed only by morphine injections, and that spring she attempted suicide.

Two months later Zelda entered the Prangins Clinic in Switzerland, one of the finest psychiatric hospitals of the day, where she would stay for the next eighteen months. Her diagnosis of schizophrenia, made in the early days of psychiatry, has since been disputed; many now argue that Zelda was more likely bipolar. Whatever the correct diagnosis, there was a frighteningly high suicide rate in her family and almost certainly a history of mental illness: her grandmother and brother both committed suicide, and her aunt may have as well; her father had 'nervous prostration' the year that Zelda and Scott Fitzgerald met, and her older sister Marjorie suffered mysterious 'breakdowns'. Decades later Scottie's son would also commit suicide. Although armchair psychiatrists continue to argue over what exactly Zelda's illness may have been, something had gone seriously wrong. It is certainly not the case, as some continue simplistically to claim, that Fitzgerald drove his wife crazy, or that he locked her up because she was a nuisance. It would have been far easier, and cheaper, to have divorced her. Instead he continued to fight on Zelda's behalf, as best he could, when he wasn't fighting against her in what rapidly became for both a genuine struggle for survival. In 1930 Scott sharply rebuked a doctor for prescribing 're-education' for Zelda: 'It is somewhat difficult to teach a person who is capable now of understanding the Einstein theory of space, that 2 and 2 actually make four.'

But reality was melting away inside her head, Zelda said: 'for months I have been living in vaporous places peopled with one-dimensional figures and tremulous buildings until I can no longer tell an optical illusion from a reality'. Zelda's periods of disorientation were terrifying, but relatively brief. Much of the time she was entirely rational, and absolutely trapped. She wrote to her doctor, rejecting his 'exalted sophistries': 'If you do cure me what's going to happen to all the bitterness and unhappiness in my heart – It seems to me a sort of castration, but since I am powerless I suppose I will have to submit, though I am neither young enough nor credulous enough to think that you can manufacture out of nothing something to replace the song I had.' In his ledger for 1930, Fitzgerald wrote: 'The Crash! Zelda + America'. Crashes had taken on a different meaning: bad drivers would no longer be the dominant metaphor – but the sense that their fortunes eerily followed the nation's would only be strengthened.

As Zelda tried to recover, the Fitzgeralds exchanged long, bitter letters, attempting to understand what had happened to them. Amid accusations, vindications and recriminations, they retold the story of their unravelling lives. Nursing old grievances and justifying himself, Scott sent Zelda an angry account of recent years: 'Those days when we came up from the south, from Capri, were among my happiest – but you were sick and the happiness was not in the home. I had been unhappy for a long time then – when my play failed a year and a half before, when I worked so hard for a year, twelve stories and novel and four articles in that time with no one believing in me and no one to see except you & before the end your heart betraying me and then I was really alone with no one I liked. In Rome we were dismal and I was still working proof and three more stories and in Capri you were sick and there seemed to be nothing left of happiness in the world anywhere I looked. Then we came to Paris and suddenly I realized it hadn't all been in vain. I was a success – the biggest one in my profession – everybody admired me and I was proud I'd done such a good thing.'

'You were going crazy and calling it genius,' Scott told her at the end of his outpouring. 'I was going to ruin and calling it anything that came to hand. And I think everyone far enough away to see us outside of our glib presentation of ourselves guessed at your almost megalomaniacal selfishness and my insane indulgence in drink ... I wish the Beautiful and Damned had been a maturely written book because it was all true. We ruined ourselves – I have never honestly thought that we ruined each other.'

Zelda's response ran to almost forty pages, an impressionistic memoir of their lives:

> You have been thinking of the past. The weeks since I haven't slept more than three or four hours, swathed in bandages sick and unable to read so have I . . . We came to New York and rented a house when we were tight. There was Val Engelicheff and Ted Paramour and dinner with Bunny in Washington Square and pills and Doctor Lackin and we had a violent quarrel on the train going back, I don't remember why. Then I brought Scottie to New York. She was round and funny in a pink coat and bonnet and you met us at the station. In Great Neck there was always disorder and quarrels: about the Golf Club, about the Foxes, about Peggy Weber, about Helen Buck, about everything . . . We gave lots of parties . . . We drank always and finally came to France because there always too many people in the house . . . You were constantly drunk. You didn't work and were dragged home at night by taxi-drivers when you came home at all. You said it was my fault for dancing all day. What was I to do? You got up for lunch.

'You didn't care,' she ended, 'so I went on and on – dancing alone, and no matter what happens, I still know in my heart that it is a Godless, dirty game; that love is bitter and all there is.'

As the months passed their letters grew by turns defensive, tender, accusatory, and grieving. Scott kept a passport photo of Zelda, he told her, 'the face I knew and loved': 'It is with me from the morning when I wake up with a frantic half dream about you to the last moment when I think of you and of death at night . . . I will take my full share of responsibility for all this tragedy but I cannot spread beyond the limits of my reach and grasp, I can only bring you the little bit of hope I have and I don't know any other hope except my own . . . I love you with all my heart.' Zelda responded, with the terrible lucidity that followed her breakdowns: 'It's ghastly losing your mind and not being able to see clearly, literally or figuratively . . . What a disgraceful mess – but if it

stops our drinking it is worth it ... if it will only work, and I can keep
sane and not a bitter maniac – '

In February 1931 Fitzgerald published 'Babylon Revisited', perhaps
his greatest story, an elegy to everything he had lost: his wife, his
daughter, his self-respect. But as that magnificent tale showed, he still
had his art, if he could keep it from washing away in the oceans of
gin and despair in which he was drowning. 'Without hope or youth or
money I sit constantly wishing I were dead,' Zelda wrote to him. 'Bitched
once more.'

Fitzgerald struggled to make any progress on his next novel, which
had ceased to be inspired by Leopold and Loeb or any other murder
cases. He no longer needed the newspapers to learn about horror.

## IN JEOPARDY

As the Depression bore down, Scott battled to earn enough to pay for
Zelda's world-class hospitals and Scottie's boarding schools. After years
of extravagance, Fitzgerald suddenly faced financial disaster. He seemed
abruptly to lose his knack for commercial fiction just when he needed
it most; he no longer believed in his frivolous, silvered tales, and the
old spontaneity began to freeze up. 'When you can't write,' Zelda told
him, 'you sit on the bed and look so woebegone like a person who's got
to a store and can't remember what they wanted to buy.' At the end of
1931, Zelda was released from Prangins. Hopeful that she could make
a full recovery and they could piece together the fragments of their
lives, they returned to America. Scott began writing retrospective
essays on the jazz age; 'it was borrowed time,' he'd realized, 'the whole
upper tenth of a nation living with the insouciance of grand dukes and
the casualness of chorus girls.'

Six months later Zelda had another breakdown and entered the
psychiatric clinic at Johns Hopkins University in Baltimore. While a
patient there, in what certainly sounds a manic burst of energy over just

a month, she finished the autobiographical novel she had barely begun a few months earlier. She was proud of *Save Me the Waltz*, she wrote to Scott. 'You will like it – It is distinctly École Fitzgerald.' Scott had not read drafts and when he realized that the novel was a barely fictionalized *roman-à-clef* of their life together he was furious. In her first draft Zelda called the artist husband Amory Blaine, the name of Fitzgerald's alter ego from *This Side of Paradise*. Fitzgerald wrote to her psychiatrist in a fury: 'This mixture of fact and fiction is simply calculated to ruin us both or what is left of us and I can't let it stand. Using the name of a character I invented to put intimate facts in the hands of the friends and enemies we have accumulated *en route* – My God, my books made her a legend and her single intention in this somewhat thin portrait is to make me a non-entity.'

In particular, he was nettled at the idea she was 'expressing herself', he told Zelda later. Self-expression 'simply doesn't exist. What one expresses in a work of art is the dark tragic destiny of being an instrument of something uncomprehended, incomprehensible, unknown – you came to the threshold of that discovery and then decided that in the face of all logic you would crash the gate', using only 'the frail equipment of a sick mind and a berserk determination'. But Zelda had written a novel in a few blazing months when Fitzgerald had been unable to complete one in seven years, and she fought hard for her book to be given a chance. In one session with her doctor, Scott told Zelda: 'The difference between the professional and the amateur is something that is awfully hard to analyse, it is awfully intangible. It just means the keen equipment; it means a scent, a smell of the future in one line ... You are a third rate writer and a third rate ballet dancer.' Zelda shot back: 'It seems to me you are making a rather violent attack on a third rate talent then.'

Scott clearly felt threatened by Zelda's incursion into what he considered his territory, but he was also affronted at the temerity of thinking that writing was easy: 'She has seen me do it as apparently some automatic function of the human machine,' he wrote to Zelda's doctor, 'lying dormant in everyone; she shares in this way, the American vulgar opinion of the arts: that they are something that people do when they have nothing else to do ... She clings to the idea that the thing has all been done with a beautiful intention rather than with a dirty, sweating, heartbreaking effort extending over a long period of time when enthusiasm and all the other flowers have wilted.' The beautiful intention, Fitzgerald knew, is merely an apparition that will slowly be murdered in the bloody effort to bring the book to life, for dreams are always more beautiful than reality.

But insisting that the novel be revised, Fitzgerald also helped Zelda to do so, and wrote to Perkins that the novel was good, and truly original. *Save Me the Waltz* was published in October 1932; it was dismissed critically, and sold poorly. The Fitzgeralds had neither the strength nor the appetite for another fight. Zelda would not try to publish another novel.

They had achieved something more than a détente, however; an accommodation had been reached with the new terms that life had set. A few days after his thirty-sixth birthday, in September 1932, Fitzgerald wrote to a friend that he and Zelda 'got through a lot and have some way to go; our united front is less a romance than a categorical imperative'. It was time to recognize that they could no longer 'insist on a world which we will willingly let die, in which Zelda can't live, which damn near ruined us both, which neither you nor any of our more gifted friends are yet sure of surviving'.

Once again, Scott could read the signs: survival was by no means a certainty. In August 1933 Zelda's brother Anthony committed suicide; a month later, Ring Lardner died at forty-eight from tuberculosis exacerbated by acute alcoholism. By the end of that year, Scott finally finished *Tender is the Night*. It was serialized in early 1934; in February, Zelda had another breakdown and was hospitalized again. She had taken up painting, and Scott helped organize an exhibition in New York that spring. On 12 April 1934, nine years and two days after the appearance of *The Great Gatsby*, Fitzgerald published *Tender is the Night*, dedicated to Gerald and Sara Murphy for 'many fêtes'. In 1933, he showed a visitor a manuscript nearly a foot high, and said: 'There's my new novel. I've written 400,000 words and thrown away three-fourths of it. Now I only have 15,000 words to write.' Then he exclaimed: 'It's good, good, good.' He pinned all his hopes on it.

Fitzgerald had plundered Zelda's personal writing for his novel once more, this time taking the letters she had written him from the depths of her breakdown and turning them to useful account in his rendering of Nicole Diver's madness. This took some effrontery, after his outrage at Zelda's daring to use their 'common store' of material in her novel. It was the writer at his most solipsistic, prepared to sacrifice anyone on the altar of his art. Doubtless he justified the betrayal with the obvious rationale, that the money earned would pay for her care. But it was also true that he had begun *Tender* much earlier and read Zelda drafts: from his perspective, *Save Me the Waltz* was often copying his original work.

Like *Gatsby*, however, *Tender is the Night* received mixed reviews, more good than bad overall, but the book sold poorly and for Fitzgerald it was a crushing disappointment. The *New York Times* said the novel displayed Fitzgerald's 'most engaging qualities': it was 'clever and brilliantly surfaced, but it is not the work of a wise and mature novelist'. Once again his readers could not see past Fitzgerald's glittering surfaces. John Bishop said the book 'was no advance on *Gatsby*'; Fitzgerald responded that its intention was entirely different. Whereas *Gatsby* was a 'dramatic novel', a 'kind of *tour de force*', *Tender* was 'a philosophical or psychological novel', a 'confession of faith'. Comparing the two was like comparing a sonnet sequence and an epic. In *Tender*, he'd underplayed his 'harrowing and highly charged material', including incest and madness, whereas in *Gatsby*, 'dealing with figures as remote as are a bootlegger-crook to most of us, I was not afraid of heightening and melodramatizing any scenes'.

*Tender*'s failure would push Fitzgerald over the edge – the edge over which Zelda, too, kept falling, as she continued intermittently to attempt suicide. In 1934, Scott wrote to Zelda's doctor, painfully trying to make sense of her illness, asking for a theory that might predict her breakdowns and discussing the psychiatric textbooks he'd been reading. The letter surely banishes any facile accusation that Fitzgerald was shoving Zelda into hospitals: 'My great worry is that time is slipping by, life is slipping by, and we have no life. If she were an anti-social person who did not want to face life and pull her own weight that would be one story, but her passionate love of life and her absolute inability to meet it, seems so tragic that sometimes it is scarcely to be endured.' But no theories to explain Zelda's illness emerged; they remained unable to help her in any consistent, meaningful way.

When *Tender* failed, Zelda wrote to Scott protectively, 'Don't worry about critics – what sorrow have they to measure by or what lilting happiness with which to compare these ecstatic passages?' Scott replied that she should focus only on recovering: 'You and I have had wonderful times in the past, and the future is still brilliant with possibilities if you will keep up your morale ... The only sadness is the living without you, without hearing the notes of your voice.' Hers was the only opinion that mattered, he said. All he hoped for was for her to come back to him: 'I can carry most of contemporary literary opinion, liquidated, in the hollow of my hand – and when I do, I see the swan floating on it and – I find it to be you and you only ... Forget the past – what you can of it, and turn about and swim back home to me, to your haven for ever and ever – even though it may seem a dark cave at times and lit with torches of fury; it is the best refuge for you – turn gently in the waters through which you move and sail back.'

---

## NOT WHOLLY "LOST"

But Zelda could only continue to eddy in her dark waters: often lucid, calm, unfathomably brave; and then suddenly withdrawn into depression, aural hallucinations, or hysteria. 'I wish I had been what I thought I was,' she wrote to Scott: 'and so debonnaire; and so debonnaire'.

Struggling to sell his writing, Fitzgerald plunged into an abyss of liquor. He was hospitalized four times by the end of 1935; trying to recover, he began to write the *Esquire* articles that would help invent confessional journalism. In the now-famous 'Crack-Up' essays, published in early 1936, Fitzgerald describes how he had suddenly 'cracked like an old plate', losing all his illusions. In the three short articles he never mentions Zelda's illness and flatly denies his own alcoholism, but spells out the effects of his defeat and tries to redefine himself as an artist. Three months later, his friend Hemingway, whose career he had helped launch and whose admiration he had always sought, mocked him publicly in 'The Snows of Kilimanjaro' as 'poor Scott Fitzgerald', pathetically defined by his 'romantic awe' of the rich. When Fitzgerald read the *Esquire* story, he demanded that Hemingway 'please lay off me in print', but his innate honesty and instinctive respect for art made him add, with his often astonishing generosity: 'It's a fine story – one of your best.'

A month later, a reporter named Michael Mok interviewed Fitzgerald on his fortieth birthday. The result was a brutal exposé, describing the former golden boy as a wasted man with trembling hands and pallid, 'twitching face with its pitiful expression of a cruelly beaten child', who made 'frequent trips to a highboy, in a drawer of which lay a bottle'. Asked to comment on his generation, Fitzgerald told Mok: '"Some became brokers and threw themselves out of windows. Others became bankers and shot themselves. Still others became newspaper reporters. And a few became successful authors . . . Successful authors!" he cried. "Oh, my God, successful authors!" He stumbled over to the highboy and poured himself another drink.' When Fitzgerald saw the headline story ('THE OTHER SIDE OF PARADISE: SCOTT FITZGERALD, 40, ENGULFED IN DESPAIR'), he swallowed a handful of morphine pills, but survived.

Zelda had moved to Highland Hospital, in Asheville, North Carolina. After years of watching her try to recover, Fitzgerald no longer had any confidence that she would be able to resume an independent life: 'I cannot live in the ghost town which Zelda has become,' he admitted. But still, he would not abandon her; they would remain joined in vital ways, and they would always love each other: 'Supposing Zelda at best would be a lifelong eccentric, supposing that in two or three years there is certain to be a sinking, I am still haunted by the fact that if it were me, and Zelda were passing judgment, I would want her to give me a chance . . . ' Zelda continued to write him loving letters from the hospital, concerned for his health, asking to see Scottie and expressing her devotion. Around the time of his breakdown she wrote to Scott remembering the days of their courtship, when they were 'gold and happy all the way home'. Then she added: 'There isn't any more happiness and home is gone and there isn't even any past . . . I wish you had a little house with hollyhocks and a sycamore tree and the after-noon sun imbedding itself in a silver-tea pot. Scottie would be running about somewhere in white, in Renoir, and you will be writing books in dozens of volumes . . . I want you to be happy – if there were any jus-tice you would be happy – maybe you will be anyway . . . I love you anyway – even if there isn't any me or any love or even any life.'

They were all clinging to the wreckage. 'Me caring about no one nothing,' Fitzgerald wrote in his ledger for April 1936, as the last of the Crack-Up essays was published. Ring Lardner was dead, Zelda was lost. Hemingway had succumbed to his own myth; his drinking and depres-sion would take longer to conquer him, but he would not escape either. Edmund Wilson was embarking on his third marriage, to Mary McCarthy; his alcoholism, while more functional than Fitzgerald's, was also gathering pace and victims. The Murphys lost two of their three children in less than two years, one to meningitis, the other to tuber-culosis. When Fitzgerald heard about the death of their second son in 1937, he wrote to the Murphys: 'I can see another generation growing up around [their daughter] Honoria and an eventual peace somewhere, an occasional port of call as we all sail deathward. Fate can't have any more arrows in its quiver for you that will wound like these.' In 1936, Burton Rascoe's twenty-two-year-old son committed suicide at their home in upstate New York; filling out a Guggenheim application three years later, Rascoe wrote that his permanent address was Ferncliff Cemetery, Scarsdale – where his son was buried. Six months before his son's suicide, Rascoe had written Fitzgerald a generous letter about the Crack-Up articles: 'it is a magnificent and salutary thing for you to have written them,' Rascoe said, not for Fitzgerald's readers but for the ther-apeutic value to Fitzgerald. They would surely inaugurate 'a new period in which your enviable talents will flower into deeper and lovelier things than you have created hitherto.' Fitzgerald saved Rascoe's letter, replying: 'That was darn nice of you to write me that letter. Those kinds of gestures mean more to the recipient than he can well say. Best wishes always, Scott Fitz.'

Amid the sadness, Fitzgerald's markets continued to shrink, and he needed to pay for Zelda's care and for Scottie's education and living expenses; she would soon enroll at Vassar. In 1937, deeply in debt, Fitzgerald went to Hollywood to try to reverse his fortunes once more. 'I feel a certain excitement,' he wrote to Scottie from the train, remembering his first 'Hollywood venture' exactly ten years earlier. 'Hollywood made a big fuss over us and the ladies all looked very beautiful to a man of thirty. I honestly believed that *with no effort on my part* I was a sort of magician with words – an odd delusion on my part when I had worked so desperately hard to develop a hard, colorful prose style. Total result – a great time & no work.' This time would be different, that was clear – not least because no one was making a fuss over Scott Fitzgerald any more; he was finding it difficult to get published at all. A train's movement had the rhythm, he wrote, of finding and losing, finding and losing.

In Hollywood Fitzgerald suddenly faced a ghost from the past. Ted Paramore had been working for some years as a screenwriter and was assigned to collaborate with Scott on an adaptation of Erich Maria Remarque's *Three Comrades*. The association was not happy. Fitzgerald would not give the dilettante he had known equal say; viewing Paramore as a hack, he was determined to retain control. 'I didn't write four out of four best sellers or a hundred and fifty top-price short stories out of the mind of a temperamental child without taste or judgment,' he told Paramore angrily. *Three Comrades* became one of the biggest hits of 1938 and would be Fitzgerald's only screen credit. When Zelda heard that they were working together after all those years, she told Scott, 'Give Paramour my regards and affectionate remembrances – Tell him how good looking he is – We used to have a lot of fun.'

In the summer of 1937, Fitzgerald met the twenty-eight-year-old Hollywood columnist Sheilah Graham. He was immediately struck by her resemblance to Zelda and would use the uncanny likeness in *The Last Tycoon*: 'Smiling faintly at him from not four feet away was the face of his dead wife, identical even to the expression. Across the four feet of moonlight, the eyes he knew looked back at him, a curl blew a little on a familiar forehead; the smile lingered, changed a little according to pattern; the lips parted – the same. An awful fear went over him, and he wanted to cry aloud.' Sheilah Graham was, as it happened, a self-invented woman, the platonic conception of Lily Shiel, a girl who had grown up in a slum in the East End of London before inventing an aristocratic background for herself as an upper-class English woman and moving to Hollywood.

Over the seven years since Zelda's breakdown, Scott had had a few brief affairs, but Sheilah Graham was the first with whom he entered a comparatively stable relationship. She tried to help him stop drinking; in the beginning these attempts always ended in failure, and often in violence: he still turned nasty when drunk. Making it clear to Sheilah and others that divorce was not in question, Scott continued to support Zelda, who was lobbying to be released from Highland Hospital and go live with her mother in Montgomery, and to travel. Fitzgerald was wary, and frustrated by the expense this would entail. He wrote her a chastising letter explaining the dire state of their finances, which ended: 'Oh, Zelda, this was to have been such a cold letter, but I don't feel that way about you. Once we were one person and always it will be a little that way.' But Zelda was turning in her isolation and despair to God, embracing a religious zeal that would colour the rest of her life.

On Christmas Eve 1938 Fitzgerald wrote to Max Perkins from California. His once-golden hair had faded to the ashy colour of dying straw; his smile was deprecating, tremulous, uncertain, his eyes wilted and bloodshot. He would have been chain-smoking, as he always did those days, a filtered Raleigh providing the slight veil through which he now viewed the scene. He was not having a merry Christmas.

I have come to feel somewhat neglected. Isn't my reputation being allowed to slip away? I mean what's left of it. I am still a figure to many people and the number of times I still see my name in *Time* and *New Yorker* etc. make me wonder if it should be allowed to casually disappear – when there are memorial double-deckers to such fellows as Farrell and Steinbeck ... The recession is over for awhile and I have the most natural ambition to see my stuff accessible to another generation ... Unless you make some gesture of confidence I see my reputation dying on its feet from lack of nourishment ... You can imagine how distasteful it is to blow my own horn like this but it comes from a deep feeling that something could be done if it is done at once, about my literary standing – always admitting that I have any at all.

What had prompted this protest was hearing that *This Side of Paradise*, which had launched his career with such verve almost twenty years earlier, had recently been allowed to go quietly out of print. 'My God I am a forgotten man,' he wrote to Zelda. '*Gatsby* had to be taken out of the Modern Library because it didn't sell, which was a blow.' Increasingly elegiac and wistful, he composed essays, letters and stories memorializing his own life. 'We have our tombstones to chisel,' he told Zelda in a letter he probably never sent, 'and can't blunt our tools stabbing you back, you ghosts, who can't either clearly remember or cleanly forget.'

Meanwhile the voices grow fainter and fainter, he added in his notebooks: How is Zelda, how is Zelda – tell us – how is Zelda.

---

## AMERICA, LAND OF GOLDEN PROMISE

As *The Great Gatsby* draws to a close, Nick decides to leave the east, where he has discovered he doesn't belong, and return home to the Middle West. West Egg now seems warped and phantasmagoric to him: 'I see it as a night scene by El Greco: a hundred houses, at once conventional and grotesque, crouching under a sullen, overhanging sky and a lustreless moon. In the foreground four solemn men in dress suits are walking along the sidewalk with a stretcher on which lies a drunken woman in a white evening dress. Her hand, which dangles over the side, sparkles cold with jewels. Gravely the men turn in at a house – the wrong house. But no one knows the woman's name, and no one cares.' The tableau resembles a bac- chanalian morality play, the spirit of the age embodied in the beautifully dressed corpse on a funeral bier, carelessness personified. Nick finds the east 'haunted for me like that, distorted beyond my eyes' power of correction'.

Before he leaves Nick feels bound to end things with Jordan, although he has not seen her since the night of the accident that killed Myrtle. He is trying to be careful, he says, 'and not just trust that oblig- ing and indifferent sea to sweep my refuse away'. The ocean may sweep you toward a new destiny, but Nick is going back, not forward. When they meet, Jordan reminds him of a conversation they once had about driving a car: 'You said a bad driver was only safe until she met another bad driver? Well, I met another bad driver, didn't I? I mean it was care- less of me to make such a wrong guess. I thought you were rather an honest, straightforward person. I thought it was your secret pride.' Jordan thinks she was careless, but that they were both bad drivers. Nick won't accept the charge of having been dishonourable: 'I'm thirty,' he says. 'I'm five years too old to lie to myself and call it honor.' But Jordan may have a point: she certainly made a wrong guess.

The last person Nick sees before he leaves is Tom Buchanan. They bump into each other, and Nick asks Tom what he said to George Wilson the afternoon that Wilson shot Gatsby and then himself. Nick is just guessing, but Tom's expression shows him that he's guessed right. On the fatal day, George Wilson came to the Buchanans' house look- ing for the driver of the yellow car, and Tom gave him Gatsby's name. Tom says defiantly: 'What if I did tell him? That fellow had it coming to him. He threw dust into your eyes just like he did in Daisy's but he was a tough one. He ran over Myrtle like you'd run over a dog and never even stopped his car.' Nick takes refuge in the incommunicable one final time: 'There was nothing I could say, except the one unutterable fact that it wasn't true.' The final mistake in identity hovers, uncorrected:

Daisy never told her husband that she was driving the car. Daisy was the person who truly sacrificed Gatsby, as she deceived even Tom.

It is at this point of silence that Nick names his world's malaise: 'It was all very careless and confused. They were careless people, Tom and Daisy – they smashed up things and creatures and then retreated back into their money or their vast carelessness or whatever it was that kept them together, and let other people clean up the mess they had made.' But again Nick keeps his judgements to himself, complicit in the lies and corruption he has just identified. He shakes Tom's hand, saying it seems silly not to, and watches Tom go into a jewellery store to buy a pearl necklace, perhaps for Daisy, or perhaps for some other woman to dangle off a funeral bier as she's carried drunkenly into the wrong house.

Nick has already discreetly planned Gatsby's funeral: 'I didn't want it to be in the papers and draw a sightseeing crowd.' He succeeds in avoiding publicity so well that when the day of the funeral arrives, neither do any mourners. Jay Gatsby, the man who was defined by his guests, has no one to grieve over him but his father, his neighbour and the one man who appears at Nick's side by the grave, Owl-Eyes, who stares, amazed that no one has come: '"Why, my God! they used to go there by the hundreds." He took off his glasses and wiped them again outside and in. "The poor son-of-a-bitch," he said.'

El Greco's distorted vision presides over the novel's ending, as Fitzgerald invokes the old master who painted because the spirits whispered madly in his head, seeing in the stars God's careless splatters.

---

## MAN'S HOPE

'I left my capacity for hoping on the little roads that led to Zelda's sanitarium,' Fitzgerald wrote in his notebooks, but in 1938 he started trying to recapture it. That summer he sent a letter to Beatrice Dance, a woman with whom he'd had a brief affair in 1935, during the worst days of the crack-up. He was currently living on Malibu Beach, he told her:

I have a cottage on the Pacific which I gaze at morning and night with a not too wild surmise – my capacity for wonder has greatly diminished. And anyway it automatically stops whenever I cross the Mississippi River. I have a grand novel up my sleeve and I'd love to go to France and write it this summer. It would be short like 'Gatsby' but the same in that it will have the transcendental approach, an attempt to show a man's life through some passionately regarded segment of it. This letter was to have been about you but there is only the old you that I knew – knew very well I think – yet I always enjoyed the thrill of surprise when you made some new romantic gesture. *Almost* you always made all your dreams plausible – so often they quivered on the edge of fulfillment, but there were ranges of mountains higher than the Rockies in the way.

The letter could be addressed to young Jimmy Gatz from North Dakota, so reverberant is it with the language and sensibility of *The Great Gatsby*. The working title for the new transcendental book was *The Last Tycoon*, which Fitzgerald told Zelda would be 'a novel *à la Flaubert* without "ideas" but only people moved singly and in mass through what I hope are authentic moods. The resemblance is rather to *Gatsby* than to anything else I've written.'

And to Scottie he wrote: 'I wish now I'd *never* relaxed or looked back – but said at the end of *The Great Gatsby*: "I've found my line – from now on this comes first. This is my immediate duty – without this I am nothing."' To find his line again, he would return to the ground of his greatest work, the book that he knew was a masterpiece, even if no one else did, and wrest out of his 'expiring talent' another magnificent novel.

For a year or more, Fitzgerald had been hearing echoes, trying to recapture his once-perfect pitch. He was reading constantly, piling up recently published books: Marjorie Kinnan Rawlings's *The Yearling* (it 'fascinated me ... just simply flows'), Steinbeck's *Of Mice and Men* ('praised all out of proportion to its merits'), John O'Hara's *Hope of Heaven* ('he didn't bite off anything to chew on. He just began chewing with nothing in his mouth') and a new book, published in the US for the first time the previous year, called *The Trial*, which he described to his friend John Biggs as 'a fantastic novel by the Czech Franz Kafka which you may have to wait for but it is worth it'.

Fitzgerald had also read André Malraux's *Man's Hope*, an eyewitness account of the Spanish Civil War. He didn't much care for it, preferring Malraux's *Man's Fate*, which he considered 'the best *individual* novel of the last five years'. *Man's Hope* was just 'hasty journalism', he said, 'about as good as Ernest's Spanish stuff'. (His erstwhile friend Hemingway's *For Whom the Bell Tolls* was a novel Fitzgerald judged to have been written for the movies, 'with all the profundity of *Rebecca*'.)

But one day between 1938 and 1940 it was *Man's Hope* that Fitzgerald picked up: perhaps he liked what its title suggested. Maybe, with memory and imagination, he could recapture the past and there find again his art, 'a delicate thing – mine is so scarred and buffeted that I am amazed that at times it still runs clear. (God what a mess of similes).' He opened the book at the back cover, and on the last fly-leaf he printed a schedule, without a date. And underneath:

It is a schedule for self-improvement, a short autobiography, a love letter to the past. It is a programmatic attempt to recover the self-made man who had been unmade by fate, a to-do list for retrieving all he had lost by the man who loved lists. He did not write it on the last fly-leaf of *Hopalong Cassidy*, but on the last fly-leaf of *Man's Hope*. Sometimes life provides better images than imagination and Fitzgerald's life had always been magically graced by symbols. 'I come across this book by accident,' as Henry Gatz told Nick. 'It just shows you, don't it?' We come across this book by accident, and it just shows us – without explaining to us what we should think about what it shows.

In 1939 Fitzgerald began work on *The Last Tycoon* in earnest. In late 1940 he would say that he had not had a drink in over a year, but his past was strewn with false claims and false starts. As late as February 1939 he had been hospitalized for what he still called going on a bat, but he was doing his best, fighting to resurrect his art. The past was all around him: 'We were the great believers,' he wrote in his 1939 essay, 'My Generation'. Ginevra King came to Hollywood; predictably Fitzgerald got drunk in order to brave the reunion and it did not go well. In October he wrote to Zelda about a party he'd attended: 'A lot of the past came into that party. Fay Wray, whose husband John Monk Saunders committed suicide two months ago; Deems Taylor whom I haven't seen twice since the days of the Swopes . . .'

By the autumn of 1940 he was telling Zelda, 'I am deep in the novel, living in it, and it makes me happy.' *The Last Tycoon* would be a '*constructed* novel like *Gatsby*, with passages of poetic prose when it fits the action, but no ruminations or side-shows like *Tender*. Everything must contribute to the dramatic movement. It's odd that my old talent for the short story vanished. It was partly that times changed, editors changed, but part of it was tied up somehow with you and me – the happy ending.'

The happy ending had dissipated into the vanished past, but tragedy was well within Scott Fitzgerald's expertise, and now perhaps he could bring to his writing a hard-earned wisdom; if the glitter had worn off his bright cleverness, it was showing the steel of his intelligence beneath. 'Twenty years ago "This Side of Paradise" was a best seller,' he wrote to Zelda in 1940. 'Ten years ago Paris was having almost its last great American season but we had quit the gay parade and you were gone to Switzerland. Five years ago I had my first bad stroke of illness and went to Asheville. Cards began falling badly for us much too early,' he concluded, but 'the world has certainly caught up in the last four weeks.' He hoped she was not too surrounded by the 'war talk' that was engulfing America.

The novel was coming, slowly but surely. 'I am digging it out of myself like uranium – one ounce to the cubic ton of rejected ideas.' In late November he told Bunny Wilson: 'I think my novel is good. I've written it with difficulty ... I am trying a little harder than I ever have to be exact and honest emotionally.' In December 1940 he wrote to Zelda: 'Everything is my novel now – it has become of absorbing interest. I hope I'll be able to finish it by February.'

On 15 December Fitzgerald sent a letter to Scottie explaining that he had recently had heart trouble, thanks to twenty-five years of cigarettes. 'You have got two beautiful bad examples of parents. Just do everything we didn't do and you will be perfectly safe.' He had, in fact, had a minor heart attack and was in bed recuperating. He urged her to be 'sweet' to Zelda over Christmas, 'despite her early Chaldean rune-worship which she will undoubtedly inflict on you. Her letters are tragically brilliant on all matters except those of central importance,' he added. 'How strange to have failed as a social creature – even criminals do not fail that way – they are the law's "Loyal Opposition", so to speak. But the insane are always mere guests on earth, eternal strangers carrying around broken decalogues that they cannot read.'

It was the last letter he would write to his daughter. On 21 December 1940, Scott Fitzgerald died suddenly of occlusive coronary arteriosclerosis in California, while sitting in an armchair at Sheilah Graham's apartment, reading about the Princeton football team and commenting on the reporter's prose in the margins. He was forty-four years old. In August Fitzgerald had received what would be his last royalty statement, reporting the sale of nine copies of *Tender is the Night* and seven copies of *The Great Gatsby*. *The Great Gatsby* had earned a total of $2.10 in royalties that year; Fitzgerald had not sold a single book outside the United States in the last twelve months of his life, and all of his books combined had earned him an unlucky total of $13.13. Life continued to shower him with symbols, right up to the bitter end.

Fitzgerald's body was put on view at a mortuary in a seedy Los Angeles neighbourhood, in the William Wordsworth Room. 'Except for one bouquet of flowers and a few empty chairs, there was nothing to keep him company,' wrote one of the few reporters who went. 'I never saw a sadder [scene] than the end of the father of all the sad young men.' John O'Hara declared, 'Scott should have been killed in a Bugatti in the south of France, and not to have died of neglect in Hollywood, a prematurely old little man haunting bookstores unrecognized.' Gerald Murphy wrote of his shock: 'I thought of him as imperishable, somehow.' The *New York Times* regarded Fitzgerald as such a minor writer that they didn't bother getting the facts right, describing *The Beautiful and Damned* as a short story. 'With the skill of a reporter and ability of an artist he captured the essence of a period when flappers and gin and "the beautiful and damned" were the symbols of the carefree madness of an age,' the *Times's* obituary said, before concluding that 'the promise of his brilliant career was never fulfilled'. The next day a brief editorial agreed: *The Great Gatsby* 'was not a book for the ages, but it caught superbly the spirit of a decade ... here was real talent which never fully bloomed'.

Notified of Scott's sudden death, Zelda gave confused instructions and collapsed. Nineteen-year-old Scottie, 'tragic and bewildered', said she had 'thought for so long that *every* day he would die for some reason'. Fitzgerald's original will, written during the days of grand extravagance, had left the seigneurial instructions that he be buried 'in accordance with my station'. Later, he'd amended the request to 'the cheapest funeral ... without undue ostentation or unnecessary expense'.

Fitzgerald's body was sent east, to be buried with his father in Rockville, Maryland, but St Mary's Church refused him burial. Scottie believed it was because his books were on a proscribed list at the time of his death, but in fact it was because he hadn't received last rites. One of the mourners was Andrew Turnbull, a Maryland friend who would later write Fitzgerald's biography and edit the first collection of his letters. Turnbull described the funeral as 'a meaningless occasion, having no apparent connection with the man, save as one of life's grim jokes ... It was the sort of *envoi* a great dramatist might attach to the end of a play.' 'Afterwards,' he finished, 'we drove to the cemetery in the rain.'

The whole day, in fact, uncannily echoed the funeral Fitzgerald had invented in 1924: 'About five o'clock our procession of three cars reached the cemetery and stopped in a thick drizzle beside the gate – first a motor hearse, horribly black and wet, then Mr Gatz and the minister and I in the limousine, and, a little later, four or five servants and the postman from West Egg in Gatsby's station wagon, all wet to the skin. As we started through the gate into the cemetery I heard a car stop and then the sound of someone splashing after us over the soggy ground', coming to offer an elegy.

Fitzgerald's old friend and drinking companion Dorothy Parker had been one of the few people to view his body in Los Angeles; she supposedly echoed the epitaph he bestowed upon his most famous character: 'The poor son of a bitch.' If she had gone east for the funeral, Parker might well also have repeated Owl-Eyes's other exclamation, 'Why, my God! they used to go there by the hundreds.' Fitzgerald's burial service was attended by about twenty people; Zelda was not permitted by her doctors to go, and only a few of the old crowd of friends made it. Gerald and Sara Murphy, Max Perkins and his wife, the Obers, Ludlow Fowler, Fitzgerald's cousin Cecilia Taylor, John Biggs and a few other friends were the only mourners. Fitzgerald was buried at Rockville Union Cemetery on 27 December 1940, eulogized by an Episcopalian rector who made the extraordinary (and rarely reported) decision to make public his disgust for the man he was burying: 'The only reason I agreed to give the service, was to get the body in the ground. He was a no-good, drunken bum, and the world was well rid of him.'

Zelda wrote to Max Perkins of her grief at realizing they wouldn't 'share again the happy possibility aspirational promise that he always seemed buoyed with', their mutual loss of Fitzgerald's courage and faith and devotion. A year earlier, she had unwittingly offered her own elegy to Scott, only slightly premature. 'Dearest: I am always grateful to all the loyalties you gave me, and I am always loyal to the concepts that held us together so long: the belief that life is tragic, that man's spiritual reward is the keeping of his faith: that we shouldn't hurt each other. And I love, always your fine writing talent, your tolerance and generosity; and all your happy endowments. Nothing could have survived our life.'

---

# A HEEDLESS NATION

## Careless of Past and Future

As he prepares to leave the east, Nick finds that he can't shake off his dreams of Gatsby's revels, 'those gleaming, dazzling parties of his were with me so vividly that I could still hear the music and the laughter faint and incessant from his garden and the cars going up and down his drive. One night I did hear a material car there and saw its lights stop at his front steps. But I didn't investigate. Probably it was some final guest who had been away at the ends of the earth and didn't know that the party was over.'

After seeing the final material trace of Gatsby's accidental parties, Nick walks over to Gatsby's house on his last night, looking 'at that huge incoherent failure of a house once more'. He erases some obscene graffiti scrawled on the steps (hinting perhaps at Nick's persistent need to idealize) and walks down to the beach for his last view of Long Island Sound. And then Fitzgerald offers his great meditation on the lost paradise of America:

Most of the big shore places were closed now and there were hardly any lights except the shadowy, moving glow of a ferryboat across the

Sound. And as the moon rose higher the inessential houses began to melt away until gradually I became aware of the old island here that flowered once for Dutch sailors' eyes – a fresh, green breast of the new world. Its vanished trees, the trees that had made way for Gatsby's house, had once pandered in whispers to the last and greatest of all human dreams; for a transitory enchanted moment man must have held his breath in the presence of this continent, compelled into an aesthetic contemplation he neither understood nor desired, face to face for the last time in history with something commensurate to his capacity for wonder.

And as I sat there brooding on the old, unknown world, I thought of Gatsby's wonder when he first picked out the green light at the end of Daisy's dock. He had come a long way to this blue lawn and his dream must have seemed so close that he could hardly fail to grasp it. He did not know that it was already behind him, somewhere back in that vast obscurity beyond the city, where the dark fields of the republic rolled on under the night.

Gatsby believed in the green light, the orgastic future that year by year recedes before us. It eluded us then, but that's no matter – tomorrow we will run faster, stretch out our arms farther . . . And one fine morning –

So we beat on, boats against the current, borne back ceaselessly into the past.

The ninth chapter of *The Great Gatsby* is Fitzgerald's ninth symphony, his ode to lost joy. Before he died, Fitzgerald wrote to Scottie about what it meant to appreciate beauty: '*The Grecian Urn* is unbearably beautiful with every syllable as inevitable as the notes in Beethoven's Ninth Symphony or it's just something you don't understand. It is what it is because an extraordinary genius paused at that point in history and touched it. I suppose I've read it a hundred times. About the tenth time I began to know what it was about, and caught the chime in it and the exquisite inner mechanics.' In the novel's final words, the deep-focus economy of Fitzgerald's prose and characterization suddenly widens from the particular details of the people we have been watching, and gathers a generalizing force that sweeps all of America before it.

Originally Fitzgerald had written this valedictory passage to end Chapter One, when Nick stands on the edge of his lawn and watches Gatsby measure the heavens. Reading the modulations of the edited draft is like hearing a familiar song in a different key: 'And as I sat there brooding on the old unknown world I too held my breath and waited, until I could feel the ~~very~~ motion of ~~the continent~~ America as it turned through the ~~dark~~ hours – my own blue lawn and the tall incandescent city on the water and beyond that the dark fields of the republic rolling on under the night.' The original first chapter finished there, until Fitzgerald moved the passage to the end of the novel, erased the towering incandescent city in the distance, and added in his first draft the idea that Gatsby had lost his dream 'long before, not here but westward, where the dark fields of the republic rolled on under the night'. Having left the dream of hope and progress behind him in the west, Gatsby finds himself stranded on the wrong side of Eden, disinherited from the promise of America.

Ultimately Fitzgerald chose not to use the word 'America' at all in the novel's concluding passage. America remains an emblem – not quite a metaphor, but a symbol, a figure, the fact as colossal as a continent – and what it represents is not a specific nation but a human capacity, our capacity for hope, for wonder, for discovery. And it also represents the corruption of that capacity into a faith in the material world, rather than the ideal one. It reminds us, too, of our careless habit of losing our paradises.

Gatsby's destiny is manifest, but he is also subject to the amnesias and ignorances that destroy the American experiment. Murder happens casually and is forgotten, the story of America told through tokens of forgotten violence. Gatsby does not understand that the American romance with the west is over. The nation's hope has been exhausted, its promise glimpsed and left for ever unrealized. There will be no triumph of hope any more than there will be a triumph of the will. The great Emersonian dream of self-reliance does not survive its encounter with the forces of society and destiny in the shape of the carelessness of the rich. The disillusionment of this novel lies not in its disappointment in romantic love, but in the outcome of our romance with America.

America, too, is a blend of fact and fiction, a story told out of the chaotic facts of an uncertain land, in which the question of who is guilty will never be determined. We never find out who did it, because no one and everyone is to blame, everyone is equally guilty. The rich did it, the poor did it, it's been a case of mistaken identity all along, America mistaking itself for something it may not be – or hasn't yet become.

The future continues to recede before us, as we are borne back into the past to find there, awaiting us, our present: recklessness and greed, waste and profligacy, trial by newspaper and manipulative media moguls, irresponsible bankers and bad investments, cronyism and corruption, media scandals and Ponzi schemes, invented celebrities and frauds, violence and cynicism, epidemic materialism and a frantic search for the values we keep losing.

Clairvoyance does not mean prophecy: it means seeing clear. Trying to see America clear, we stand amid the debris, looking at the old hopes of the vagrant dead as they scatter across our tattered Eden.

# ENVOI

## THE ORGASTIC FUTURE

After Scott Fitzgerald's sudden death, Edmund Wilson, who by 1940 had become one of America's most influential literary critics, decided that although Fitzgerald had not lived long enough to finish *The Last Tycoon*, it merited publication, and took on the task of editing it. To add length and gravitas to his 1941 volume, he included *The Great Gatsby*, and a reassessment began.

Four years later, Wilson published *The Crack-Up and Other Essays*, a collection of Fitzgerald's essays, letters and selections from his notebooks. Other eminent critics began arguing for Fitzgerald's significance. *The Great Gatsby*, declared the critic Lionel Trilling, remained 'as fresh as when it first appeared; it has even gained in weight and relevance, which can be said of very few American books of its time.' Although it was a 'record of contemporary manners', this had not dated the novel, thanks to the 'specifically intellectual courage' that Fitzgerald brought to it. Trilling compared Fitzgerald to the French novelists of the nineteenth century, to the English Romantic poets and to Goethe, comparisons he insisted were legitimate, although he knew they would surprise his readers. Most important was Fitzgerald's voice, in which could be heard, said Trilling, 'the tenderness toward human desire that modifies a true firmness of moral judgment. It is,' he added, the 'ideal voice of the novelist.'

In 1945 Malcolm Cowley wrote, 'Fitzgerald had the sense of living in history', trying to 'catch the color of every passing year'; he cultivated a 'double vision' that let him simultaneously celebrate glamour and view it from the outside, a 'little Midwestern boy with his nose to the glass'. 'It is a difficult technical problem to tell the truth in fiction,' Cowley added, but Fitzgerald 'had both the technique and the need for being honest.' A year later John Berryman called *Gatsby* a masterpiece, and Trilling published his introduction to a new edition of *Gatsby*, declaring, 'Fitzgerald is now beginning to take his place in our literary tradition.' A renaissance had begun.

'I always feel that Daddy was the key-note and prophet of his generation and deserves remembrance as such,' Zelda told Scottie. In 1941 she published a formal tribute to Scott, lamenting that their era had been 'lost in its platonic sources': 'He endowed those years that might have been so garishly reckless with the dignity of his bright indicative scene, and buoyed the desperation of a bitter day with the spontaneity of his appreciation ... The meter being waltz time which moves nostalgic twilights to their rendezvous, the world believes again in sentiment and turns to fairy tale; whereas those years haunted by the more aggressive sadness of march time produce a more dynamic, tragic spiritual compensation.' Fitzgerald's 'tragic tales' were of the 'plaintive deaths [of] the gilded aspirations of a valiant and protesting age'.

'In retrospect,' she wrote to Harold Ober, 'it seems as if he was always planning happinesses for Scottie, and for me. Books to read – places to go. Life seemed so promissory when he was around.' Over the years after Scott's death, Zelda continued to move in and out of Highland Hospital, trying to live at home with her mother in Montgomery and then returning to the medical support of the hospital. She worked intermittently on an autobiographical novel she never finished, *Caesar's Things*, and painted. Her religious zeal intensified, and she wrote letters to old friends hoping for their salvation.

In March 1948 Zelda was in her room on the top floor of Highland Hospital, locked in at night with the other patients. A fire began in the kitchen below, and blazed through the whole building, killing nine women who could not be rescued in time. Zelda's body was burned beyond recognition, identified only by a slipper that survived the flames. She was forty-seven years old.

Over the years several 'true crime' books about the murders of Hall and Mills were published. One book argued that the Ku Klux Klan committed the murders; another that the culprit was Willie Stevens, protecting the honour of his family, and that his sister was covering up for him. A former judge told a *New York Times* reporter in 1992 that he was 'confident that the Stevens family were responsible for the murders' of Hall and Mills. 'The reason the prosecution couldn't win the trial was because the case wasn't well tried. They had lousy witnesses and the defense was excellent.' The New Brunswick district attorney's office continues to give talks about the case, suggesting that the Stevens family committed the crimes. But no new evidence has ever come to light and the mystery of who murdered Eleanor Mills and Edward Hall was never solved.

'Fitzgerald was a better just plain writer than all of us put together. Just words writing,' John O'Hara told John Steinbeck. The first biography of Fitzgerald, Arthur Mizener's *The Far Side of Paradise*, appeared in the same year as the first full-length critical study, Alfred Kazin's *F. Scott Fitzgerald: The Man and His Work*, and just after Budd Schulberg's *roman-à-clef* about his time with Fitzgerald in Hollywood at the end of his life, *The Disenchanted* (1950). In 1949 Hollywood released a film version of *Gatsby* starring Alan Ladd, a film noir in which Jordan Baker reforms and marries Nick, Tom Buchanan has a change of heart and tries to warn Gatsby that Wilson is on his way to shoot him, and Gatsby delivers a remarkably incoherent speech before he is shot saying that he's going to turn himself in, as a moral exemplum for lost young men: 'What's going to happen to kids like Jimmy Gatz if guys like me don't tell them we're wrong?'

Scottie Fitzgerald donated all of her parents' papers in her possession, which she had steadfastly refused to sell or scatter, to Princeton University in 1950. The following year Malcolm Cowley edited a revised *Tender is the Night*, rearranging the novel's three sections into chronological order, a decision prompted by some tinkering Fitzgerald had been doing with the novel before he died, trying to account for its critical failure. Cowley also published a new edition of Fitzgerald's stories, including some that had never been collected before. *The Great Gatsby* had by now become required reading in many American schools, and the subject of theses, dissertations and journal articles; as early as 1952, readers were seeing in *Gatsby* a study of carelessness. The legend of Scott Fitzgerald continued to grow, entangling itself with ideas about *Gatsby* and with another idea that was taking root over the same period, called the American dream, an idea that America grabbed hold of in 1931, the same year that it named 'The Star-Spangled Banner' its national anthem.

Before 1931, the phrase 'American dream' as we know it did not exist, but that year a popular historian named James Truslow Adams wrote a book called *The Epic of America*, which spoke of 'the American dream of a better, richer and happier life for all our citizens of every rank, which is the greatest contribution we have made to the thought and welfare of the world. That dream or hope has been present from the start. Ever since we became an independent nation, each generation has seen an uprising of ordinary Americans to save that dream from the forces that appear to be overwhelming it.' Adams's book sparked a great national debate in the early years of the Great Depression about the promise of America, and the idea of the American dream has become as familiar as the novel that is held to exemplify it, but actually helped prophesy it into existence.

It is not a coincidence that *The Great Gatsby* began to be widely hailed as a masterpiece in America during the 1950s, as the American dream took hold once more, and the nation was once again absorbed in chasing the green light of economic and material success.

*The Great Gatsby* is a stranger novel than some of the bromides about it admit. Dig deep and you will not find the perfection that some sigh about – but you will find a nearly incorruptible style purifying and controlling the incoherence of Fitzgerald's raw material. The novel's small imperfections do not disappoint for long: it is so rich and unexpected, so slight and so unfathomable, so much a story of its moment and yet so much a story of ours.

It is a reckoning of the nation's hopes and its failures, and Scott Fitzgerald has long been hailed as one of America's most important, and best loved, writers. In addition to that remarkable voice, his uncanny prescience has long been recognized and celebrated. But there are still aspects of his faculty for guessing right that we have yet to see, such as that in his 1929 story 'The Swimmers', Fitzgerald predicted the metaphor of the '99 per cent' that has so dominated recent conversations about economic inequality. Two years earlier Fitzgerald told a *World* reporter that America would face a great 'national testing' in the near future: 'The idea that we're the greatest people in the world because we have the most money in the world is ridiculous. Wait until this wave of prosperity is over! Wait ten or fifteen years! Wait until the next war on the Pacific, or against some European combination! ... The next fifteen years will show how much resistance there is in the American race.' It was 1927, and he was right again. 'There has never been an American tragedy,' Fitzgerald ended. 'There have only been great failures.'

What Fitzgerald once called 'the opportunistic memory' of Americans abounds in popular readings of *The Great Gatsby*. Fitzgerald's first readers could only see one half of the meaning of the book, its entanglement with the facts and contexts of the day, and were blind to its transcendent meanings. We tend now to focus on those universal meanings, letting our myths and misapprehensions about the 1920s take the place of facts about Fitzgerald's world. Each moment mistakes the part for the whole, seeing only one side of his book, the other side obscured by the darkness of the era's own blind spots, the lustre of the moon half hidden by the shadows of the earth.

But Fitzgerald's genius was in seeing it whole, in having it both ways, which is what fiction is for: the eternal *as if*, the world suspended in a conditional mood, awaiting its intricate and indeterminate destiny.

# NOTES

## Abbreviations

| | |
|---|---|
| FSF | F. Scott Fitzgerald |
| NYT | *New York Times* |
| PUL | Princeton University Library |
| *Tribune* | *New York Tribune* |
| *World* | *New York World* |
| ZF | Zelda Fitzgerald |

## Preface

1  'I want to write something new . . .': *Correspondence of F. Scott Fitzgerald*, 112.

'the very best I am capable of . . .': *A Life in Letters*, 65.

3  'the murder of the decade', 'The Hall–Mills case . . .', 'It was an illiterate . . .': Allen, *Only Yesterday*, 4.

4  'You pick up your morning paper . . .': Bryer (ed.), *The Critical Reception*, 242

6  'I insist on reading meanings into things': *Correspondence of F. Scott Fitzgerald*, 577.

7  'Fitz argued about various things . . .': Milford, *Zelda Fitzgerald*, 84.

'for all your superior observation . . .': *Dear Scott, Dearest Zelda*, 65.

9  'inebriate', 'animosities develop, quarrels arise . . .': NYT, 27 June 1922.

## 1924

15  on board the SS Minnewaska: The *NYT* reported on 3 May 1924 when

the SS *Minnewaska* set sail and its passenger list. The rest is from Bruccoli, *Some Sort of Epic Grandeur*, 229.

16 '*We were going to the Old World* ...': 'How to Live on Practically Nothing a Year', 20 September 1924, in *Afternoon of an Author*, 102.

*they drank champagne cocktails and had to apologize*: 'A Short Autobiography', *New Yorker*, 25 May 1929, in *In His Own Time*, 223.

17 '*rose in wild stimulation on the barbaric* ...': *Save Me the Waltz*, in *The Collected Writings*, 82.

*drank Graves Kressmann* ... *and got into political arguments*: 'A Short Autobiography', 223.

'*My novel grows more and more extraordinary* ...': *Correspondence of F. Scott Fitzgerald*, 141.

## I. Glamour of Rumseys and Hitchcocks

22 '*Bonds were the thing now* ...': 'The Popular Girl', *Saturday Evening Post*, 11 February 1922.

23 '*Arrive Wednesday tell no one*': PUL, Charles Scribner's Sons Papers.

24 *they had 'a violent quarrel'*: *A Life in Letters*, 191.

'*there is a feeling of accomplishment* ...': 'A Millionaire's Girl', in *The Collected Writings*, 331.

'*hard and emerald eyes*': Wilson, *Night Thoughts*, 121.

'*sophomore face and troubadour heart*': Ben Hecht, *A Child of the Century* (New York: Simon & Schuster, 1954), 395.

'*such a sunny man*': Milford, *Zelda Fitzgerald*, 120.

'*Fitzgerald was pert and fresh and blond* ...': John Peale Bishop, 'Fitzgerald at Princeton', in *An F. Scott Fitzgerald Companion*, 2.

'*that he might even have been called beautiful*': H. L. Mencken, *My Life as Author and Editor* (New York: Knopf, 1992), 256–7.

'*Fitzgerald is romantic* ...': Edmund Wilson, *The Shores of Light* (New York: Farrar, Straus, and Young, 1952), 31

25 '*haunted [their] generation like a song* ...': Churchill, *The Literary Decade*, 72.

'*astonishing prettiness*': Wilson, *Letters on Literature and Politics*, 478.

'*any real sense of what she looked like* ...': Ring Lardner, Jr, quoted in Taylor, *Sometimes Madness is Wisdom*, 26.

26 '*an artist in her particular field* ...': *The Collected Writings*, xxi.

'*Called on Scott Fitz and his bride* ...': Milford, *Zelda Fitzgerald*, 75

'*full of felicitous phrases and unexpected fancies* ...': Wilson, *Letters on Literature and Politics*, 478.

28 'discreetly hooded', 'a degree of privacy in pairs': NYT, 1 July 1923.

29 'New York is a good place to be on the upgrade': The Collected Writings, 49.

30 a comical piece about an 'Old Soak': Tribune, 15 September 1922.

30–1 'Laughed with a sudden memory of Hopkins . . .': Notebooks, 224.

31 putting on a show of 'the cat's pajamas': NYT, 16 November 1922.
current adjectives, "hectic and delirious and killing"': The Collected Writings, 361.
'the new and really swagger things': New Yorker, 2 May 1925.
'It was slick to have seen you': PUL, Charles Scribner's Sons Papers.
'Thank you again for the slick party . . .': ZF to Carl Hovey. Huntington Library, ALS.

34 'a chorus of pleasant envy followed . . .': Bits of Paradise, 311.
I can feel my ears growing pointed . . .': Wilson. The Twenties, 66.

35 'She was an original . . .': Milford, Zelda Fitzgerald, 98.
'Fitz blew up drunk, as usual . . .': Wilson, The Twenties, 115.
'Unfortunately, liquor sets him wild . . .': Mencken, The Diary of H. L. Mencken, 45.
Suggested to Scott and Zelda they save . . .': Milford, Zelda Fitzgerald, 80.

36 'eccentric': NYT, 19 September 1922.
'two children': NYT, 17 September 1922.
'MRS HALL, THE "WOMAN IN A POLO COAT" . . .': NYT, 18 September 1922.
'Mrs Mills, twenty-eight and the mother . . .': Daily World, 17 September 1922.

37 'rich wife', 'a pale, nervous little man', 'never did understand': Tribune, 17 September 1922.
'clawed', 'deep finger-nail scratches', 'killed by a companion . . .': NYT, 18 September 1922.
'The marks on the clergyman's hands and arms . . .': Ibid.
'Something terrible is going to happen . . .': Ibid.

38–9 'The Long and Short of New York': NYT, 17 September 1922.

39 'the first abortive shortening of the skirts': 'Echoes of the Jazz Age', in The Crack-Up, 22.
'the smartest summer color . . .': NYT, 11 June 1922.

40 'gentlemen's clothes', 'symbol of "the power . . ."': 'Echoes of the Jazz Age', 14.

41 'looked into Emily Post and [was] inspired . . .': Edmund Wilson, quoted in Berman, The Great Gatsby and Modern Times, 73.

42 'four bulging scrapbooks full of all the things . . .': Save Me the Waltz, in The Collected Writings, 58.

'We are accustomed enough to this . . .': Milford, *Zelda Fitzgerald*, 96

43 'to experiment with herself as a transient . . .': *The Collected Writings*, 392–3.

'dancing happily about . . .': *Save Me the Waltz*, 46.

'as proudly careless about money . . .': Cowley, *A Second Flowering*, 36.

'If ever there was a pair whose fantasies . . .': Quoted in Taylor, *Sometimes Madness is Wisdom*, 36.

'You can order it in four sizes . . .': *Notebooks*, 33.

44 'I liked your interview immensely . . .': Bruccoli and Baughman (eds), *Conversations with F. Scott Fitzgerald*, 26–7.

'the recognized spokesman of the younger generation . . .': Ibid, 6.

'Yes, The Beautiful and Damned is true . . .': *World*, 5 March 1922.

45 'I like the ones that are like me . . .': *Louisville Courier-Journal*, 30 September 1923.

46 'plagiarising their existence': Churchill, *The Literary Decade*, 68.

46–7 'Mrs Mills was slain by a bullet . . .': *NYT*, 21 September 1922.

48 'looked like Flanders Field': Wilson, *The Twenties*, 115.

'the room was always swimming in gin . . .': Ibid., 116.

'he was tickled to death . . .': Ibid., 204.

'You couldn't have in in the room . . .': Ibid., 116.

'wishbone' diaphragms: Quoted in Kinney, *James Thurber*, 379.

'I suppose I'd be a nicer girl . . .': *Town Topics*, 7 December 1922.

48–9 'One of Ted's principal pastimes . . .': Wilson, *The Twenties*, 52.

49 'very pretty and languid': Ibid., 64.

'the rumorous hum of summer': Ibid., 110.

'Fitz goes about soberly transacting his business . . .': Wilson, *Letters on Literature and Politics*, 97.

You could only tell the story of the Fitzgeralds: Ibid., 478.

50 'any scholar of the future shall seek to learn . . .': Bryer (ed.), *The Critical Reception*, 161.

'fiction will be the treasure trove of the antiquarian . . .': PUL, FSF Scrapbooks.

'In this book Mr F has developed his gifts . . .': *A Life in Letters*, 59–60.

'a certain phase of life that has not been portrayed . . .': PUL, FSF Scrapbooks.

'I want to be one of the greatest writers . . .': Edmund Wilson, 'Thoughts on Being Bibliographed', *Princeton University Library Chronicle*, 5.2 (1944): 54.

'even then he was determined to be a genius . . .': John Peale Bishop, 'Fitzgerald at Princeton', in *An F. Scott Fitzgerald Companion*, 1.

51  When I'm with John [Bishop], I say . . .': Wilson, *The Twenties*, 64–5.

52  'the flapper springs full grown, like Minerva . . .': *The Collected Writings*, 397.

'The unholy finger of jazz holds nothing sacred . . .': PUL, FSF Scrapbooks.

53  When Harriman died in 1909: Abramson, *Spanning the Century*, 22.

55  'research is in the chronicles of the big business juntos . . .': John C. Mosher, 'That Sad Young Man', *New Yorker*, 17 April 1926.

55–6  'Rockefeller Center: that it all came out . . .': *Correspondence of F. Scott Fitzgerald*, 461.

56  'would always cherish an abiding distrust . . .': 'The Crack-Up', in *The Crack-Up*, 77.

57  hiring Zelda to add some 'sparkle' to his pages: PUL, ZF Scrapbook.

Rascoe also wrote a weekly Sunday column: Rascoe's Day Book column, wrote Malcolm Cowley later, 'gave a better picture of that frenzied age than any historian could hope to equal. He was distinguished among literary journalists by really loving his profession, by speaking with hasty candor and being absolutely unself-protective in his hates and enthusiasms.' Cowley, *Exile's Return*, 176.

'Aspiration and discontent are the parents . . .': *Tribune*, 24 September 1922.

58  'proved too generous a host . . .': *Tribune*, 1 October 1922.

## II. Ash Heaps. Memory of 125th. Gt Neck

60  ledger . . . put the lunch in September: *Ledger*, 177.

61  'gaudy Liberty silk necktie', 'selfindulgent mouth', 'Scott always . . .': Dos Passos, *The Best Times*, 130.

62  'also had an act as Prince Charming . . .': Wilson, *The Twenties*, 90.

'Their gambit was to put you in the wrong . . .': Dos Passos, *The Best Times*, 128.

63  'a humble man of an unusually credulous . . .': NYT, 23 September 1922.

'before his wife's death' . . . Mills had been 'dominated': Ibid.

64  'Mrs Hall does not like flappers . . .': Ibid.

'highly imaginative', 'fond of reading . . .', 'nobody': Ibid.

'a hotbed of trouble', 'Mrs Mills was the cause . . .': NYT, 24 September 1922.

65  'the triumphant put-put of their cut-outs . . .': 'Dice, Brassknuckles & Guitar', *Short Stories*, 252.

66  'a cross movement or side-shoot of some kind': NYT, 8 November 1922.

'traffic signal uniformity . . .': NYT, 1 September 1924.

'*as he struck a Swedish match and lit . . .*': FSF, 'How to Live on Practically Nothing a Year', in *Afternoon of an Author*, 113

67   '*Life is slipping away, crumbling all round us . . .*': *New Yorker*, 18 May 1929.

*Astoria, where Nick and Gatsby would scatter light*: Fitzgerald was later told that, technically, Nick and Gatsby were scattering light through Long Island City, but as he was not trying to map New York he continued to call it Astoria, retaining the symbolic meaning of a neighbourhood that had been named for America's richest man, in an effort to persuade him to invest some of his vast wealth in the area. Astor sent the district five hundred dollars and never set foot in it.

68   *Refuse stretched in all directions*: NYT, 15 April 1923.

*ash-heaps, looming like a corner of the Inferno*: Lionel Trilling, introduction to *The Great Gatsby* (1925. New York: New Classics, 1945).

69   '*With the general trend of opposition to billboards . . .*': NYT, 9 November 1922.

'*We grew up founding our dreams on the infinite promise . . .*': *Save Me the Waltz*, in *The Collected Writings*, 195.

70   '*almost all the superfluous wealth of America . . .*': 'Paint and Powder', in *The Collected Writings*, 416–17.

'*Because of the carelessness with which the authorities . . .*': *World*, 25 September 1922.

71   '*convinced that jealousy was the motive . . .*': NYT, 25 September 1922.

'*The precise manner in which the bodies were laid out . . .*': *World*, 25 September 1922

72   *only learned about the murder by reading the newspapers*: NYT, 25 September 1922.

73   '*Great Neck is becoming known as "the Hollywood of the East" . . .*': *Town Topics*, 10 August 1922.

'*implies that you belong to a very rudimentary state of life*': *A Life in Letters*, 235.

74   '*authentic American*' voice: Yardley, *Ring*, 170.

'*the best prose that has come our way*': Woolf, 'American Fiction'.

76   '*basic fissure in her mental processes . . .*': Dos Passos, *The Best Times*, 129–30.

78   '*While Dr Cronk says she was shot three times . . .*': NYT, 27 September 1922.

'*admitted yesterday that their investigation had failed . . .*': NYT, 29 September 1922.

'*remove all doubt as to the manner . . .*': NYT, 28 September 1922.

79 '*Following this discovery . . .*': NYT, 30 September 1922.

'*the position of the bullet holes in the woman's head . . .*': Ibid.

80 '*Finding him out, we climbed into his studio . . .*' Tribune, 8 October 1922.

80–2 *Drawbell . . . was in an expensive speakeasy in Manhattan*: In *The Sun Within Us*, Drawbell offers only scattered dates, but a few clues enable the timing of this encounter to be reconstructed. He was born in 1899 and spent the year he was twenty-three (1922) in the US, before sailing for London in April 1923. He says the encounter with Fitzgerald took place in 'early autumn', after Fitzgerald had written *The Beautiful and Damned*. The Fitzgeralds weren't in New York before 20 September and Drawbell mentions the Carpentier fight around the same time, which was on 24 September, Scott's birthday. This encounter was probably in late September 1922.

82 '*trail murderers by day and writer short stories by night*': 'Who's Who – And Why', *Saturday Evening Post*, 18 September 1920. Reprinted in Bruccoli, Smith and Kerr, *Romantic Egoists*, 71.

'*advertising is a racket, like the movies . . .*': *Dreams of Youth*, 107.

82–3 '*one room in a high, horrible apartment-house . . .*': 'The Sensible Thing', in *Short Stories*, 290.

83 '*He pictured the rooms where these people lived . . .*': *This Side of Paradise* (Oxford, 2009), 217.

'*a male gossip, an artistic edition of* Town Topics': *Louisville Courier-Journal*, April 1922. Reprinted in *In His Own Time*, 410.

84 '*The women are jealous of Zelda's looks and of her soft voice . . .*':*Town Topics*, 17 August 1922.

86 '*looked round mockingly. The party was over . . .*': Drawbell, *The Sun Within Us*, 179.

### III. Goddards, Dwans, Swopes

90 *Goddard, for example, may have been . . .*: Bruccoli, *F. Scott Fitzgerald's The Great Gatsby*, 55.

93 '*well-advertised gin-swigging, finale-hopping . . .*': NYT, 1 October 1922.

94 *set sail for Cherbourg in May 1924*: NYT, 3 May 1924.

'*Think of the ride through the dusty blue twilight . . .*': PUL, ZF Papers.

95 '*Fitz and Zelda have struck their perfect milieu . . .*': Wilson, *Letters*, 106.

'*and since then I have had the Baby myself . . .*': PUL, ZF Papers.

'*See if there is any bacon . . .*': *The Collected Writings*, 401.

'*Mr Fitzgerald – I believe that is how he spells his name . . .*': 'Friend

Husband's Latest', *Tribune*, 2 April 1922. Bryer (ed.), *The Critical Reception*, 111.

96 'Went to Fizgeralds. Usual problem there . . .': Milford, *Zelda Fitzgerald*, 78–9.

'What'll we do, David . . .': *Save Me the Waltz*, in *The Collected Writings*, 79.

'I always felt a story in the Post was tops . . .': Bruccoli, *Some Sort of Epic Grandeur*, 225.

Fitzgerald blew into New York last week . . .': Letter to James Branch Cabell. Quoted in Milford, *Zelda Fitzgerald*, 98.

'had something to live for beside a high standard of living': Wilson, *The Twenties*, 78.

97 'That is to say, five years ago we had no money at all . . .': 'How to Live on $36,000 a Year', *Saturday Evening Post*, 31 May 1924. Reprinted in *Afternoon of an Author*, 90.

'Even when you were broke, you didn't worry about money . . .': Ibid., 95.

'checks written in disappearing ink': Quoted in Bruccoli, *Some Sort of Epic Grandeur*, 219.

97–8 police finally began canvassing the area: NYT, 1 October 1922.

98 'tore down the front porch of the old house . . .': Kunstler, *The Hall–Mills Murder Case*, 42.

'Dr Long notified me on Monday . . .': NYT, 1 October 1922.

'a woman lawyer', Florence North: NYT, 3 October 1922.

98–9 Miss North had been a boxing promoter: *Tribune*, 9 November 1922.

99 Charlotte and her 'good looking young, smartly dressed lawyer': NYT, 17 October 1922.

'authorities have shown themselves guilty . . .': *Town Topics*, 5 October 1922.

'I am sorry you bought me that spicy book . . .': NYT, 7 October 1922.

100 'pushes me off a piano stool, & breaks my arm': Van Vechten, *The Splendid Drunken Twenties*, 12.

'There were many mock speeches . . .': *Tribune*, 15 October 1922.

'Suppose the idea of the book is the contrast . . .': Quoted in Thomas C. Beattie, 'Moments of Meaning Dearly Achieved: Virginia Woolf's Sense of an Ending', *Modern Fiction Studies* 32.4 (1986), 529.

101 'Half of my ancestors came from just such an Irish strata . . .': 25 June 1922, *A Life in Letters*, 61.

'The Satyricon is a keen satire . . .': NYT, 28 September 1922.

'a prize remark', 'a literary and documentary classic . . .': *Tribune*, 29 October 1922.

'ancient *Rome* and *Nineveh*': PUL, ZF Papers.

101–2 'regular orgy', 'a Roman banquet or something': Wilson, *The Twenties*, 117.

102 'Trimalchio's famous dinner party . . .': NYT, 22 October 1922.

'he emerald green, the glass bauble . . .': Petronius, *The Satyricon*, 86–7.

'It's O.K. but my heart tells me . . .': *A Life in Letters*, 95.

104 *The police had a culprit at last*: NYT, 10 October 1922.

105 'We seem to have achieved a state . . .': PUL, ZF Papers.

106 *Engalitcheff's death certificate*: New York Hall of Records; author's collection

'Everybody said to everybody else . . .': *Save Me the Waltz*, 49.

'They went out on a party . . .': NYT, 28 August 1922.

107 'Perhaps the most light on "parties" . . .': NYT, 27 June 1922.

'"The Boozeful and Damned," . . .': 'Fitzgerald's Flapper Grows Up', *Columbus Dispatch*, 19 March 1922. Reprinted in Bryer (ed.), *The Critical Reception*, 97.

107–8 'As "cocktail", so I gather . . .': Letter to Blanche Knopf, *A Life in Letters*, 135.

108 'lawless drinker of illegally made . . .': 'Are You a Scofflaw?', *Boston Globe*, 16 January 1924.

'exceedingly popular among American prohibition dodgers': *Chicago Tribune*, 27 January 1924.

'the night before it went into effect . . .': Lardner, *What of It?*, 107.

109 'Month by month, Ring is getting . . .': *Tribune*, 1 October 1922.

110 'Mr Swope of the World . . .': Yardley, *Ring*, 261.

'Herbert Bayard Swope operated a continual . . .': Ben Hecht, *Charlie: The Improbable Life and Times of Charles MacArthur* (New York: Harper & Bros, 1957), 96.

'seems inadequate, ineffectual, limp . . .': Burton Rascoe Papers, Rare Book & Manuscript Library, University of Pennsylvania.

113 'happened to be hungry at four . . .': Pegolotti, *Deems Taylor*, 101.

114 'framing' of Clifford Hayes: NYT, 11 October 1922.

'Truth? We are not trying . . .': Ibid.

'shiftless at twenty-three', 'mentally deficient': *World*, 11 October 1922.

'has exhibited a willingness . . .': NYT, 11 October 1922.

'abuse', 'stop bothering me', 'Father never wanted . . .': Ibid.

'the most despicable that can be . . .': *Tribune*, 22 October 1922.

*admitted to carrying a .45 revolver*: NYT, 11 October 1922.

114–15 'he would bring to bear . . .': Ibid.

115 He liked to sing a mock-tragic song: Wilson, The Twenties, 164.
'Fitzgerald, Wilson said, composed . . .': Tribune, 10 March 1923.
116–17 'Soon across the space booms . . .': PUL, FSF Scrapbooks.
117 'There was even a recurrent idea . . .': 'The Swimmers', in Short Stories, 506.
118 'what a skunk I was . . .': NYT, 13 October 1922.
'Happy' Bahmer . . . brought in for questioning: NYT, 15 October 1922.
The jury decided the homicide was justifiable: Tribune, 22 October 1922.
'considered the height of absurdity . . .': NYT, 13 October 1922.
119 'committed to a correctional facility . . .': NYT, 25 October 1922.
'jauntily out of the courthouse . . .': Kunstler, The Hall–Mills Murder Case, 71.
120 'a cartoon carries its story . . .': NYT, 15 October 1922.
radio had added more than three thousand words: NYT, 27 August 1926.
sudden explosion of branded goods: NYT, 6 August 1922.
'the author of the latest bestseller . . .': Ibid.
121 'delete the man who says . . .': 8 July 1925, A Life in Letters, 124.
'Gilda Gray, Ziegfeld Follies beauty . . .': Town Topics, 28 September 1922.
'I had never seen anything like it . . .': 'The Dance', reprinted in Bits of Paradise, 136.
'prancing into favor': NYT, 30 August 1925. The New Yorker similarly noted on 8 August 1925 that New Yorkers were suddenly seeking 'enlightenment about the intricacies of this newest and most puzzling dance'.
123 exchange that is said to have originated with Zelda: West, The Perfect Hour, 96.
124 'a driver of many eccentricities . . .': The Beautiful and Damned (1922. Oxford: Oxford University Press, 1998), 141.
'There were people all along . . .': Save Me The Waltz, 54.
driving Max Perkins into a pond: FSF and Perkins, Dear Scott/Dear Max, 74.
124–5 Posters and badges had been organized: NYT, 15 August 1922.
125 out of over four hundred deaths: NYT, 7 October 1922.

## IV. A. Vegetable Days in N.Y.
## B. Memory of Ginevra's Wedding

128 a skeleton in a taxicab: Wilson, The Twenties, 114.
they ended their festivities at the morgue: Morris, Incredible New York, 316; Morris gives no source for this anecdote.
130 'We are established in the above town . . .': Correspondence of F. Scott Fitzgerald, 117.
130–1 solemnly recorded a list of current slang: Wilson, The Twenties, 102.

131 'A Lexicon of Prohibition': Wilson, *The American Earthquake*, 89.

132 'On the Fourth of July . . .': Elder, *Ring Lardner*, 200.

133 'Tragedy of LIES . . .': *World*, 18 October 1922.
'really immoral book': In His Own Time, 170.

134 'from a woman in humble life . . .': NYT, 18 October 1922.
mocking . . . trying to become a literary critic: *World*, 18 October 1922.
'SLAIN RECTOR AND CHOIR SINGER FOUND . . .': *World*, 19 October 1922.
'Was this the logic . . .': *World*, 20 October 1922.

135 'is the kind of book that certain men . . .': NYT, 20 October 1922.
'may lead to a further effort . . .': Ibid.

135–6 'In Chap II of my book . . .': FSF and Perkins, *Dear Scott/Dear Max*, 85.

137–8 'Art invariably grows out of a period . . .': *Notebooks*, 162.

138 'no doubt, the best American comedy . . .': Wilson, *Letters on Literature and Politics*, 84.

139 'modest and self-contained': NYT, 26 May 1926.

140 'though no club membership is required for admission': NYT, 22 January 1922.
'Two months ago they were serving cocktails . . .': O. O. McIntyre, 'New York Day By Day', *Providence News*, 7 October 1922.
'furnished with a sufficient number of chairs . . .': Van Vechten, *Parties*, 28–9.

141 'When you want something, telephone him . . .': Kellner, *Carl Van Vechten and the Irreverent Decades*, 48.
it was the boom, after all: *New Yorker*, 4 June 1927.

142 'loaded down with the cards . . .': Quoted in Kinney, *Thurber*, 379.
Chemists . . . analyzed the liquor: Blum, *The Poisoner's Handbook*, 51.
police raided the White Poodle on Bleecker Street: NYT, 18 October 1922.
'were stoned by angry residents': NYT, 26 October 1922.

143 'the intoxication of policemen . . .': NYT, 16 October 1922.

144 'wine enough flowed to float a battleship': NYT, 15 October 1922.
'Well I've a good mind . . .': Wilson, *The Twenties*, 96.

145 'The curiosity seekers took everything . . .': NYT, 23 October 1922.
'a spectral line against the sky': *Tribune*, 26 October 1922.
'Fakers from New Brunswick flocked . . .': NYT, 19 July 1925.
'unearthed some of the choicest bootleggers . . .': PUL, ZF Papers.

146 'Fleischman was making a damn ass of himself . . .': Wilson, *Discordant Encounters*, 280.
'Bunny appreciates feeling ...': May 1924, *Letters*.

146–7 'to acquire works of art . . .': NYT, 16 April 1922.

147   *Ted Paramore's favourite hangover cures*: Wilson, *The Twenties*, 112.
      '*Most of my friends drank too much . . .*': 'My Lost City', in *The Crack-Up*, 30.
      '*1929: A feeling that all liquor has been drunk . . .*': 'A Short Autobiography',
      in *In His Own Time*, 223.
      '*A great many drugstore proprietors . . .*': Rascoe, *We Were Interrupted*, 166–7.
148   *Fitzgerald's recipe for bathtub gin*: PUL, FSF Papers.
      '*based on a neighbor named Von Guerlach . . .*': Kruse, 'The Real Jay
      Gatsby: Max von Gerlach, F. Scott Fitzgerald, and the Compositional
      History of *The Great Gatsby*', 46.
      *another cutting of the same photo*: In his edited version of the scrapbooks,
      *The Romantic Egoists*, Matthew J. Bruccoli states that this 'old sport' clip-
      ping is in the Fitzgerald scrapbook, but the clipping in the scrapbook is
      unsigned. It is not clear where the original clipping that Bruccoli found
      was from, or what has become of it since.
      *Max Gerlach has haunted Fitzgerald scholars for decades*: Ibid., 52.
150   '*Gatsby was never quite real to me . . .*': Bruccoli and Baughman (eds), *F.
      Scott Fitzgerald in the Marketplace*, 4.
151   '*A writer had better rise above . . .*': Quoted in Christopher Ricks, *T. S.
      Eliot and Prejudice* (Berkeley: University of California Press, 1988), 46.
      '*five weeks of inexpert investigation*': *Tribune*, 22 October 1922.
      '*was willing to join in . . .*': NYT, 22 October 1922.
152   '*New York suddenly became very brilliant . . .*': Kellner, *Carl Van Vechten
      and the Irreverent Decades*, 47.
      '*hints at a sort of charitable regret . . .*': *Tribune*, 25 October 1922.
      *the Mills family had been receiving letters*: NYT, 24 October 1922.
      '*If you do not stop your silly activities . . .*': Ibid.
153   '*mistreated' his wife*: NYT, 17 November 1922.
153–4 '*What should have been done . . .*': NYT, 24 October 1922.
156–7 '*After careful searching of files . . .*': FSF and Perkins, *Dear Scott/Dear
      Max*, 89.
157   '*to fit a given mood or "hauntedness" . . .*': *Dreams of Youth*, 571.
158   '*aroused over this double murder*': *Town Topics*, 26 October 1922.
      '*in harmony with the loving care . . .*': NYT, 28 October 1922.
159   '*had never seen so much publicity . . .*': NYT, 2 November 1922.
      '*commented on the lack of corroboration . . .*': NYT, 16 October 1922.
      '*the clergyman's expensive garments . . .*': NYT, 21 October 1922.
      '*the contrast between the social status . . .*': NYT, 26 October 1922.
      '*dissatisfaction*', '*drab apartment*': *Tribune*, 26 October 1922.
161   '*had been reading a passage in a romantic novel . . .*': *World*, 24 October 1922.

162   'Fell in love on the 7th, with Zelda': Ledger.

163   'Jordan of course was a great idea . . .': FSF and Perkins, Dear Scott/Dear Max, 90.

164   'Even the grief he could have borne . . .': FSF, 'Winter Dreams', in Short Stories, 235–6.
       'At last we were one with New York . . .': 'My Lost City', 28–9.

164–5  'because as a restless and ambitious man . . .': Milford, Zelda Fitzgerald, 319.

165   'about Zelda & me. All true': FSF and Perkins, Dear Scott/Dear Max, 113.
       'She was something desirable and rare . . .': 'The Sensible Thing', in Short Stories, 301.
       'You are right about Gatsby being blurred . . .': A Life in Letters, 101, 126.

166   'Splendor . . . was something in the heart': Tender is the Night (1934. London: Penguin Classics, 2010), p. 68.

## V. The Meeting all an invention. Mary

170–1  'There was a kindliness about intoxication . . .': The Beautiful and Damned (1922. London: Penguin Classics, 2010) 338.

171   'in an offhand manner that the case . . .': Tribune, 1 November 1922.
       'astonishing, rambling statement': World, 1 November 1922.
       'forced to believe [her] in other aspects': Ibid.

172   local officials started looking for fingerprints: Tribune, 2 November 1922.
       'Embittered by poverty': Baltimore News, November 1922.

173   'poise', 'perfect self-control', 'an inexplicable phenomenon . . .': Tribune, 5 November 1922.
       'Not even the tutoring of a lifetime . . .': Ibid.
       'There has been so much criticism here . . .': Town Topics, 9 November 1922.
       'has been called all sorts of names . . .': Ibid.

174   'Petronius is Sunday School literature . . .': New Republic, 1 November 1922.
       'Well, I guess the children have left . . .': Turnbull, Scott Fitzgerald, 130.
       'Dearest Lud – I'm running wild . . .': PUL, ZF Papers.

175   'I told them you were richer than God . . .': PUL, ZF Papers.
       reported the game in his column: Adams, The Diary of Our Own Samuel Pepys, 362.
       'think of that horse's ass F.P.A. . . .': A Life in Letters, 140.
       advertisement . . . declaring that it had hired Lothrop Stoddard: Tribune, 2 November 1922.
       'this man Goddard': During Fitzgerald's time at Princeton he may also have encountered a professor named Goddard, confusingly enough, who also gave a series of eugenicist lectures, which may be the 'Stoddard

Lectures' that Owl-Eyes pulls from Gatsby's shelves in Chapter Three. It is quite possible that Fitzgerald intended to name names, and mixed the two up. He had cheerfully given other real-life miscreants their own names in the novel, and one eugenicist does sound much like another. 'Look for the Fay Cab . . .': *Tribune*, 2 November 1922.

176  *Fay expanded his taxi fleet*: See Peretti, *Nightclub City*, Chapter 1.

177  '*the societies which rally . . .*': *NYT*, 30 July 1922.
Swastika Fruit Company, rumoured to be a bootlegging front: *NYT*, 3 July 1922.

178  '*a particularly brilliant day*': Van Vechten, *The Splendid Drunken Twenties*, 14.
'*stood on her head, disrobed . . .*': Ibid., 11

179  'All the literary, theatrical and cinema world . . .': *Tribune*, 12 November 1922.
'The food was execrable . . .': Ibid.

181  'One hundred per cent Americanism': *Tribune*, 10 November 1922.
'all the kept women & brokers in New York: Van Vechten, *The Splendid Drunken Twenties*, 14.
'it was on the train . . .': Quoted in Crunden, *Body and Soul*, 208.

182  'It started out with a weird, spinning sound . . .': *Trimalchio*, 42.

183  'which accounts for her agility at midnight . . .': *Tribune*, 27 October 1922.
'It has been established to the satisfaction . . .': *Tribune*, 4 November 1922.
'It's an amazing story . . .': Kunstler, *The Hall–Mills Murder Case*, 80.
'romantic inaccuracies in her story . . .': *Tribune*, 4 November 1922.

183–4  'gave a vivid account of hearing a man's voice . . .': *NYT*, 31 October 1922.

184  'What difference does it make . . .': Ibid.

185  'filled his house at this time . . .': Pegolotti. *Deems Taylor*, 101.
'one of the most forceful men I have ever met . . .': Ibid., 72.

186  'beglamored by the idea of Scott Fitzgerald': Wilson, *The Twenties*, 62.
'there was something petulant': Milford, *Zelda Fitzgerald*, 68.
'rush after New Year's Eve': Quoted in Kinney, *Thurber*, 379.
'I couldn't seem to get sober enough . . .': Turnbull, *Scott Fitzgerald*, 125.

187  'Zelda and her abortionist': In Milford, *Zelda Fitzgerald*, 88; Taylor, *Sometimes Madness is Wisdom*, 114; Cline, *Zelda Fitzgerald*, 125; Mellow, *Invented Lives*, 147; Wagner-Martin, *Zelda Sayre Fitzgerald*, 64.
Scott wrote in his notebooks of a son: *Notebooks*, 244.

188  'We find them both rather changed . . .': Wilson, *Letters on Literature and Politics*, 78–9.

'Your catalogue is not complete . . .': A Life in Letters, 51.

189 'a thing of bitterness and beauty . . .': Tribune, 5 November 1922.
'reflect our present condition of disruption . . .': Saturday Literature Review, 25 November 1922.

190 'Mr Eliot's trivialities are more valuable . . .': Ibid.
'In fact, it seems to me the first step . . .': The Crack-Up, 310.

191 'the Yale Bowl, with lamps': Pegolotti, Deems Taylor, 267.
'We have been having a hell of a time . . .': PUL, ZF Papers.

192 'in Great Neck there was always disorder . . .': The Collected Writings, 452.
'where Zelda and Helen became drunk . . .': Bruccoli, Some Sort of Epic Grandeur, 208.
'For Helen and Jean . . .': Bruccoli and Baughman (eds), Fitzgerald in the Marketplace, 80.
'Helen – not of Troy . . .': Ibid., 81.

193 'Gene didn't make any comment . . .': PUL, FSF Papers.

194 Beauty fires us with the faith: Sparrow, 'Footloose Philosophy', 130.
'because it interfered with the neatness of the plan': A Life in Letters, 76.

195 'Imagination, not invention . . .': Conrad, A Personal Record: Some Reminiscences, ed. Zdzisław Naider and J. H. Stape (Cambridge: Cambridge University Press, 2008), 35.

196 'synchronized clocks on the north and south . . .': NYT, 13 December 1922.
'haunted by time': Cowley, 'The Romance of Money.'

197 'We do love the centre of things . . .': The Collected Writings, 201.
'Can't you come? Dos Passos . . .': Wilson, Letters on Literature and Politics, 98.

198 Swope told reporters: Tribune, 8 November 1922.
changing the channels of their avidity: Notebooks, 322.
'because it shows classes in movement': Ibid.

200 'You danced elbow to elbow . . .': 'My Lost City', in The Crack-Up, 28.
'May Hay – that is, she differs . . .': Bruccoli, Some Sort of Epic Grandeur, 337.
Fitzgerald said was based on Mary Hay: FSF and Ober, As Ever, Scott Fitz, 146.

201 'I never saw her again until after . . .': The Collected Writings, 317–25.
'imagine the divergent New Yorks . . .': Tribune, 6 August 1922.

202 'statements and romantic stories . . .': Tribune, 10 November 1922.
'no greater calamity could befall workers . . .': NYT, 7 November 1922.
'in the court of public opinion . . .': World, 11 November 1922.
'a formal court trial as a rank extravagance': Ibid.

203 'at the hour the pig-raising Amazon . . .': Tribune, 13 November 1922.
'talks in bunches. I don't think she's reliable': NYT, 14 November 1922.

204 'the Star-Spangled Banner can never . . .': Tribune, 11 June 1922.
'The critics, one and all . . .': Reprinted in Bruccoli and Baughman (eds), Conversations with F. Scott Fitzgerald, 34.

204–5 'prefers piquant hors d'oeuvres . . .': Ibid., 34.

### VI. Bob Kerr's Story. The 2nd Party

208 'The thing which sets off . . .': George Jean Nathan and H. L. Mencken, The American Credo: A Contribution Toward the Interpretation of the Modern Mind (New York: Alfred Knopf, 1920).

209 'but he is unable to get seats . . .': Van Vechten, The Splendid Drunken Twenties, 15.
'half a quart of my best bourbon . . .': Ibid., 16.

210 'was very spectacular and . . .': PUL, ZF Papers.

210–11 'This is a very drunken town . . .': In A Life in Letters, Bruccoli dates this letter some time 'after November 18, 1923', but the Yale game, which Princeton won 3–0, was played on 18 November 1922. By November 1923 the Kalmans had already visited New York, as Zelda wrote to them in July 1923 about their recent visit. Thus, the internal evidence of this letter suggests strongly that the correct year is 1922 and that the date 1923 in the published letters is a mistake (or a misprint, given the correct date of 18 November for the Yale game).

211 'lured John Dos Passos back to New York . . .': PUL, ZF Papers.
would not be reported in America: NYT, 10 December 1922.
'Biography as Fiction': NYT, 19 November 1922.

211–12 Witnesses would include . . .: Ibid.

212 'The motive accepted by Mr Mott . . .': World, 20 November 1922.
'A jury will decide between . . .': Tribune, 16 November 1922.
ambassador to Britain had given a talk: NYT, 24 October 1922.

213 Ring Lardner said: Tribune, 25 October 1922
Paul Hamborszky: Tribune, 18 November 1922.

214 become a used-car salesman: NYT, 18 November 1922.
'the authorities do not consider . . .': Ibid.
'murder museum', 'soda water . . .': NYT, 17 November 1922.
The crab-apple tree had disappeared: NYT, 19 November 1922.
'burned up New Jersey roads . . .': Tribune, 19 November 1922.

214–15 'having read much about . . .': World, 20 November 1922.

216 'from Chicago by the dirty channels . . .': NYT, 19 November 1922

'*there are too many common people . . .*': Ibid.

218  *long list of books he recommended*: Sheilah Graham, *College of One: The Story of How F. Scott Fitzgerald Educated the Woman He Loved* (London: Weidenfeld & Nicolson, 1967), 123.

'*Scott and I were "buzzing" . . .*': Corso, 'One Not-Forgotten Summer Night: Sources for Fictional Symbols of American Character in *The Great Gatsby*', 18.

*most celebrated piece of investigative journalism*: Tribune, 28 January 1922.

*implied that Nelly Bly was not his only mistress*: See Corso, 'One Not-Forgotten Summer Night', 8–33.

219  '*The part of what you told me . . .*': A Life in Letters, 75.

'*Dear Bob, Keep reading . . .*': Ibid., 102.

'*not praise a book like that beautiful . . .*': PUL, FSF Scrapbooks.

220  '*If an author wants 2 cols . . .*': FSF files, Huntington Library.

'*The Wild West's Own New York*': NYT, 5 March 1922.

221  'FICTION PUT TO SHAME . . .': Tribune, 20 November 1922.

222  '*the cold, proud woman of Southern blood . . .*': Tribune, 11 November 1922.

'*a pathetic little salamander . . .*': Tribune, 20 November 1922.

'*like the salamander . . .*': NYT, 18 June 1922.

'*I believed I was a Salamander*': Milford, Zelda Fitzgerald, 176.

'*Seats selling eight weeks in advance . . .*': World, 20 November 1922.

225  '*probably does not know himself . . .*': NYT, 21 November 1922.

'*sophisticated politicians . . .*': NYT, 22 November 1922.

226  '*I protect pocketbook as well as person*': 'Dice, Brassknuckles & Guitar', in Short Stories, 246.

'*He drives on to his Elizabethan villa . . .*': Ibid., 237.

227  '*Ronald here'd no more think . . .*': Ibid., 249–50.

'*the number of feminine witnesses called*': Tribune, 23 November 1922.

'*a thin, emaciated, drooping man . . .*': NYT, 23 November 1922.

'*James Mills sat stonily . . .*': Tribune, 23 November 1922.

*requested his witness fee*: NYT, 23 November 1922.

228  '*as lugubrious as usual . . .*': Tribune, 27 November 1922.

'*hoping for a "break" . . .*': World, 25 November 1922.

229–30  *Daisy draws the line at sharing her hairdresser*: Trimalchio, 85.

231  '*Paul Whiteman played . . .*': The Collected Writings, 48.

232  '*In the real dark night of the soul . . .*': 'Pasting it Together', in The Crack-Up, 63.

*she found her novel's title*: Dear Scott, Dearest Zelda, 207

'Listen . . . you're not keeping time': Save Me the Waltz, in The Collected Writings, 48.

all women's colleges should be burned: NYT, 23 November 1922.

'To one large turkey add one gallon . . .': Notebooks, 183.

233 champagne 'flowed like the Rhine . . .': World, 7 June 1922.

234 'Gold and Cocktails': NYT, 22 November 1926.

235 'My mentioning our having had lunch . . .': Tribune, 26 November 1922.

'The substance of the conversation . . .': Farrar (ed.), Literary Spotlight, 257.

235–6 'he quoted me so much and so inaccurately . . .': Wilson, Letters on Literature and Politics, 97.

236 'I enclose Burton Rascoe's report . . .': PUL, FSF Papers.

'I told her, full of hope . . .': Wilson, The Twenties, 147–8. In the published version, Wilson changes the Rascoes' names to 'Belle and Clem', but Wilson's biographer Lewis Dabney identifies them from the manuscripts as the Rascoes.

'engaged in combat with Mr Burton Rascoe . . .': Meyers, Edmund Wilson, 46.

Rascoe bit Bunny Wilson on the nose: Dabney, Edmund Wilson, 100–1.

237 'never gets full credit now . . .': Wilson, Letters on Literature and Politics, 168.

238 'The great novel of the past fifty years . . .': FSF, '10 Best Books I Have Read', in Bruccoli and Baughman (eds), F. Scott Fitzgerald on Authorship, 86.

'the meaning of an episode was not . . .': Joseph Conrad, Heart of Darkness (1899. London: Penguin Classics, 2007), 6.

'it is an exact portrayal of a very notorious . . .': Rascoe, A Bookman's Daybook, 31.

239 'Fiction is history, human history . . .': Joseph Conrad, 'Henry James: An Appreciation', North American Review (1916).

'until today her movements had been . . .': Tribune, 28 November 1922.

He claimed it was just coincidence: NYT, 28 November 1922.

grand jury withdrew in mid-afternoon: NYT, 29 November 1922.

240 'the expense of a trial that might . . .': Ibid.

'there was not the remotest possibility . . .': World, 29 November 1922.

241–2 'who invented an entirely fictitious career . . .': Claridge (ed.), Critical Assessments, vol. II, 166–7.

242 'the newspapers with thin copy . . .': Van Vechten, Parties, 212.

Fania Marinoff, hated it: Van Vechten, The Splendid Drunken Twenties, 299, 286.

*Fitz drew up a household budget*: Bruccoli, *Some Sort of Epic Grandeur*, 224.

'*literary and artistic tea party . . .*': Rascoe, *A Bookman's Daybook*, 291.

## VII. The Day in New York

248 '*Nobody knew whose party it was . . .*': *Save Me the Waltz*, in *The Collected Writings*, 95.

249 '*Rules For Guests At the Fitzgerald House*': Boyd, *Portraits*, 223.

'*The remarkable thing about the Fitzgeralds . . .*': Wilson, *Letters on Literature and Politics*, 478.

'*I guess so. We were awfully good showmen*': Milford, *Zelda Fitzgerald*, 275.

249–50 '*we had retained an almost theatrical innocence*': *My Lost City*, 111.

250 '*Scott loved to recount the episode . . .*': George Jean Nathan, 'The Golden Boy of the Twenties', *Esquire* (October 1958), 148–53.

'*Nothing about you ever fades . . .*': PUL, ZF Papers.

'*I accordingly took him to a house . . .*': Nathan, 'The Golden Boy of the Twenties', 148–53.

250–2 *Edmund Wilson's 1923 essay*: Edmund Wilson, 'The Delegate from Great Neck: Mr F. Scott Fitzgerald and Mr Van Wyck Brooks', *New Republic*, 30 April 1924. In Claridge (ed.), *Critical Assessments*, vol. I, 400–8.

252 '*natural idealist, a spoiled priest*': Mizener, *The Far Side of Paradise*, 345.

'*fell asleep over the soup . . .*': Brooks, *Days of the Phoenix*, 109.

253 '*what I might ironically call our "private" life*': *Letters*, 380.

254 '*party must be arranged . . .*': Boyd, *Portraits*, 226.

255 '*fight for a real investigation*': *NYT*, 2 December 1922.

*Conan Doyle wrote to the* New York Times: *NYT*, 10 December 1922.

'*There is a trend . . .*': *NYT*, 4 December 1922.

256 '*A monkey was shot near Babylon . . .*': *World*, 6 December 1922.

257 '*human sympathy has it curious limits . . .*': *Trimalchio*, 104.

258 '*preserve the sense of mystery*': Turnbull, *Scott Fitzgerald*, 515.

259 '*I didn't go into the ethics . . .*': *NYT*, 28 November 1922.

*In the early months of 1920*: *Tribune*, 25 October 1922.

'*the Snyder–Gray and Hall–Mills murder cases*': Rascoe, *We Were Interrupted*, 218.

259–60 '*the world seemed to have gone mad . . .*': Ibid., 265.

260 '*venturesome souls . . . from the days of Columbus . . .*': *NYT*, 16 January 1921.

*a story from Scott entitled* '*Recklessness*': Some have speculated that the story might have been published as 'Dice, Brassknuckles & Guitar', although

Fitzgerald's ledger always refers to 'Dice, Brassknuckles' by that title and so does Zelda's 1930 letter reminiscing about the Great Neck days.

'The girl is excellent of course . . .': FSF and Perkins, *Dear Scott/Dear Max*, 52.

261  'We thoroughly believe that if . . .': *World*, 11 December 1922.

'Quite a lot of the frenzy . . .': PUL, FSF Scrapbooks.

262  'It serves to purge the hero . . .': PUL, FSF Scrapbooks.

'clip for preservation . . .': Burton Rascoe Papers, Rare Book & Manuscript Library, University of Pennsylvania.

263  'That winter to me is a memory . . .': 'A Millionaire's Girl', in *The Collected Writings*, 330.

'When people fail in the national viewpoint . . .': NYT, 14 December 1922.

'her daughter was driving fast . . .': NYT, 16 November 1922.

'Gains Weight, Gets Damages': NYT, 14 December 1922.

'American Civilization on the Brink': NYT, 12 June 1921.

264  'Everybody followed it . . .': *Tribune*, 10 December 1922.

'shielded by the cloak of anonymity . . .': NYT, 10 December 1922.

'I note what you say with reference . . .': Ibid.

265  'Imagine that doctor not reporting . . .': NYT, 19 December 1922.

'than the public suspect': NYT, 13 December 1922

'delve into New Brunswick's . . .': NYT, 11 December 1922.

266  'with springs so perfectly adjusted . . .': *Town Topics*, 2 February 1922.

267  '"Gossip" Real Murderer of Mrs Meadows': *Evening World*, 2 August 1922.

268  'supplementing her former story': NYT, 20 December 1922.

'The crime was committed . . .': Ibid.

269  'leading a cow near where the collision . . .': NYT, 27 January 1922.

Davies made headlines again: NYT, 26 June 1922.

270  'the State then put the teeth in evidence': NYT, 21 December 1922.

'This "Minnie McGluke" stands for . . .': Bruccoli and Baughman (eds), *Conversations with F. Scott Fitzgerald*, 51.

The World was highly amused: *World*, 22 December 1922.

271  'Highball Epic': NYT, 21 December 1922.

'Our literature seemed to me . . .': Brooks, *Days of the Phoenix*, 170.

'Things are always beginning . . .': Wilson, *The Twenties*, 95.

'You may have spoken in jest . . .': FSF (ed. Bruccoli), *A Life in Letters*, 47.

'Your time will come, New York . . .': 'Three Cities', *Brentano's Book Chat* 1 (September–October 1921), 15, 28. In *His Own Time*, 126.

272  'They don't know whether to begin . . .': *Tribune*, 20 August 1922.

'If this fellow Sandburg will us slang . . .': Ibid.

*American slang was so incomprehensible*: NYT, 17 December 1922.

272–3  *a helpful glossary, including*: NYT, 12 December 1922.

274   'The story of our national life . . .': NYT, 24 December 1922.
'*speed production*': Ibid.
'*Want truer history books . . .*': NYT, 19 December 1922.

275   '*In Great Neck there was always disorder . . .*': *Dear Scott, Dearest Zelda*, 68.
'*just for a moment, the "younger generation" . . .*': 'My Lost City', in *The Crack-Up*, 27.

276–7  '*astounding holidays*', '*about a week before Christmas*': PUL, ZF Papers.

277   '*fiction writers have emancipated themselves . . .*': NYT, 24 December 1922.
'*Reading it over one can see . . .*': FSF, introduction to 1934 Modern Library edition of *The Great Gatsby*.
'*by the power of the written word . . .*': Joseph Conrad, *The Nigger of the Narcissus: A Tale of the Forecastle* (New York: Doubleday, 1914), xiv.
'*As Conrad says in his famous preface . . .*': unpublished letter, privately owned, ALS. Quoted by Christie's catalogue, 1997.

278   '*take the Long Island atmosphere . . .*': 'My Lost City', 29.
'*strong draughts on Zelda's and my . . .*': *A Life in Letters*, 170.
'*There is no materialist . . .*': *The Collected Writings*, 57.
'*dig up the relevant, the essential . . .*': *Letters*, 447.

279   '*did not stop, because we believed . . .*': *Tribune*, 27 December 1922.
*justification for running Carberry over*: NYT, 27 December 1922.
'*thinks that when he is arrested . . .*': *In His Own Time*, 186–7.

281   '*the theater is no longer what it used to be . . .*': *Tribune*, 17 December 1922.

282   '*on a course like "English Prose since 1800" . . .*': *A Life in Letters*, 457.
'*Like all your stories there was . . .*': *Dear Scott, Dearest Zelda*, 210.

## VIII. The Murder (inv.)

286   *Fitzgerald wrote to his agent*: FSF and Ober, *As Ever, Scott-Fitz*, 51.
'*Life is not dramatic; only art is that . . .*': *Tribune*, 31 December 1922.

287   '*Perhaps all this fidgeting that we call change . . .*': Ibid.
'*The new world couldn't possibly be . . .*': 'Early Success', reprinted in *Afternoon of an Author*, 161.

288   '*by throwing everybody's hat . . .*': PUL, ZF Papers.
'*Come and bring a lot of drunks*': Carr, *Dos Passos*, 192.
'*it seems so much longer*': PUL, ZF Papers.

289   '*but it is fashionable only as Rolls-Royces . . .*': NYT, 5 November 1923.

289–90  '*February: Still drunk . . .*': *Ledger*, 177–8.

290   '*we were no longer important . . .*': 'My Lost City', in *The Crack-Up*.

'As a boy and a youth Fitzgerald . . .': *Town Topics*, 22 March 1923.

290–1 *'I'm not sure that I told my right name . . .'*: PUL, ZF Papers.

291 *'all the pools and even the Sound reek . . .'*: PUL, ZF Papers.

'It was an exquisite summer . . .': 'How to Live on $36,000 a Year', in *Afternoon of an Author*, 93.

'We drank always . . .': *A Life in Letters*, 191.

*a quip that Burton Rascoe repeated*: Rascoe, *A Bookman's Daybook*, 248.

292 *'Fitzgerald showed us some card tricks . . .'*: *Tribune*, 15 July 1923.

'Ring is drinking himself . . .': PUL, ZF Papers.

293 *Burton Rascoe correctly guessed*: *Tribune*, 14 December 1923.

*he has a saving quality of wit . . .'*: Rascoe, *A Bookman's Daybook*, 50.

'as a creator of a cheap type of fiction . . .': NYT, 19 June 1921.

'Just one more great . . .': PUL, FSF Scrapbooks.

'Scott's play went so badly . . .': Wilson, *Letters on Literature and Politics*, 118–19.

294 *'I went over there . . .'*: Van Vechten, *The Splendid Drunken Twenties*, 45.

'There were many changing friends . . .': Milford, *Zelda Fitzgerald*, 103.

'No detective story ever written . . .': NYT, 8 April 1923.

295 *'inspired by a desire to make some money . . .'*: NYT, 31 May 1923.

'And if anybody had come to the door . . .': Ibid.

296 *She would go on stage*: NYT, 14 September 1923.

297 *put the temptations of the new world behind them*: 'How to Live on Practically Nothing a Year', in *Afternoon of an Author*, 100–16.

298 *'Horsey, Keep Your Tail Up . . .'*: PUL, Charles Scribner's Sons Papers.

*sent a telegram . . . to Max Perkins*: PUL, Charles Scribner's Sons Papers.

*'nearly a scandal about Bunny Burgess'*: *A Life in Letters*, 191.

*passenger list for the* Minnewaska: NYT, 3 May 1924.

*'found a good nurse . . .'*: PUL, Charles Scribner's Sons Papers.

299 *'boarded the train for the Riviera . . .'*: 'How to Live on Practically Nothing a Year', 104.

'where people do not need to see . . .': *Save Me the Waltz*, in *The Collected Writings*, 71.

'the loveliest piece of earth . . .': *A Life in Letters*, 68.

'I shall be obligated to snatch . . .': PUL, Charles Scribner's Sons Papers.

*The villas they saw at Hyères . . .*: 'Show Mr and Mrs F to—', in *The Collected Writings*, 421.

'for the monotony': *Save Me the Waltz*, 87.

300 *'protruded insistently from their white . . .'*: Ibid., 80–2.

'we warmed our sunburned backs . . .': 'Show Mr and Mrs F to—', 421.

'*It is twilight as I write this* ...': 'How to Live on Practically Nothing a Year', 116.

301 '*often leads to perversion*': NYT, 1 June 1924.

'*several things, one of which* ...': FSF and Perkins, *Dear Scott/Dear Max*, 120.

'*that girl who shot her mother* ...': *A Life in Letters*, 140–1.

302 '*a particularly sordid and degraded* ...': 'Jacob's Ladder', in *Short Stories*, 350.

'*Hall–Mills Case Recalled*': NYT, 25 June 1924.

303 '*I am so anxious for people to see* ...': *Correspondence of F. Scott Fitzgerald*, 139.

304 '*Everything would be perfect* ...': Milford, *Zelda Fitzgerald*, 107.

*an undated letter from Olive Burgess*: PUL, FSF Papers.

'*Zelda swimming every day* ...': Ledger.

305 '*The table at Villa Marie* ...': *Notebooks*, 106.

*Olive would divorce Bunny Burgess*: NYT, 10 December 1926.

'*I've been unhappy but my work* ...': *A Life in Letters*, 80.

307 '*We've had a quiet summer* ...': Ibid., 78.

'*Zelda and I are contemplating* ...': Ibid., 80.

'*It is like nothing I've read before*': PUL, Charles Scribner's Sons Papers.

307–8 '*That September 1924, I knew* ...': FSF (ed. Bruccoli), *Notebooks*, 113.

308 '*Under separate cover I am sending* ...': *A Life in Letters*, 84.

'*I have now decided to stick to* ...': Ibid., 85.

*were leaving St Raphaël in two days*: Matthew Bruccoli dates the letter c. 7 November, but it is headed Sunday, saying they will leave Tuesday; the Sunday was 9 November 1924.

'*ill feeling with Zelda*': Ledger.

'*an operation to enable [her]* ...': Bruccoli, *Some Sort of Epic Grandeur*, 245.

309 '*the strange incongruity of the words* ...': FSF and Perkins, *Dear Scott/Dear Max*, 82.

'*In no other way could your irony* ...': PUL, Charles Scribner's Sons Papers.

'*He was supposed to be a bootlegger* ...': PUL, Charles Scribner's Sons Papers.

310 '*careful searching of the files* ...': FSF and Perkins, *Dear Scott/Dear Max*, 89–90.

'*I'm a bit (not very – not dangerously)* ...': Ibid.

'*The Plaza Hotel scene* ...': *Correspondence of F. Scott Fitzgerald*, 151.

310–11  *'clearing up that bum Plaza Hotel scene . . .'*: FSF and Ober, *As Ever, Scott-Fitz*, 75.

311  *'title is bad'*: Ibid., 78.

*'it may hurt the book's popularity . . .'*: FSF and Perkins, *Dear Scott/Dear Max*, 88–90.

*'I am quite drunk I am told . . .'*: *A Life in Letters*, 98–9.

*'represents about a year's work . . .'*: *Dreams of Youth*, 498.

312  *'I read your article (very nice too) in Van . . .'*: PUL, John Peale Bishop Papers.

*'Like Gatsby I have only hope'*: *Dreams of Youth*, 504.

313  *'dignified by an ardent pursuit'*: John Keats, *Selected Letters*, ed. Grant F. Scott and Hyder Edward Rollins (Cambridge, MA: Harvard University Press, 2005, revised edn), 100.

*'Premature success . . .'*: 'Early Success', in *The Crack-Up*.

314  *'This is very important. Be sure . . .'*: FSF and Perkins, *Dear Scott/Dear Max*, 93.

*what he really meant was the leg of a compass*: See Dilworth, 'Donne's Compass at the Death Scene in Fitzgerald's *The Great Gatsby*'.

317  *'I look out at it . . .'*: *Notebooks*, 332.

## IX. Funeral an Invention

322  *'Begin with an individual . . .'*: 'The Rich Boy', in *Short Stories*, 317.

*'The book comes out today . . .'*: FSF and Perkins, *Dear Scott/Dear Max*, 100.

*'Sales situation doubtful excellent reviews'*: *A Life in Letters*, 106n.

*'It is too ripe for us . . .'*: Bruccoli, *Some Sort of Epic Grandeur*, 254.

322–3  *'F. Scott Fitzgerald's Latest a Dud'*: Bryer (ed.), *The Critical Reception*, 195.

323  *'one woman, who could hardly have . . .'*: FSF, introduction to 1934 Modern Library edition of *The Great Gatsby*

*'a strange mixture of fact and fancy'*: Leonard Baird, *Life* 85 (30 April 1925), 33.

*'melodramatic, a detective story . . .'*: *Literary Digest International Book Review*, 3 May 1925, 426–7.

*Heywood Broun's wife, Ruth Hale, wrote*: *Brooklyn Daily Eagle*, 18 April 1925.

*'a snotty (and withal ungrammatical)'*: *A Life in Letters*, 127.

*'most decidedly, not a great novel . . .'*: *Galveston Daily News*, 26 April 1925.

*'"The Great Gatsby," certainly, is written . . .'*: Bryer (ed.), *The Critical Reception*, 232.

'*a curious book, a mystical, glamorous story of today*': NYT, 19 April 1925.

324 'As for the drama of the accident . . .': *In His Own Time*, 353–4.

'*Some day they'll eat grass . . .*': PUL, Charles Scribner's Sons Papers.

'*mastered his talent and gone soaring . . .*': Claridge (ed.), *Critical Assessments*, vol. I, 179.

'*The Long Island [Fitzgerald] sets before us . . .*': *In His Own Time*, 351.

324–5 '*Without making any invidious comparisons . . .*': *A Life in Letters*, 109.

325 '*What has never been alive cannot very well . . .*': Bryer (ed.), *The Critical Reception*, 202.

'*Burton Rascoe says* The Great Gatsby *is . . .*': *Dreams of Youth*, 503. *Nedra* is a 1905 novel of love among the upper classes by George Barr McCutcheon. There is no evidence of a writer named Harold Nigrath, although a Harold MacGrath was a bestselling writer of romances such as *The Princess Elopes*.

'*little tribute is a result of our having snubbed . . .*': *A Life in Letters*, 117.

325–6 '*has never been known to refuse an invitation . . .*': *Dreams of Youth*, 204.

326 '*that cocksucker Rascoe*': Bruccoli, *Scott and Ernest*, 62.

327 '*I give you my word of honor . . .*': Rascoe, 'Contemporary Reminiscences', 66.

327–8 '*triumphs by technique rather than by theme . . .*': Ibid., 68.

328 '*It's just four o'clock in the morning . . .*': PUL, FSF Scrapbooks.

331 '*Gatsby's life seemed to have had . . .*': *Trimalchio*, 137.

'*creating the contemporary world*': *Correspondence of F. Scott Fitzgerald*, 164

332 '*rather a bitter dose . . .*': Wilson, *Letters on Literature and Politics*, 121.

'*My present quarrel with you is only this . . .*': *Correspondence of F. Scott Fitzgerald*, 164.

332–3 '*Gatsby was far from perfect in many ways . . .*': *A Life in Letters*, 112.

333 '*We had a great trip together . . .*': Hemingway (ed. Baker), *Selected Letters 1917–1961*, 163.

*Hemingway told Ezra Pound*: Donaldson, *Hemingway vs. Fitzgerald*, 61.

'*Most people are dull, without distinction . . .*': PUL, FSF Papers.

'*We went to Antibes to recuperate . . .*': PUL, ZF Papers.

334 '*Let me tell you about the very rich . . .*': 'The Rich Boy', 318.

*These are not the words of a man in thrall to riches*: Ten years later, Hemingway would claim in 'The Snows of Kilimanjaro' that someone told Fitzgerald the only difference between the rich and other people is that the rich have more money. In fact, someone told it to Hemingway: he had announced at a dinner with Max Perkins that he was getting to know the rich, and the sharp Irish critic Mary Colum informed Hemingway that the rich just have more money. Characteristically, Hemingway turned his own humiliation into an arrow to shoot down the competition.

'*sense of carnival and impending disaster*': PUL, Charles Scribner's Sons Papers.

334–5 '*he suddenly realized the meaning of the word . . .*': 'Babylon Revisited', in *Short Stories*, 620.

335 '*the most glamorous place in the world*': *Dreams of Youth*, 100.
'*Now Ludlow, take it from an old souse . . .*': Turnbull, *Scott Fitzgerald*, 168.
'*Is there any man present . . .*': Ibid.
'*Dear Adolph, Please let Mr Fitzgerald . . .*': PUL, FSF Papers.
'*back in America – further apart than ever before*': *A Life in Letters*, 193.
'*The parties were bigger . . .*': 'My Lost City', in *The Crack-Up*, 30.

336 '*to increase the paper's circulation*': Morris Markey, 'A Mystery Revived', *New Yorker*, 7 August 1926, 25.

337 *The trial lasted just under a month*: Brazil, 'Murder Trials, Murder, and Twenties America'.

338 '*She's a liar! Liar, liar, liar! . . .*': NYT, 19 November 1926.

338–9 '*After reading pages of testimony . . .*': *New Yorker*, 4 December 1926, 23.

339 '*My mother was a good woman . . .*': Kunstler, *The Hall-Mills Murder Case*, 309.

340 '*engaged in flagrantly sentimental relations . . .*': *A Life in Letters*, 193.
'*Success was the goal . . .*': *The Collected Writings*, 408–9.
'*I was in the insistent mood . . .*': Turnbull, *Scott Fitzgerald*, 168.

341 *the dancing madness of the Middle Ages*: Ibid.
'*wanted to have something for herself . . .*': Milford, *Zelda Fitzgerald*, 149.
'*Great ladies, bourgeoises, adventuresses . . .*': *Short Stories*, 498–9.

341–2 '*she has given me the greatest joy that can exist . . .*': Bruccoli, *Some Sort of Epic Grandeur*, 342.

342 *calmed only by morphine . . . attempted suicide*: Milford, *Zelda Fitzgerald*, 159.
*high suicide rate in her family . . . history of mental illness*: Ibid., 19.
'*It is somewhat difficult to teach . . .*': *A Life in Letters*, 203.
'*for months I have been living . . .*': *Dear Scott, Dearest Zelda*, 83.

343 '*If you do cure me what's going to happen . . .*': Milford, *Zelda Fitzgerald*, 185.
'*Those days when we came up . . .*': *Dear Scott, Dearest Zelda*, 63.
'*You were going crazy and calling it genius . . .*': Ibid., 65.

344 '*You have been thinking of the past . . .*': Ibid., 67–9.
'*You didn't care . . .*': Ibid., 73.
'*It is with me from the morning . . .*': Ibid., 88–9.

344–5 '*It's ghastly losing your mind . . .*': Ibid., 89–90.

345 'Without hope or youth or money . . .': Ibid., 96–7.
'When you can't write . . .': Ibid., 103.
'it was borrowed time . . .': 'Echoes of the Jazz Age', in The Crack-Up, 21.
346 'You will like it . . .': Dear Scott, Dearest Zelda, 156.
'This mixture of fact and fiction . . .': Ibid., 165.
'simply doesn't exist. What one expresses . . .': Milford, Zelda Fitzgerald, 255.
'the frail equipment of a sick mind . . .': Ibid., 271.
'It seems to me you are making . . .': Ibid., 273.
346–7 he wrote to Zelda's doctor: PUL, Craig House Medical Records on ZF.
347 'got through a lot and have some way to go . . .': Letters, 506.
348 'It's good, good, good': Malcolm Cowley, introduction to Tender is the Night: A Romance. With the Author's Final Revisions. Preface by Malcolm Cowley (New York: Charles Scribner's Sons, 1951).
'clever and brilliantly surfaced . . .': NYT, 15 April 1934.
Fitzgerald responded that its intention was entirely different: PUL, FSF Papers.
349 'My great worry is that time is slipping by . . .': PUL, Craig House Medical Records on ZF.
'Don't worry about critics . . .': Dear Scott, Dearest Zelda, 187.
'You and I have had wonderful times . . .': Ibid., 193–4.
'I wish I had been what I thought . . .': Ibid., 222.
350 Hemingway . . . mocked him publicly: Ernest Hemingway, 'The Snows of Kilimanjaro', Esquire (August 1936).
'please lay off me in print . . .': A Life in Letters, 302.
'Some become brokers and threw . . .': Bruccoli and Baughman (eds), Conversations with F. Scott Fitzgerald, 120–6.
350–1 'Supposing Zelda at best . . .': Milford, Zelda Fitzgerald, 319.
351 'There isn't any more happiness . . .': Dear Scott, Dearest Zelda, 212–13.
'I can see another generation . . .': FSF (ed. Turnbull), Dreams of Youth, 446.
filling out a Guggenheim application: Hensley, Burton Rascoe, 33.
351–2 'it is a magnificent and salutary thing . . .': Burton Rascoe Papers, Rare Book & Manuscript Library, University of Pennsylvania.
352 'That was darn nice of you . . .': Burton Rascoe Papers, Rare Book & Manuscript Library, University of Pennsylvania.
'Hollywood made a big fuss over us . . .': A Life in Letters, 330.
'I didn't write four out of four best sellers . . .': Dreams of Youth, 580.
'Give Paramour my regards . . .': Quoted in Mellow, Invented Lives (Houghton Mifflin), 462.
353 'Smiling faintly at him . . .': The Last Tycoon (1941. London: Penguin, 2001), 26.

'Oh Zelda, this was to have been . . .': *Dear Scott, Dearest Zelda*, 249.

354   'I have come to feel somewhat neglected . . .': FSF and Perkins, *Dear Scott/Dear Max*, 250–2.

'My God I am a forgotten man . . .': *Dear Scott, Dearest Zelda*, 331.

'We have our tombstones to chisel . . .': Ibid., 314.

How is Zelda, how is Zelda . . .: *Notebooks*, 66.

356   'I left my capacity for hoping . . .': Ibid., 204.

357   'I have a cottage on the Pacific . . .': *Correspondence of F. Scott Fitzgerald*, 516–17.

'a novel à la Flaubert . . .': *A Life in Letters*, 470.

'I wish now I'd never relaxed . . .': Ibid., 451.

'expiring talent': *Dear Scott, Dearest Zelda*, 313.

'fascinated me . . . just simply flows': *A Life in Letters*, 358

'praised all out of proportion to its merits': *Correspondence of F. Scott Fitzgerald*, 483.

358   'a fantastic novel by the Czech Franz Kafka . . .': *A Life in Letters*, 389.

'the best individual novel of the last five years': Ibid.

'a delicate thing . . .': Ibid., 431.

359   'We were the great believers': In *Zelda Fitzgerald*, Nancy Milford quotes Fitzgerald as having written in the then-unpublished essay 'My Generation': 'So you see that old libel that we were cynics and skeptics was nonsense from the beginning. On the contrary we were the great believers.' In fact, in that essay Fitzgerald writes only 'We were the great believers.' (See 'My Generation', in *My Lost City*, 192). The credit for the rest of the quotation, which has widely circulated, appears to belong to Milford.

'A lot of the past came into that party . . .': PUL, FSF Papers.

'I am deep in the novel . . .': *A Life in Letters*, 467, 469.

360   'Twenty years ago "This Side of Paradise" . . .': Ibid., 470.

'I am digging it out . . .': Ibid.

'I think my novel is good . . .': Ibid., 471–2.

'Everything is my novel now . . .': Ibid., 474.

'You have got two beautiful bad examples . . .': Ibid., 475.

commenting . . . in the margins: Daniel, 'The Last Thing He Wrote'.

360–1   his last royalty statement: PUL, FSF Papers.

361   'Except for one bouquet . . .': Frank Scully, 'Death of a Genius', in PUL, John Peale Bishop Papers.

'Scott should have been killed . . .': O'Hara (ed. Bruccoli), *Selected Letters*, 279.

'I thought of him as imperishable, somehow': Murphy, *Letters from a Lost Generation*, 259.

'With the skill of a reporter . . .': NYT, 23 December 1940.

'was not a book for the ages . . .': NYT, 24 December 1940.

'thought for so long that every day . . .': Murphy, *Letters from the Lost Generation*, 259.

'the cheapest funeral . . .': *Baltimore Evening Sun*, 22 January 1941.

361–2  Scottie believed . . . books on a proscribed list: Eleanor Lanahan, introduction to *Dear Scott, Dearest Zelda*, xxv.

362  'a meaningless occasion . . .': Turnbull, *Scott Fitzgerald*, 286.

'The poor son of a bitch': Wilson, *The Twenties*, 62.

'The only reason I agreed . . .': Lanahan, *Scottie*, 132.

362–3  'share again the happy possibility . . .': PUL, Charles Scribner's Sons Papers.

363  'Dearest: I am always grateful . . .': *Dear Scott, Dearest Zelda*, 277.

364  'The Grecian Urn is unbearably beautiful . . .': *A Life in Letters*, 460.

365  'long before, not here but westward . . .': Bruccoli (ed.), *The Great Gatsby: A Facsimile Manuscript*.

## Envoi

368  'I always feel that Daddy was the key-note . . .': Quoted in Mellow, *Invented Lives*, 490.

'He endowed those years . . .': *The Collected Writings*, 440–1.

'In retrospect . . . it seems as if . . .': Quoted in Mellow, *Invented Lives*, 488

370  a study of carelessness: Burnam, 'The Eyes of Dr Eckleburg', 9.

371  'The idea that we're the greatest . . .': Bruccoli and Baughman (eds), *Conversations with F. Scott Fitzgerald*, 86.

# A NOTE ON SOURCES

In addition to the notes and bibliography, readers may find helpful a few additional remarks about sources. All scholars of the Fitzgeralds and *The Great Gatsby* are indebted to the publications of Matthew J. Bruccoli and James L. W. West III, in particular, whose archival work and textual scholarship have been invaluable. I relied upon both their detective work and their analysis throughout this book. In addition, Fitzgerald specialists such as Jackson Bryer, Ruth Prigozy and Ronald Berman, and Zelda's first biographer Nancy Milford, to name just a few of the most prominent, have greatly enhanced our knowledge of Scott and Zelda Fitzgerald, *The Great Gatsby* and their world. Because this book already has a cast of hundreds, I decided not to ask the reader to juggle the names of scholars as well, but their contribution to the field must be acknowledged at the outset.

No person can claim to have read all of the scholarship on *The Great Gatsby* in English alone, much less globally. Our understanding of *Gatsby* has evolved and grown culturally over the decades, and many of the stories that I include in *Careless People* have taken their place in the tales told by others: the memoirs and recollections of Edmund Wilson, John Peale Bishop, John Dos Passos, Ernest Boyd, James Drawbell, Gerald Murphy and many other of the Fitzgeralds' legion of friends have been recycled in various accounts over the years. In addition, the possible relation of Jay Gatsby to Max Gerlach, Larry Fay and George Remus has been discussed by others (see the notes and bibliography). Scott and Zelda's correspondence has, of course, been reprinted often (although it has too often been misprinted), but it has not all been published, and each of the volumes of published correspondence includes different letters, sometimes in different versions. Where possible I tried always to go back to original documents as a first principle.

The Hall–Mills case has been related to *Gatsby* in two primary scholarly articles (as well as in a handful of references, including a footnote on the Hall–Mills Wikipedia page): 'Literary History/Unsolved Mystery: *The Great Gatsby* and the Hall–Mills Murder Case' by Henry C. Phelps (2001) and '"He Fell Just Short of Being News": Gatsby's Tabloid Shadows' by Christopher Wilson (2012). Readers can judge for themselves, but I will mention now just a few examples of aspects of the story that these articles did not address. Phelps never refers to Mrs Gibson at all, while Wilson mentions her once in passing, as a witness in the case; neither article connects her to Fitzgerald's November 1922 interview that demonstrates he was following the case. Nor does either article explore the submerged themes that I believe *The Great Gatsby* shares with this case in particular, including mistaken identity, fraudulent pasts, social climbing and class resentment, to name perhaps the most salient. (Wilson does mention Myrtle's class resentment, but not its parallel with the unfolding Hall–Mills case, which is only one of several tabloid cases his article examines.)

In addition to the original newspaper research throughout this book (including the addition of Burton Rascoe's Day Book columns to the story of the Fitzgeralds) and my dating and sourcing of the Fitzgerald scrapbook clippings identified in the text, the *Town Topics* articles I found that mention the Fitzgeralds had not been identified as of 2010, according to an article published that year in the *F. Scott Fitzgerald Review*; Burton Rascoe's 1925 *Gatsby* review had never been located, and therefore its quoted letter from Scott Fitzgerald about his intentions in *Gatsby* is also new. Most of the unpublished archival material mentioned in the text is to be found in the marvellous archives at

Princeton University's Firestone Library. I particularly relied upon the F. Scott Fitzgerald Papers, the Zelda Fitzgerald Papers, the John Peale Bishop Papers, the Craig House Medical Records on Zelda Fitzgerald, and the Archives of Charles Scribner's Sons.

# BIBLIOGRAPHY

**Newspapers and Magazines**
*Harper's Magazine*
*The New Republic*
*The New Yorker*
*The New York Times*
*The New York Tribune*
*The New York World* and *The New York Evening World*
*The Saturday Evening Post*
*Town Topics*
*Vanity Fair*

**Articles and Essays**
Antolin, Pascale, 'New York in *The Beautiful and Damned*: "A City of Words"', *The F. Scott Fitzgerald Review*, 7 (2009): 113–25

Berman, Ronald, 'American Dreams and "Winter Dreams": Fitzgerald and Freudian Psychology in the 1920s', *The F. Scott Fitzgerald Review*, 4 (2005): 49–64

Beuka, Robert and James L. W. West III, 'The Fifth Guest in *The Great Gatsby*: An Online Symposium', *The F. Scott Fitzgerald Review*, 8 (2010): 24–32

Bicknell, John W., 'The Waste Land of FSF', *Virginia Quarterly Review*, 30 (1954): 556–72

Birch, Thomas D., '"In Arithmetical Progression": Shaw, Wells, and Fitzgerald', *The F. Scott Fitzgerald Review*, 6 (2008): 55–68

Bishop, John Peale, 'The Missing All', *Virginia Quarterly Review*, 13 (1937): 106–21

Blair, Stephen, 'Homer, Daedalus, and the Petronian Narrative', *Undergraduate Library Research Award*, Paper 2 (8 April 2008)

Bourgeois, Pamela and John Clendenning, 'Gatsby, Belasco, and Ethnic Ambiguity', *The F. Scott Fitzgerald Review*, 6 (2008): 105–20

Boyer, Allen, '*The Great Gatsby*, The Black Sox, High Finance, and American Law', *Michigan Law Review*, 88.2 (1989): 328–42

Brauer, Stephen, 'Jay Gatsby and the Prohibition Gangster as Businessman', *The F. Scott Fitzgerald Review*, 2 (2003): 51–71.

Brazil, John R., 'Murder Trials, Murder, and Twenties America', *American Quarterly*, 33.2 (1981): 163–84

Bufkin, E. C., 'A Pattern of Parallel and Double: The Function of Myrtle in *The Great Gatsby*', *Modern Fiction Studies*, 15 (1969–70): 517–24

Burnam, Tom, 'The Eyes of Dr Eckleburg: A Re-Examination of *The Great Gatsby*', *College English*, 14.1 (1952): 7–12

Cochoy, Nathalie, 'New York as a "Passing Stranger" in *The Beautiful and Damned*', *The F. Scott Fitzgerald Review*, 4 (2005): 65–83

Coleman, Dan, '"A World Complete in Itself": Gatsby's Elegiac Narration', *The Journal of Narrative Technique*, 27.2 (1997): 207–33

Corso, Joseph, 'One Not-Forgotten Summer Night: Sources for Fictional Symbols of American Character in *The Great Gatsby*', *Fitzgerald/Hemingway Annual* (1976): 9–34

Cowley, Malcolm, 'Fitzgerald: The Double Man', *Saturday Review of Literature*, 34 (24 February 1951): 9–10, 42–4

Cowley, Malcolm, 'F. Scott Fitzgerald: *The Romance of Money*', *Western Review*, 17 (Summer 1953): 245–55

Cowley, Malcolm, 'The Scott Fitzgerald Story', *New Republic*, 124 (1951): 17–20

Daniel, Anne Margaret, 'The Last Thing He Wrote', *Princeton Alumni Weekly*, 20 October 2004

DeKoven, Marianne, 'The Politics of Modernist Form', *New Literary History* 23.3 (1992): 675–90

Del Gizzo, Suzanne, 'The American Dream Unhinged: Romance and Reality in *The Great Gatsby* and *Fight Club*', *The F. Scott Fitzgerald Review* 6 (2008): 69–94

DiBattista, Maria, 'The Aesthetic of Forbearance: Fitzgerald's *Tender is the Night*', *NOVEL: A Forum on Fiction*, 11.1 (1977): 26–39

Dilworth, Thomas, '*The Great Gatsby* and the Arrow Collar Man', *The F. Scott Fitzgerald Review*, 7 (2009): 81–93

Dilworth, Thomas, 'Donne's Compass at the Death Scene in Fitzgerald's *The Great Gatsby*', *The Explicator*, 68:1 (2010): 55–7

Donaldson, Scott, 'The Crisis of Fitzgerald's "Crack-Up"', *Twentieth Century Literature*, 26.2 (1980): 171–88

Donaldson, Scott, 'Possessions in *The Great Gatsby*', *The Southern Review*, 37.2 (2001): 187–210

Dos Passos, John, 'Fitzgerald and the Press', *New Republic*, 104 (1941): 213

Duffy, Dennis, 'Owl Eyes and Incinerators: Ring Lardner's Role in *The Great Gatsby* Revisited', *American Notes & Queries*, 22.4 (2009): 42–6

Eble, Kenneth, 'The Craft of Revision: *The Great Gatsby*', *American Literature*, 36 (1964): 315–26

Edwards, A. S. G., 'F. Scott Fitzgerald, *The Great Gatsby*: "Like an Angry Diamond"', *American Notes & Queries*, 19.2 (2006): 54–5

Endres, Nikolai, 'Petronius in West Egg: *The Satyricon* and *The Great Gatsby*', *The F. Scott Fitzgerald Review*, 7 (2009): 65–79

Fahey, William A., 'Fitzgerald's Eggs of Columbus', *American Notes & Queries*, 8:4 (1995): 26–7

Fisher, Maxine P., 'F. Scott Fitzgerald and Marcel Proust: Literary Soul Mates', *The F. Scott Fitzgerald Review*, 9 (2011): 146–60

Fitzgerald, F. Scott, 'The Most Pampered Men in the World', *The F. Scott Fitzgerald Review*, 5 (2006): 22–7

Fitzgerald, F. Scott, 'What I Think and Feel at 25', *The American Magazine* (September 1922)

Fraser, John, 'Dust and Dreams and *The Great Gatsby*', *English Literary History*, 32.4 (1965): 554–64

Friedrich, Otto, 'Reappraisals – F. Scott Fitzgerald: Money, Money, Money', *American Scholar*, 29 (1960): 392–405

Fussell, Edwin S., 'Fitzgerald's Brave New World', *English Literary History*, 19 (1952): 291–306

Geismar, Maxwell, 'F. Scott Fitzgerald: Orestes at the Ritz', in *The Last of the Provincials: The American Novel 1915–1925* (Boston: Houghton Mifflin, 1947) 287–352

Godden, Richard, 'Glamor on the Turn', *Journal of American Studies*, 16.3 (1982): 343–59

Goldleaf, Steven, 'Our Local Heavens: F Scott Fitzgerald's Years on Long Island and in New York City, 1922–1924' (New York: Hofstra Museum of Art, 2005)

Gross, Dalton and Mary-Jean Gross, 'F. Scott Fitzgerald's American Swastika: The Prohibition Underworld and *The Great Gatsby*', *Notes and Queries*, 41.3 (1994): 377

'Hall–Mills Murder Case', *Life Magazine Special Issue: American Life and Times 1900–1950*, 2 January 1950: 68–70

Hamilton, Sharon, 'Mencken and Nathan's *Smart Set* and the Story behind Fitzgerald's Early Success', *The F. Scott Fitzgerald Review*, 4 (2005): 20–48

Hamilton, Sharon, 'The New York Gossip Magazine in *The Great Gatsby*', *The F. Scott Fitzgerald Review*, 8 (2010): 34–56

Hays, Peter L., 'What the Dickens? *Great Expectations* and *The Great Gatsby*', *The F. Scott Fitzgerald Review*, 3 (2004): 128–39

Hewitt, Jessica L., '"Owl Eyes" in *The Great Gatsby*', *American Notes & Queries*, 9.1 (1996): 26–7

Horowitz, Evan, 'Narrative Accidents and Literary Miracles', *Philosophy and Literature*, 35.1 (2011): 65–78

Kehl, D. G., 'Fitzgerald's "Unbroken Series of Successful Gestures": From Gestural Tableau to Emotion and Idea', *The F. Scott Fitzgerald Review*, 2 (2003): 116–33

Kruse, Horst, 'Gatsby and Gadsby', *Modern Fiction Studies*, 15 (1969–1970): 539–41

Kruse, Horst, 'Reading *The Great Gatsby* in New Jersey: Responses to Fitzgerald in Richard Ford's Bascombe Trilogy: *The Sportswriter* (1986), *Independence Day* (1995), and *The Lay of the Land* (2006)', *The F. Scott Fitzgerald Review*, 8 (2010): 208–17

Kruse, Horst, '*The Great Gatsby*: A View from Kant's Window – Transatlantic Crosscurrents', *The F. Scott Fitzgerald Review*, 2 (2003): 72–84

Kruse, Horst, 'The Real Jay Gatsby: Max von Gerlach, F. Scott Fitzgerald, and the Compositional History of *The Great Gatsby*', *The F. Scott Fitzgerald Review*, 1 (2002): 45–83

Kuehl, John, 'Scott Fitzgerald's Reading', *The Princeton University Library Chronicle*, 22.2 (1961): 58–89

Kuehl, John, 'Scott Fitzgerald: Romantic and Realist', *Texas Studies in Literature and Language*, 1 (1959): 412–26

Kunce, Catherine and Paul M. Levitt, 'The Structure of *Gatsby*: A Vaudeville Show, Featuring Buffalo Bill and a Cast of Dozens', *The F. Scott Fitzgerald Review*, 4 (2005): 101–28

Kunz, Heidi M., '"Love in the Night," Without Polish Eyes to See It', *The F. Scott Fitzgerald Review*, 7 (2009): 37–51

Lena, Alberto, 'The Seducer's Stratagems: *The Great Gatsby* and the Early Twenties', *Forum Modern Language Studies*, 34.4 (1998): 303–13

Levitt, Paul M., 'Point of View, Telephones, Doubling, and Vicarious Learning in *The Great Gatsby*', *The Midwest Quarterly*, 53.3 (2012): 299–306

Lewis, Niko, 'Fitzgerald's Mythical Manhattan: Coming of Age in "May Day" and "My Lost City"', *The F. Scott Fitzgerald Review*, 5 (2006): 109–32

Liston, William T., 'Not Just Personal: Platonism in *The Great Gatsby*', *The Midwest Quarterly*, 35.4 (1994): 378–91

Luft, Joanna and Thomas Dilworth, 'The Name Daisy: *The Great Gatsby* and Chaucer's Prologue to *The Legend of Good Women*', *The F. Scott Fitzgerald Review*, 8 (2010): 79–91

MacKendrick, Paul L., 'The Great Gatsby and Trimalchio', *The Classical Journal*, 45.7 (1950): 307–14

Makowsky, Veronica, 'Bad Driving: Jordan's Tantalizing Story in *The Great Gatsby*', *The F. Scott Fitzgerald Review*, 9 (2011): 28–40

Makurath, Paul A., Jr, 'Another Source for "Gatsby"', *Fitzgerald/Hemingway Annual*, 7 (1975): 115–16

McCall, Dan, 'The Self-Same Song That Found a Path: Keats and *The Great Gatsby*', *American Literature*, 42 (1971): 521–30

McConnell, Gordon B., 'Sane Crooks, Mad Puritans: Fitzgerald, Modernist Sociology, and Poor Material for a Socialist', *The F. Scott Fitzgerald Review*, 2 (2003): 85–115

Mintler, Catherine R., 'From Aesthete to Gangster: The Dandy Figure in the Novels of F. Scott Fitzgerald', *The F. Scott Fitzgerald Review*, 8 (2010): 104–29

Monteiro, George, 'Carraway's Complaint', *Journal of Modern Literature*, 24.1 (2000): 161–71

Mosher, John C., 'That Sad Young Man', *New Yorker*, 17 April 1926

Ornstein, Robert, 'Scott Fitzgerald's Fable of East and West', *College English*, 18.3 (1956): 139–43

Phelps, Henry C., 'Literary History/Unsolved Mystery: *The Great Gatsby* and the Hall–Mills Murder Case', *American Notes & Queries*, 14.3 (2001): 33–9

Plath, James, 'In an Odd Light: Kipling's Maisie and Fitzgerald's Daisy', *The F. Scott Fitzgerald Review*, 6 (2008): 95–104

Podis, Leonard A., 'The Unreality of Reality: Metaphor in *The Great Gatsby*', *Style*, 11 (1977): 56–72

Quirk, William J., 'Living on $500,000 a Year', *The American Scholar* (September 2009)

Raleigh, John Henry, 'F. Scott Fitzgerald's *The Great Gatsby*: Legendary Bases and Allegorical Significance', *University of Kansas City Review*, 24 (1957): 55–8

Rascoe, Burton, 'Contemporary Reminiscences', *Arts and Decoration* (June 1925): 66–8

Raubicheck, Walter, 'Hollywood Nights: The Filmmaker as Artist in "Crazy Sunday"', *The F. Scott Fitzgerald Review*, 7 (2009): 53–64

Rawson, Eric, 'The Telephonic Logic of *The Great Gatsby*', *The F. Scott Fitzgerald Review*, 8 (2010): 92–103

Rule-Maxwell, Lauren, 'The New Emperor's Clothes: Keatsian Echoes and American Materialism in *The Great Gatsby*', *The F. Scott Fitzgerald Review*, 8 (2010): 57–78

Sanders, J'aimé L., 'Discovering the Source of Gatsby's Greatness: Nick's Eulogy for a "Great" Kierkegaardian Knight', *The F. Scott Fitzgerald Review*, 3 (2004): 108–27

Scribner, Charles, III, 'Celestial Eyes: From Metamorphosis to Masterpiece', *Princeton University Library Chronicle*, 53 (1992): 104–55

Seguin, Robert, '*Ressentiment* and the Social Poetics of *The Great Gatsby*: Fitzgerald Read Cather', *Modern Fiction Studies*, 46.4 (2000): 917–40

Seidel, Kathryn Lee, Alexis Wang and Alvin Y. Wang, 'Performing Art: Zelda Fitzgerald's Art and the Role of the Artist', *The F. Scott Fitzgerald Review*, 5 (2006): 133–63

Sklenar, R., 'Anti-Petronian Elements in *The Great Gatsby*', *The F. Scott Fitzgerald Review*, 6 (2008): 121–8

Sparrow, Carroll Mason, 'Footloose Philosophy', *Virginia Quarterly*, 2.1 (winter 1926): 125–30

Stallman, R. W., 'Conrad and *The Great Gatsby*', *Twentieth Century Literature*, 1 (1955): 5–12

Stenberg, Doug, 'Lights from a Distance: The Ghostly Hearts of Fitzgerald's Gatsby and Chekhov's Riabovich in "The Kiss"', *The F. Scott Fitzgerald Review*, 7 (2009): 95–112

Sutton, Brian, 'Fitzgerald's *The Great Gatsby* and "Babylon Revisited"', *The Explicator*, 65.3 (2007): 164–7

Tanselle, G. Thomas and Jackson R. Bryer, '*The Great Gatsby*: A Study in Literary Reputation', *New Mexico Quarterly*, 33 (1963–64): 409–25

Thomas, J. D., 'F. Scott Fitzgerald: James Joyce's "Most Devoted' Admirer"', *The F. Scott Fitzgerald Review*, 5 (2006): 65–85

Trilling, Lionel, 'F. Scott Fitzgerald', in *The Liberal Imagination: Essays on Literature and Society* (New York: Viking, 1950), 243–54

Turlish, Lewis Afton, 'The Rising Tide of Color: A Note on the Historicism of *The Great Gatsby*', *American Literature*, 43 (1971): 442–3

Vince, Raymond M., '*The Great Gatsby* and the Transformations of Space–Time: Fitzgerald's Modernist Narrative and the New Physics of Einstein', *The F. Scott Fitzgerald Review*, 5 (2006): 86–108

Wagenknecht, Edward, 'Our Changing Literary Temper', *College English*, 6.8 (1945): 423–30

Watkins, Floyd C., 'Fitzgerald's Jay Gatz and Young Ben Franklin', *New England Quarterly*, 27 (1954): 249–52

West, James L. W., III, 'Polishing Up "Pampered"', *The F. Scott Fitzgerald Review*, 5 (2006): 13–21

Wilson, Christopher P., '"He Fell Just Short of Being News": Gatsby's Tabloid Shadows', *American Literature*, 84 (2012): 119–49

Wilson, Edmund, 'The Literary Spotlight – VI: F. Scott Fitzgerald', *The Bookman*, 55 (1922): 20–5

Woolf, Virginia, 'American Fiction', *Saturday Review of Literature*, 2.1 (1 August 1925): 1–2.

## Books

Abramson, Rudy, *Spanning the Century: The Life of W. Averell Harriman 1891–1986* (New York: William Morrow, 1992)

Adams, Franklin Pierce, *The Diary of Our Own Samuel Pepys 1911–1925* (New York: Simon and Schuster, 1935)

Aldrich, Nelson W., Jr, *Tommy Hitchcock: An American Hero* (London: Fleet Street, 1985)

Allen, Frederick Lewis, *Only Yesterday: An Informal History of the Nineteen-Twenties* (1931. New York: Harper, 1964)

*An F. Scott Fitzgerald Companion* (New York: Bookspan, 2000)

Asbury, Herbert, *The Great Illusion: An Informal History of Prohibition* (New York: Doubleday, 1950)

Behr, Edward, *Prohibition: The 13 Years That Changed America* (London: BBC Books, 1997)

Berg, A. Scott, *Max Perkins: Editor of Genius* (1978. New York: Riverhead, 1997)

Berger, Meyer, *The Story of The New York Times 1851–1951* (New York: Simon and Schuster, 1951)

Berman, Ronald, *Fitzgerald, Hemingway, and the Twenties* (Tuscaloosa: University of Alabama Press, 2001)

Berman, Ronald, *Fitzgerald's Mentors: Edmund Wilson, H. L. Mencken, and Gerald Murphy* (Tuscaloosa: University of Alabama Press, 2012)

Berman, Ronald, *Fitzgerald–Wilson–Hemingway: Language and Experience* (Tuscaloosa: University of Alabama Press, 2003)

Berman, Ronald, *The Great Gatsby and Fitzgerald's World of Ideas* (Tuscaloosa: University of Alabama Press, 1997)

Berman, Ronald, *The Great Gatsby and Modern Times* (Urbana: University of Illinois Press, 1994)

Bessie, Simon Michael, *Jazz Journalism: The Story of the Tabloid Newspapers* (New York: Dutton, 1938)

Beuka, Robert, *American Icon: Fitzgerald's The Great Gatsby in Critical and Cultural Context* (New York: Camden House, 2011)

Bishop, John Peale and Edmund Wilson, *The Undertaker's Garland* (New York: Knopf, 1922)

Bloom, Harold (ed.), *F. Scott Fitzgerald's The Great Gatsby* (New York: Chelsea House, 1986)

Blum, Deborah, *The Poisoner's Handbook: Murder and the Birth of Forensic Medicine in Jazz Age New York* (New York: Penguin, 2010)

Bogdanovich, Peter, *Allan Dwan: The Last Pioneer* (New York: Praeger, 1971)

Boyd, Ernest, *Portraits: Real and Imaginary* (1924. New York: AMS, 1970)

Boylan, James (ed.), *The World and the 20s: The Best From New York's Legendary Newspaper* (New York: Dial, 1973)

Broer, Lawrence R. and John D. Walther. *Dancing Fools & Weary Blues: The Great Escape of the Twenties* (Bowling Green: Bowling Green State University Popular Press, 1990)

Brooks, Van Wyck, *Days of the Phoenix: The 1920s I Remember* (New York: Dutton, 1957)

Bruccoli, Matthew J., *Fitzgerald and Hemingway: A Dangerous Friendship* (1994. London: André Deutsch, 1995)

Bruccoli, Matthew J., *F. Scott Fitzgerald's The Great Gatsby: A Literary Reference* (2000. New York: Carroll & Graf, 2002)

Bruccoli, Matthew J., *Scott and Ernest: The Authority of Failure and the Authority of Success* (New York: Random House, 1978)

Bruccoli, Matthew J., *Some Sort of Epic Grandeur: The Life of F. Scott Fitzgerald* (1981. London: Cardinal, 1991)

Bruccoli, Matthew J. and Judith S. Baughman (eds), *Conversations with F. Scott Fitzgerald* (Jackson: University of Mississippi Press, 2004)

Bruccoli, Matthew J. and Judith S. Baughman (eds), *F. Scott Fitzgerald in the Marketplace: The Auction and Dealer Catalogues 1935–2006* (Columbia: University of South Carolina Press, 2009)

Bruccoli, Matthew J. and Judith S. Baughman (eds), *F. Scott Fitzgerald on Authorship* (Columbia: University of South Carolina Press, 1996)

Bruccoli, Matthew J., Scottie Fitzgerald Smith and Joan P. Kerr, *The Romantic Egoists: A Pictorial Autobiography from the Scrapbooks and Albums of F. Scott Fitzgerald and Zelda Fitzgerald* (1974. Columbia: University of South Carolina Press, 2003)

Bryer, Jackson R. (ed.), *F. Scott Fitzgerald: The Critical Reception* (New York: Burt Franklin, 1978)

Bryer, Jackson R., *New Essays on F. Scott Fitzgerald's Neglected Stories* (Columbia: University of Missouri Press, 1996)

Bryer, Jackson R., *The Short Stories of F. Scott Fitzgerald: New Approaches in Criticism* (Madison: University of Wisconsin Press, 1982)

Bryer, Jackson R., Alan Margolies and Ruth Prigozy, *F. Scott Fitzgerald: New Perspectives* (Athens: University of Georgia Press, 2000)

Bryer, Jackson R., Ruth Prigozy and Milton R. Stern, *F. Scott Fitzgerald in the Twenty-First Century* (Tuscaloosa: University of Alabama Press, 2003)

Buller, Richard, *A Beautiful Fairy Tale: The Life of Actress Lois Moran* (Pompton Plains: Limelight, 2005)

Canterbury, E. Ray and Thomas Birch, *F. Scott Fitzgerald: Under the Influence* (St Paul: Paragon House, 2006)

Carr, Virginia Spencer, *Dos Passos: A Life* (Evanston: Northwestern University Press, 2004)

Castronovo, David and Janet Groth, *Critic in Love: A Romantic Biography of Edmund Wilson* (Washington: Shoemaker & Hoard, 2005)

Charyn, Jerome, *Gangsters & Gold Diggers: Old New York, the Jazz Age, and the Birth of Broadway* (New York: Four Walls Eight Windows, 2004)

Churchill, Allen, *The Literary Decade: A Panorama of the Writers, Publishers, and Litterateurs of the 1920s* (Englewood Cliffs: Prentice-Hall, 1971)

Claridge, Henry (ed.), *F. Scott Fitzgerald: Critical Assessments*, vols I–IV (Mountfield: Helm, 1991)

Cline, Sally, *Zelda Fitzgerald: Her Voice in Paradise* (2002. London: John Murray, 2003)

Coffey, Thomas M., *The Long Thirst: Prohibition in America 1920–1933* (New York: Norton, 1975)

Collins, Joseph, *Taking the Literary Pulse: Psychological Studies of Life and Letters* (New York: Doran, 1924)

Coover, Robert, *Gerald's Party* (New York: Grove, 1985)

Cowley, Malcolm, *Exile's Return: A Literary Odyssey of the 1920s* (New York: Viking, 1951)

Cowley, Malcolm, *A Second Flowering: Works and Days of the Lost Generation* (1956. London: André Deutsch, 1973)

Crunden, Robert M., *Body and Soul: The Making of American Modernism; Art, Music and Letters in the Jazz Age, 1919–1926* (New York: Basic Books, 2000)

Cummings, E. E., *Selected Letters of E. E. Cummings*, ed. F. W. Dupee and George Stade (London: André Deutsch, 1972)

Curnutt, Kirk, *A Historical Guide to F. Scott Fitzgerald* (Oxford: Oxford University Press, 2004)

Dabney, Lewis M., *Edmund Wilson: A Life in Literature* (New York: Farrar, Straus and Giroux, 2005)

Dash, Mike, *Satan's Circus: Murder, Vice, Police Corruption and New York's Trial of the Century* (London: Granta, 2011)

Donaldson, Scott, *Fitzgerald & Hemingway: Works and Days* (New York: Columbia University Press, 2009)

Donaldson, Scott, *Fool For Love: F. Scott Fitzgerald* (New York: Congdon & Weed, 1983)

Donaldson, Scott, *Hemingway vs. Fitzgerald: The Rise and Fall of a Literary Friendship* (New York: Overlook, 1999)

Dos Passos, John, *The Best Times: An Informal Memoir* (New York: NAL, 1966)

Douglas, Ann, *Terrible Honesty: Mongrel Manhattan in the 1920s* (1995. London: Picador, 1996)

Drawbell, James, *The Sun Within Us* (London: Collins, 1963)

Drowne, Kathleen, *Spirits of Defiance: National Prohibition and Jazz Age Literature, 1920–1933* (Columbus: Ohio State University Press, 2005)

Dunbar, Robin, *Grooming, Gossip, and the Evolution of Language* (1996. Cambridge, MA: Harvard University Press, 1998)

Elder, Donald, *Ring Lardner* (New York: Doubleday, 1956)

Ellard, Robert A., 'Old Great Neck: A Stroll in Memories' Lane', 28 June 1963. Available via the Great Neck Library website

Fadiman, Clifton, *Party of One* (New York: World, 1955)

Farrar, John (ed.), *Literary Spotlight* (New York: Doran, 1924)

Fischler, Marcelle S., *TM Design's Ultimate Book of Great Neck: Fabled Tales & Fabulous Images* (Great Neck: Glenn Bucalo, 2003)

Fitzgerald, F. Scott, *Afternoon of an Author: A Selection of Uncollected Stories and Essays*, ed. Arthur Mizener (New York: Scribner, 1957)

Fitzgerald, F. Scott, *Before Gatsby: The First Twenty-Six Stories*, ed. Matthew J. Bruccoli and Judith S. Baughman (Columbia: University of South Carolina Press, 2001)

Fitzgerald, F. Scott, *The Best Early Stories of F. Scott Fitzgerald*, ed. Bryant Mangum (New York: Random House, 2005)

Fitzgerald, F. Scott, *The Collected Short Stories* (1986. London: Penguin, 2000)

Fitzgerald, F. Scott, *The Collected Short Stories of F. Scott Fitzgerald* (London: Penguin, 1986)

Fitzgerald, F. Scott, *Correspondence of F. Scott Fitzgerald*, ed. Matthew J. Bruccoli and Margaret M. Duggan (New York: Random House, 1980)

Fitzgerald, F. Scott, *The Crack-Up*, ed. Edmund Wilson (1945. New York: New Directions, 1993)

Fitzgerald, F. Scott, *Dreams of Youth: The Letters of F. Scott Fitzgerald*, ed. Andrew Turnbull (London: Little Books, 2011)

Fitzgerald, F. Scott, *Flappers and Philosophers: The Collected Short Stories* (London: Penguin, 2010)

Fitzgerald, F. Scott, *F. Scott Fitzgerald: In His Own Time*, ed. Matthew J. Bruccoli and Jackson R. Bryer (New York: Popular Library, 1971)

Fitzgerald, F. Scott, *F. Scott Fitzgerald's Ledger: A Facsimile* (Washington, DC: NCR/Microcard, 1972)

Fitzgerald, F. Scott, *The Great Gatsby*, ed. Matthew J. Bruccoli (1991. Cambridge: Cambridge University Press, 1999)

Fitzgerald, F. Scott, *The Great Gatsby* (1925. Notes and preface by Matthew J. Bruccoli. New York: Scribner, 1995)

Fitzgerald, F. Scott, *The Great Gatsby: A Facsimile of the Manuscript*, ed. Matthew J. Bruccoli (Washington: Microcard Editions, 1973)

Fitzgerald, F. Scott, *The Letters of F. Scott Fitzgerald*, ed. Andrew Turnbull (1963. New York: Bantam, 1971)

Fitzgerald, F. Scott, *A Life in Letters*, ed. Matthew J. Bruccoli (New York: Scribner, 1994)

Fitzgerald, F. Scott, *The Love of The Last Tycoon*, ed. Matthew J. Bruccoli (New York: Scribner, 1994)

Fitzgerald, F. Scott, *My Lost City: Personal Essays, 1920–1940*, ed. James L. W. West III (Cambridge: Cambridge University Press, 2005)

Fitzgerald, F. Scott, *The Notebooks of F. Scott Fitzgerald*, ed. Matthew J. Bruccoli (New York: Harcourt Brace Jovanovich/Bruccoli Clark, 1978)

Fitzgerald, F. Scott, *The Pat Hobby Stories* (1962. New York: Scribner, 1995)

Fitzgerald, F. Scott, *The Price Was High: The Last Uncollected Stories of F. Scott Fitzgerald*, ed. Matthew J. Bruccoli (New York: Harcourt Brace Jovanovich/Bruccoli Clark, 1979)

Fitzgerald, F. Scott, *The Short Stories of F. Scott Fitzgerald*, ed. Matthew J. Bruccoli (1989. New York, Scribner: 2003)

Fitzgerald, F. Scott, *Tales of the Jazz Age*, ed. James L. W. West III (Cambridge: Cambridge University Press, 2002)

Fitzgerald, F. Scott, *Tender Is the Night* (1934. New York: Bantam, 1962)

Fitzgerald, F. Scott, *This Side of Paradise* (1920. Oxford: Oxford University Press, 2009)

Fitzgerald, F. Scott, *This Side of Paradise* (1920. New York: Collier, 1986)

Fitzgerald, F. Scott, *This Side of Paradise, Flappers and Philosophers* (Avenel: Gramercy, 1996)

Fitzgerald, F. Scott, *Trimalchio: An Early Version of The Great Gatsby*, ed. James L. W. West III (Cambridge: Cambridge University Press, 2000)

Fitzgerald, F. Scott, *The Vegetable, Or From President to Postman* (1923. New York: Collier, 1987)

Fitzgerald, F. Scott and Harold Ober, *As Ever, Scott-Fitz: Letters Between F. Scott Fitzgerald and His Literary Agent, Harold Ober 1919–1940*, ed. Matthew J. Bruccoli (London: Woburn, 1973)

Fitzgerald, F. Scott and Maxwell E. Perkins, *Dear Scott/Dear Max: The Fitzgerald–Perkins Correspondence*, ed. John Kuehl and Jackson Bryer (London: Cassell, 1973)

Fitzgerald, F. Scott and Zelda Fitzgerald, *Bits of Paradise: Twenty-One Uncollected Stories*, ed. Matthew J. Bruccoli and Scottie Fitzgerald Smith (1973. Harmondsworth: Penguin, 1982)

Fitzgerald, F. Scott and Zelda Fitzgerald. *Dear Scott, Dearest Zelda: The Love Letters of F. Scott and Zelda Fitzgerald*, ed. Jackson R. Bryer and Cathy W. Barks (London: Bloomsbury, 2002)

Fitzgerald, Zelda, *The Collected Writings*, ed. Matthew J. Bruccoli (1991. London: Abacus, 1993)

Fitzpatrick, Kevin C., *A Journey into Dorothy Parker's New York* (Berkeley: Roaring Forties Press, 2005)

Garnett, David, *Lady into Fox* (1922. London: Hesperus, 2008)

Goldhurst, William, *F. Scott Fitzgerald and His Contemporaries* (Cleveland: World, 1963)

Goldstein, Judith S., *Inventing Great Neck: Jewish Identity and the American Dream* (New Brunswick, NJ: Rutgers University Press, 2006)

Graham, Sheilah, *The Real F. Scott Fitzgerald* (London: Comet, 1976)

Graham, Stephen, *New York Nights* (New York: George H. Doran, 1927)

Green, Henry, *Party Going* (1939. London: Vintage, 2000)

Hammill, Fay, *Sophistication: A Literary and Cultural History* (Liverpool: Liverpool University Press, 2010)

Hemingway, Ernest, *Ernest Hemingway: Selected Letters 1917–1961*, ed. Carlos Baker (New York: Scribner, 1981)

Hensley, Donald M., *Burton Rascoe* (New York: Twayne, 1970)

Hindus, Milton, *F. Scott Fitzgerald: An Introduction and Interpretation* (New York: Holt, Rinehart and Winston, 1968)

Hutchens, John K., *American Twenties: A Literary Panorama* (New York: Lippincott, 1952)

Kahn, E. J., Jr, *The World of Swope: A Biography of Herbert Bayard Swope* (New York: Simon and Schuster, 1965)

Katcher, Leo, *The Big Bankroll: The Life and Times of Arnold Rothstein* (1959. New York: Da Capo, 1994)

Keable, Robert, *Simon Called Peter* (New York: E. P. Dutton, 1921)

Kellner, Bruce, *Carl Van Vechten and the Irreverent Decades* (Norman: University of Oklahoma Press, 1968)

Kinney, Harrison, *James Thurber: His Life and Times* (New York: Henry Holt, 1995)

Kuehl, John, *F. Scott Fitzgerald: A Study of the Short Fiction* (Boston: Twayne, 1991)

Kunstler, William M., *The Hall–Mills Murder Case: The Minister and the Choir Singer* (1964. New Brunswick, NJ: Rutgers University Press, 1996)

Lanahan, Eleanor, *Scottie, The Daughter of . . .: The Life of Frances Scott Fitzgerald Lanahan Smith* (New York: HarperCollins, 1995)

Lanahan, Eleanor (ed.), *Zelda – An Illustrated Life: The Private World of Zelda Fitzgerald* (New York: Abrams, 1996)

Lardner, Ring, *The Best of Ring Lardner* (London: Dent, 1984)

Lardner, Ring, *What of It?* (New York: Scribner, 1925)

Lerner, Michael A., *Dry Manhattan: Prohibition in New York City* (Cambridge, MA: Harvard University Press, 2007)

Le Vot, André, *F. Scott Fitzgerald: A Biography* (1979. Trans. William Byron. London: Allen Lane, 1984)

Lewis, Alfred Allan, *Man of the World: Herbert Bayard Swope: A Charmed Life of Pulitzer Prizes, Poker and Politics* (Indianapolis: Bobbs-Merrill, 1978)

Long, Robert Emmet, *The Achieving of The Great Gatsby: F. Scott Fitzgerald, 1920–1925* (1979. London: Associated University Press, 1981)

Longstreet, Stephen, *The Crime* (1959. Greenwich: Crest, 1961)

MacElhone, Harry, Andrew and Duncan MacElhone, *Harry's ABC of Mixing Cocktails* (London: Souvenir, 2006)

March, Joseph Moncure and Art Spiegelman, *The Wild Party: The Lost Classic* (New York: Pantheon, 1994)

Meade, Marion, *Bobbed Hair and Bathtub Gin: Writers Running Wild in the Twenties* (Orlando: Harcourt, 2004)

Meade, Marion, *Dorothy Parker: What Fresh Hell Is This?* (New York: Villard, 1988)

Mellow, James R., *Invented Lives: F. Scott & Zelda Fitzgerald* (1984. London: Condor/Souvenir, 1985)

Mellow, James R., *Invented Lives: F. Scott & Zelda Fitzgerald* (New York: Houghton Mifflin, 1984)

Mencken, H. L., *The American Language: A Preliminary Inquiry Into the Development of English in the United States* (New York: Knopf, 1919)

Mencken, H. L., *The Diary of H. L. Mencken*, ed. Charles A. Fecher (New York: Alfred A. Knopf, 1990)

Meyers, Jeffrey, *Edmund Wilson: A Biography* (Boston: Houghton Mifflin, 1995)

Meyers, Jeffrey, *Scott Fitzgerald: A Biography* (1994. New York: Cooper Square, 2000)

Milford, Nancy, *Zelda Fitzgerald* (1970. Harmondsworth: Penguin, 1974)

Miller, Nathan, *New World Coming: The 1920s and the Making of Modern America* (Boston: Da Capo, 2004)

Mizener, Arthur, *The Far Side of Paradise: A Biography of F. Scott Fitzgerald* (Boston: Houghton Mifflin, 1951)

Moore, Lucy, *Anything Goes: A Biography of the Roaring Twenties* (2008. London: Atlantic, 2009)

Morris, Jan, *Manhattan '45* (London: Faber and Faber, 2011)

Morris, Lloyd, *Incredible New York: High Life and Low Life from 1850 to 1950* (1951. New York: Syracuse University Press, 1996)

Murphy, Gerald and Sara, and friends. *Letters from the Lost Generation*, ed. Linda Patterson Miller (New Brunswick, NJ: Rutgers University Press, 1991)

North, Michael, *Reading 1922: A Return to the Scene of the Modern* (Oxford: Oxford University Press, 1999)

Noyes Hart, Frances, *The Bellamy Trial* (1928. Kingswood: Windmill, 1930)

O'Hara, John, *Selected Letters of John O'Hara*, ed. Matthew J. Bruccoli (New York: Random House, 1978)

Okrent, Daniel, *Last Call: The Rise and Fall of Prohibition* (New York: Scribner, 2010)

Parker, Dorothy, *Laments for the Living: Collected Stories* (New York: Quality Paperback Book Club, 1939)

Parkinson, Kathleen, *F. Scott Fitzgerald: The Great Gatsby* (1987. London: Penguin, 1988)

Pegolotti, James A., *Deems Taylor: A Biography* (Boston: Northeastern University Press, 2003)

Peretti, Burton W., *Nightclub City: Politics and Amusement in Manhattan* (Philadelphia: University of Pennsylvania Press, 2007)

Petronius, Gaius, *The Satyricon*, trans. W. C. Firebaugh (New York: Boni & Liveright, 1922)

Phelps, William Lyon, *As I Like It* (1923. New York: Scribner, 1926)

Pietrusza, David, *Rothstein: The Life, Times and Murder of the Criminal Genius who Fixed the 1919 World Series* (New York: Carroll & Graf, 2003)

Pincus, Roberta (ed.), *This Is Great Neck: A History of the Great Neck Community From 1600 to the Present* (1975. Great Neck: Great Neck Library, 1983)

Piper, Henry Dan, *Fitzgerald's The Great Gatsby: The Novel, The Critics, The Background* (New York: Scribner, 1970)

Piper, Henry Dan, *F. Scott Fitzgerald: A Critical Portrait* (1965. London: The Bodley Head, 1966)

Prigozy, Ruth. *F. Scott Fitzgerald* (2001. Woodstock: Overlook, 2004)

Procter, Ben, *William Randolph Hearst: The Later Years, 1911–1951* (Oxford: Oxford University Press, 2007)

Rascoe, Burton, *A Bookman's Daybook* (New York: Horace Liveright, 1929)

Rascoe, Burton, *Before I Forget* (New York: Doran, 1937)

Rascoe, Burton, *We Were Interrupted* (New York: Doubleday, 1947)

Ring, Frances Kroll, *Against the Current: As I Remember F. Scott Fitzgerald* (San Francisco: Donald S. Ellis, 1985)

Roulston, Robert and Helen H. Roulston, *The Winding Road to West Egg: The Artistic Development of F. Scott Fitzgerald* (Lewisburg: Bucknell University Press, 1995)

Seldes, Gilbert, *The 7 Lively Arts: The Classic Appraisal of the Popular Arts* (1924. Mineola: Dover, 2001)

Sinclair, Andrew, *Prohibition: The Era of Excess* (London: Faber and Faber, 2009)

Sklar, Robert, *F. Scott Fitzgerald: The Last Laocoön* (1967. Oxford: Oxford University Press, 1969)

Spacks, Patricia Meyer, *Gossip* (1985. Chicago: University of Chicago Press, 1986)

Spear, Devah and Gil Spear, *The Book of Great Neck* (Great Neck: privately printed, 1936)

Speare, Dorothy, *Dancers in the Dark* (New York: George H. Doran Co., 1922)

Steel, Ronald, *Walter Lippmann and the American Century* (Boston: Little, Brown, 1980)

Sullivan, Mark, *Our Times, The Twenties* (New York: Scribner, 1935)

Tate, Mary Jo, *Critical Companion to F. Scott Fitzgerald: A Literary Reference to His Life and Work* (New York: Facts on File, 2007)

Taylor, Kendall, *Sometimes Madness is Wisdom: Zelda and Scott Fitzgerald, A Marriage* (New York: Ballantine, 2001)

Tomlinson, Gerald, *Fatal Tryst: Who Killed the Minister and the Choir Singer?* (Lake Hopatcong: Home Run, 1999)

Turnbull, Andrew, *Scott Fitzgerald: A Biography* (London: The Bodley Head, 1962)

Vaill, Amanda, *Everybody Was So Young: Gerald and Sara Murphy – A Lost Generation Love Story* (Boston: Houghton Mifflin, 1998)

Van Doren, Carl, *Many Minds* (New York: Knopf, 1924)

Van Vechten, Carl, *Parties: Scenes from Contemporary New York Life* (1930. Freeport: Books for Libraries Press, 1971)

Van Vechten, Carl, *The Splendid Drunken Twenties: Selections from the Daybooks 1922–1930*, ed. Bruce Kellner (Urbana: University of Illinois Press, 2003)

Wagner-Martin, Linda, *Zelda Sayre Fitzgerald: An American Woman's Life* (New York: Palgrave Macmillan, 2004)

Way, Brian, *F. Scott Fitzgerald and the Art of Social Fiction* (New York: St Martin's Press, 1980)

West, James L. W., III, *The Perfect Hour: The Romance of F. Scott Fitzgerald and Ginevra King, His First Love* (2005. New York: Random House, 2006)

Wilson, Edmund, *The American Earthquake: A Documentary of the Jazz Age, the Great Depression, and the New Deal* (New York: Doubleday, 1958)

Wilson, Edmund, *Discordant Encounters: Plays and Dialogues* (New York: Albert and Charles Boni, 1926)

Wilson, Edmund, *Edmund Wilson: Letters on Literature and Politics 1912–1972*, ed. Elena Wilson (1957. New York: Farrar, Straus and Giroux, 1977)

Wilson, Edmund, *The Twenties: From Notebooks and Diaries of the Period* (London: Macmillan, 1975)

Wilson, Edmund, *Wilson's Night Thoughts* (New York: Farrar, Straus and Cudahy, 1961)

Yardley, Jonathan, *Ring: A Biography of Ring Lardner* (New York: Random House, 1977)

Zeitz, Joshua, *Flapper: A Madcap Story of Sex, Style, Celebrity, and the Women Who Made America Modern* (New York: Crown, 2006)

Zhang, Aiping, *Enchanted Places: The Use of Setting in F. Scott Fitzgerald's Fiction* (Westport: Greenwood, 1997)

# ACKNOWLEDGEMENTS

This book began in 2009, when I told my agent, Peter Robinson, that I wanted to write about Scott Fitzgerald and *The Great Gatsby*, and that I thought there was more to say about its relation to a crazy, unsolved murder mystery from 1922. It is largely thanks to Peter that an actual book has emerged, many entertaining and searching conversations later, from that amorphous concept, and I am deeply grateful for his unwavering belief in this idea, his material assistance in bringing it to life and his friendship.

This was not a straightforward book to write, or to research, and I have been extremely fortunate in the support I have had during the years I worked on it. In addition to Peter's insights and suggestions, the book benefited tremendously from not one but two brilliant editors. Lennie Goodings at Virago in London and Ann Godoff at Penguin Press in New York both understood from the outset what I was trying to do, and offered wise, perceptive counsel that helped immensely in shaping my resistant material into something that more closely resembled the apparition I'd had in my head. If I have done something better than I am capable of, it is largely thanks to these three. My thanks to Zoe Gullen at Virago and Benjamin Platt at Penguin for their unstinting help with extremely complicated permissions and copy-editing, and to everyone at Virago and Penguin for their intelligence and enthusiasm in helping us produce the book we all wanted to publish. Special thanks are also due to Melanie Jackson for representing the book so superbly in the United States.

Many friends also offered brilliance, energy and that most precious commodity of all, their time, in reading drafts and talking ideas over. I am immensely grateful to Heather Brooke, Jon Cook, Tamsin Todd Defriez, Natalie Haynes, David Miller, John Mitchinson, Lyndsey Stonebridge and Dana Wildman for reading so carefully and for so many sparkling conversations, and especially to Helen Brocklebank, who read draft after draft, talked over every detail with me and never once threw a chapter at my head: our conversations solved many thorny problems, and always raised flagging spirits. Special thanks are due to Nicholas Pierpan, who gave the book a ruthlessly painstaking reading from which it benefited greatly, and to Anne Margaret Daniel, who unstintingly offered not only her time, but also her considerable expertise on the Fitzgeralds and Gatsby, as well as detailed notes on an enormous first draft – not to mention a home in the Village for my many research trips to Princeton and New York, and an always interested ear at the end of a long day in the archives. James Pethica offered the suggestions of an experienced biographer, and helped me track down the answers to several difficult questions. Thanks to Nancy Allen, for chauffeuring me around Great Neck one beautiful July day while I took photographs, and to Ellen and Bill Allen for their hospitality on Long Island, and for sharing stories about prohibition. Steven Goldleaf generously shared his research into the topography of Gatsby, while offering me an expert guided tour around Queens and Great Neck, while I took more photographs. David Miller read an early draft with the working title 'The Dying Fall', and suggested the infinitely superior Careless People, which has been the name of this book ever since. Thanks to Sadaf Fahim-Hashemi for her astute, scrupulous help compiling and fact-checking the bibliography, endnotes and images. Thanks also to the staff and librarians at the University of Pennsylvania, which houses the Burton Rascoe papers, and to the staff at the Huntington Library, particularly to Molly Gipson for her help in tracking down Fitzgerald references. Every Fitzgerald scholar relies especially upon the wonderful librarians who care for the Fitzgerald archive at Princeton University; I am particularly grateful to AnnaLee Pauls for her help with reproductions and other tricky aspects of long-distance research, and to Charles E. Greene and Ben Primer for their help and generosity with permissions. I am grateful to the Fitzgerald Estate, Princeton University, the

University of Pennsylvania, the Huntington Library, Judith Rascoe and the Dorothy Parker Estate for permission to reproduce the various images and quotations in these pages. The New York Historical Society has a fascinating collection of speakeasy and bootlegger's cards, as well as restaurant and hotel menus from the 1920s, and the New York Public Library's collection of *Town Topics* was a treasure trove. Many newspapers from 1922 are now available digitally, including via the *New York Times* archive and the wonderful Library of Congress website, *Chronicling America*, both of which were immensely helpful in researching this book. Some alterations have been made between the US and UK edition in order to comply with US copyright restrictions.

I was fortunate to be invited to share my research and developing ideas at numerous lectures, seminars and conferences around the UK, US and Europe while I was writing. My thanks for their enthusiastic support especially to the brilliant guests at Julia Hobsbawm's annual Names Not Numbers conference, who made me trust that this might indeed be more than a book about *Gatsby*, and to Bruno Giussani for the invitation to speak at a TED Salon in London in 2010. Thanks also to audiences at Birkbeck, Birmingham, Cambridge, Edinburgh, Glasgow, Liverpool, Nottingham, St Anne's College Oxford, Plymouth, Portsmouth, Sheffield, Southbank Centre London, Southampton, UEA Norwich and UEA London, the University of Southern California, Wymondham College and John Cabot University, Rome. I am grateful to UEA for the financial support it provided for research trips, and to the friends there who have supported my work on the book in other ways, especially John, Lyndsey, Yvonne, and Jenni. This book is for Wyndham, who heartened me, and it, every day, and who will see how the blue of Arcadia found its way into these pages.

It is also, of course, for Scott and Zelda, who have been such dazzling company for the last four years. I hope they might think I got at least part of it right.

# CREDITS

297, 301, 302, 305, 305, 307, 312, 315, 321, 328, 331, 335, 339 (bottom), 349, 354, 356, 363

*The New Yorker*: 332

*New York Tribune*: 71, 77, 118, 138, 160, 176, 214

*New York World*: 44, 46, 53, 78, 98, 103, 113, 117, 133, 144, 145 (top), 151, 158, 184, 202, 210, 221, 233, 239, 267

Sporting News via Getty Images: 109

TEXT

Previously unpublished archive material by F. Scott Fitzgerald and Zelda Fitzgerald is reproduced by permission of David Higham Associates Limited.

Extracts from Zelda Fitzgerald, *Save Me the Waltz* (1932. London: Random House, 2001); F. Scott Fitzgerald and Zelda Fitzgerald (ed. Jackson R. Bryer and Cathy W. Barks) *Dear Scott, Dearest Zelda: The Love Letters of F. Scott and Zelda Fitzgerald* (London: Bloomsbury, 2002); and Zelda Fitzgerald (ed. Matthew J. Bruccoli), *The Collected Writings* (1991. London: Abacus, 1993) are reproduced by permission of David Higham Associates Limited.

'The Flapper' by Dorothy Parker is quoted by permission of Gerald Duckworth & Co. Limited.

The letter on pages 351–2 is in the Burton Rascoe Papers, Rare Book & Manuscript Library, University of Pennsylvania. Quoted with the permission of Judith Rascoe.

George Jean Nathan's note to Zelda Fitzgerald is quoted by permission of Patricia Angelin, The George Jean Nathan Literary Estate.

*Every reasonable effort has been made to contact copyright holders before publication, but in some cases this has not been possible. If notified, the publisher will be pleased to rectify any errors or omissions at the earliest opportunity.*

# INDEX